FULL DISCLOSURE

Which SUVs are most likely to roll over? What cities have the unhealthiest drinking water? Which factories are the most dangerous polluters? What cereals are most nutritious? In recent decades, governments have sought to provide answers to such critical questions through public disclosure to force manufacturers, water authorities, and others to improve their products and practices. Corporate financial disclosure, nutritional labels, and school report cards are examples of such targeted transparency policies. At best, they create a light-handed approach to governance that improves markets, enriches public discourse, and empowers citizens. But such policies are frequently ineffective or counterproductive. Using an analysis of eighteen U.S. and international policies, *Full Disclosure* shows that the information provided is often incomplete, incomprehensible, or irrelevant to consumers, investors, workers, and community residents. To be successful, transparency policies must be accurate, must keep ahead of disclosers' efforts to find loopholes, and, above all, must focus on the needs of ordinary citizens.

Archon Fung, Mary Graham, and David Weil codirect the Transparency Policy Project at Harvard's John F. Kennedy School of Government, http://www.transparencypolicy.net.

Archon Fung is Associate Professor of Public Policy at Harvard's John F. Kennedy School of Government. His research examines the impacts of civic participation, public deliberation, and transparency on public and private governance. He has authored three books, including *Empowered Participation: Reinventing Urban Democracy* (2004), and edited three collections; more than fifty of his articles have appeared in journals, including *Political Theory, Journal of Political Philosophy, Politics and Society, Governance, Journal of Policy and Management*, and *American Behavioral Scientist*.

Mary Graham is a Research Fellow at Harvard's John F. Kennedy School of Government and a Visiting Fellow in Governance Studies at the Brookings Institution, Washington, D.C. Her research focuses on the use of information strategies to foster social change, the politics of public information, innovative approaches to health and safety regulations, and new trends in environmental policy. She is the author of *Democracy by Disclosure* (2002) and *The Morning After Earth Day* (1999). Graham has written for the *Atlantic Monthly, Financial Times, Environment, Issues in Science and Technology*, the *Brookings Review*, and other publications.

David Weil is Professor of Economics and Everett W. Lord Distinguished Faculty Scholar at Boston University School of Management. His research spans labor market policy, industrial and labor relations, occupational safety and health, and regulatory policy. He has published widely in these areas and has also served as adviser to the U.S. Department of Labor, the Occupational Safety and Health Administration, and other agencies. He has written two other books, including the award-winning *A Stitch in Time: Lean Retailing and the Transformation of Manufacturing* (1999), and his articles have appeared in numerous journals, including the *RAND Journal of Economics, Industrial and Labor Relations Review, Harvard Business Review*, and the *Journal of Policy Analysis and Management*.

Full Disclosure

The Perils and Promise of Transparency

ARCHON FUNG

John F. Kennedy School of Government,
Harvard University

MARY GRAHAM

John F. Kennedy School of Government,
Harvard University

DAVID WEIL

Boston University School of Management

CAMBRIDGE
UNIVERSITY PRESS

CAMBRIDGE UNIVERSITY PRESS
Cambridge, New York, Melbourne, Madrid, Cape Town, Singapore, São Paulo

Cambridge University Press
32 Avenue of the Americas, New York, NY 10013-2473, USA

www.cambridge.org
Information on this title: www.cambridge.org/9780521876179

First published 2007

Printed in the United States of America

A catalog record for this publication is available from the British Library.

Library of Congress Cataloging in Publication Data
Fung, Archon, 1968–
Full disclosure : the perils and promise of transparency / Archon Fung,
Mary Graham, David Weil.
p. cm.
Includes bibliographical references and index.
ISBN 978-0-521-87617-9
1. Government information – Access control – United States.
2. Transparency in government – United States.
3. Disclosure of information – Government policy – United States.
4. Disclosure of information – Law and legislation.
I. Graham, Mary, 1944– II. Weil, David, 1961–. III. Title.
JK468.S4.F86 2007
352.3′8 – dc22   2006029588

ISBN 978-0-521-87617-9 hardback

To our parents

Contents

Figures and Tables

Figures

Tables

Preface

Five years ago, we set out to explore a question of growing importance in public life: can government legislate transparency policies that reduce risks to health, safety, and financial stability, or improve the performance of major institutions such as schools, hospitals, and banks?

We were an unlikely trio – a political scientist, an economist, and a lawyer, each busy with our own research concerning new trends in participatory democracy, workplace practices, and regulatory policy. But all of us were based, serendipitously, at the Kennedy School's Taubman Center for State and Local Government at Harvard University. We began meeting every couple of weeks to talk about an intriguing development that each of us had noted separately in our work. Faced with challenges to reduce serious risks or improve public services, legislators were no longer simply setting standards or imposing taxes. They were also creating scores of public disclosure policies.

In effect, policymakers were honing transparency – a widely shared but amorphous value – into a refined instrument of governance. This trend raised a fundamental question that no one seemed to be asking: does transparency work? Can new information – placed in the public domain and structured by government mandate – improve consumers', investors', and voters' choices and, in turn, create new incentives for manufacturers, hospitals, schools, and other organizations to bring their practices more in line with public priorities? We decided to examine that question together.

As we framed our research project, transparency policy failures with devastating consequences helped convince us that the inquiry was important. In 2001, Enron Inc., the world's largest energy trading firm, collapsed. To prosecutors, Enron's demise represented fraudulent efforts by executives to hide huge losses from investors. To many investors, it represented the loss of life savings. To us, however, the Enron debacle also signaled a failure of the nation's oldest and most trusted transparency system – the detailed federal requirements that publicly traded companies disclose their profits and losses. Enron's demise was followed quickly by the sudden collapse of other respected companies – WorldCom and Tyco, for example – incidents that underscored the flaws in financial reporting.

Over the next two years, the Bush administration's attempt to employ transparency to reduce risks of death and injury from terrorist attacks also failed. The tragedy of the terrorist attacks of September 11, 2001, was leavened by the grace and courage of citizen heroes. Firefighters rushed into the World Trade Center towers as company managers ushered their fellow workers out of the doomed buildings, saving thousands of lives. Passengers aboard United Airlines Flight 93 attacked their hijackers and sacrificed themselves to halt a terrorist attack on the nation's capital.[1] On September 11, as in many other emergencies, citizens were the first to respond.

Perhaps recognizing the importance of public awareness and mobilization, the Bush administration created a color-coded ranking system for terrorist threats early in 2002.[2] That system was designed to encourage government agencies, the private sector, and members of the public to take steps at each threat level to minimize attacks and their consequences. Instead, announced increases in the threat level created confusion, leaving millions of Americans uncertain what they should do to protect themselves. Before long, terrorism threat ranking degenerated into fodder for late-night comedians.

These and other instances of transparency gone awry drove home three important points. First, transparency policies were always limited by politics. They represented compromises forged from conflict, as people and organizations with diverging interests and values battled over how much information should be made public and in what forms. Some of the issues raised by the accounting scandals – whether and how companies should have to report on stock options and off–balance sheet entities – had been the subject of decades of intense lobbying. Thus, in public policy, there was no such thing as full disclosure – only varying degrees of partial transparency that might or might not serve the public's needs.

Second, the transparency measures we observed were fundamentally different from the more familiar right-to-know policies that dated from the 1960s in the United States and became contentious once again as George W. Bush expanded executive branch secrecy during his two terms as president. Right-to-know laws, a cornerstone of democratic governance, required general openness in federal, state, and local government in order to hold officials accountable for their actions. The transparency measures we observed, by contrast, required disclosure of specific factual information, usually by corporations or other private organizations. Their aims, too, were specific: to reduce needless economic losses to investors from corporate deception, to prevent deaths and injuries, to improve the quality of public services, or to fight corruption. We developed a name for this second generation of public disclosure: targeted transparency.

Third, the consequences of failed transparency could be devastating. The underreporting and misreporting of financial data by Enron and WorldCom cost thousands of workers their pension savings and millions of stockholders their investment funds. The ambiguity of the terrorist threat ranking system ultimately led many individuals and organizations to ignore it, creating the potential for a disastrous boy-who-cried-wolf scenario.

We began our inquiry into the effectiveness of targeted transparency as skeptics. We could think of many reasons from each of our disciplines to predict that new information would not in fact reduce risks. At the same time, the idea of transparency remained appealing. Who could oppose providing more information to the public? The spread of these targeted policies made it especially important to understand their strengths and drawbacks.

Over coffee, covering blackboards and papers with arrows and boxes, we explored how targeted transparency might further specific policy objectives and how obstacles might block the way. When we searched for studies by other researchers, we found almost no literature analyzing targeted transparency across a range of policy areas. There were, however, new and interesting empirical studies that explored the effectiveness of individual transparency systems in domains such as financial policy, environmental regulation, public health, and product safety. Supplementing these studies with our own research, we began to examine and compare specific transparency policies to see how they worked.

The evidence we developed turned us from skeptics into pragmatists. Certainly, some targeted transparency policies were costly failures. But others were clearly effective. What made the difference between success and failure?

With foundation funding as well as support from the Kennedy School's Taubman Center, its Environment and Natural Resources Program, and what is now the Ash Institute for Democratic Governance and Innovation, we organized the Transparency Policy Project to explore that question. We examined a carefully chosen array of fifteen targeted transparency systems in the United States to determine their purposes, politics, effects, and effectiveness. We also examined three international transparency policies to see whether targeted transparency could further nations' shared aims.

As our research progressed, we tested the emerging ideas in papers, seminars, and articles. We found that diverse transparency policies shared common roots, characteristics, and challenges, and therefore represented a single policy innovation.[3] We also found that the dynamics of targeted transparency were of central importance; that transparency systems were more likely to grow weaker than to improve over time; and that the systems that grew stronger featured strong groups representing information users, offered benefits to at least some information disclosers, and provided comprehensible content.[4]

Finally, we created a framework for analyzing the effectiveness of targeted transparency policies. We constructed a stylized "action cycle" to describe the steps from information disclosure to risk reduction in order to see at what point policies failed. At each step, we found that the linchpin of effective transparency was the connection between information and action. Targeted policies were effective only when they provided facts that people wanted in times, places, and ways that enabled them to act. That is, effective policies were those that succeeded in embedding new information in users' and disclosers' existing decision-making routines.[5] That meant that the starting point for any transparency policy was an understanding of the priorities and capacities of diverse audiences who might use the new information. Effective policies did not simply increase information. They increased knowledge that informed choice.

We presented our ideas to audiences at the Kennedy School, the Brookings Institution, the American Enterprise Institute, Georgetown University, the Association for Public Policy Analysis and Management, Boston University, and the American Political Science Association, among other venues, and received valuable feedback. In three occasional papers for the Ash Institute for Democratic Governance and Innovation, we set forth our emerging ideas. We also introduced our ideas to broader audiences in articles for the *Financial Times*, *Environment*, *Issues in Science and Technology*, the *Atlantic Monthly*, the *Journal of Policy Analysis and Management*, and other publications.

This book is an effort to bring together what we have learned in order to offer the first systematic account of the political economy of targeted transparency systems. Because targeted transparency has been applied to such a diverse range of problems, we have based our conclusions on a rich variety of cases. Like biologists collecting and comparing specimens of flora and fauna to derive common classifications, we have examined individual policies to gain insights into the common elements of their operation and consequences.

Our multidisciplinary approach recognizes that transparency policies arise from real-world compromises rather than from pristine public policy analyses, and that the resulting incentive systems are dynamic, evolving under pressure from the shifting economic and political interests of affected parties. We provide an analytical structure for understanding how such policies work and what makes the difference between success and failure.

We speak to three audiences. First, we hope to inform the work of scholars in many disciplines. Targeted transparency is of interest to economists, political scientists, regulatory analysts, cognitive psychologists, specialists in business administration, information technology analysts, and many others.

Second, we hope to provide useful insights that provoke debate among those engaged in framing and responding to targeted transparency policies. These groups include not only policymakers but also business executives, consumer groups, and advocacy organizations.

Finally, we hope to alert interested citizens to both the promise and the perils of targeted transparency. Ultimately, the effectiveness of transparency policies depends on the needs and capacities of ordinary citizens. The provision of information doesn't automatically enable people to make more informed choices. That requires an alert and engaged public that understands the dynamics of transparency and is ready to participate energetically in using new information and in shaping more effective policies.

This book could not have been completed without the contributions of many at the Kennedy School of Government. First among these is Alan Altshuler, who, as director of the Taubman Center for State and Local Government, supported our work from the beginning. Alan offered insightful comments at every stage and created that rare environment that fosters truly interdisciplinary work. The Taubman Center provided a fortuitous home for our project. State and local governments proved to be true laboratories of democracy in the development of targeted transparency policies. Many of the most innovative policies we studied began as state or local mandates – among them, school performance reporting, nutritional labeling, patient safety reporting, restaurant hygiene grades, workplace chemicals reporting, and sex offender community notification. Wherever policies originated, nearly all succeeded or failed because of their impact (or lack of it) on the choices of people going about their everyday lives in their communities.

We also owe a great deal to Henry Lee, director of the school's Environment and Natural Resources Program, for his early and enthusiastic interest and for keeping the research project afloat at key moments. Gowher Rizvi, director of the Roy and Lila Ash Institute for Democratic Governance and Innovation, offered not only financial support and a venue for publication of three of our papers but also invaluable personal encouragement.

The Brookings Institution in Washington, D.C., and in particular Carol Graham and Pietro Nivola, successive directors of Governance Studies, also supported the project from the outset. They offered valuable insights, provided crucial research support for the development of international cases, offered Mary Graham a Visiting Fellow appointment, and published (with the Governance Institute) her in-depth analysis of three public disclosure systems, *Democracy by Disclosure.*

We also received essential financial support at key junctures from the William and Flora Hewlett Foundation, from another major foundation, and from the Center for Business and Public Policy at Georgetown University.

We have benefited from the intellectual and financial support as well as the warm friendship of colleagues at the Taubman Center, including Ed Glaeser, Arn Howitt, David Luberoff, and Sandy Garron. The insights of Cass Sunstein, a dean of the American regulatory state, led us to ask important questions that we otherwise might have missed. We are also indebted to the editors and four anonymous reviewers of the *Journal of Policy Analysis and Management* for their comments on "The Effectiveness of Regulatory Disclosure Policies," the article that forms the basis of the fourth chapter of this book.

A host of individuals provided us with insights, detailed comments, observations, and camaraderie in our ongoing discussions. We owe a special debt to Richard J. Zeckhauser, Frank Plumpton Ramsey Professor of Political Economy at the Kennedy School, whose detailed and insightful comments we pondered and debated for months with the result that our analysis was enriched in many ways. We are also very grateful for several conversations with the late Daniel Patrick Moynihan, whose distinguished career included an investigation of the issues of secrecy and transparency, summarized in his last book, *Secrecy.* We thank Dara O'Rourke, Charles Sabel, Michael Dorf, Bradley Karkkainen, Amy Shapiro, William Simon, James Liebman, Cary Coglianese, Jennifer Nash, Rob Stavins, Lori Snyder, James Hamilton, Ron Mitchell, the late Vicki Norberg Bohm, and John Mayo.

Two Kennedy School graduates, Elena Fagotto and Khalisha Banks, joined our research team at the Taubman Center. They helped enormously in documenting and analyzing the transparency policies on which this book is based. Elena Fagotto, the project's senior research associate, has participated in our intellectual journey from almost its beginning and joins us as coauthor of the book's chapter on effectiveness. At the Brookings Institution, Andrew Eggers offered exceptional research support as well as original insights that contributed greatly to the development of the international cases.

Several individuals assisted us in finalizing the manuscript. Karl Weber took on the formidable task of editing our chapter drafts to make the book comprehensible to those in many disciplines. Terri Gallego-O'Rourke gave us the benefit of her legal expertise, attention to detail, and indefatigable good humor in completing the fact-checking and sourcing of the manuscript. Martha Nichols provided important feedback on a very early draft.

The book benefited enormously from the wise counsel, experience, and enthusiasm of Cambridge University Press senior editor Scott Parris, who shepherded it through the publication process. We are grateful to Marielle Poss for managing the publication process with alacrity on a very tight schedule. As copy editor, Janis Bolster improved the manuscript and saved us from several inconsistencies. Melissanne Scheld, Gene Taft, and Greg Houle worked to bring the book to the attention of many specialized audiences.

Finally, we would not be fully transparent if we did not gratefully acknowledge our families for their ongoing support and willingness to listen to and critique our ideas and musings on this project over the last five years.

ONE

Governance by Transparency

THE NEW POWER OF INFORMATION

On September 12, 2000, Masatoshi Ono, the chief executive of leading U.S. tire manufacturer Bridgestone/Firestone, faced a panel of senators and a battery of television cameras in a packed hearing room. The senate panel was investigating mounting deaths from a mysterious series of auto accidents in which tires blew out without warning, causing vehicles – many of them Ford Explorer SUVs – to roll over. Addressing the senators and the room full of victims' families, auto safety advocates, and industry representatives, as well as a nationwide television audience, Ono uttered words that no CEO wants to say: "I come before you to express my deep regret and sympathy to you, the American people and especially to the families who have lost loved ones in these terrible rollover accidents."[1]

The Firestone scandal remained national news during the summer and fall of 2000 because auto companies and tire makers had failed to inform the public about deadly risks. Documents from Firestone/Bridgestone and Ford indicated that both companies had been aware of a pattern of fatal accidents caused by a combination of tire tread separation and top-heavy SUVs but had done nothing to alert drivers. Bridgestone/Firestone executives knew that its plant in Decatur, Illinois, where most of the problem tires were made, had long had quality-control problems. When the count was finally complete, 271 people had been killed in accidents involving problematic SUV design and defective tires.[2]

The public, however, learned about these problems only by chance – and only after many of the deaths and injuries. In early February of 2000, Houston station KHOU-TV reported that lawsuits claimed that exploding Firestone tires and associated Explorer rollovers had caused thirty deaths. It took another six months for Bridgestone/Firestone executives to acknowledge the problem and recall 6.5 million tires, the largest tire recall since the 1970s.[3]

More troubling, the Senate investigation revealed that the problem was larger than a limited number of defective tires. In the 1990s, many people bought SUVs because they thought they were safer than smaller cars. The Firestone/Explorer revelations showed that, to the contrary, SUVs were more likely to roll over than other cars – and some SUV models were much more prone to roll over than others. That was important because rollovers remained the most deadly auto accidents, accounting for nearly a third of auto fatalities in the United States even though they represented less than 4 percent of all accidents.[4] Nonetheless, information about which SUVs were prone to roll over – like the facts about the unusual Firestone tire blowouts – remained locked in company files.

As reports of deaths and injuries mounted, congressional committees debated what action to take. Regulators had authority only to mandate recalls and impose modest fines on automakers and tire companies for safety defects. States could prosecute officials for criminal negligence, of course, and injured passengers could sue for damages. But such actions would not reduce the likelihood of future deadly accidents.

Circling around contentious issues concerning how to mandate safer design, Congress instead legislated targeted transparency. The Transportation Recall Enhancement, Accountability, and Documentation (TREAD) Act, approved in November 2000, required auto companies for the first time to give car buyers the facts about each model's rollover risks so that they could make their own safety choices.[5]

The idea was not just that the public deserved better information. It was that the power of information would create a chain reaction of new incentives. Armed with new rollover ratings, buyers would choose safer cars. Confronted with declining sales of the most top-heavy SUVs, auto companies would improve design. Safer design would save lives and prevent injuries. The new law thus made transparency into a precise policy tool.

Information had new power because policymakers did not stop at simply placing facts about risks in the public domain – where they could easily be lost in the cacophony of new-car hype. Instead, policymakers required that information be presented in a format that was designed to be user-centered. They distilled the complex probabilities of rollovers into simple five-star ratings based on government tests of each new model (see Figure 1.1). In a few seconds, car buyers, regardless of their math or language skills, could compare risks and identify rollover-prone models. A five-star vehicle, with a 10 percent or less chance of rolling over in a single-vehicle crash, was much safer than a one-star vehicle, with a 40 percent or more chance of rolling

Save vehicles	Vehicle	Frontal Star Rating (based on risk of head & chest injury)		Side Star Rating (based on risk of chest injury)		Rollover Rating	
		Driver	Passenger	Front Seat	Rear Seat	2 wheel drive	4 wheel drive
▷	2006 Acura MDX 4-DR. w/SAB (SUV)	☆☆☆☆	☆☆☆☆☆	☆☆☆☆☆	☆☆☆☆☆	Not rated	☆☆☆
▷	2006 Buick Rendezvous 4-DR. w/SAB (SUV)	☆☆☆	☆☆☆☆	☆☆☆☆☆	☆☆☆☆☆	Not rated	Not rated
▷	2006 Cadillac Escalade 4-DR. w/SAB (SUV)	☆☆☆☆	☆☆☆☆☆	Not rated	Not rated	☆☆☆	☆☆
▷	2006 Cadillac Escalade ESV 4-DR. w/SAB (SUV)	☆☆☆☆	☆☆☆	Not rated	Not rated		☆☆☆

Figure 1.1. Rollover Star Rating Graphic. *Source:* http://www.SaferCar.gov

over. Buyers could also customize information to suit their needs. Anyone interested in more detail could delve deeper into narratives and Web site links. In 2005, Congress made the policy even more user-centered. A new law required that information be presented by September 2007 *where* car buyers most needed it, on showroom new-car stickers.[6]

The policy also included an interesting built-in mechanism intended to increase the chances that transparency would be sustainable. It required that ratings become more accurate over time. The initial scores would be based on simple mathematical modeling of rollover propensity combining each model's center of gravity and track width. But the law required that safety regulators also work toward a road test that would more accurately mimic real-world driving conditions, and it directed the National Academy of Sciences to study possible tests and required regulators to consider the academy's recommendations. As a result, regulators instituted a new test in 2004 that combined modeling with driving maneuvers.[7]

Congress added other disclosure-based incentives. The TREAD Act required tire pressure monitoring sensors by 2003;[8] safety regulators required automakers to disclose information on customer complaints and other early indications of safety defects;[9] and new labels made it easier for car owners to see if their tires had been recalled.[10]

This, then, was the concept: government would use the power of information to drive better choices by car buyers, which in turn would improve vehicle designs and reduce risks. But would it work?

Five years after the release of the first set of rollover ratings, the answer appeared to be yes. Initially, SUV models had widely varying rollover rates – and most performed poorly. In 2001, thirty models received only one or two stars, meaning that they had a greater than 30 percent chance of rolling over, while only one model (the Pontiac Aztek 4-DR) earned a four-star rating, meaning that it had a less than 20 percent chance of rolling over. By 2005, however, only one model (the Ford Explorer Sport Trac) received as few as two stars, while twenty-four models earned four stars.[11]

Transparency also created pressures that ended a generation of industry lobbying against a rollover safety standard. The national attention that rollover accidents received in 2000 and the new star ratings spurred automakers to accelerate their introduction of stability-control technology. By 2005, 20 percent of new vehicles were equipped with sensors that triggered corrective braking, compared with fewer than 5 percent in 2000. Voluntary adoption of new technology changed the political dynamic. In 2005, Congress approved the Safe, Accountable, Flexible, Efficient Transportation Equity Act: A Legacy for Users (SAFETEA-LU), which directed regulators to issue minimum performance standards for auto rollovers.[12]

TRANSPARENCY INFORMS CHOICE

In recent years public attention has focused mainly on struggles over broad transparency in government – President Clinton's championing of a broader public right to know and President George W. Bush's controversial moves to increase government secrecy, for example. Few have recognized that a second generation of targeted transparency has been rapidly gaining ground.

Instead of aiming to generally improve public deliberation and officials' accountability, targeted transparency aims to reduce specific risks or performance problems through selective disclosure by corporations and other organizations. The ingeniousness of targeted transparency lies in its mobilization of individual choice, market forces, and participatory democracy through relatively light-handed government action.

Since the mid-1980s, scores of targeted transparency policies have percolated up through the political system in the United States – usually without any awareness by their creators that they were participating in a more general innovation in governance. After a deadly chemical accident in Bhopal, India, killed thousands of people, Congress required in 1986 that manufacturers tell the public about the toxic pollutants they released – factory by factory and chemical by chemical. After scientists confirmed that unhealthy eating habits were contributing to millions of deaths from heart disease and cancer each year, Congress required in 1990 that food companies inform the public about the levels of fat, sugar, and other nutrients in each can of soup and box of cereal. After a series of revelations about the surprising frequency of serious medical mistakes, Congress considered proposals in 2000 to require hospitals to inform the public about such mistakes, and several states required hospitals and doctors to tell the public their mortality rates for specific procedures. After the corporate accounting scandals of 2001 and 2002, Congress required that public companies improve their financial disclosure.

Targeted transparency policies have also been crafted to improve the fairness and quality of public services. In response to continuing concern about financial institutions' discrimination against inner-city borrowers, Congress strengthened requirements in 1989 and 1992 that banks report on their mortgage loans according to the race, gender, and income level of borrowers in each geographical area they serve. In response to continuing concern about the quality of public schools, Congress required in 2001 that school performance reporting demonstrate school improvement as a condition of federal aid.

Each of these laws wrested from the files of corporations, nonprofit organizations, or public agencies some of the facts that executives would often like to keep confidential – information about the risks they create and about flaws in the quality of goods and services they provide. Each offered sunlight in a format that poor performers would most like to avoid – in labels, reports, or Web sites that allowed consumers, investors, employees, and community residents to compare products and practices.

Though the problems they address vary widely, the idea behind all these new laws is the same. A generation of research by economists and political scientists has shown that markets and deliberative processes do not automatically produce all the information people need to make informed choices among goods and services. When hidden risks or service flaws create serious problems for the public at large, the government can help reduce those risks or improve services by stepping in to require the disclosure of missing information.

Why is government action needed? Three reasons: First, only government can compel the disclosure of information from private and public entities. Second, only government can legislate permanence in transparency. Third, only government can create transparency backed by the legitimacy of democratic processes.

The core characteristics of targeted transparency policies are also the same. It is hard to imagine that nutritional labeling, school performance ratings, and corporate financial reporting have much in common. Yet all targeted transparency policies include these characteristics:

- mandated public disclosure
- by corporations or other private or public organizations
- of standardized, comparable, and disaggregated information
- regarding specific products or practices
- to further a defined public purpose.

When they achieve their objectives, these policies all work in the same way, incorporating the following sequence of events or "action cycle":

- Information users perceive and understand newly disclosed information
- and therefore choose safer, healthier, or better-quality goods and services.
- Information disclosers perceive and understand users' changed choices
- and therefore improve practices or products
- that in turn reduce risks or improve services.

While new in its broad information-age applications, targeted transparency is not a new idea in governance. In 1913 Louis D. Brandeis, the "people's attorney" and later Supreme Court justice, wrote in *Harper's Weekly* that "sunlight is... the best of disinfectants." Brandeis recommended new laws to require public companies to disclose their profits and losses in order to stop insider deals that deceived investors. He pointed to an even earlier law, the 1906 Pure Food and Drug Act, which required listing ingredients on interstate shipments of foods, as an example of government-mandated "sunlight" to reduce public risks.[13]

President Franklin D. Roosevelt quoted Brandeis's words twenty years later when he urged Congress to require new corporate financial disclosure rules after millions of Americans lost their savings in the stock market crash of 1929. The 1933 and 1934 Securities and Exchange Acts ordered publicly traded companies to disclose assets and liabilities at regular intervals and in a standardized format.[14] Corporate financial disclosure as required by those laws, which remains at the core of U.S. securities policy, has become the United States' most sophisticated – though still imperfect – example of targeted transparency policy.

TRANSPARENCY AS MISSED OPPORTUNITY

However, targeted transparency policies can also do more harm than good. Such policies are always the products of political compromise. When the information from the tug and pull among many interests is incomplete, inaccurate, obsolete, confusing, or distorted, it can contribute to needless injuries or deaths or to large economic losses.

Four years before successful use of targeted transparency to reduce auto rollovers, Congress tried to enlist the power of information to reduce another serious safety risk – disease outbreaks from contaminated public water supplies. This time Congress failed.

Drinking water safety became national news in 1993 when a microbe called cryptosporidium infested the drinking water of Milwaukee, Wisconsin, sickening an astounding 400,000 individuals and killing as many as 110 within a matter of weeks. Congress responded in 1996 by demanding that water authorities inform their customers about contaminants in the water supply.[15]

That time, though, Congress crafted a requirement that employed technical terms, produced inaccurate and out-of-date information, failed to link contaminant data to health risks, and did not provide comparability from one community to another. Instead of receiving clear information that was comprehensible at a glance, like the five-star auto rollover rankings, consumers seeking information about the relative safety of their tap water faced

City of Cambridge Water Department
2005 Annual Drinking Water Quality Report

250 Fresh Pond Parkway
Cambridge, MA 02138

DEP PWS ID#3049000   June 2006

24 Hour Emergency/Customer Service
Phone Number   1-617-349-4770

Cambridge Water Department - Consumer Confidence Report 2005 Data								
Lead and Copper	Units	90% Value	Range	Action Level(AL)90%	MCLG	Violation	Sites exceeding AL	
Copper	ppm	0.035	0.001-1.09	1.3	0	NO	0 of 60	Corrosion of household plumbing.
Lead	ppb	7	0 - 157	15	0	NO	2 of 60	Corrosion of household plumbing.
Regulated- Inorganic Contaminants		Highest	Range	MCL	MCLG	Violation		
Barium	ppm	0.047	0.035-0.047	2	2	NO		Erosion of natural deposits.
Fluoride	ppm	1.3	0-1.3	4	4	NO		Water additive to promote strong teeth.
Nitrate as Nitrogen	ppm	0.74	0.29-0.74	10	10	NO		Runoff from fertilizer use.
Nitrite as Nitrogen	ppm	0.015	0-0.015	1	1	NO		Runoff from fertilizer use.
Unregulated - Inorganic Contaminants		Average	Range					
Sulfate	ppm	25	23-27					Erosion of natural deposits.
Sodium	ppm	70	60-92					road salt.
Unregulated - Organic Contaminants		Average	Range					
Bromodichloromethane	ppb	2.8	1.6-4.6					By-product of drinking water chlorination.
Bromoform	ppb	1.8	0.9-3.4					By-product of drinking water chlorination.
Chloroform	ppb	1.4	0.7-3.0					By-product of drinking water chlorination.
Dibromodichloromethane	ppb	3.9	2.3-6.3					By-product of drinking water chlorination.
Regulated -Volitale Organic Contaminants		Highest Ave	Range	MCL	MCLG	Violation		
Total Trihalomethanes(THMs)	ppb	10.3	4.8-18	80	0	NO		By-product of drinking water chlorination.
Haloacetic Acids(HAA5)	ppb	8.7	3.5-20	60	0	NO		By-product of drinking water chlorination.
		Highest Ave	Range	MRDL	MRDLG	Violation		
Chlorine as Chloramine	ppm	3	1.3 - 3.0	4	4	NO		Water additive used to control microbes.
Regulated - Radioactive Contaminants (2002)						Violation		
Gross Alpha Activity	pCi/L	0.3	n/a	15	0	NO		Erosion of natural deposits.
Gross Beta Activity	pCi/L	14	n/a	AL = 50	0	NO		Decay of naturally occurring deposits.
Turbidity	TT	Lowest Monthly %		Highest Daily Value		Violation		
Daily Compliance(NTU)	1			0.16		NO		Suspended matter from soil runoff.
Monthly Compliance	At least 95%	100				NO		Suspended matter from soil runoff.
Bacteria	Highest % Positive in a Month			Total # positive	MCL	Violation	MCLG	
Total Coliform	1%(April)			1	>5%	NO	0	Naturally occurring in the environment.

Figure 1.2. Drinking Water Safety Report – Cambridge, Massachusetts. *Source:* Excerpts from City of Cambridge report, June 2006, http://www.cambridgema.gov/ CityOfCambridge_Content/documents/CCR2005_web.pdf

the daunting task of interpreting complex documents like that shown in Figure 1.2. Just at the time when electronic monitoring and the Internet made real-time reporting feasible, water authorities' lobbying as well as careless planning by policymakers produced partial and hard-to-decipher information that was as much as a year out of date.[16]

As a result, some customers who relied on assurances that tap water was safe actually suffered *increased* health risks. In a particularly troubling series of incidents, media reports in 2004 revealed that tens of thousands of children in Washington, D.C., Boston, and other big cities were drinking water contaminated with unreported high levels of lead, an especially dangerous toxin that could cause severe neurological damage in children. In the nation's capital, federal and local officials admitted they had known about the lead contamination for years but had neither informed customers nor taken steps to remedy the problem. Instead, the city's contaminant reports assured customers, "Your Drinking Water Is Safe." One reason that risks remained hidden was because contaminant reports did not include information about microbes or toxins that entered water after it left the filtration plant – as it passed through hundreds of miles of old lead pipes.[17]

Drinking water reports represent a missed opportunity with serious consequences. According to the National Centers for Disease Control and Prevention, up to 30 percent of reported disease outbreaks each year can be attributed to problems of public water systems, affecting as many as nine hundred thousand people. In 2005, Stephen L. Johnson, the new administrator of the federal Environmental Protection Agency, estimated that at least 10 percent of Americans regularly drink unhealthy water.[18] All in all, as many as 50 million Americans drink water containing industrial solvents and related chemicals that may have long-term health effects.[19]

In the largest water systems, the mixture and levels of contaminants vary greatly from week to week as weather and waste discharges change. Accurate and current contaminant reporting can be critical for those most vulnerable – the very young, the very old, and people on chemotherapy, suffering from AIDS, or with otherwise compromised immune systems. Such individuals – who together make up roughly 20 percent of the U.S. population – are at special risk from bacteria or toxins in drinking water.

Meanwhile, the public's trust in the nation's water supply continues to erode. A quarter of Americans reported in 1999 that they never drank tap water. Sixty-five percent of those who did drink tap water reported that they drank bottled water or filtered tap water some of the time.[20]

Transparency gaps that increase serious risks are common. Some other prominent examples:

- Millions of investors lost savings and retirement funds in 2001 and 2002 not only because corporate executives at some of the nation's largest and best-known companies fraudulently withheld information but also because the financial accounting system allowed them to hide – and profit from – information about financial risks in their companies.
- Millions of people have unknowingly increased their risk of heart disease because nutritional labels have not told consumers when cookies, muffins, and other fast foods contain trans fats, the most dangerous fats on the market. For two decades, scientists have known and warned of trans fat risks.

- Despite twenty years of alarming evidence that more people in the United States die from medical errors in hospitals than from auto accidents and findings that some institutions are ten times safer than others, hospitals are still not required to disclose mistakes that cause death or serious injury.
- Five years after the September 11, 2001, terrorist attacks in New York City and Washington, D.C., government officials still rely on a five-color terrorist threat warning system that does not provide the public with needed information for self-protection – leaving information gaps that could cost thousands of lives.

The cases we have drawn together illustrate both the promise and the perils of a new generation of targeted transparency. By requiring auto rollover ratings, Congress invented a means of communicating complex information in a simple format that helps car buyers compare models and make safe choices. By requiring reports on drinking water safety, Congress settled for a compromise that produced out-of-date and incomplete information that confuses and sometimes misleads customers. Such distorted disclosure not only impairs public health. It also undermines one of democracy's central tenets – that citizens can trust their government as a source of reliable, timely information.

A REAL-TIME EXPERIMENT

What makes the difference between transparency success and failure and how can its effectiveness be improved? We have written this book to answer these questions.

We have scrutinized a carefully selected group of transparency policies using a multidisciplinary approach. We have analyzed the effectiveness of fifteen major targeted transparency policies in the United States and three international policies. Out of the universe of policies that fit our definition of targeted transparency, we chose a set of relatively mature cases, distributed across a range of public policy areas, with potentially important consequences, and whose varied effectiveness has been assessed in rigorous empirical studies.

We reviewed the legislative history and legal requirements of each policy and examined the politics surrounding initial approval and later amendments. We assessed each policy's regulatory structure and the incentives that structure provided for accurate reporting by disclosers, as well as the kind of information it ultimately provided to users. We also analyzed the decision-making processes of users and disclosers in order to understand their actual responses to newly released information. Finally, we identified the drivers of effectiveness by analyzing hundreds of empirical studies and by interviewing policymakers, scholars, and diverse users and disclosers of information. This approach has allowed us to develop a theory of targeted transparency effectiveness that explains the varying outcomes of existing policies and can provide the basis for future research. Table 1.1 provides an overview of the eighteen targeted transparency policies that form the analytic core of this book, and the Appendix contains our detailed descriptions of them.

Our analysis has limitations. We did not attempt to construct a random sample of all targeted transparency policies or undertake a formal meta-analysis of studies. Such approaches were neither tenable nor desirable given the diversity of transparency policies we examined. The benefits of using a multidisciplinary approach and rooting our conclusions in well-grounded studies outweighed the inevitable biases that arose from choosing a subset of all possible cases.

We conclude that the effectiveness of targeted transparency depends heavily on two factors that form the book's two major themes.

- First, targeted transparency policies succeed when they are *user-centered*. Successful policies focus first on the needs and interests of information users, as well as their abilities to comprehend the information provided by the system. Such policies also focus on the needs, interests, and capacities of disclosing organizations. They seek to embed new facts in the decision-making routines of information users and to embed user responses into the decision making of disclosers. Successful transparency policies thus place the individuals and groups who will use information at center stage.
- Second, effective transparency policies must be *sustainable* to be effective. Sustainable policies are those that gain in use, accuracy, and scope over time. Such improvement is important because policies inevitably start as flawed compromises, because markets and public priorities change, and because policymakers constantly need to fill loopholes discovered by reluctant information disclosers.

The sudden bankruptcies of Enron, WorldCom, and other large and respected companies in the 2001 and 2002 illustrate how costly transparency failure can be. While no disclosure system can prevent fraud or intentional

Table 1.1. *Targeted Transparency Systems: Overview of Eighteen Transparency Policies*

Disclosure System	Year Enacted	Public Policy Objective	Information Disclosed	Primary Disclosers	Primary Users
U.S. Targeted Transparency Systems					
Corporate Financial Disclosure[a]	1933, 1934	Reduce hidden risks to investors, improve corporate governance	Company financial data	Public companies trading in U.S.	Investors, financial intermediaries
Union Finances Disclosure[b]	1959	Reduce corruption, increase accountability of labor union officers	Financial revenues and expenditures, union governance information	Labor unions	Labor union members, prospective members
Campaign Finances Disclosure[c]	1971	Reduce corruption, increase accountability of national political candidates	Contributions to candidates by individuals, organizations	Candidates for national office	Opposing candidates, journalists, political parties, interest groups
Mortgage Lending Disclosure[d]	1975	Reduce mortgage lending discrimination	Lending activity demographics	Banks, other lending institutions	Community groups, regulators
Workplace Hazards Disclosure[e]	1983	Reduce worker exposures to chemical hazards	Information on workplace hazardous chemicals	Manufacturers, employers	Workers, employers
Toxics Releases Disclosure[f]	1986	Reduce toxic pollution	Quantities of releases by chemical and factory	Chemical manufacturers, users	Regulators, environmental groups, communities
Plant Closing, Mass Layoff Disclosure[g]	1988	Lower costs of major economic dislocations from closures/layoffs	Plans of large-scale layoffs/ facility closings	Large companies	Affected workers, communities
Nutritional Labeling[h]	1990	Reduce risks of chronic disease	Nutrients in most processed foods	Manufacturers of packaged foods	Consumers, schools, employers, hospitals
Patient Safety Disclosure (NY, PA)[i]	NY: 1990 PA: 1992	Improve cardiac surgery performance	Mortality rates, etc., in patient treatment	Hospitals, doctors	Patients, doctors, insurers, governments
School Performance Disclosure[j]	1994 (federal); various years (states)	Improve school performance and accountability	School-level performance data	Schools, school districts	Parents, prospective residents, governments

12

Policy	Date	Goal	Information Disclosed	Disclosers	Users
Sex Offender Place of Residences[k]	WA: 1990 (Other states – various years)	Reduce public safety risks from released sex offenders and other felons	Place of residence of dangerous ex-offenders	Police departments, sex offenders	Community residents
Drinking Water Contaminant Disclosure[l]	1996	Improve quality of public drinking water supplies	Water supply contaminants	Public, private water authorities	Consumers, schools, employers, hospitals
Restaurant Hygiene Disclosure[m]	Los Angeles County: 1997	Reduce risk of food-borne illnesses	Letter grades reflecting hygiene inspection results	Restaurants	Consumers
Automobile Rollover Disclosure[n]	2001	Lower risk of death, injuries from auto rollovers	5-star ratings of new-model rollover propensity	Auto companies selling in U.S.	Consumers, fleet purchasers
Terrorism Threat Disclosure[o]	2002	Reduce risks of, minimize damage from terrorist attacks	Color-coded national, local terrorist threat levels	Department of Homeland Security	Federal, state, local governments, companies, public
International Targeted Transparency Systems					
International Corporate Financial Disclosure[p]	2002	Reduce hidden investor risks, improve corporate governance	Company financial data	Public multinational, EU-headquartered companies	Investors, financial intermediaries
Genetically Modified Foods Labeling[q]	2004	Increase food safety, environmental protection	Presence/absence of genetic modification of crops	Farmers, exporters, importers, consumers, grocery stores	Consumers, national governments
Infectious Disease Surveillance[r]	2005	Reduce international spread of serious infectious diseases	Location, character of disease outbreaks	National governments, public health personnel, citizens	World Health Organization, public health personnel, citizens

Note: Dates are years of initial policy enactment; see the Appendix for a discussion of amendments or supplemental legislation in subsequent years.
[a] Securities Act (1933) and Securities and Exchange Act (1934); [b] Labor Management Reporting and Disclosure Act; [c] Federal Election Campaign Act; [d] Home Mortgage Disclosure Act; [e] Hazard Communication Standard – promulgated under the Occupational Safety and Health Act; [f] Emergency Planning and Community Right-to-Know Act – the Toxics Release Inventory is a database established by the act; [g] Worker Adjustment and Retraining Notification Act; [h] Nutrition Labeling and Education Act; [i] New York Cardiac Surgery Reporting System and Pennsylvania Guide to Coronary Artery Bypass Graft Surgery; [j] Federal School Report Card law; [k] Megan's Law; [l] Amendments to the Safe Drinking Water Act of 1974; [m] Los Angeles County Restaurant Hygiene Grade Cards; [n] Transportation Recall Enhancement, Accountability, and Documentation Act; [o] Homeland Security Presidential Directive 3 (HSPD-3), as amended by Homeland Security Presidential Directive 5 (HSPD-5); [p] International Accounting Standards Board reorganization; [q] European Union labeling system; [r] International Health Regulations.

misrepresentation, those scandals represent a failure of the corporate financial disclosure policy – the nation's most respected targeted transparency system – to keep pace with changing markets. A proliferation of off–balance sheet entities, unreported stock options, and other arguably legal market innovations hid risks and inflated reported earnings. As a result, millions of investors lost their savings while a few executives profited from inside knowledge. The 2002 Sarbanes-Oxley Act represented a belated and still controversial attempt by Congress to repair the financial transparency system so that it could catch up with market innovations.

TRANSPARENCY SUCCESS AND FAILURE

Whether effective or not, targeted transparency is likely to proliferate as the preferred remedy for a wide variety of public risks and service flaws. That is why it is worth taking the time and effort to understand how these policies work and how to improve their effectiveness. The legislative histories of the policies we have studied suggest that three long-term trends help explain why such an unlikely innovation is occurring now and why it is likely to last.[21]

First, transparency policies are gaining strength because conventional forms of government intervention – for example standards-based regulatory systems or performance-based tax policies – are sometimes ill suited to the kinds of risks and performance flaws that policymakers now identify for action. Problems that are widely dispersed and locally variable, or characterized by wide differences in consumers' and citizens' preferences, may not lend themselves to uniform rules, subsidies, or taxes. For example, Congress required auto rollover ratings in 2000 when national publicity about hidden risks created a demand for public action, when no immediate consensus could be reached about the feasibility and provisions of a minimum rollover performance standard, and when car buyers' safety preferences varied widely. Congress required nutritional labeling in 1990 when scientists linked deaths from heart disease and cancer to unhealthy diets, consumers' food choices varied widely, and outlawing saturated fats or taxing donuts was neither feasible nor desirable. Congress required disclosure of drinking water contaminants, albeit ineffectively, when existing minimum safety standards proved inadequate to prevent locally variable spikes in contamination. In such circumstances, transparency policies often represent pragmatic compromises.

Second, transparency policies have been propelled by the transforming power of computers and the Internet. Even as large corporations employ information technology to gather personal data about their customers, the public – through transparency laws – is using technology to mine the files of public companies, chemical manufacturers, hospitals, schools, water authorities, banks, and other public and private organizations.

The Internet provides new ways to customize and share information about the risks companies create and the quality of the products and services they provide. In the public domain as in the private sector, electronic capabilities to layer, customize, and share information have shattered the settled assumption that in-depth information can be communicated only among small groups of experts while broad audiences should receive only superficial ideas or simple warnings.[22] Internet users can now search for toxic pollution by zip code and factory, chemical, or health effect, with opportunities to add comments or communicate with members of Congress.[23] Likewise, Internet users can quickly compare airlines' safety records and on-time and baggage-handling records before buying a ticket – or add information about a safety problem they have observed.[24] The Internet may ultimately help create a new generation of more effective collaborative transparency policies.[25]

Third, transparency policies are becoming more prevalent because they represent a politically viable means of responding to emerging risks or public service flaws in the context of widespread skepticism about the capacity of government alone to solve those problems.[26] When party loyalty and trust of elected representatives are declining and opportunities to participate in public decisions are taking new forms, it makes sense that voters and community residents would demand better factual information on which to base decisions about community services or candidates for office. Targeted transparency offers an opportunity to harness the decisions of private individuals and organizations to achieve public purposes. As we will see, many transparency policies successfully operate in this political middle ground. Others, however, create an illusion that a problem has been addressed while producing minimal impact.

HOW THE BOOK IS ORGANIZED

We begin by placing targeted transparency in context. Chapter 2 documents the increasing use of targeted transparency as a policy instrument in the United States through a survey of Federal Register entries from 1996 to 2005. The chapter explains how this political innovation evolved from first-generation "right-to-know" requirements that aimed to inform the public about the workings of government. We find that both first- and second-generation policies defy assumptions that transparency is simple and inevitably beneficial. Instead, openness evolves through political struggle in continuous competition with values that favor secrecy, beset by practical difficulties in making information truly accessible, outpaced by disclosers' discoveries of new loopholes, and challenged by changing markets and public priorities.

We explain that recent research has helped to provide a rationale for government intervention to correct information imbalances. Targeted transparency policies have drawn strength from recent economic analysis challenging the idea that markets efficiently provide all the information that participants need. In addition, cognitive psychologists and economists have persuasively challenged the notion that individuals and groups automatically use available information to make rational choices, documenting an array of cognitive shortcuts that distort the processing of new data. Legislated transparency is intended to help remedy these problems.

In Chapter 3, we describe the architecture of targeted transparency policies and distinguish them from more conventional forms of government intervention. Targeted transparency employs communication as a regulatory vehicle, works through both market and political channels, and purposefully does *not* provide clear guidance to target organizations concerning what actions they should take. Conventional mandates, by contrast, employ rules and penalties or financial incentives, work through market channels, and do provide clear guidance to organizations concerning what actions they should take.

We then turn to the book's central question: what makes transparency policies effective? In Chapter 4, we construct a model showing the steps by which the mandated provision of new information can reduce risks or improve the performance of public institutions. We find that effective targeted transparency policies embed new information in the decision routines of both information disclosers and users. Our research suggests why it is difficult to achieve this goal. Because information disclosers and users have limited time and energy, they are likely to act on new information only if it has value to them, is compatible with the way they make choices, and is easily comprehensible. Providing information at a convenient time and place and in a useful format can improve chances of effectiveness. Even when new information is well embedded, however, conflicting preferences, distortions, and other obstacles may interfere with its effective use. Nonetheless, we find that some transparency policies prove highly effective and others moderately so.

To be effective, targeted transparency policies must also become sustainable, meaning that they improve over time in scope, accuracy, and usefulness. Chapter 5 explains that all transparency policies are inherently dynamic. However, they may be more likely to weaken than to improve. That is because information disclosers usually have stronger motivations and better capacity to influence transparency policies than do information users. Our research suggests that effective intermediaries who represent users' interests, the presence of some disclosers who find improved transparency advantageous, and periodic crises that concentrate users' interests can lead to improvement in transparency policies over time.

In Chapter 6, we examine whether targeted transparency can work across national boundaries and how the analytical framework we have developed can help in analyzing international policies. We find that both the structure and the functioning of international targeted transparency policies parallel those of national systems. However, because many international transparency policies emerge outside the usual structures of international law, such policies struggle to gain legitimacy – a formidable challenge to their effectiveness. Nonetheless, analyses of the improving systems of international corporate accounting and infectious disease surveillance suggest that international transparency policies can sometimes succeed.

Finally, we look to the future. Leaps in information technology are making possible a third generation of collaborative transparency in which communities of information users play an active role in shaping the content and format of information they need and in acting as disclosers themselves. Chapter 7 suggests that collaborative transparency policies will create both new potential benefits and potential dangers. Constantly updated access can increase accuracy and informational coverage, but it can also ignite public scares based on false or misleading facts. As information users take charge, government must still play an important role as the steward of transparency policies by compelling disclosure of needed information when participants cannot obtain it, fostering common definitions and accurate metrics, and providing feedback and analysis to encourage transparency improvement. Because we foresee growing use of targeted transparency in the future, Chapter 8 concludes with our recommendations for crafting policies to further crucial public priorities.

A detailed Appendix summarizes the eighteen cases we have analyzed. It describes each policy's government mandate, public purpose, targeted disclosers and users, information structure, and vehicle for communication. It also summarizes the politics that surrounded the creation of each policy, how each works, and whether and how each has changed over time.

The future of targeted transparency remains uncertain. The next generation of technology-enhanced transparency holds promise. However, technology won't untangle gerrymandered or poorly designed policies that squander the public's trust. Transparency's future remains a matter of political choice. Without leadership, imagination, and public scrutiny, the disinfecting power of disclosure soon fades.

TWO

An Unlikely Policy Innovation

The emergence of targeted transparency as mainstream policy represents an unlikely political innovation. In recent years, national, state, local, and international policymakers have overcome political obstacles to require both private-sector organizations and public agencies to collect and share new facts about the risks they create and the quality of their performance. Legislators have mandated new transparency despite enduring values and political interests that usually favor secrecy. They have also overcome the resistance to innovation that generally characterizes democratic systems of government.[1] Their actions are all the more surprising because they have invented new transparency systems without any central direction and usually without knowledge that their actions are contributing to a broader policy change.

In this chapter we explore why such an unexpected development in governance has occurred at this moment in history by examining the growth of targeted transparency policies in the United States in recent decades. We begin by documenting the frequency with which targeted transparency has been legislated in recent years across many major policy areas.

We then review the development of government-mandated transparency in the United States. We find that three factors have helped to propel this new generation of transparency into mainstream policy. First, the maturing of an early generation of right-to-know transparency measures helped to prepare the way for targeted transparency policies. Second, crises that called for urgent responses to suddenly revealed risks or performance problems helped to overcome political forces that favored secrecy and that limited innovation. Finally, a generation of research by economists and cognitive psychologists concerning information failures and communication complexities helped to provide a rationale for government action. This chapter's study of the roots of targeted transparency provides a backdrop for our detailed evaluation of effectiveness in subsequent chapters.

AN UNPLANNED INVENTION

In the last twenty years, targeted transparency policies have played a prominent role as a chosen policy response to a surprising number of national crises. In fact, ten of the fifteen U.S. targeted transparency policies analyzed in this book were created since 1986 (see Table 1.1), with a range of goals including improving the nutritional content of foods, reducing discrimination against minority groups in bank lending, minimizing sudden disruptions for workers and communities from plant closures, furthering patient safety, improving restaurant hygiene to reduce food poisoning, and cutting toxic pollution. These recent initiatives join long-standing disclosure requirements such as those designed to reduce financial risks faced by investors and to reduce risks of political corruption associated with campaign contributions by special interests.

A detailed review of federal regulations in the United States over the last decade reveals the importance of targeted transparency as a form of government intervention. In order to measure the extent of its use, we surveyed the Code of Federal Regulations for the calendar years 1996 to 2005, recording each final federal rule adopted during that period that employed targeted transparency. Using a variety of search terms and then applying a strict definition of targeted transparency, we found a total of 133 targeted transparency rules promulgated during this period.[2] Although it is difficult to estimate the total number of final regulations using other forms of government intervention over the same period, the absolute number itself underscores the importance of this approach as mainstream policy.

The scope of policies where targeted transparency has been applied is also quite striking. Table 2.1 provides examples from each of the ten years, illustrating the range of final regulations issued during this period.

Almost a quarter of the final regulations pertain to financial disclosure, with the majority of those regulations issued after 2000, in the wake of corporate reporting scandals. Regulations dealing with food and with drugs each account for about 15 percent of the total approved during the ten-year period. Disclosure policies related to consumer products – ranging from automobile crash and rollover risks to energy and water consumption of home appliances – also constitute a significant proportion of the final regulations, about 23 percent. The remaining policy areas include transparency requirements relating to the environment (about 7 percent), the workplace (about 5 percent), and an array of other topics.

This survey of recent federal regulations also points to several of the recurring themes of the book. First, as the examples in Table 2.1 suggest,

Table 2.1. *Selected Final Federal Regulations Regarding Targeted Transparency, Issued Between 1996 and 2005*

Year	Policy Area and Title of Final Rule	Description of Final Rule	Who Discloses?
1996	Drug safety – Sodium Labels for Over-the-Counter Drugs	Provides information on sodium content in OTC drugs similar to that found in nutritional labels	Drug manufacturers
	Consumer products – Energy Consumption and Water Use of Certain Home Appliances	Describes methods for the disclosure of energy-related operating costs of 8 categories of home appliances	Appliance manufacturers
1997	Food labeling – Serving Sizes Reference Amount for Specified Substances	Amends nutritional labeling to change reference amounts for customarily consumed food	Manufacturers of packaged foods
	Financial disclosure – Accounting Policies for Derivative Financial Instruments and Quantitative and Qualitative Information About Market Risk	Provides enhanced disclosure regarding accounting for derivatives found in financial statements	Domestic and foreign issuers of derivative financial instruments
1998	Food labeling – Irradiation in Production, Processing, and Handling of Food	Provides labeling of foods treated with radiation	Food manufacturers
	Water quality – National Primary Drinking Water Regulation – Consumer Confidence Reports	Requires community water systems to provide customers with annual reports of contaminants	Community water suppliers
1999	Consumer products – Consumer Information for Utility Motor Vehicles	Modifies rollover warnings required for small and mid-sized utility vehicles by requiring "alert" symbol to accompany previous text regarding possibility of rollover	Auto manufacturers

(continued)

Table 2.1 *(continued)*

Year	Policy Area and Title of Final Rule	Description of Final Rule	Who Discloses?
	Financial disclosure – Audit Committee Function	Requires that companies disclose in proxy statements the function of audit committees	Publicly traded companies
2000	Workplace disclosure – Enhanced Pension Plan Summary Descriptions Regarding Eligibility, Retirement Age, Cost-Sharing, and Other Provisions	Provides greater information to employees covered by pension plans about their benefits and coverage	Employers providing pension plans
	Workplace disclosure – Ergonomics Health Standard	Provides information regarding employee health risks (particularly musculoskeletal) associated with certain jobs and activities	Employers covered by OSHA
2001	Financial disclosure – Disclosure of Mutual Fund After-Tax Returns	Improves disclosure to investors of tax effects on mutual funds' performance	Mutual fund providers
2002	Consumer products – Consumer Complaints About Potential Defects in Automobiles	Requires auto manufacturers to collect and report consumer complaints	Auto manufacturers
	Mortgage lending – Loan Pricing Information	Provides information on mortgage lending practices that exceed certain benchmark levels	Banks/mortgage lenders
	Workplace disclosure – Hazardous Chemical Exposure to Miners	Requires mine operators to provide a written hazard communication program and material safety data sheets to employees	Mine operators
2003	Nutritional labeling – Trans-Fatty Acids	Requires that trans fats be disclosed in nutrition labels of purchased foods and dietary supplements	Food and supplement manufacturers

Year	Policy Area and Title of Final Rule	Description of Final Rule	Who Discloses?
	Labor union disclosure – Labor Union Annual Financial Information Regarding Revenues and Expenditures	Provides more extensive information on receipts, disbursements, and time allocation by union officers and employees toward specified activities	Labor unions
2004	Environmental protection – Hazardous Material Exposure in Communities	Increases requirements for hazard communication in the transportation of certain substances, including potential exposures in transportation incidents	Companies transporting hazardous chemicals
	Financial disclosure – Market Timing and Selective Disclosure of Portfolio Holdings	Requires disclosure regarding risks to shareholders of frequent purchases and redemptions of investment company shares	Investment management companies
2005	Financial disclosure – Accounting and Financial Reporting for Public Utilities	Requires enhanced financial reporting by public utilities information	Public utility companies

targeted transparency as an innovative form of regulation has been applied to virtually the full range of public policy problems that other forms of intervention – standards- and market-based regulation – have traditionally been deployed to address. These include reducing public exposure to health risks, reducing organizational corruption, and improving the provision of public goods like clean water and air.

Second, transparency has often been chosen as an initial – often tentative – response to emerging and thorny policy problems. For example, several years before tire malfunctions and auto rollovers gained national attention in a rash of Firestone Tire/Ford Explorer fatalities, regulators approved a rule to require auto manufacturers to collect and report consumer complaints to the government. Similarly, several narrowly constructed disclosure rules dealing with corporate governance appeared in the years immediately before major corporate scandals at Enron and WorldCom.

A third and related point is that targeted transparency policies are subjected to ongoing refinement long after enactment. Many of the disclosure rules that deal with food refine provisions of the nutritional labeling law approved in 1990, providing specific guidance on what dietary outcomes are included (e.g., the addition of labeling regarding trans fats approved in 2003) or the basis for calculating daily allowances of different nutrients. The specific changes shown in Table 2.1 often arose from political battles between information disclosers, users, and government officials.

The large number of disclosure rules adopted in recent years to flesh out broad public policies like nutritional labeling, financial disclosure, and environmental toxic releases also demonstrate that crafting effective transparency policies is far from a simple matter. It is one thing to advocate that Congress give the public "more information" and quite another to devise systems that actually deliver the public benefits they set out to accomplish.

THE STRUGGLE TOWARD OPENNESS

The notion that public access to information is central to democratic governance has a long history in the United States. In often-quoted phrases that are carved into the exterior of the Library of Congress in Washington, D.C., James Madison declared: "A popular government without popular information or the means of acquiring it, is but a Prologue to a Farce or a Tragedy or perhaps both. Knowledge will forever govern ignorance and a people who mean to be their own Governours, must arm themselves with the power knowledge gives."[3] John Stuart Mill noted the importance of permitting "the widest participation in the details of judicial and administrative business . . . above all by the utmost possible publicity and liberty of discussion."[4]

However, political thinkers have also long understood that powerful forces stand in the way of the public's access to information. Sociologist Max Weber warned that "[e]very bureaucracy seeks to increase the superiority of the professionally informed by keeping their knowledge and intentions secret."[5] Senator Daniel Patrick Moynihan argued that "secrecy is an institution of the administrative state that developed during the great conflicts of the twentieth century."[6] Political scientist Alan Altshuler noted that "people in government fear nothing more than newsworthy failure."[7]

As a result, government action to increase transparency has remained a struggle. A first generation of legislated transparency, *right-to-know policies,* gradually improved government openness. By the 1960s, national policies provided access to most government processes and files with the general aim of informing the public and guarding against arbitrary government action. A second generation of legislated transparency, *targeted transparency policies*, evolved from these right-to-know policies. Targeted transparency policies are more specific in their requirements and goals. They mandate access to precisely defined and structured factual information from private or public sources with the aim of furthering particular policy objectives. A nascent third generation of *collaborative transparency policies* has the potential to employ computer power and the Internet to combine information from first- and second-generation policies with a new user-centered orientation and a government facilitating role in order to create adaptable, real-time, customized information that reduces risks and public service flaws.

These three generations of transparency policy in the United States have proven complementary and overlapping. Targeted transparency did not lessen the need for right-to-know laws, nor will technology-enhanced collaborative transparency lessen the need for targeted disclosure requirements.

The generations of transparency policy also have much in common. Each has gained strength by a slow, evolutionary process with many setbacks. Each has been challenged by sometimes compelling arguments in defense of secrecy. Each has been dogged by persistent gaps between the public's legal right to data and the public's practical access to usable information. Each has also given rise to unintended consequences.

A Slow March Toward Right-to-Know

In practice, the march toward government openness in the United States began early but proceeded slowly. Although the proceedings that created the U.S. Constitution were held in secret, with sentries posted at the State House doors in Philadelphia to turn away onlookers, the Constitution itself required that most deliberations of Congress be public. Article 1, Section 5, states: "Each House shall keep a Journal of its Proceedings, and from time to time publish the same, excepting such Parts as may in their Judgment require Secrecy." Likewise, Supreme Court arguments, from the first sessions held in 1790, were open to spectators.[8]

However, it was not until 1946 that Congress opened the regulatory proceedings of the executive branch to public view and participation. The Administrative Procedure Act of that year represented a belated and controversial response to mounting concerns about fairness and accountability that accompanied the extraordinary growth of federal agencies during the

New Deal and war years. The new law required executive branch agencies to publish the substance of and rationale for proposed and final regulations and to allow opportunity for public comment.[9]

More right-to-know laws adopted between 1960 and 1990 sought to further open the increasingly complex and voluminous proceedings and records of government to public view. The most far-reaching of these laws, the federal Freedom of Information Act (FOIA), initially adopted in 1966 and strengthened by later amendments, created a broad presumption that the public had a right to information held by government. It was enacted after a decade of debate as an acknowledgment that the Administrative Procedure Act had fallen short of its goals and "had come to be looked upon as more of a withholding statute than a disclosure statute."[10]

In the Freedom of Information Act, Congress ambitiously tried to compress into a few paragraphs of legal prose the problematic balance between the need for open government and the need for secrecy in some deliberations. The law granted "any person" a right to receive data, transcripts, and other "agency records" in response to a formal request, unless disclosure threatened national security, personal privacy, or other interests specified in nine exemptions.[11] In time, all fifty states adopted right-to-know laws modeled after the federal statute.

Congress amended FOIA in the 1970s to narrow exemptions, speed disclosure, and increase oversight. An important further amendment in 1996 required agencies to make new records available electronically within a year of their creation and to make frequently sought records available on the Internet.[12]

Later federal right-to-know laws elaborated on the dual themes of informing the public about the workings of government and reducing the influence of narrow interests. In 1971, Congress required candidates for federal office to disclose campaign contributions and expenditures in order to reduce the political influence of large contributors, requirements that were substantially strengthened in later amendments.[13] The next year, Congress required that advisory committees appointed by agencies to help develop or implement policy make public their meetings and records in the hopes of reducing the influence of special interests.[14] In 1976, Congress required that government regulatory commissions also open their meetings to the public.[15]

Nonetheless, government transparency remained contentious. By the mid-1990s, nearly four thousand disclosure disputes involving the Freedom of Information Act had been decided by the courts, including nearly three dozen that were litigated all the way to the Supreme Court. Some centered on where to draw the line between openness and other competing values like national security, privacy, and corporate trade secrets. Others challenged the administrative chasm between the law's promise and agency practice. Information seekers could gain information only if they could correctly identify its substance and location, and agencies sometimes took months or years to respond to FOIA requests.[16]

The drive toward transparency was also challenged by periodic executive branch efforts to expand secrecy. Executive orders and reinterpretations of right-to-know reduced public access to information during the Cold War with the Soviet Union, the Vietnam War, and other international conflicts.

Presidential leadership remained critical in establishing a climate of openness or secrecy. Beginning in 2001, for example, President George W. Bush created an extended period of retrenchment in public access to government information, driven both by national security concerns and by politics and bureaucratic instincts. After the terrorist attacks of September 11, 2001, federal agencies quickly removed thousands of pages about health and safety risks from government Web sites. They included reports about accidents, risks, and emergency plans at factories that handled dangerous materials, information about security breaches at airports, and reports on reservoirs and other water resources. Administration officials argued that making such information available on the Web created mosaics of opportunity for terrorists.[17]

But even before the attacks of September 11, the Bush administration had taken unprecedented steps to expand official secrecy. Early in 2001 Vice President Dick Cheney provoked the first-ever suit by Congress's General Accounting Office against the executive branch by refusing to reveal the names of energy-industry executives who had advised a task force he headed on energy policy. Also before September 11, the Justice Department began work on a policy to reverse a presumption in favor of disclosure by supporting agency actions to keep any information secret when there was a "sound legal basis" for withholding it. These unilateral executive branch actions, typically adopted without public debate, demonstrated once again how much discretion officials had to foster or restrict public access to information.[18]

Right-to-know policies also produced unexpected consequences. Open government proved surprisingly costly. By the mid-1990s, the executive branch was processing more than half a million requests for information each year at a cost of about $100 million. Even more surprising, few individual citizens used the law to gain information about their government. Nearly all FOIA requests came from businesses seeking to gather information about other businesses. Fifteen years after the law was passed, the General Accounting Office reported that 82 percent of requests came from business, nine percent from the press, and only 1 percent from individuals or public interest groups.[19]

Targeted Transparency Emerges

Targeted transparency policies grew out of right-to-know measures but were more ambitious in their goals and requirements. While right-to-know policies aimed generally to create a more informed public, targeted transparency policies aimed to reduce specific risks or improve particular aspects of public services. While right-to-know policies required simply that existing government reports and other documents be made available to the public, targeted transparency policies required that government agencies, companies, and other private-sector organizations collect, standardize, and release factual information to inform public choices. Sometimes such information was new even to the agency or corporation that collected it.

Most targeted transparency policies overcame political obstacles because they were serendipitous inventions that responded to perceived crises. They were the creations of stock market crashes, toxic chemical accidents, bank discrimination, and perceived public school failure. They were adopted as last-ditch compromises or as eleventh-hour add-ons to larger legislative measures. Their inventors were executive branch officials, senators or House members, congressional staffers, advocacy groups, and scholars.

With rare exceptions, those who drafted the requirements did not know they were helping to create a mainstream policy tool. Like most lasting changes in democratic governance, transparency policies percolated up through the political system as pragmatic responses to problems that seemed to call for public action. Newly revealed risks or service flaws momentarily caught the public's attention, creating a political opportunity for innovative remedies. The policies' creators were simply solving pressing problems.

If these policies in one sense represented a surprising political innovation, in another sense they represented the next logical step in a long progression of government mandates to place vital information in the public domain. Like first-generation transparency policies, the second-generation policies that became common in the 1980s and 1990s had important historic precursors that created a foundation for political innovation.

In the early 1900s, Congress began requiring accurate product labeling and adding statutory requirements to the common-law duty that held manufacturers responsible for warning the public about foreseeable harm from their products. The Pure Food and Drug Act of 1906 required the accurate labeling of packaged foods shipped in interstate commerce, and the

Insecticide Act of 1910 required labeling of pesticide products, for example. Among the best-known legislated product safety warnings are the statements prominently printed on labels of alcoholic beverages and tobacco products.[20]

In what remains the United States' most sophisticated and familiar targeted transparency policy, Congress required companies to inform investors about financial risks after the collapse of American financial markets in 1929. In the Securities and Exchange Acts of 1933 and 1934, Congress required publicly traded companies to disclose financial information to investors in quarterly and annual accounts.[21]

In the mid-1980s, growing concern about pollution and workplace hazards led to issue-specific right-to-know requirements that represented a bridge between first-generation and second-generation transparency policies. In *A Citizen's Right to Know*, Susan G. Hadden traces parallel efforts by labor unions and environmental groups beginning in the 1970s to gain access to information about toxic chemicals in the workplace and in communities. By the mid-1980s, those efforts had merged. Philadelphia, Cincinnati, and several cities in California required public disclosure of both workplace and public chemical hazards. California voters also approved Proposition 65 in 1986, which required businesses that exposed the public to more than minimal levels of certain toxins to inform the public of those risks.[22]

These disclosure requirements for toxic hazards featured all the characteristics of targeted transparency policies but cloaked them in right-to-know language. For instance, a 1983 federal Occupational Safety and Health Administration (OSHA) rule required employers to inform workers of chemical risks in the workplace by posting structured factual information (material safety data sheets) about specific chemicals for the purpose of improving employees' safety and health.[23] In 1986, Congress required manufacturers to make annual disclosures of toxic pollution released into the environment, factory by factory and chemical by chemical. The results of this little-noticed right-to-know mandate surprised the federal regulators and environmental groups that had been working for decades to reduce such pollution. Even before the first company reports, executives of some large companies made commitments to reduce this pollution by as much as 90 percent. The mere *anticipation* of bad publicity had created strong incentives to improve environmental protection. Ten years later, reported toxic releases had been reduced by half, and federal environmental officials were referring to this modest right-to-know measure as one of the nation's most effective environmental safeguards. Targeted transparency, an accidental innovation, had become accepted as part of mainstream environmental policy.[24]

WHY DISCLOSURE?

Why have policymakers turned to targeted transparency policies in the last twenty years – particularly in a market-based economy, where companies presumably have significant incentives to provide sufficient information on their own?

In fact, a number of economists have argued *against* the need for such policies on precisely these grounds. The logic behind their view is straightforward. On one hand, if a firm has favorable information about its products or services, it will benefit from voluntary disclosure. On the other hand, if a firm has unfavorable information that it fails to disclose, that refusal should lead consumers to draw negative conclusions about the firm and its products or services. These consumer responses will either cause the price of the goods to fall (because of the lower quality implied by the failure to disclose) or create an incentive for the firm to improve its products or services and then disclose.[25] In the world described by this theory, transparency policies are at best redundant and at worst costly mandates that force organizations to disclose information they would readily release on their own.

Ronald Coase's seminal paper "The Problem of Social Cost" provided a different argument for a limited information-focused approach to address problems like environmental damage. Coase showed that parties facing low transactions costs should be able to resolve problems like pollution privately and reach socially desirable outcomes through bargaining. In particular, if both polluters and those harmed by pollution had information about the problem, self-interested negotiations could lead to a solution that left both parties – and society – better off. If information was readily available to the parties, legislated transparency was not necessary.

A generation of research, however, points out why these theoretical conclusions may seldom apply in practice and therefore why transparency policies may be socially beneficial. Markets alone often do not provide the information needed by consumers, investors, and employees to make informed choices. And even when sufficient information is available, people do not always process that information accurately and logically when making decisions. As a result, bargaining over pollution and other risks may not lead to the socially optimal outcomes Coase described.[26]

Together, these insights indicate that the natural flow of information in an unfettered marketplace and its application by individuals to real-world decision making may not always lead to the optimal outcomes predicted by economic theory. Understanding these problems of information processing provides insight into how transparency policies might help redress them. But it also suggests why such policies may be difficult to implement.

Imperfections of Real-World Information

One of the fundamental assumptions underlying classical economic theory is the availability of perfect information to the actors in an economic system. Armed with all the information they need, individuals, firms, and markets allocate scarce social resources efficiently in transactions mediated principally by signals sent by prices.[27] This picture is appealingly simple and clear – but it is also inaccurate.

A wide-ranging set of theoretical and empirical papers produced in recent years demonstrates that even relatively small imperfections in information can dramatically change the behaviors of businesses, consumers, workers, and other economic actors, producing inefficiencies that scuttle the neat predictions of social welfare economics.[28]

There are three major problems that lead to imperfect information in the marketplace and, in turn, to the misallocation of financial and social resources. The first arises because of the peculiar nature of information itself.

New information has one of the central characteristics of a so-called public good: its consumption is *non-rival*, meaning that new information can be consumed by one party without diminishing its value to another party. Consequently, actors in private markets will either produce less-than-optimal amounts of information or attempt to limit access to information in order to capture economic value from its production. Either way, private incentives lead to the dissemination of too little information, and so society as a whole should benefit from policies that lead to its increased provision.[29]

Disparities in information – *information asymmetries* – among the actors and organizations of a market economy lead to two additional problems.

The first problem, known as *adverse selection*, arises in cases where the underlying characteristics of the subject of a transaction vary, with one party to the transaction having more information about those characteristics than the other. The subject of a transaction might be a product, a service, a job, or an investment – anything being traded for money in the marketplace. Its characteristics might include its quality, productivity, or risks associated with it.

Adverse selection reflects the fact that there is considerable uncertainty in markets about the underlying characteristics of products or services beyond those expressed in price or readily observable by a consumer. The classic example is the so-called lemons problem described by George Akerlof.[30] Because the seller of a used car knows much more about its underlying characteristics than any buyer, a buyer must make guesses about the car's quality, which will tend to lower its perceived value. Furthermore, used cars on the market are likely to be of relatively low quality, because owners are more likely to hold onto cars with fewer problems. As a result, even if one is selling a high-quality used car, information asymmetry leads it to have a lower market value than it would have if complete and accurate information were generally available.

In similar fashion, because sellers of health insurance are unable to observe the underlying state of health of those seeking insurance policies, and because those with more severe health problems will be more likely to seek coverage, premiums will tend to be priced higher than they would be in a world of perfect information. Adverse selection, then, leads to market transactions that are less optimal than would be the case if all parties were fully informed.

Information asymmetries also lead to a second class of problems, related to *moral hazard.* Moral hazard occurs when one party to a market transaction cannot directly observe the actions of another party. Many economic transactions involve one party agreeing to act in return for payment – for example, employees work in exchange for wages, while managers run a company in exchange for salaries. But because it is costly for the party contracting for the services to observe the party who has been hired to carry them out, the actual behavior of the executing party may diverge from the desired behavior – employees may nap rather than work, managers may run the company to maximize their incomes rather than long-term shareholder value, and so on.

Similar perverse incentives may exist in non-employment transactions. For example, households purchasing fire insurance may become less vigilant about fire safety, leaving the insurer more vulnerable to claims. As a result of moral hazard, contracting parties must seek means to monitor behavior or create incentives to compensate for their inability to do so, while other contracting parties have incentives to take advantage of the fact that observing their behavior is costly.

These three problems imply that (1) information will tend to be underproduced in markets; (2) real-world market transactions will differ significantly from those in a world where information is costless to obtain; and (3) individuals, firms, and companies will have different incentives to resolve information asymmetries. In the words of economist Joseph Stiglitz, "[R]esults of information economics show forcefully that the long-standing hypothesis that economies with imperfect information would be similar to economies with perfect information – at least so long as the degree of information imperfection was not too large – has no theoretical basis."[31]

Of course, government intervention is not the only possible response to information asymmetries. Private parties and institutions often use different types of contracts and organizational forms to compensate for these problems. For example, "efficiency wage" theory predicts that wages in certain settings will be set above what would be predicted under a model with perfect information about worker activity as a means of boosting productivity. However, the economics of information literature does suggest the potentially important role that government-mandated disclosure may play in some instances.

Difficulties of Comprehension

Information, then, is neither costless to acquire and share nor equally available to all parties in market transactions. But even if it were, a second set of insights offered by cognitive and behavioral psychologists, sociologists, and economists challenge the notion that people with access to information will use it to make rational decisions. Building on the pioneering work of Herbert Simon, these researchers use the term *bounded rationality* to describe how people make decisions individually, in groups, and in organizations. Even in the presence of seemingly objective information, individuals are prone to a host of cognitive distortions that may lead them to make decisions far different from those predicted in a world of perfect rationality.[32]

Consider the following examples of the kinds of cognitive errors people tend to commit when making decisions with uncertain outcomes:[33]

- People tend to substantially overestimate risks associated with unlikely events over which they have little control (such as chemical accidents or airplane crashes). By contrast, they tend to underestimate risks posed by events in which they perceive themselves as having greater control (such as smoking, eating high-fat foods, or speeding on the highway).[34]
- People are more likely to take action to reduce risks when outcomes are described in graphic (rather than clinical) terms. In the extreme case, they will pay little attention to different probabilities of risk if the outcomes have highly emotional and negative consequences.[35]
- People do not seek or use information about risks even when making risk-related purchases. For example, when buying product warranties,

customers do not seek out information about the probabilities of repair, even when it is available.[36]

- People regard a loss of a given magnitude as having a much higher value than an equivalent gain. This form of "loss aversion" applies even to gains and losses of relatively small amounts.[37]

These and other behavioral responses mean that information – whatever its source – may not always lead people to make decisions in their individual or collective best interest. This finding has direct implications for policies that mandate information disclosure.

First, people may make decisions contrary to the public interest in response to information about risks. For example, the public may over-react to information about a potential terrorist threat whether provided by "voluntary" media reporting or by an announcement from the Department of Homeland Security.

Second, organizations have incentives to "game" the release of information to take advantage of common cognitive distortions. This dynamic applies to companies seeking to expand demand for their products, policy advocates seeking to affect political outcomes, candidates seeking votes, and government agencies attempting to expand public support for their programs. It also implies that transparency policies create both opportunities and dangers.

Third, even when some compelling public interest supports disclosure, providing information in a way that leads to desired changes in behavior may be very difficult. As political scientist Cass Sunstein notes with regard to disclosure of information concerning health risks:

An understanding of the nature of fear raises cautionary notes about disclosure policies.... The problem is not simply that people may well misunderstand risk disclosures, seeing the hazard as far greater than it is in fact. The problem is also that the disclosure may greatly alarm people, causing various kinds of harms, without giving them any useful information at all.[38]

So it may not be enough for disclosure systems to provide, in the words of Sergeant Joe Friday of *Dragnet*, "Just the facts, ma'am." Such systems may need to aggregate, translate, simplify, or benchmark the facts so that resulting decisions fit the objectives that motivated disclosure in the first place. One reason these systems often fall short is that their creators fail to recognize that potential users may not respond in the ways that models of rational behavior predict.

THREE

Designing Transparency Policies

IMPROVING ON-THE-JOB SAFETY: ONE GOAL, MANY METHODS

Federal and state governments in the United States have grappled with the problem of occupational safety and health in various ways for more than a century. As far back as 1916, John R. Commons, one of the first social scientists to study and help design workplace regulations, commented:

Prominent among the problems which the Industrial Revolution brought in its wake is that of maintaining safety and health in workplaces. As long as industry was chiefly agricultural, or carried on about the family hearth, with tools relatively few and simple, the individual laborer might control the physical conditions under which he worked.[1]

The range of government responses to the problem of safety in the newly industrialized workplace has made this area a kind of real-world laboratory in which differing policy approaches to the same broad objective may be observed and compared. These include, most recently, targeted transparency.

Early factory laws in the United States, beginning with one enacted by Massachusetts in 1886, created dedicated agencies to reduce the toll of workplace fatalities and serious injuries. These early regulatory systems relied on enforcement of specific safety standards (such as requirements for safety shields on machinery or limits on the amount of dust in the air). They also raised questions about regulatory design that have long since become familiar to policymakers and the general public – questions like these:

- What safety standards should be adopted to improve workplace conditions?
- How many inspectors should be hired, and what skills and training do they need?

- To which industries and workplaces should inspectors be sent, and what should they do once there?
- What penalties should be assessed when violations are detected?
- How should repeat offenders be treated?

As workplace health and safety problems persisted, legislators devised additional regulatory approaches to augment standards-based systems. The most striking example was workers compensation insurance, adopted first by Maryland in 1902 in the form of a cooperative insurance law covering a narrow set of industries. Workers compensation systems provide benefits to injured workers by requiring companies in specified industries to pay into a common insurance fund. Premiums paid into the system by firms varied both by industry and by the employer's prior injury performance. This system of "experience rating" was intended to create financial incentives for employers to improve safety practices.

The workers compensation insurance premium serves as a kind of "injury tax" on employers. As Commons noted, linking safety outcomes to private financial interests dramatically changed the dynamic of regulation: "State agencies can order the application of mechanical safeguards. . . . But their inspectors can do but little in comparison with what the employer and employee can do, under the stimulus of an adequate compensation system."[2]

Not surprisingly, workers compensation raised a new set of regulatory design questions that differed considerably from those required for standards-based systems. For example:

- For the purpose of setting insurance premiums, how should an injury event be defined?
- How can accurate reports of injuries by employers be ensured?
- How should the profile of insurance premium rates change with different injury levels?
- How should the inherently variable and partially random nature of injuries and fatalities be managed? For example, how should premiums be set for a very small employer whose injury rate may vary widely from year to year?

Consider now the use of targeted transparency to reduce workplace injuries and illnesses. The earliest factory safety legislation included requirements that employers maintain and disclose information on injury rates. However, the audience for this information was the government, not the workforce. Thus, true targeted transparency didn't become part of the workplace safety toolkit until 1983. In that year, OSHA promulgated workplace hazard reporting that sought to reduce workers' exposure to dangerous chemicals by providing them with information about those chemicals.[3] Once again, a new approach raised a new set of design questions. For example:

- What specific information on chemical risks should employers be required to provide? How often should this information be updated and how should it be presented?
- How can employees' receipt and comprehension of relevant risk information be ensured?
- What sanctions should be administered if employers fail to provide material information in a timely, accurate fashion?
- Since government does not play a direct role as enforcer of specific chemical exposure rules in a targeted transparency regime, instead leaving that role to workers informed by disclosure about workplace hazards, which parties should be vested with responsibility for seeing that health risks decline?

The story of government efforts to improve workplace health and safety illustrates two important points about the design of targeted transparency policies. First, those policies build on and often complement prior regulatory efforts in an area of public concern. Workplace hazard disclosure does not replace workers compensation or OSHA standards but potentially extends the reach of both to new types of health problems.

Second, just as market-based intervention raises distinctive design questions, targeted transparency policies also share a common set of design features. These common features underlie our conclusion that targeted transparency represents a coherent system of government intervention.

In this chapter, we will review the architecture of targeted transparency, starting by comparing it with other policies that also draw on information. We will then lay out the five common features shared by the transparency systems studied in this book. Finally, we will compare targeted transparency with traditional standards-based and market-based forms of regulation. Understanding the architecture and distinctive character of targeted transparency provides a basis for understanding where and why policies succeed or fail, the focus of Chapters 4 and 5.

DISCLOSURE TO CREATE INCENTIVES FOR CHANGE

Targeted transparency represents a distinctive category of public policies that, at their most basic level, mandate disclosure by corporations or other actors of standardized, comparable, and disaggregated information regarding specific products or practices to a broad audience in order to achieve a public policy purpose.

Thus, targeted transparency does not require specific technologies, performance targets, or taxes. Instead, it relies on thousands of individual choices by information disclosers and users who interact to establish acceptable risk levels or improve organizational performance.

Targeted transparency policies represent a subset of transparency measures, as that term is commonly used. We can distinguish the various types of information disclosure that are often lumped together as transparency measures by their purposes, the kind of information they provide, and the role played by government in disclosure.

Voluntary disclosure by businesses and other organizations involves no direct government intervention. Firms and other institutions have incentives to provide factual information to customers, employees, and investors voluntarily through advertising, reports, labels, or public relations efforts. Such information often has value for the public. Liability laws can increase the incentives for firms to voluntarily disclose risk information to consumers, workers, or potential investors.[4] Publicized crises, shifts in public attitudes, and competitive dynamics can further augment incentives. Yet as the literature on the economics of information discussed in Chapter 2 makes clear, the quantity and quality of information that a company voluntarily provides is often inadequate for informed decision making by the public. In targeted transparency, then, policymakers push organizations to reveal more than they otherwise would choose to do.

As noted in Chapter 2, *warnings* represent a second form of transparency.[5] Here, government requires auto companies, cigarette makers, and other organizations to provide specific, prescriptive instructions for consumers, motivated by a clear regulatory intent – usually to prevent or curtail a specific type of behavior by information users. For example, provisions in the Child Safety Protection Act of 1994 require labels on packages of balls, balloons, marbles, and other toys and games intended for children at least three years of age, warning against choking hazards.[6] Other familiar government-mandated warnings caution auto passengers to fasten their safety belts, parents to keep household chemicals out of the reach of their children, and consumers that smoking may prove harmful to their health.

Like targeted transparency, warnings leave decisions about what actions to take to information users – that is, there is no enforcement mechanism to insure that parents keep balloons or toys out of reach of their children; the label itself is regarded as sufficient to achieve the public purpose. However, warnings, unlike targeted transparency, omit factual information to enable users to make informed choices. Instead, government experts make judgments based on some unseen body of information and provide a prescriptive admonishment to consumers.[7]

Compared with warnings, the information conveyed by *right-to-know* policies is typically more complex and less focused. As discussed in Chapter 2, right-to-know policies attempt to improve public awareness about the activities, financial flows, or decision-making processes of government agencies and other institutions as an end in itself, rather than attempting to achieve specific risk-reducing or service-improving objectives. Thus, for example, the Freedom of Information Act provides citizens with access to government documents that show how decisions were made or reveal factual information gathered by a particular agency.

Targeted transparency differs from warnings and right-to-know policies. Whereas warnings provide information that is simple and prescriptive, targeted transparency provides information that is complex and factual. Whereas warnings urge users to take a particular course of action, targeted transparency encourages users to make reasoned judgments of their own. And whereas right-to-know policies aim to generally inform public discourse, targeted transparency aims to influence specific choices.

WHAT TARGETED TRANSPARENCY POLICIES HAVE IN COMMON

Disclosure of information to the public is often thought to be a simple matter, especially compared to the complexities of other forms of government intervention. But just as traditional regulatory systems require policymakers to develop legal standards, inspection protocols, and penalty procedures, targeted transparency policies are characterized by a distinctive and demanding architecture. Such policies share five basic design features that distinguish them from other forms of regulation. All five are needed to translate a general policy purpose into a specific transparency requirement for disclosers and users to act upon:

- a specific policy purpose
- specified discloser targets
- a defined scope of information
- a defined information structure and vehicle
- an enforcement mechanism.

Some of these design features, like a defined policy purpose and an enforcement mechanism, are basic to any system of regulation. Others are distinctive and present design challenges quite different from those that characterize conventional regulation.

Policy Purpose

Targeted transparency policies are designed to change the behavior of information users and/or disclosers in specified ways. Their particular aims vary widely. But in general, the regulatory rationale for transparency presupposes the existence of some type of information asymmetry between disclosers and users. The aim of government intervention is to provide the public with adequate information to make more informed and more socially beneficial decisions. Information asymmetry alone is not sufficient to trigger government intervention, however. The cases we have analyzed suggest that government intervenes when such gaps create one of four public problems.

First, government intervenes when information imbalances substantially increase the risks borne by the public. For example, Enron's failure to reveal its enormous losses in off–balance sheet entities substantially increased risks faced by its investors. Likewise, manufacturers' exclusive knowledge of hazardous chemicals in the workplace and toxic pollutants emitted into surrounding communities left workers and neighborhood residents exposed to hidden health risks.

Second, government intervenes when lack of information seriously impairs the quality of critical services provided by public or private organizations. For example, as long as public schools kept confidential student test scores, attendance and failure rates, teacher qualifications and achievements, and other measures of performance, families could not judge the relative quality of available schools.[8] Likewise, hospitals' exclusive knowledge of the prevalence of medical errors has prevented patients from choosing relatively safe facilities. Thus, targeted transparency policies can provide organizational "report cards" to enhance performance. People with more complete performance information can better match the benefits and costs of public services as they decide where to live and work.[9]

Third, government intervenes when information imbalances perpetuate unacceptable patterns of discrimination or other social inequities. Unfair practices that are hidden can deny social benefits to some people. So long as the number and size of mortgage loans made by local banks, savings and loans, and other lending institutions to inner-city residents, minorities, women, and other groups were not made public, neighborhoods experiencing systematic discrimination in lending could not fight back. Similarly, the inability of workers or state and local officials to find out about pending plant closures or large-scale layoffs kept them from either attempting to contest closure decisions or adequately preparing for their impacts.[10]

Fourth, government intervenes when information imbalances allow corruption to persist in important institutions that serve the public. For example, the inability of union members to find out about governance practices or financial spending by their elected leaders reduced the pressure on union officials to be responsive or in some cases to act with integrity. Likewise, confidentiality of campaign contributions prevents voters from judging whether candidates are beholden to well-heeled interests.

Specified Targets

Targeted transparency policies designate specific organizations that are viewed as responsible for some public risk or performance problem (and therefore have unique access to information about it) as disclosers. As in other areas of government intervention, the designated disclosers are frequently businesses. For example, corporate financial disclosure targets companies that issue securities in public capital markets where the "lemon problem" (adverse selection), described in Chapter 2, may lead to distortions in the signals capital markets send to investors. Toxic pollution disclosure targets large manufacturers and users of toxic chemicals to reveal their emissions. Mortgage lending disclosure targets banks to disclose the demographics of their lending.

Other transparency policies target disclosers that are not-for-profit or public organizations. Thus, drinking water safety reporting targets both public and private water authorities, campaign finance disclosure targets candidates for national public office, school performance report cards focus on public schools, and patient safety reporting targets hospitals.

Defining who must disclose is almost always politically controversial. For example, nutritional labeling requirements exempted fast-food outlets and full-service restaurants even though U.S. consumers spend about half of their food budgets there. Political attempts to limit the universe of disclosers can persist over time. Early versions of toxic pollution reporting exempted power plants and mining operations despite their release of significant amounts of toxic chemicals. The pollution reporting requirement also initially exempted firms that used less than ten thousand pounds or produced less than twenty-five thousand pounds of listed chemicals in a year.[11] In 2005, the Bush administration attempted to reduce the frequency, depth, and scope of reporting for many firms.[12]

Although targeted transparency policies specify classes of disclosers, they do not usually define intended information users. In fact, most policies describe potential users in the most general language. For example, campaign finance reporting legislation in 1971 defined the audience for disclosure as the electorate.[13] Most often, users are defined simply as "the public." As a result, actual users in most cases are self-selected by their own interests.

Not specifying users makes policies adaptive to changes in the makeup of user groups. However, it may also keep policymakers from assuring that policies are designed for easy use by diverse audiences.

Sometimes intermediaries – community groups, environmental advocates, or political parties, for example – act as agents for users, translating complex information into metrics for diverse audiences. In corporate financial disclosure, mortgage lending disclosure, and toxic release reporting, for example, intermediaries played a pivotal role in the effectiveness and long-term development of transparency systems. However, the conditions under which such groups form and become engaged as agents of information users are often very demanding and may be governed by factors outside legislators' control.[14] We examine such conditions in Chapter 5.

Defined Scope

Targeted transparency policies specify the universe of practices, substances, activities, or other information that must be disclosed. The content of disclosure – what information must be released – relates to the character of the information imbalance that the policy seeks to redress. Investors need reliable information to be able to assess financial risk; parents need information about school performance in order to select a community or school for their children. Targeted transparency policies therefore explicitly specify the boundaries of disclosure – never a simple matter.

In defining what must be disclosed, targeted transparency policies sometimes require organizations to provide information that is already available to the discloser, typically data generated for internal purposes or for experts or other limited classes of users. For example, financial disclosure required companies to make available to the public information created for managerial decision making and for specific investor groups. Disclosure of the current address of released sex offenders mandated by state-level Megan's Laws required local police departments to provide information to state agencies – and ultimately to the public – that many departments already collected on a regular basis as part of other law enforcement activities.

In other cases, the mandated scope of information may require disclosers to generate new data that are not readily available to the organization.

Businesses may be forced to establish new systems of monitoring, measuring, review, and reporting. Toxic chemical reporting, for example, required companies to establish systems to measure and track and add up, often for the first time, the quantity of toxic pollutants released by plants.[15] In such instances, disclosers may change their practices in response to new knowledge as well as to public pressure.

Whether they require organizing and sharing existing information or generating new information not formerly collected, design decisions regarding the scope of information impose costs – often very significant costs – on disclosers. As a result of these costs, the boundaries of disclosure often become a focal point for intense political wrangling. In the passage of a targeted transparency policy, efforts by potential disclosers to limit the scope of what must be disclosed quickly become a second line of defense once the political will to require disclosure has become clear. The recent battle over expanding the scope of corporate executive compensation disclosure is typical. Despite long-standing requirements that companies provide information on compensation, efforts to include information on stock options and on the compensation of the five highest-paid executives quickly became contentious.

Structure and Vehicles for Information

In order to make the information comparable from product to product and institution to institution, transparency policies specify a framework that standardizes content and format. This framework generally standardizes information formats to ensure comparability among products or practices. It also specifies the time, place, and means by which information will be provided. Thus, the transparency framework always specifies metrics, frequency of disclosure, and a communication vehicle.

First, policies specify what quantitative or qualitative *metrics* must be used and what level of accuracy in those metrics is required. Specific disclosure metrics for toxic pollution reporting are quite narrow: annual reports of the amounts (measured in pounds) of specific chemicals released by each covered facility into air, water, or ground. The law does *not*, for example, require manufacturers to characterize the toxicity, exposure, or relative risks created by different chemicals or to provide information on the pathways by which chemicals could infiltrate surrounding communities. The requirement allows companies to employ a variety of estimating techniques to determine pollution quantities. In the past, companies' changes in estimating techniques sometimes led to sudden drops in reported pollution levels that were not necessarily associated with true reductions.[16]

Second, policies specify the *frequency* with which disclosers must update information. In principle, the frequency of updates should coincide with changes in the underlying conditions of policy concern, and many policies do require periodic provision of new information in reports to the public. For example, corporate financial reporting and restaurant hygiene disclosure are updated multiple times during the year, as is consistent with the volatile nature of financial risks or hygiene practices. In other cases, policies require less frequent updates. School report cards are typically updated each academic year, and auto rollover reports are updated for each model year. However, reporting can lag months or years behind changes in risks or service quality.

Finally, policies specify the *vehicles* to be used in communicating information. These vary widely, from public announcements via the news media (as with the Department of Homeland Security's terrorist threat alerts) and information postings directly on products (as with nutritional labels on foods and rollover ratings on new-car stickers) or in places where services are provided (as with restaurant hygiene report cards) to printed materials available upon request (as with material data safety sheets that describe workplace hazards) or Web sites (as with hospital safety reports and campaign finance disclosure). The vehicles of disclosure are more than administrative details. They have profound impacts on policy effectiveness because they determine when a user encounters information that influences decision making.

Cognitive psychologists and behavioral economists have shown that people's ability to use information varies according to its presentation. For example, in a wide-ranging set of studies, Daniel Kahneman and Amos Tversky showed that people tend to make decisions that minimize their exposure to losses, even if this minimization requires reduction of significant upside gains (a phenomenon that they called, not surprisingly, "loss aversion"). Loss aversion, coupled with another widely shared trait – that people tend to want to keep what has been given them ("endowment effects") – means that manipulation of signals to individuals regarding the potential of losses can have significant effects on behavior. This research suggests that *how* information is presented can have as much influence on people's behavior as the factual content of the data.[17] François Degeorge, Jayendu Patel, and Richard Zeckhauser document a striking example of the impact of cognitive biases on corporate financial disclosure. Reviewing quarterly financial performance data, the researchers found a much larger than expected incidence of zero reported earnings in a sample of publicly traded companies. They also found almost no cases of small losses relative to reported instances of small positive earnings. These skewed results reflected corporate accounting decisions that allowed companies to show zero or slightly positive returns to deal with investors' loss aversion and the consequent negative market consequences of reports of even trivial earnings losses.[18] Not surprisingly, structural features of disclosure are a frequent source of tension between disclosers and users and are an important part of the ongoing politics surrounding targeted transparency policies.

Enforcement

Although some advocates suggest that transparency policies eliminate the need for costly efforts to ensure compliance that are typical of traditional regulation, in practice targeted transparency policies do not work unless they are enforced. Monitoring nonreporting or misreporting and then levying penalties for those who violate disclosure requirements remain essential. In economic terms, disclosers' assessments of costs and benefits from transparency policies include expected costs of noncompliance – that is, the costs associated with failing to report accurately, factoring in the likelihood of getting caught.

In a few policies, enforcement is simplified because a public entity itself gathers and posts information. Thus, the terrorism threat alerts draw on information collected and disclosed by the federal government. Auto rollover rankings are generated and posted by the National Highway Traffic Safety Administration. In Los Angeles County, restaurant hygiene grades are formulated as part of the public health inspection process.

Most policies, however, rely on data generated and posted by disclosing organizations. As a result, the government must develop methods to monitor compliance with disclosure requirements. Enforcement of campaign finance reporting, for example, includes substantial civil and criminal penalties for failing to disclose contributions or disclosing inaccurately. The McCain-Feingold amendment to campaign finance disclosure approved in 2002 attempted to close reporting loopholes that allowed candidates and their supporters to use "soft money" to circumvent campaign spending limitations. Under that policy, anyone who "knowingly and willfully" violates disclosure provisions could face a maximum penalty of five years in prison.[19] Failure to provide accurate corporate financial information similarly results in substantial civil and criminal penalties. Under the plant closure disclosure system, the penalties facing companies that fail to provide advance notice of closure or major layoffs include compensating affected workers with back pay for the period of time when notice was not provided as well as paying fines of up to five hundred dollars for each day of violation.[20] Under sex offender disclosure rules, released offenders risk felony charges if they do not apprise police officials of their current residences or provide advance notice when they move.[21]

By contrast, there is no systematic mechanism for auditing the toxic pollution data provided by companies, although the nominal penalties for failing to disclose are significant (twenty-five thousand dollars for each violation of reporting requirements).[22] Thus, while estimated compliance is fairly high, the pressure to file accurate reports is less acute.[23] Enforcement of union financial practices was similarly weak until recently. Although the disclosure law included significant penalties for failing to file reports and for misreporting, in practice the U.S. Department of Labor reviewed the accuracy of only a small percentage of reports and imposed only modest penalties. The result was a high rate of late filings and incomplete reporting.[24] The George W. Bush administration substantially augmented enforcement, however, by increasing resources for the division of the Department of Labor in charge of the policy.[25]

The structure of enforcement has important consequences for both the effectiveness and the improvement of policies over time, as we will see later.

STANDARDS, MARKET INCENTIVES, OR TARGETED TRANSPARENCY?

Policy discussions often describe two broad means of government intervention to encourage private and public organizations to further public priorities. The first relies on government-promulgated standards enforced by inspectors. Those standards are traditionally thought of as prescribing particular technology- or design-based solutions to public policy problems, but they may also be based on broader performance goals that regulated parties must attain. A second category constructs market-based incentives to compel organizations to move in desired directions by means of either carrots (e.g., subsidies) or sticks (e.g., taxes or trading regimes). As we saw with the example of workplace safety, legislators have often used a combination of these tools over time.[26]

In our view, targeted transparency policies represent a distinctive third form of government intervention to further important public priorities. Just as standards- and market-based tools have certain preconditions for success, transparency policies rely on users and disclosers of information, as well as government officials, to fulfill distinct roles in order to improve chances of success. Our classification differs from that of others who have tended to describe transparency policies as a subset of financial incentive–based approaches.[27] It also differs from the approach of scholars who have focused on the importance of transparency-based systems as responses to particular categories of policy problems.[28] Finally, our analysis contrasts with those that view transparency policies as examples of the more general trend toward deregulation.[29]

Targeted transparency differs from standards- and market-based approaches in two major respects. First, it uses a broader set of pathways to affect the behavior of targeted organizations, and second, it uses communication as a regulatory mechanism.

Most regulatory systems work through economic pathways. Standards-based approaches aim to change the behavior of targeted organizations by requiring that they adopt certain practices or attain certain goals. If they fail to comply, organizations face civil and/or criminal penalties that take an economic toll.[30] Market-based systems work by connecting behavior explicitly to economic incentives via performance-linked taxes or subsidies. Economic pathways are also important to the operation of many targeted transparency systems. Restaurant hygiene disclosure, auto rollover rankings, and nutritional labeling operate by providing consumers with information that can inform and change product choices and in turn alter the incentives faced by the businesses providing those goods and services.

However, *political* pathways are also important to many of the policies we review. For example, mortgage lending and toxic pollution disclosure help empower community organizations to press disclosers to improve practices. Similarly, parental pressure on school systems is critical to the success of school performance disclosure systems. Frequently economic and political pathways are intertwined – for example, as community pressure translates into reputational damage. Several studies document how community pressure to reduce toxic pollution can become economic pressure exerted through capital markets.

Targeted transparency policies also differ from the other forms of government intervention in the combination of signals they send to disclosing organizations and the latitude of responses available to those organizations. The differences between regulatory interventions in this respect are captured in Figure 3.1.

Standards-based interventions – whether they require specific practices ("design standards") or mandate particular regulatory goals ("performance standards") – provide the targets of regulation with guidance that defines acceptable behavior. For example, under the Occupational Safety and Health Act, company managers know whether or not they have complied with

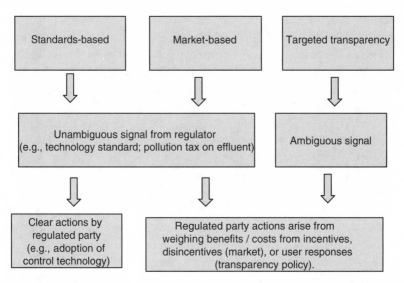

Figure 3.1. Standards-Based, Market-Based, and Transparency Signals and Responses

workplace safety requirements regarding practices such as machine guarding. Performance standards, while providing greater latitude to organizations to decide *how* to achieve a target, stipulate that goal clearly and gauge performance according to it (e.g., reduction of auto safety risks to certain targeted levels). Similarly, when government employs market-based policies using taxes, subsidies, or trading regimes to regulate business behavior, it also specifies clear outcomes. For example, the system of sulfur dioxide (SO_2) trading devised to reduce acid rain, created under the Clean Air Act Amendment of 1990, requires the establishment and careful monitoring of emission goals.[31]

Unlike these regulatory approaches, targeted transparency policies employ communication as a regulatory mechanism and send more ambiguous signals to target organizations regarding whether they are behaving satisfactorily. Signals arise from changes in consumer, investor, or employee behavior as they respond to new information. Although regulators may have some preexisting belief about how people will respond to new information, those reactions – and the ability of disclosers to perceive those reactions – are never assured.

Targeted transparency systems resemble market-based regulatory systems (and systems employing performance-based standards) by providing choices to targeted organizations. Under systems that set overall performance goals and rely on market-based incentives to achieve those goals, targeted organizations enjoy wide latitude in choosing what actions to take. Under the SO_2 trading system, utilities know how many allowances they need to purchase in order to meet maximum emission levels, how much they will be willing to pay to purchase allowances given those targets, and the value of selling allowances given a decision to reduce emissions below prescribed levels.[32] With this information, they can make their own decisions about the course of action to follow. By contrast, under design- or technology-based standards, firms receive very clear guidance regarding actions they should take. Manufacturers and utilities under the original Clean Air Act Amendments of 1970 were required to adopt certain types of "scrubber" technology to remove effluents from smokestacks.[33] Many of the original workplace safety standards promulgated by OSHA required adoption of particular technologies, work practices, or worker protection accessories.[34]

Targeted transparency policies provide even broader choice. Both users and disclosers are free to take no action at all. In contrast to performance- or market-based systems, target organizations receive their signals from the behavior of users rather than the actions of regulators or financial incentives from markets. That means that signals may work through a wide variety of pathways: through consumer purchasing patterns; via capital markets; or through organized political activity of users or their agents, for example. Therefore, predicting those pathways is more complicated than predicting the pathways through which compliance- or market-based interventions work.

Targeted transparency therefore represents a distinctive form of government intervention. As we have seen, it is characterized by unique design features. Furthermore, its reliance on signals sent by users via market, political, organizational, or combined pathways makes its operation far more complex than perceived by the public or even its proponents.

FOUR

What Makes Transparency Work?

(With Elena Fagotto)

In Los Angeles County, as in other localities, public health inspectors visit restaurants to make sure they comply with local hygiene codes. In most communities, however, the information they collect is locked away in government files. In a few, inspection results are posted in searchable electronic databases that foresighted and tech-savvy restaurant-goers may learn to access. But Los Angeles County goes much further. Since 1998, restaurant managers there have been required to post in their windows a letter grade ranging from A to C that reflects the results of their most recent hygiene inspection. Would-be patrons needn't call the public health office or visit a Web site. A glance at the restaurant's storefront tells them how clean it is and lets them incorporate that information into one of the most common of daily decisions – figuring out where to eat.[1]

These restaurant hygiene reports have created powerful incentives for restaurateurs to clean up their premises. Early research has found significant revenue increases for restaurants with high grades and revenue decreases for C-graded restaurants (a powerful *effect*). More important, research results suggest that the policy has caused a measurable increase in restaurant hygiene and a significant drop in hospitalizations from food-related illnesses (a clear sign of *effectiveness*). Thus, more-informed choices by consumers appear to be improving restaurant cleanliness, rewarding restaurateurs who practice good hygiene, and stimulating a new dimension of beneficial competition among restaurants.[2]

This restaurant grading system illustrates how a thoughtful public policy can generate information that is genuinely helpful to people in their everyday decisions. What makes the Los Angeles County system so successful? More generally, what separates the transparency policies that succeed from those that fail? In this chapter, we try to answer these questions by examining eight major U.S. targeted transparency policies: corporate financial reporting, restaurant hygiene disclosure, mortgage lending disclosure, nutritional labeling, toxic pollution reporting, workplace hazardous chemicals disclosure, patient safety reporting, and plant closing reporting (shown in Table 4.1 and explored in subsequent tables).[3]

We focus on this subset of the full database of policies because we can take advantage of a significant body of quantitative policy evaluations and other literature that has developed in recent years. Although these evaluations examine specific policies, they provide us with a means to look deeply at the crosscutting drivers of success.[4] Thus the eight policies provide a particularly sharp means of evaluating the effectiveness of targeted transparency.

As we have seen, all targeted transparency policies share certain underlying design features. However, it is the variations in their design and the problems they address that shape their evolution and ultimately help to determine their success or failure.

A COMPLEX CHAIN REACTION

Like other forms of regulation, transparency policies aim to change the behavior of individuals and organizations in ways that policymakers believe will advance the public interest. But not all transparency policies achieve this objective. In this analysis, we divide transparency policies into three categories:

(A) Some transparency policies fail to alter behavior because few act on the information they generate.

(B) Other policies alter the behavior of individuals or organizations, but not necessarily in ways that are consistent with policy objectives.

(C) Still other policies alter behavior in ways that ultimately advance core public policy objectives.

Transparency policies in category (C) are successful, while those in categories (A) and (B) are failures or are only marginally effective.

To illustrate, consider the nutritional labeling of packaged foods mandated by Congress in 1990 with the goal of reducing the risk of heart disease, cancer, and other chronic illnesses. Suppose shoppers responded to the availability of nutrition information on packaged cookies by continuing to choose cookies based only on price and taste, with no regard for the nutrition data provided under the policy. In this case, the policy would fall into category (A) and be deemed a failure.

Table 4.1. *Overview of Eight Selected Transparency Policies*

Disclosure System	Year Enacted	Public Policy Objective	Information Disclosed	Primary Disclosers	Primary Users
Corporate Financial Disclosure[a]	1933, 1934	Reduce hidden risks to investors, improve corporate governance	Company financial data	Public companies trading in U.S.	Investors, financial intermediaries
Restaurant Hygiene Disclosure[b]	Los Angeles County: 1997	Reduce risk of food-borne illness	Letter grades reflecting hygiene inspection results	Restaurants	Consumers
Mortgage Lending Disclosure[c]	1975	Reduce mortgage lending discrimination	Lending activity demographics	Banks and other lending institutions	Community groups, regulators
Nutritional Labeling[d]	1990	Reduce risks of chronic disease	Nutrients in most processed foods	Manufacturers of packaged foods	Consumers
Toxic Releases Disclosure[e]	1986	Reduce toxic pollution	Quantities of toxic releases by chemical and factory	Chemical manufacturers, users	Regulators, environmental groups, communities
Workplace Hazards Disclosure[f]	1983	Reduce worker exposures to chemical hazards	Information on workplace hazardous chemicals	Manufacturers, employers	Workers, employers
Patient Safety Disclosure (NY, PA)[g]	NY: 1990 PA: 1992	Improve cardiac surgery performance	Mortality rates, etc., in patient treatment	Hospitals, doctors	Patients, doctors, insurers, governments
Plant Closing, Mass Layoff Disclosure[h]	1988	Lower costs of major economic dislocations from closures/layoffs	Plans of large-scale layoffs/facility closings	Large companies	Affected workers, communities

Note: Dates are years of initial policy enactment; see the Appendix for a discussion of amendments or supplemental legislation in subsequent years.
[a] Securities Act (1933) and Securities and Exchange Act (1934); [b] Los Angeles County Restaurant Hygiene Grade Cards; [c] Home Mortgage Disclosure Act; [d] Nutrition Labeling and Education Act; [e] Emergency Planning and Community Right-to-Know Act – the Toxics Release Inventory is a database established by the act; [f] Hazard Communication Standard – promulgated under the Occupational Safety and Health Act (1971); [g] New York Cardiac Surgery Reporting System and Pennsylvania Guide to Coronary Artery Bypass Graft Surgery; [h] Worker Adjustment and Retraining Notification Act.

Suppose shoppers responded by switching to cookies that were somewhat lower in sugar but higher in saturated fat. Or suppose they switched to cookies that were lower in both sugar and fat but increased their consumption of cookies enough to more than offset the health benefits. In these cases, nutritional labeling would have had effects on consumers' behavior, but it would not have furthered the policy aim of reducing heart disease. The policy would fall into category (B) in that it had an effect on behavior but was not effective.

But if shoppers responded by choosing cookies low in sugar and fat, and thereby increased the healthfulness of their overall diets, the policy would fall into category (C) and we would judge it to be successful. In examining our inventory of transparency policies, therefore, we must ask both whether new information changes user and discloser behavior and whether it does so in a way that moves that behavior in a desired policy direction.

As we have noted, simply placing information in the public domain does not guarantee that it will be used or used wisely. Individuals' and groups' responses to information are inseparable from their interests, desires, resources, cognitive capacities, and social contexts. Owing to these and other factors, people may ignore information, misunderstand it, or misuse it.[5] Whether and how new information is used to further public objectives depends upon its incorporation into complex chains of comprehension, action, and response.

In transparency systems, those chains of actions and responses have two primary actors: those who are compelled by public policies to provide that information and whose behavior policymakers hope to change (disclosers), and those who receive the new information produced by transparency policies and whose choices policymakers hope to improve (users). These information disclosers and users are typically connected in an action cycle (see Figure 4.1).[6]

When disclosers provide information voluntarily to customers, investors, and employees through advertising, reports, or other means, as shown on the left side of the diagram, users and disclosers are linked through an action cycle that conceptually begins with the provision of information by disclosers to potential users. Users draw on information that they find relevant, which affects their perceptions about the product, service, or outcome of concern and in turn informs their actions or behavior. User behavior changes (for example, purchases of a new "healthy" snack) are interpreted by disclosers, who may adjust their behaviors on the basis of user activity (such as by producing more or fewer healthy product lines in response to consumer preferences).

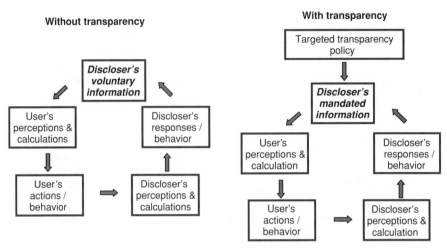

Figure 4.1. Targeted Transparency Action Cycle

As Chapter 2 described, there are many incentives for disclosers to provide less-than-complete information, so that the action cycle produces less than the socially desired outcomes. Targeted transparency policies attempt to redress the resulting information asymmetries in order to reduce public risks and improve public services. As depicted on the right side of Figure 4.1, such policies compel corporations, government agencies, or other organizations to provide information about their practices or products to the public at large. If this additional information is useful, accessible, and understood by consumers, investors, employees, community residents, or other individuals or groups, they may incorporate it into their decision-making processes in ways that alter their actions. The original disclosers of information, in turn, observe the changed choices of information users and, if policymakers are successful, respond by altering practices and products to reduce public risks or improve services.

The action cycle can be used to describe the effects and effectiveness of transparency policies across various policy domains as follows: A policy has *effects* when the information it produces enters the calculus of users and they consequently change their actions. Further effects may follow when information disclosers notice and respond to user actions. A system is *effective*, however, only when discloser responses significantly advance policy aims.

NEW INFORMATION EMBEDDED IN USER DECISIONS

Let us assume that, because of a targeted transparency policy, a new body of valued and accurate information is available to the public. Whether and how people respond to that information depends on how easily it fits into their routine ways of making choices.

As we have seen, the concept of bounded rationality helps explain the limitations of typical decision making.[7] People want to act rationally to advance their various, usually self-interested, ends. But because they are willing to invest only so much time and attention (and rightfully so), they don't seek out all of the information necessary to make optimal decisions. Instead, they try to make decisions that are good enough, using time-tested rules of thumb. (Economists call this *satisficing*.) Only information that penetrates these sometimes severe economies of decision making affects their calculations and actions.

Transparency systems alter decisions only when they provide pertinent information that enables people to substantially improve their choices without imposing significant additional costs. That is one reason diners are more likely to use the window-front grades in Los Angeles than Internet databases with similar information: the added cost of obtaining new information (in time, energy, and planning) is very low.

When new information becomes part of users' decision-making routines, we say that it is *embedded* in user decisions. For transparency systems to be effective, it is necessary but not sufficient that information become embedded in existing decision-making processes. Embedded information is not sufficient for effectiveness because conflicting preferences, cognitive challenges, and other constraints may still keep users from taking action that furthers public policy objectives.

What determines whether information will become embedded in users' decision making? We have identified three key factors:

- the information's perceived value in achieving users' goals;
- its compatibility with users' decision-making routines; and
- its comprehensibility.

Let us consider these factors in a bit more detail.

Value

Few people spend time and energy obtaining information for its own sake. Most people must perceive that the information will be valuable in achieving their goals. We assume that the underlying goals of users are not altered by most transparency systems. There are instances, however, where intensive education, training, or widely publicized crises change preferences; hence an accompanying transparency system can help users act on those changed preferences. The Enron and WorldCom corporate scandals and no-smoking educational campaigns illustrate such synergies between preference changes and transparency systems.[8]

Making good decisions is a goal that all people share, and we all know that good information can sometimes improve our decisions: no one wants to eat in a restaurant with a filthy kitchen or buy a car that is unsafe. But consumers who feel they already know everything they need to know about restaurant quality or auto safety will ignore the data that transparency policies generate.

Similarly, additional information won't help users who believe they have few meaningful choices to make. A restaurant grade might be of little value in a town with only one restaurant (although a C rating might persuade more people to eat at home). Requirements that employers clearly label hazardous substances in their workplaces have had little impact in part because many workers find it daunting either to change jobs or to persuade managers to use different chemicals.[9]

In addition, the cost of acquiring and using new information must be low enough to justify users' efforts in relation to expected benefits. Users may be more willing to invest time and effort in integrating new information into their choices when they perceive substantial immediate or long-term gain. Car buyers who care about safety may seek out safety rankings even though such ratings are not available in showrooms. Home buyers who care about school quality may be willing to invest time in searching newspapers, magazines, or Web sites for school rankings. Investors making important financial decisions may be willing to seek information about the risks of publicly traded companies even if the search is costly. In general, though, if users incur a substantial cost in either time or material resources to acquire information generated by transparency systems, they are unlikely to embed that information into their everyday choices.[10]

Compatibility

Information must also be compatible with the usual ways that people go about making their decisions. People have settled routines and habits for making choices. Some carefully compare the price-per-pound labels for different brands of pasta at the grocery before buying; others don't bother. Some browse reviews of products and services in publications like *Consumer Reports* or on Internet sites before making large purchases; others shop on impulse. Information generated by transparency policies can become embedded only if it is compatible with these settled routines.

Compatibility ordinarily includes two elements: *format* and *time and place of availability*. The Los Angeles restaurant ratings excel on both: everyone who attended grade school understands the meaning of A, B, and C letter grades (format); and because grades are posted at the entrance of every restaurant, they are available to patrons *when and where* they make dining decisions (time and place).

Information is compatible in format if users can easily take note of new facts to make more-informed choices. Large miles-per-gallon stickers on new-car windows in dealer showrooms are easy to read and hard to miss. On the other hand, home buyers are unlikely to wade through technical government reports to determine which neighborhoods have high levels of toxic pollution.

As we have seen, one way to simplify the format of complex information is by creating a rating system. The Los Angeles restaurant hygiene grades and the auto rollover ratings described in Chapter 1 provide good illustrations. Both systems convert data and expert interpretation into simple normative signals such as stars or letter grades (see Figure 4.2). In both systems, underlying details can be accessed by those who want to study them. (Note that rating systems that lack access to such underlying facts would not constitute transparency systems as we define them.) In other systems, simple graphics – a pie chart or a clock face, for example – provide similar shortcuts.

Significantly, rating systems involve two sets of trade-offs: (1) simple presentation versus accurate communication of complex facts, and (2) normative judgments by policymakers versus normative judgments by users. If the information is not amenable to a simple rating formula or the rating organization is not widely trusted, then a rating system is unlikely to be effective.

Making information available at a time and place where users are accustomed to making decisions also maximizes the chances that information will become embedded. Grades in restaurant windows and fuel economy ratings on new-car stickers are familiar examples of such compatibility. Sometimes it takes careful planning to ensure that information is available when choices are actually occurring. Thus, if school performance report cards and information about toxic pollution from nearby factories are intended to inform the decisions of would-be home buyers, the data should be aggregated and made available in real estate offices or Web sites rather than being stored in different public databases. Similarly, campaign finance disclosures are more likely to facilitate opposing candidates' and voters' responses if they are available in real time, and hospital safety ratings are more likely to support doctors' and patients' choices if they are available in doctors' offices.

In some cases, decisions are made by agents acting on behalf of other people. When this is the case, information must be presented in a format

Figure 4.2. Restaurant Hygiene Quality Cards. *Source:* Restaurant hygiene cards, Fairfax area, Los Angeles. November 2005. Photos by Elizabeth Schetina

that fits in with those agents' routines. For example, travel agents are more likely to pay attention to government-required airline safety and on-time data if they are prominently displayed on travel reservation Web sites that travel agents frequent. Community groups representing neighborhood residents are more likely to press banks to improve their lending practices if the relevant information is posted on Web sites they normally access or emailed to them. Parents acting for their children are more likely to consider new information about school performance if it is sent home with reenrollment forms. Of course, additional problems can arise when the goals of agents and those they represent are not congruent. For example, agents may have incentives to exaggerate information in order to pursue their own aims.

Comprehension

Even if valuable and compatible with users' routines, information is unlikely to become embedded in everyday choices unless it is *comprehensible*. Information is comprehensible when users have the capacity to relate it to the decisions they face. The complexity of information often creates a barrier to comprehension by diverse groups of users.[11]

The disclosure system for workplace chemical hazards illustrates the challenge of comprehensibility. Since 1983, federal regulations have required employers to inform employees about various hazardous substances at their workplaces. Employers must post material safety data sheets (MSDS) that describe the characteristics, hazards, precautions, and appropriate emergency responses for each hazardous chemical used.

Unfortunately, as the image of a typical MSDS shows (Figure 4.3), these data sheets are extremely difficult to understand. One study found that workers were able to grasp only about 60 percent of the information they contain.[12] In addition, workers have limited resources available for interpretation. In a unionized setting, they may be able to turn to local representatives or health and safety committees for assistance in responding to the information.[13] However, in nonunion settings (which make up far more than 90 percent of all workplaces), workers must find other resources to help them interpret the technical data contained in data sheets. Compounding these difficulties, cognitive biases may affect workers' ability to act on information about low-level risks.[14]

In some cases, as we have noted, it is possible to dramatically simplify complex data to make them comprehensible and actionable. Restaurant hygiene grades in the Los Angeles system, for example, are a simple letter

The MSDS format adheres to the standards and regulatory requirements
of the United States and may not meet regulatory requirements
in other countries.

DuPont   Page 1
Material Safety Data Sheet

10110PP
        "Teflon" Advanced
        Revised 16-FEB-2001
CHEMICAL PRODUCT/COMPANY IDENTIFICATION
Material Identification

"Teflon" is a registered trademark of DuPont.

    Corporate MSDS Number : DU007357

Company Identification

MANUFACTURER/DISTRIBUTOR
        DuPont
        1007 Market Street
        Wilmington, DE 19898

PHONE NUMBERS
    Product Information : 1-800-441-7515 (outside the U.S.
                          302-774-1000)
    Transport Emergency : CHEMTREC 1-800-424-9300(outside U.S.
                          703-527-3887)
    Medical Emergency   : 1-800-441-3637 (outside the U.S.
                          302-774-1000)

COMPOSITION/INFORMATION ON INGREDIENTS
Components

Material   CAS Number   %
Fluorinated Polyurethane   3-5
  (NJ Trade Secret Registry # 0085020l001-5418P)
Acrylic Copolymer   1-2
  (NJ Trade Secret Registry # 0085020l001-5516P)

Hexylene Glycol   107-41-5   1-4
Water   7732-18-5   89-95

HAZARDS IDENTIFICATION
Potential Health Effects

    Skin contact may cause skin irritation with discomfort or
    rash. The product diluted 1:4 with water was not a skin
    irritant or a skin sensitizer in human patch testing.

    Eye contact with the product may cause eye irritation with
    discomfort, tearing, or blurring of vision.

    Inhalation may cause irritation of the upper respiratory
    passages or lung irritation effects with cough, discomfort,

---

10110PP   DuPont   Page 2
                   Material Safety Data Sheet

              (HAZARDS IDENTIFICATION - Continued)

    difficulty breathing, shortness of breath, or pulmonary
    edema (body in the lungs). Symptoms may be modest
    initially, followed in hours by severe shortness of breath
    requiring prompt medical attention.

    Ingestion may cause nonspecific discomfort, such as nausea,
    headache, or weakness, heartburn, vomiting, or diarrhea.
    Ingestion of Hexylene Glycol may cause temporary nervous
    system depression with anaesthetic effects such as
    dizziness, headache, confusion, incoordination, and loss of
    consciousness.

Carcinogenicity Information

    None of the components present in this material at concentrations
    equal to or greater than 0.1% are listed by IARC, NTP, OSHA or ACGIH
    as a carcinogen.

FIRST AID MEASURES
First Aid

    INHALATION

    If inhaled, remove to fresh air. If not breathing, give
    artificial respiration. If breathing is difficult, give oxygen.
    Call a physician.

    SKIN CONTACT

    In case of contact, immediately wash skin with soap and water.
    Wash contaminated clothing before reuse.

    EYE CONTACT

    In case of contact, immediately flush eyes with plenty of water
    for at least 15 minutes. Call a physician.

    INGESTION

    If swallowed, do not induce vomiting. Immediately give 2 glasses
    of water. Never give anything by mouth to an unconscious person.
    Call a physician.

Notes to Physicians

    Activated charcoal mixture may be administered. To prepare
    activated charcoal mixture, suspend 50 grams activated charcoal in
    400 mL water and mix thoroughly. Administer 5 mL/kg, or 350 mL
    for an average adult.

Figure 4.3. Material Safety Data Sheet for Teflon Exposures. *Source:* Material Safety Data Sheet Excerpt, DuPont Corporation, pp. 1–2 (of 7),
February 2001

grade based upon one hundred criteria that include not only the presence of rodent droppings but also food temperature, twice-served food, and utensil sanitation.[15] Letter grades work in this case because most people trust health inspectors to combine the many different measures into a single metric that captures how we should judge a restaurant. In the same way, the five-star ranking system for automobile rollovers distills complicated engineering calculations and crash-test results into a simple yet credible scale. Most car shoppers are glad that someone in the National Highway Traffic Safety Administration has taken the time to test car models and inform them about this important aspect of safety.

In other cases, however, simple scales fail to make the crucial data more comprehensible. The five-color scheme designed to inform Americans about changing levels of threat of a terrorist attack fails notoriously in this regard. In this system, red indicates the most severe level of threat, green specifies low threat, and blue, yellow, and orange designate intermediate levels.[16] But terrorist threat reporting differs from restaurant hygiene grading and automobile rollover ratings in two important ways.

First, terrorist threats are unfamiliar and diverse. Most people can clearly visualize what a filthy restaurant kitchen or an overturned car looks like and imagine the dire consequences they can produce. But what is a terrorist threat? Does it mean that terrorists are planning to crash planes into buildings near us, send suicide bombers to shopping malls, release noxious chemicals or infectious microbes into the environment, or disrupt telephone and Internet service? Or does it mean merely that some people in faraway countries seem to be talking about such actions? Without a more specific notion of threat, it is unlikely that any color-coded system could make this public risk more transparent.

Second, terrorist threat levels fail to guide individuals' actions meaningfully. Restaurant and auto rollover ratings help users make clear and straightforward choices – Should I eat at this restaurant? Should I buy this car? The choices with respect to terrorist threats are much more complicated. Citizens' objectives are multifaceted and may include staying alive and uninjured, protecting friends and family, helping authorities to identify threats, and aiding those in distress. Because it is not associated with specific threats or even particular locations, the color-coded scheme provides only vague suggestions for the public, such as "be alert to suspicious activity" (blue level) and "stay tuned to TV or radio for current information" (red level).[17]

When transparency systems produce complex information, intermediaries can sometimes translate it into user-friendly messages. The toxic pollution disclosure system, for example, produces factory-by-factory data on releases of a list of toxic chemicals each year. It is difficult for untrained users to navigate this extensive database or relate emissions to relative levels of risk.[18] More sophisticated users – such as owners and managers of industrial plants, environmental organizations, and regulators themselves – have the analytic capacities to comprehend this information. They use it to inform management goals, shape agendas for action, and target enforcement actions, respectively. Such intermediaries also create user-friendly Web sites searchable by chemical, facility, or zip code.[19]

The mortgage lending reporting system provides another example of intermediary action. The Home Mortgage Disclosure Act (HMDA) of 1975 (substantially strengthened in 1989) requires banks to disclose their mortgage loans by race, gender, census tract, and income level.[20] Intermediaries such as community organizations, economists, bank regulators, and bank managers used the mortgage lending data to gather evidence of lending patterns, leaving little doubt about the prevalence of racial discrimination in lending.[21] National and local advocacy groups then pressed banks to increase their lending to disadvantaged customers, compiled public cases against particular banks, and negotiated with them to improve their practices.[22]

As these varied cases suggest, making information generated by transparency policies comprehensible is no simple matter. When policies address an issue on which experts agree and for which most information users have similar goals, it is often possible to reduce complex information into a simple guiding metric. But when the knowledge itself is evolving quickly or subject to controversy, or when users have very different uses for the same kinds of information, this shortcut can create confusion rather than transparency. In such cases, transparency policies that produce more complex, disaggregated data are often comprehensible only to sophisticated users who then act as translators and advocates.

Table 4.2 summarizes the key dimensions of user embeddedness – value, compatibility, and comprehensibility – for eight of the transparency policies we have studied. In the final column of the table, we assess each policy's overall level of user embeddedness as high, moderate, or low on the basis of these components.

Two of the eight policies produce information that has become highly embedded in users' decisions: corporate financial disclosure and restaurant hygiene grades. As noted, the information in restaurant grades is highly relevant to users and is provided at an appropriate time, place, and format that is readily understood at relatively low cost. The information in corporate financial reports is also highly relevant, reasonably timely, and

Table 4.2. *User Embeddedness in Eight Selected Transparency Policies*

Disclosure System	Relevance of Information to User Decision	Compatibility with User Decision-Making Process			Comprehensibility of Information	Cost of Information Access for Users	User Embeddedness
		Format of Information	Timeliness of Information	Location of Information			
Corporate Financial Disclosure	High: directly related to assessing risk/return of investments	Detailed: multiple levels of content	Timely: available at time of investment; updated quarterly	Web; brokers, other intermediaries	Complex: typically requires third-party interpretation	Moderate cost to obtain; high cost to process	High (third party important)
Restaurant Hygiene Disclosure	High: directly related to assessing health risks	Simplified (letter grade, A–C)	Timely: available at time of choice; updated multiple times per year	Restaurant window/entry area	Simple: customer can interpret	Low cost to obtain and process	High
Mortgage Lending Disclosure	Low: not directly related to individual mortgage applicants; high: directly related to aims of community groups	Detailed: community-level microdata regarding bank lending	Timely: available at all times; updated annually	Web and lending institutions	Complex: typically requires third-party interpretation	Moderate cost to obtain; high cost to process	Moderate to high (third party important)
Nutritional Labeling	High: directly related to nutritional and dietary concerns	Simple format; complex vocabulary	Timely: available at point of sale; updated infrequently	Product labels	Complex: requires knowledge of nutrition	Low cost to obtain; high cost to process	High for some users; low for others

(continued)

63

Table 4.2 (*continued*)

Disclosure System	Relevance of Information to User Decision	Compatibility with User Decision-Making Process			Comprehensibility of Information	Cost of Information Access for Users	User Embeddedness
		Format of Information	Timeliness of Information	Location of Information			
Toxic Releases Disclosure	Low: not directly related to most individual decisions; moderate: variable for third parties	Detailed: pounds of chemical releases by plant	Timely: available at all times; updated annually	Web	Complex: typically requires third-party interpretation	Moderate cost to obtain; high cost to process	Low
Workplace Hazards Disclosure	Moderate: directly related to employment decisions	Detailed: information related to workplace chemicals	Timely/limited: available at the worksite, not available to job seekers; updated infrequently	Workplace posted sheets; Web for some information	Complex: multiple chemicals; exposure, risk data	Moderate cost to obtain; high cost to process	Low for workers; moderate for manufacturers selecting suppliers
Patient Safety Disclosure (NY, PA)	High: directly related to risk of medical treatment when facing decision	Moderate detail: multiple measures of medical safety	Timely: available to patients at all times; updated annually	Web; media reports	Complex: multi-attribute, technical information	High cost to obtain and process	Low
Plant Closing, Mass Layoff Disclosure	High: directly related to employee, community decisions	Simple: posting of pending closing/layoff	Not timely: 60 days prior to closing/layoff	Workplace/ community leaders notification	Simple	Low cost to obtain and process	Low for workers, communities

64

designed for comparability. However, because the data are complex and accounting vocabulary is hard to understand, users often rely on intermediaries (brokers, analysts, fund managers, and Web-based programs) to aid in embedding information in their investment choices.

Nutritional labeling and mortgage lending disclosure only moderately embed information in users' decisions – for differing reasons. Nutritional labels provide information to consumers conveniently available on products when and where they make purchasing decisions. However, as scientific advances make nutritional advice more complex, many shoppers have a difficult time comprehending how to use that information to improve food choices.[23]

Mortgage lending data are only moderately embedded in users' decisions because few applicants seek such data when making choices about lenders. However, community organizations and federal regulators serve as the key agents, embedding the information in activities that aim to reduce discrimination.

Finally, four policies – toxic pollution reporting, workplace hazardous chemicals reporting, patient safety disclosure, and plant closing reporting – have not become embedded into most users' decisions for a variety of reasons. Information on factories' toxic pollution is seldom available to home buyers or renters at the time and place where it might have its greatest impact on behavior – searching for a home to purchase or an apartment to rent. Untrained users, furthermore, have difficulty translating complex data on pollution into understandable levels of risk. Workplace hazards reporting generally lacks intermediaries to clarify the risk information for employees. Even if intermediaries were available, many workers have very constrained workplace choices (exit) or limited abilities to translate concerns about exposure into changes in workplace practices or human resource policies (voice).

NEW INFORMATION EMBEDDED IN DISCLOSER DECISIONS

Changes in information users' behavior usually are not enough to make transparency policies effective. Information disclosers must also alter their decisions and actions. When disclosers incorporate user responses to information into their decision calculus, we say that new information has become embedded in discloser decision-making processes. Highly effective transparency policies, then, are doubly embedded.

Though the social context of discloser decisions differs from that of user decisions, they can be understood using the same analytic concepts. Disclosers are more likely to incorporate user responses into their decisions if those responses have value in relation to their goals, are compatible with the way they make decisions, and are comprehensible to them.

It is important to keep in mind that disclosers' decisions to make improvements in products or practices sometimes anticipate rather than respond to users' changed choices resulting from transparency policies. Corporate managers concerned with protecting market share or reputation may try to predict the behavior of their customers, employees, or investors by introducing lines of healthy products, reducing toxic pollution, tightening corporate governance, or otherwise improving performance *before* the public demands such changes. Likewise, government officials may take anticipatory action to improve schools, purify drinking water, or improve other services before a new transparency system begins to drive users' responses.

Let us look in some detail at how the value, compatibility, and comprehensibility of users' responses to information affect the embedding of those responses in disclosers' decisions.

Response Value

In general, disclosers will change their practices only if they perceive that shifts in user behavior will have an impact on their core organizational goals. That is, for information to become embedded in disclosers' decisions, user actions must be perceived to substantially affect disclosers' interests or be likely to do so in the future. For companies, core objectives often include enhanced profitability, market share, and reputation. For public agencies, objectives may include increased constituency support, legitimacy, and trust.

If users respond to information in ways that do not directly affect disclosers, the behavior of disclosers is unlikely to change. Companies required to disclose specifics of toxic pollution have made commitments to reduce pollution in response to bad publicity, embarrassing demonstrations, and employee dissatisfaction. But they would be unlikely to respond to community residents' decisions to move away, since these actions do not directly affect the polluting companies. In the same way, elementary schools with poor report cards would be likely to make changes in response to pressure from local politicians and enrollment declines. But they would be unlikely to respond to students' failures to get high-paying jobs after graduation.

Furthermore, user behavior is relevant to disclosers only if the disclosers perceive that they have choices about how to respond. For example, a small food manufacturer might believe it lacks the resources to respond to shoppers' desire for healthier products. A cash-strapped school might lack the capacity to respond to parent demands for smaller classes or more extracurricular activities.

Overall, the cost to disclosers of integrating user responses into management decisions must be sufficiently low to justify their efforts in relation to expected benefits, defined in their own terms. Disclosers may be more willing to invest time and effort when they perceive opportunities to beat the competition or avoid reputational damage.[24]

Response Compatibility

Second, user responses are more likely to become embedded in disclosers' decisions if such responses are compatible with the ways in which managers receive, process, and act on new information.

Compatibility mismatches are sometimes process-oriented. For example, political candidates may have no way of perceiving and reacting to voter dissatisfaction with their disclosed sources of financing because no feedback process exists. Hospitals may not discern the character and degree of patients' concerns about medical errors because no patient-response mechanism exists.

Compatibility mismatches may also be temporal. Auto manufacturers, for instance, could not respond quickly to drops in sales of cars with high rollover ratings because their design cycle is slow, often three to four years.

Occasionally transparency systems actually alter disclosers' decision-making processes, thereby transforming a compatibility mismatch into a match. For example, when legislation forced chief executives to sign off on their companies' toxic pollution reports, some executives said that the requirement forced them to focus on and respond to total toxic pollution for the first time.[25]

Response Comprehensibility

Finally, user responses must be comprehensible to disclosers. If user responses are misunderstood, they can't become effectively embedded in disclosers' decisions. For example, a food manufacturer might assume that declining sales of its high-sugar cereals are due to unusually effective advertising by a competitor, whereas shoppers are actually responding to nutritional information. A chemical company faced with negative publicity about toxic releases might conclude that communities are demanding general reductions in pollution, whereas residents may be concerned only about levels of carcinogens.

Evidence suggests that such misunderstandings of user behavior are relatively common. For example, studies have shown that many retailers have traditionally conducted only rudimentary analysis of sales data from point-of-sale information they collect.[26] As transparency policies become more common and communication technology advances, disclosers can design new ways of studying user responses to information before planning their own responses.

Table 4.3 summarizes the key aspects of discloser embeddedness – value, compatibility, and comprehensibility – for eight transparency policies. As with user embeddedness, we have evaluated the overall level of discloser embeddedness as high, moderate, or low for each policy.

Only two of the eight policies – corporate financial disclosure and restaurant hygiene quality standards – have become highly embedded in discloser decisions. In these cases, disclosers have much at stake and a refined ability to discern changes in user behavior in response to disclosed information. For example, executives of public companies know that investors and their advisers base their decisions in large part on the data produced by financial disclosure requirements. These stock purchase decisions strongly affect the primary objectives that managers pursue. Company stock prices determine the cost of raising investment capital, and top managers are frequently compensated in part on the basis of the performance of their company's stock. Thus, responses to stock movements have been deeply incorporated into many management decisions.[27]

Other policies are only moderately embedded in discloser decision making. Banks and other financial institutions are unlikely to be actively aware of disparate lending practices that might form patterns of discrimination in their day-to-day activities. However, during attempts to merge with other banks, executives become highly sensitive to these decisions because they must comply with the community lending requirements of the Community Reinvestment Act. For several other transparency policies – nutritional labeling and patient safety, for example – the difficulty of discerning the causes of customers' or investors' changed choices impedes disclosers' capacity to adapt to those changes.

Finally, user responses to plant closing reporting could hardly be less embedded in the decisions of employers. The required sixty days' advance notice of plant closures or large-scale layoffs is linked to decisions made well in advance of the required disclosure period, which are almost certainly unaffected by responses to reporting. Notice generally comes too late for workers, unions, or community organizations to try to change employers' decisions.

Table 4.3. *Discloser Embeddedness in Eight Selected Transparency Policies*

Disclosure System	Impact of User Decisions on Discloser Goals	Compatibility of Response with Discloser Decisions	Ability to Discern User Changes in Behavior	Cost of Collecting Information Regarding Change in User Behavior	Discloser Embeddedness
Corporate Financial Disclosure	High: investor decisions directly affect capital market flows to disclosers	High: discloser companies highly attuned to investor decisions	High: firms, investment advisers attuned to changes in flows arising from new information	Moderate	High
Restaurant Hygiene Disclosure	High: customer decisions directly affect restaurant revenues	High: restaurants highly attuned to customer decisions	Moderate: direct observation possible, but imperfect; ability to perceive reduction/increase in traffic over time	Low to moderate	High
Mortgage Lending Disclosure	Low: ongoing activity; high: merger/acquisition	Low: ongoing activity; high: merger/acquisition	High: challenges using disclosed data directly observable by banks	Low: challenges brought as part of regulatory review for mergers	Low: ongoing activity; high: merger/acquisition
Nutritional Labeling	Moderate: consumer choice driven by price, taste, as well as nutrition	Moderate: consumer choice based on many factors	Moderate: difficult to discern sales shifts from label responses; large number of products for typical food processor	Moderate to high: sales data analysis or focus group reactions	Moderate
Toxic Releases Disclosure	Moderate: reactions to TRI dispersed (e.g., capital markets, reputation, sales, regulation)	Low to moderate: pollutant releases related to multiple decisions and firm objectives	Low to moderate: unclear pathway to perceive reactions, except from regulators	Moderate: no single data source or mechanism for gauging effects	Low to moderate

(continued)

Table 4.3 (*continued*)

Disclosure System	Impact of User Decisions on Discloser Goals	Compatibility of Response with Discloser Decisions	Ability to Discern User Changes in Behavior	Cost of Collecting Information Regarding Change in User Behavior	Discloser Embeddedness
Workplace Hazards Disclosure	Low for labor market behavior, which arises from multiple sources; moderate for supplier decisions more directly related to profitability	Low: nonunion worker response diffuse; union response may be more focused; moderate for supplier choice	Low to moderate: multiple reasons for potential hires to say "no," but more direct information for current workforce, supplier responses	Moderate: difficult to discern for potential hires; more discernible for current workers and suppliers	Low to moderate
Patient Safety Disclosure (NY, PA)	Moderate: patient choice driven by price, expertise, as well as safety	Low: patient choices based on many factors	Low: difficult to discern whether patient decision arising from reaction to report cards or other factors (e.g., health-care coverage)	High: no single source or mechanism for gauging effects of report cards	Low to moderate
Plant Closing, Mass Layoff Disclosure	Low: plant closing/layoff decisions made in advance of notification; incentives to change very low at time of information provision	Low: unrelated to core reasons for closings or layoffs	High: reaction of users easy to perceive	Low: users directly notify discloser	Low

OBSTACLES: PREFERENCES, BIASES, AND GAMES

Even policies that manage to embed information may fail to become effective. Users or disclosers may integrate information into decision-making routines but decide, on balance, that new data do not justify changing their decisions. Alternatively, they may make changes in their behavior that frustrate rather than serve policy objectives. Or users and disclosers may misunderstand and misuse new information.

Our research suggests that two kinds of obstacles can prevent successfully embedded transparency systems from effectively advancing policy objectives:

- lack of congruence between the goals of policymakers and those of information disclosers and users
- misinterpretation of information by disclosers or users, often owing to various kinds of cognitive bias.

Let us consider these obstacles more closely.

Goal Conflict

As we have discussed, both information users and disclosers employ newly revealed facts to advance their own aims, which may not be identical to or even consistent with public policy goals. For this reason, transparency policies are more likely to be effective when they tap into user goals that are consistent with public goals and create pressures to encourage disclosers to take actions that fit those same public goals.

Users' goals are more likely to be congruent with policy objectives than are disclosers' goals since, in principle, transparency systems are legislated to protect users' interests. Sometimes, however, public goals and the goals of at least some users do not coincide. Such lack of congruence may weaken a transparency system's effectiveness. For example, the public goal of nutritional labeling was to reduce the risk of heart disease and cancer. Many shoppers, however, were focused on the goal of losing weight. When they responded to information about fat but not calories, they complicated the signals to food companies about whether to introduce low-fat or low-calorie products. State laws that require disclosure of sex offenders' residences offer an even more striking case where public policy objectives and user interests can collide. The state laws (often referred to collectively as "Megan's Laws") aim to reduce the potential risks faced by communities from the release of dangerous sex offenders by informing residents of their current addresses.

However, since passage of these laws in the 1990s, some individuals have used that information to harass offenders, to force them to move out of their homes, or in several extreme cases to murder them.[28]

Disclosers' goals are still less likely to be congruent with policy aims. In our stylized action cycle, disclosers alter their behavior primarily to satisfy the external demands of market pressures or political actions by users. Since disclosers usually report favorable news about their activities voluntarily, government mandates that aim to minimize risks or improve services generally force disclosure of unfavorable information.

As a result, in deciding both what to disclose and how to respond to user pressures, disclosers usually weigh conflicting interests – minimizing use of resources, maximizing competitive advantage, and avoiding reputational harm, for example. And because all transparency systems represent political compromises, they nearly always have loopholes that provide disclosers with choices about how to comply while pursuing their own interests. Therefore, disclosers may respond in ways that policymakers consider negative. While many disclosers act in good faith, others minimize or hide problems. In other words, they game the system.

To return to a recent example with national and international consequences, Enron, WorldCom, and other well-respected public companies manipulated disclosed earnings to attract investors. In some cases, executives moved substantial expenses off their reported balance sheets to avoid having to justify zigs and zags in their quarterly earnings reports. When media revelations of these practices in 2001 and 2002 forced these companies into bankruptcy, Congress created new disclosure requirements to close such loopholes.

Research on toxic pollution disclosure suggests that some companies engage in "paper reductions" of pollution by changing estimating techniques or definitions.[29] A commonly raised concern about school performance report cards is that administrators and teachers may alter curricula and pedagogical methods to boost the appearance of improved performance without necessarily improving education – by "teaching to the test," or even helping students cheat on crucial exams.[30] Likewise, doctors and health-care administrators may game hospital reporting requirements by "creaming" – avoiding the most difficult-to-treat patients and seeking out healthier ones.[31]

Sometimes, of course, the goals of at least some disclosers do coincide with transparency policy aims. Executives of public companies generally support corporate financial reporting as a means of lowering the cost of capital, gaining competitive advantage, and securing investors' trust. Many major producers of packaged foods ultimately favored government-mandated nutritional labeling so that they could reap benefits in higher prices and improved image from products shown by labels to be reasonably healthy. Some food companies favored government-mandated organic labeling for similar reasons.

It is also possible for transparency systems to change organizations' internal priorities. Managers charged with improving environmental, safety, or financial practices may use new disclosure regulations to advocate changes they would like in company policy that also support public objectives.

However, it is important to note that congruence of policymakers', users' and disclosers' goals is *not* necessary for a transparency system to be effective. What is essential is that there be congruence between policy goals and the *behavioral changes* of users and disclosers. At their best, transparency policies trigger user actions that cause disclosers to advance some public good (such as public health) while pursuing private goals (such as profit). In this sense, transparency policies act as a "visible hand" that, like Adam Smith's invisible hand, harnesses private incentives for public benefits.

Misinterpretation

Even when goals are congruent, inaccurate interpretation of information may damage the effectiveness of transparency policies.

As we have already discussed, some misinterpretations are the result of cognitive errors. For example, most people tend to overestimate risks from rare, cataclysmic events while underestimating risks associated with ongoing problems or hazard exposures.[32]

Other misinterpretations result from a failure to understand the scientific implications of information or the metrics of the transparency system itself. For example, journalists (one important category of information users) widely misinterpreted factory managers' disclosure of toxic pollution measured in pounds as equivalent to a ranking of health risks to the public. This led to headlines that mistakenly labeled particular factories as the "worst" polluters and encouraged companies to change their waste emission policies based on pounds of toxins rather than other metrics – such as exposure or toxicity – that more accurately reflected public health risks.[33]

Misinterpretations of information by shoppers, investors, or community residents can also lead to unintended discriminatory effects. Researchers have shown that the ability to understand and use certain types of risk information varies with age, educational background, and other socioeconomic factors. Older and less well-educated consumers have more trouble understanding nutritional labels than younger and better-educated consumers.[34] Higher educational levels also have a positive impact on workers' understanding of information about exposure to hazardous chemicals.

Disclosers, too, may misinterpret new information in ways that create barriers to transparency's effectiveness. Restaurants concerned about users' response to hygiene grades may focus on one data point (employee hand-washing, for example) when patrons are actually more concerned about another (rodent droppings or stale food). Banks may increase lending to relatively prosperous inner-city businesses or residents while community groups may be more concerned about those that are struggling. When misunderstood information becomes embedded in disclosers' decision-making processes, the resulting systemic distortion impedes transparency effectiveness.

In summary, lack of congruence in goals and misinterpretations of new information can reduce the effectiveness of transparency systems even when information becomes embedded in routines. Sometimes such distortions mean that new information does more harm than good to specific public aims. As a practical matter, such gaps between policy goals and actual effects often become evident only after some time has passed. Thus, mid-course corrections become essential. Periodically analyzing and updating metrics increases the chances that obstacles will not cripple a promising transparency system.[35]

Table 4.4 details the extent of goal congruence, misinterpretation, and cognitive bias for each of the eight policies we focus on in this chapter. In the right-most column, we offer a prediction regarding the strength of the link between the actions of users and disclosers on the one hand and policy outcomes on the other, basing our prediction on this analysis of the major obstacles to policy effectiveness. The strength of the connection between action and effectiveness should be high when there is strong congruence between user goals and policy objectives and when the potential for misinterpretation, cognitive error, and discloser gaming is low.

HOW DO TRANSPARENCY POLICIES MEASURE UP?

How well do various transparency policies incorporate the logic of the action cycle and successfully embed information into the decision-making routines of users and disclosers? And, as we have argued, is embeddedness the key to the effectiveness of transparency policies? Using a broad survey of existing research on these eight policies, we categorized them into three general groups according to how well they accomplished their policy objectives:

- *Highly effective:* The transparency policy has significantly changed the behavior of most users and disclosers in the direction intended by public policies. We regard three of the eight policies as highly effective:

Table 4.4. Obstacles to Effectiveness in Eight Selected Transparency Policies

Disclosure System	Congruence of User and Public Policy Goals		Users: Chance of Misinterpretation and Cognitive Biases	Disclosers: Chance of Misinterpretation and Strategic Action	Predicted Link of User/Discloser Actions and Policy Outcomes
	User Goals	Public Policy Goals			
Corporate Financial Disclosure	Evaluate risk and return of potential investments	Capital market efficiency; reduce risks to investors; improve corporate governance	Low: highly developed channels and third parties for evaluation of information	Moderate: unintended consequences from reporting; gaming system through loopholes	High
Restaurant Hygiene Disclosure	Lower risk of exposure to bad health outcomes from eating out	Reduction of public health risk	Moderate: simple system of reporting may neglect risks not included in rating	Moderate: restaurants may not address practices not included in ratings	Moderate to high
Mortgage Lending Disclosure	Improve access to mortgages for groups facing discrimination	Reduce housing market discrimination through home lending practices	Low to moderate: third parties evaluate statistical information but may have strategic reasons to misinterpret	Low: statute sets clear definitions of discriminatory practices relating to disclosed data	High
Nutritional Labeling	Improve nutrition; reduce risks of disease; lose weight	Reduce risks of disease; improve nutrition	Moderate to high: confusion of nutritional and dietary objectives; conflicting preferences	Moderate: incentives to market products that appeal to multiple, conflicting user preferences	Low to moderate
Toxic Releases Disclosure	Reduce exposure to harmful chemicals	Reduce toxic pollution	High: difficulty in translating tonnage release information into risk measures; cognitive problems associated with low-level-risk perception	Moderate: allows paper reductions in tonnage releases unrelated to risk reduction	Low to moderate

(continued)

Table 4.4 (continued)

Disclosure System	Congruence of User and Public Policy Goals		Users: Chance of Misinterpretation and Cognitive Biases	Disclosers: Chance of Misinterpretation and Strategic Action	Predicted Link of User/Discloser Actions and Policy Outcomes
	User Goals	Public Policy Goals			
Workplace Hazards Disclosure	Lower exposure to risks at workplace	Reduce worker exposures to risks	High: cognitive biases associated with low-level-risk perception	Low to moderate: switching work assignments to those less concerned (aware) of exposures	Moderate
Patient Safety Disclosure (NY, PA)	Reduce risks of death, serious injury from selection of hospital/surgeon	Improve performance of cardiac surgery procedures	High: difficult to weigh risk of error in multi-attribute selection problem facing patient; high-pressure and low-frequency decision compounds problem	Moderate: systemic mistakes hard to correct; selection and sorting for healthy patients may be common	Low
Plant Closing, Mass Layoff Disclosure	Workers: find new jobs as quickly as possible; community: find potential alternatives to shutdown/mass layoff	Lower the costs associated with major economic dislocation from closures/layoffs	Low	Low: closure decision already made (few repercussions from disclosure); firms can avoid reporting layoff if fewer than 50 workers involved (spread layoffs over time)	High

corporate financial reporting, the Los Angeles restaurant hygiene grading system, and mortgage lending disclosure under the Home Mortgage Disclosure Act.

- *Moderately effective:* The transparency policy has changed the behavior of a substantial portion of users and disclosers in the intended direction but has also left gaps in behavior change and produced unintended consequences. We judged three policies as moderately effective: nutritional labeling requirements, toxic pollution reporting, and workplace hazardous chemicals disclosure.
- *Ineffective:* The transparency policy has failed to appreciably change the behavior of users and disclosers or has changed behavior in directions other than those intended. Two of the eight policies were ineffective: patient safety disclosure and plant closure and layoff notification requirements.

Table 4.5 summarizes our effectiveness findings. The sixth and seventh columns provide a summary assessment of each policy's effects and effectiveness based upon the relevant evaluation literature. That literature is voluminous. Table 4.6 (found at the end of the chapter) summarizes the studies on which we've relied.

Overall, the literature assessing the effectiveness of each policy comports well with the expectations derived from our conceptual analysis of embeddedness and the obstacles to effectiveness. Column five of Table 4.5 offers our overall prediction of each system's effectiveness based on component assessments of user embeddedness, discloser embeddedness, and various obstacles. The table shows that the highly effective policies – those that achieved their intended objectives – embedded information strongly into the decision-making processes of both users and disclosers. Moderately effective policies, by contrast, embedded information strongly into the decision making of select groups of users and/or disclosers but failed to diffuse information more broadly. Ineffective policies failed to embed information into the calculations of either disclosers or users and consequently did not alter their behavior substantially.

Highly Effective Systems

According to our review of available research, three of the eight transparency systems have contributed to significant, long-term behavior changes by users and disclosers in the direction intended by policymakers. Although these systems have encountered problems and required major adjustments over time, evidence suggests that they share core strengths.

Table 4.5. *Summary Evaluation of Effect and Effectiveness in Eight Selected Transparency Policies*

Disclosure System	Embeddedness in Users' Decisions (Table 4.2)	Embeddedness in Disclosers' Decisions (Table 4.3)	Predicted Link of Effect to Effectiveness Owing to Obstacles (Table 4.4)	Evaluation of Transparency System Effectiveness	Key Studies: Effect/No Effect	Key Studies: Effectiveness
Corporate Financial Disclosure	High	High	High	Highly effective	*Effect* • Bushee and Leuz, 2004 • Gomes, Gorton, & Madureira, 2004 *No effect* • Stigler, 1964 • Benston, 1973	*Effective* • Simon, 1989 • Lang & Lundholm, 1996 • Botosan, 1997 • Bushman & Smith, 2001 • Ferrell, 2003 • Greenstone, Oyer, & Vissing-Jorgensen, 2004 • Hail & Leuz, 2006
Restaurant Hygiene Disclosure	High	High	Moderate to high	Highly effective	*Effect* • Jin & Leslie, 2003	*Effective* • Jin & Leslie, 2003 • Simon et al., 2005 • Jin & Leslie, 2006

					Effect	Effective / Moderately effective
Mortgage Lending Disclosure	Moderate to high (third party important)	Low: ongoing activity; high: merger/acquisitions	High	Highly effective	*Effect* • Munnell et al., 1996	*Effective* • Bostic et al., 2002 • Joint Center for Housing Studies, Harvard University, 2002 *Moderately effective* • Bostic & Surette, 2001
Nutritional Labeling	High for some users; low for others	Moderate	Low to moderate	Moderately effective	*Effect* • Kristal et al, 1998 • Moorman, 1998 • Nayga, Lipinski, & Savur, 1998 • Mathios, 2000	*Moderately effective* • Derby & Levy, 2001 • Kim, Nayga, & Capps, 2001 • Variyam & Cawley, 2006
Toxic Releases Disclosure	Low	Low to moderate	Low to moderate	Moderately effective	*Effect* • Hamilton, 1995 • Konar & Cohen, 1997 • Khanna, Quimio, & Bojilova, 1998 • EPA, 2000 • Bui, 2002 • Patten, 2002	*Moderately effective* • Graham & Miller, 2001 • Oberholzer-Gee & Mitsunari, 2002

(continued)

Table 4.5 *(continued)*

Disclosure System	Embeddedness in Users' Decisions (Table 4.2)	Embeddedness in Disclosers' Decisions (Table 4.3)	Predicted Link of Effect to Effectiveness Owing to Obstacles (Table 4.4)	Evaluation of Transparency System Effectiveness	Key Studies: Effect/No Effect	Key Studies: Effectiveness
Toxic Releases Disclosure *(cont.)*					*Effect* • Grant & Jones, 2004 • Decker, Nielsen, & Sindt, 2005	*Ineffective* • Bui & Mayer, 2003
Workplace Hazards Disclosure	Workers: low; manufacturers selecting suppliers: moderate	Worker-related decision: low; supplier-related decision: moderate	Moderate	Moderately effective	*Effect* • Robins et al., 1990 • Kolp, Williams, & Burtan, 1995	*Moderately effective* • GAO, 1992a • Kolp et al., 1993 • OSHA, 1997 • Phillips et al., 1999
Patient Safety Disclosure (NY, PA)	Low	Low to moderate	Low	Ineffective	*Effect* • Romano, Rainwater, & Antonius, 1999 • Dranove et al., 2003 • Werner, Asch, & Polsky, 2005 • Jha & Epstein, 2006	*Effective* • Hannan et al., 1994 • Chassin, 2002 • Hannan et al., 2003 • Cutler, Huckman, & Landrum, 2004

		Moderately effective	No effect
	High		*No effect* • Green & Wintfeld, 1995 • Chassin, Hannan, & DeBuono, 1996 • Schneider & Epstein, 1996 • Peterson et al., 1998 • Schneider & Epstein, 1998 • Marshall et al., 2000 • Mukamel & Mushlin, 2001	*Moderately effective* • Mukamel & Mushlin, 1998 • Mukamel et al., 2002
	Low	Ineffective	*Ineffective* • Addison & Blackburn, 1997
Plant Closing, Mass Layoff Disclosure	Low		*No effect* • Addison & Blackburn, 1994 • Levin-Waldman, 1998 • GAO, 2003b

Corporate Financial Disclosure

Financial disclosure by publicly traded companies – with all of its flaws – deeply embeds information into the decision processes of both information users and corporations. Institutional and individual investors use key indicators from quarterly and annual reports to inform stock purchases and sales. Securities analysts, brokers, financial advisers, and other intermediaries translate these reports into user-friendly data for clients. Internet-based systems customize information to suit the needs of investors, and search-facilitating technologies improve its readability. Government requirements assure formats that allow investors to compare one company with another. Company managers, in turn, track investor responses to their financial disclosures as a routine practice and respond to perceived investor concerns.

While some economists have questioned the need for mandated financial transparency and its effectiveness, a growing literature suggests that financial reporting has been effective both in reducing investor risks and in improving corporate governance.[36] Research concludes that financial reporting limits investors' risks by reducing investment errors and reducing costs of identifying appropriate investment opportunities.[37] Financial reporting also reduces information asymmetries between more and less sophisticated investors.[38] In addition, public reporting reduces firms' cost of capital and attracts the attention of analysts who may then recommend the stocks for purchase.[39]

Reporting improves corporate governance by reducing information asymmetries between shareholders and managers, encouraging managerial discipline, reducing agency costs, supporting enforceable contracts, and disciplining corporate compensation.[40] Researchers have also found that foreign companies that switch to using more rigorous U.S. disclosure rules experience market benefits. Newly disclosed information reduces investor errors in achieving their investment goals and improves companies' stock liquidity and access to capital, explaining why some foreign companies decide to adopt more transparent accounting standards.[41] Comparative studies have concluded that investors are less likely to buy stocks during financial crises in companies with relatively low transparency and that investors leave less transparent markets for more transparent ones.[42]

Restaurant Hygiene Disclosure

Publicly posted hygiene scores reduce search costs for consumers and provide restaurants with competitive incentives to improve. In Los Angeles, grades posted at restaurant entrances have become highly embedded in customers' and restaurant managers' existing decision processes. A restaurant's grade is available *when* users need it, at the time when they make a decision about entering the establishment; *where* they need it, at the location where purchase of a meal will take place; and in a *format* that makes complex information quickly comprehensible.[43] Grades promote comparison-shopping in situations where most consumers have real choices. Most important, the information tells consumers something that they want to know but did not know before – the comparative cleanliness of restaurants. Restaurant managers, accustomed to local health regulations, have both market and regulatory incentives to discern customers' perceptions of food safety.

A comprehensive study of the Los Angeles transparency system suggests that the restaurant grading system has been highly effective. Researchers found significant effects in the form of revenue increases for restaurants with high grades and revenue decreases for C-graded restaurants. More important, they found measurable increases in hygiene quality and a consequent significant drop in hospitalizations from food-related illnesses.[44] The rating system also improved hygiene at franchised restaurants, which tended to have lower hygiene standards than company-owned restaurants in the same chain.[45] Overall, more informed choices by consumers appear to have improved hygiene practices, rewarded restaurants with good grades, and generated economic incentives that stimulated competition among restaurants.[46] A more recent study similarly concludes that the restaurant grading system successfully reduced the number of food-borne disease hospitalizations in Los Angeles County.[47]

Mortgage Lending Disclosure

Bank reporting of home loan information broken down by race, gender, and income level has become highly embedded in the decision processes of both information users and banks. National and local advocacy groups have used the information to advance their long-standing goal of reducing discrimination by financial institutions. They have compiled public cases against particular banks in specific communities and negotiated with those banks to improve their practices. Bank regulators, another significant group of users, have used the information to promote new rules to fight discrimination in credit access, to monitor improvements in lending, and to tighten enforcement.

This transparency system works synergistically with conventional regulations to promote fair lending. Under the Community Reinvestment Act, federal regulators use disclosed data to check that financial institutions meet the credit needs of the communities they serve, an important factor in approving requests for bank mergers. This regulatory requirement creates added incentives for banks to respond to the demands of advocacy groups. Some banks have also employed government-mandated lending data to identify important new market opportunities in inner-city communities and have then specialized in financial products targeted at low-income clients.

Researchers have found that mortgage lending disclosure contributed to increasing access to mortgage loans for blacks and minority groups during the 1990s.[48] Disclosures demonstrated that discrimination was a common practice, and information helped spur regulatory action.[49] Financial institutions tended to improve their lending to meet communities' needs prior to merger applications.[50] Furthermore, mandated transparency contributed to an increase in home ownership for all racial groups.[51]

Moderately Effective Systems

Three of the transparency policies we studied – nutritional labeling, toxic pollution reporting, and disclosure of workplace hazards – have proven moderately effective. They are characterized by more limited changes in discloser behavior to reduce public risks or by mixed responses that sometimes advance regulatory aims but sometimes frustrate them as well.

Nutritional Labeling

Medical research has established that overconsumption of saturated fats, sugar, and salt increases risks of chronic illnesses, including heart disease, diabetes, and cancer. Congress required that nutritional labels be displayed on packaged foods, using standardized formats, metrics, and recommended consumption levels in order to promote comparability. However, this transparency system, available on every can of soup, candy bar, and box of cereal, is only moderately embedded in consumers' decisions for several reasons.

First, many consumers do not consider nutritional information relevant to their purchasing goals. They make choices based mainly on price and taste. Second, the scope of nutritional disclosure excludes large categories of food – fast food, full-service restaurant meals, and delicatessen foods, for example – even though they make up roughly one-half of household food expenditures.[52] Finally, although information on packaged foods is available when and where consumers need it, the label has not proven comprehensible to many consumers.

Research on the effectiveness of nutritional labeling also reveals the complexities of shoppers' and food companies' responses to a sophisticated transparency system. Researchers have found that some consumers, especially those who are well educated and interested in health, have understood and responded to new information by changing purchasing habits, while others groups, such as older consumers and shoppers with lower incomes, have not changed their behavior.[53] Some consumers misinterpret labels. Dieters, for example, tend to emphasize fat content more than total calories and give up on labels when they don't lose weight.[54]

Analyses suggest that food companies have tried to anticipate consumers' responses to nutritional labels and to react strategically, but their responses have been only partially congruent with the aims of policymakers. Most companies have continued to market traditional high-fat, high-sodium, high-sugar products, sometimes adding more healthy ingredients such as fiber or introducing brand extensions of low-fat or low-sodium products, so that at least there are increased product choices.[55]

Whether there have been positive effects on public health is not yet clear. Americans reduced their fat consumption during the early 1990s but did not reduce total calorie consumption, leading to concerns about obesity.[56] One study found a slight improvement in diet quality; another suggested that introduction of nutritional labels was associated with a decrease in body weight and in the probability of obesity for non-Hispanic white women.[57] However, overall per capita fat consumption has increased markedly, and sugar and calorie consumption has continued to rise.

Toxic Releases Disclosure

Initially enacted as a public right-to-know measure in 1986, the toxic pollution reporting requirement soon became viewed by regulators as one of the federal government's most effective pollution-control measures. As soon as disclosure was required, executives of some major companies announced plans to reduce toxic pollution by as much as 90 percent. Reported pollution declined substantially during the next decade.

Nonetheless, factory-by-factory and chemical-by-chemical data produced by the system remain minimally embedded in the decisions of most potential users of such information. Most home buyers, renters, job seekers, consumers, and investors do not consider toxic pollution when they decide what neighborhood to live in, where to send children to school, where to work, or in what companies to buy stock. In contrast to experience with the transparency system for mortgage lending, advocacy groups have not for the most part incorporated toxic pollution data into their core strategies.

While newly disclosed information about toxic pollution has remained relatively unembedded in market transactions and community action, it did become quickly embedded in important regulatory and administrative processes, particularly in actions by Congress and federal regulators. Existing goals and decision processes made those officials highly responsive to the new information. Some had been urging stricter regulation of toxic chemicals for more than a decade, struggling with the lack of reliable information to support their efforts. Their initial responses – in the form of stricter laws or regulations – did help to strengthen incentives for companies to reduce toxic releases.[58] Enforcement officials also found the data useful as a basis for their actions.

As a result, *anticipated* reputational and regulatory threats quickly embedded newly disclosed information in some manufacturers' routine decision processes. Many targeted companies, especially those with national reputations to protect, made commitments for long-term reduction of toxic pollution in response to the first disclosures of shocking information. Some companies sought to reduce their emissions by engaging in pollution-prevention strategies, while others substituted different chemicals.[59]

However, there were serious flaws in the system. Reporting of lead and nitric acid emissions showed inaccuracies that raised doubts about the quality of the data.[60] Some reported decreases reflected changes only in reporting procedures, substituted chemicals were not necessarily less toxic, and reported decreases and increases of pollution varied widely by state, industry, and year.[61]

As noted earlier, researchers have suggested that the effectiveness of this transparency system has been more limited than it appears. National news coverage created time-limited investor responses (company stock prices declined) to the first round of disclosures of surprisingly high levels of toxic releases by many publicly traded companies.[62] And firms with large amounts of toxic releases became more forthcoming in disclosing environmental data in their reports to the federal Securities and Exchange Commission.[63] There is, however, little evidence of lasting responses by community residents and other potential users of the information. One study suggested that pollution reporting had an exceedingly low impact on housing prices and failed to stimulate the expected community response to pressure polluters, while other research found only limited impact on more expensive properties or homes located very close to facilities.[64]

Workplace Hazards Disclosure

Researchers have found contradictory evidence about whether workplace hazardous chemicals disclosure, which imposed substantial new reporting burdens on employers and manufacturers, has improved worker safety. Despite its compatibility with workers' goals of limiting their own risks or seeking higher wages to compensate for risks, new information about chemical hazards has not become embedded in most employees' routine decision making. Accessible only within the workplace and generally only in technical and non-comparable form, information usually is not available at a time and place or in a format to inform job seekers' decisions. For workers already on the job, data sheets have often been too complex to be comprehensible, and therefore have not been good indicators of comparability of the magnitude of health and safety risks. In addition, the quality of required safety training has varied widely from workplace to workplace, with small workplaces often lacking the capacity to provide employees with sufficient risk information and training.[65]

Exercising broad discretion permitted by regulators, employers have produced information sheets that vary widely in quality, detail, and technical vocabulary. Research on the quality of data sheets has shown that only 51 percent of analyzed sheets were even partially accurate in all their sections.[66] Workers were generally able to understand only about 60 percent of the information on such sheets.[67]

The high cost of understanding information has discouraged workers from using the safety sheets to change work habits. Even in cases where workers seemed to comprehend safety information, they used it only in limited fashion.[68]

It should be noted that all of the documented cases of the impact of training and disclosure of information occurred within unionized establishments where unions could play a key intermediary role.[69] The absence of unions in more than 90 percent of private-sector workplaces raises questions about the wide applicability of these results.

Nonetheless, workplace chemical hazard information has become embedded in some employers' decision-making processes. Limited evidence suggests that the awareness of risks associated with certain chemicals has led some employers to switch to safer substances. One early analysis of the disclosure requirement found that 30 percent of surveyed employers had adopted safer chemicals.[70] Concerns about potential liability claims brought against employers by customers and/or workers may have contributed to substitution.[71] In addition, material safety data sheets have become such a useful tool for the exchange of information between manufacturers of hazardous chemicals and their corporate customers that some have extended the sheets' use to nonhazardous chemicals. Overall, workplace chemical hazards reporting has functioned more as a communication tool and incentive system between companies that are chemical producers and those that are chemical users than as a device to help employees reduce their risk exposure.

Ineffective Systems

Ineffective transparency systems lead to little or no change in the behavior of users or disclosers and so do not advance policy objectives. Two of the transparency systems we studied – medical mistakes disclosure (Pennsylvania)[72] and plant closing reporting – proved ineffective because new information was not compatible with the preexisting decision processes of would-be information users, because many users faced a limited set of choices and so could not act on new information, or because users' goals differed from those of policymakers. In some instances, they also proved ineffective because disclosers responded to user demands in ways that actually exacerbated the public problem that the system sought to address.

Patient Safety Disclosure

Research results to date suggest that Pennsylvania's patient safety disclosure system for cardiac surgery may be ineffective and New York's may be moderately effective, although researchers remain divided about the specific effects and effectiveness of both systems. In all reporting of patient safety problems, metrics have proven particularly problematic. The state systems' narrow focus on mortality rates, as well as the complexities of risk adjustment, may undermine their credibility. Hospital managers and physicians, focused on liability issues and unaccustomed to aggregating patient safety data to address systemic problems, often resist information sharing and traditionally have had limited institutional mechanisms for learning from past mistakes.[73]

Although some research on the New York reporting system found that ratings reliably predicted risk-adjusted mortality rates,[74] other research concluded that patient safety reports may have had low predictive accuracy and may have been based on data with internal inconsistencies.[75]

In Pennsylvania, one survey suggested that the state's reporting system had little or no influence on the referrals of most cardiologists (87 percent). Respondents expressed concern about the narrow focus of reporting on mortality, inadequate risk adjustment, and questionable reliability of data. More than half of cardiac surgeons also reported that they were less willing to operate on severely ill patients after the report card was introduced.[76] Survey data also suggested that coronary bypass patients had limited knowledge of the state-mandated report card, both before and after surgery.[77]

By contrast, early research in New York State found that the introduction of the state's reporting system was associated with significant declines in risk-adjusted mortality rates in the first three years, giving New York the lowest risk-adjusted bypass mortality rate of any state in 1992.[78] A later evaluation of the first ten years of reporting found that both patient volume and mortality rates declined in relatively high-mortality hospitals.[79] Hospitals that received very poor ratings had improved their performance, while below-average hospitals had not responded as strongly.[80]

Interestingly, researchers also found that improvements in cardiac surgery under the New York system could not be attributed to market forces, since managed-care companies and patients did not seem to use the information and better performance was not associated with changes in market share.[81] Researchers also found that new information initially widened the gap between whites and black and Hispanic patients receiving cardiac surgery in New York State, but that the effect declined over time.[82]

More general analysis of Medicare data from 1994 to 1999 found lower risk-adjusted mortality rates in regions – including New York and Pennsylvania – where information on certain surgical procedures is publicly reported.[83] However, other analyses of Medicare claims data suggested that the introduction of report cards was associated with a decline in the illness severity of bypass surgery patients, perhaps because of selection bias by doctors and/or hospitals,[84] and that more highly educated patients made greater use of reported information.[85]

On the whole, these limited and inconsistent research findings underscore the need for more systematic evaluation of regulatory transparency systems aimed at improving patient safety in hospitals. Such evaluation would help lay the groundwork for the design of more effective reporting systems.

Plant Closing, Mass Layoff Disclosure

Plant closing reporting aims in part to enable workers to respond to economic dislocation by providing information about long-term layoffs at or shutdown of manufacturing facilities. However, evidence suggests that the information generated by this transparency system has failed to materially affect the decision-making processes of workers who face these disruptive events. Disclosure has provided little assistance to affected workers in how to seek new employment and has had no effect on the availability of other options.

The timing of disclosure may be mismatched with workers' needs. Since the sixty-day notice required by the reporting system starts running when workers are still employed, their capacity to engage in full job searches upon notification is very limited. The required information may also come too late for labor unions, community groups, or other intermediaries to create political pressures that might change the company's decision to close. In addition, such advocates often lack capacity and/or experience to help facilitate job searches.[86]

Finally, the objectives of users, intermediaries, and disclosers may prove quite diverse in the face of closures, leading them to pursue different strategies once they receive information about the imminent event. Not surprisingly, there are few documented cases of employers changing closure or layoff decisions in the wake of community and/or union notification of their plans.[87]

Studies of the impact of plant closure reporting on reemployment prospects of displaced workers have consistently shown limited effects. Several studies have found that the disclosure requirement has only modest impact on the provision of advanced notice information beyond what had been voluntarily provided before the act.[88] In those cases where new information was provided, workers did somewhat better in finding new employment in the immediate wake of displacement. However, for those who did not find jobs immediately following closures or layoffs, spells of unemployment tended to last longer than for workers who were not notified. Thus, if there were effects on reemployment, they were modest and restricted to a subset of workers.[89]

CRAFTING EFFECTIVE TRANSPARENCY POLICIES

Targeted transparency policies have the potential to introduce important new information about risk and the quality of public services into established decision-making processes of buyers and sellers, community residents and institutions, voters and candidates, or other participants in markets or collective action. To be effective, however, the information they provide must become an intrinsic part of the decision-making routines of users and disclosers. Even if information is embedded in everyday decisions, policies must still avoid or overcome obstacles that lead to misunderstanding or gaming of the system. Our analyses of individual transparency policies confirm the importance of these drivers across a range of policies.

Simply providing more information to consumers, investors, employees, and community residents will not assure that risks are diminished or that schools, banks, and other institutions improve their practices. Without careful design and implementation, transparency policies can do more harm than good. This chapter suggests that it is possible to predict the conditions needed to make transparency an effective tool of governance. In our final chapter, we suggest ten principles for crafting effective transparency policies.

Much depends on how policies evolve over time, however. The next chapter explores why some transparency policies grow more rigorous and effective while others degenerate into costly charades.

Table 4.6. *Summary of Effectiveness Research in Eight Selected Transparency Policies*

Disclosure System	Key Studies: Effect/ No Effect	Key Studies: Effectiveness
Corporate Financial Disclosure	*Effect* • When SEC reporting requirements were extended to firms quoted on the Over the Counter Bulletin Board, smaller firms decided not to comply and were pushed to a less-regulated market. Stock returns of noncompliant or newly compliant firms were negative around announcement dates, whereas already compliant firms experienced positive returns. (Bushee & Leuz, 2004) • Analysis of cross-sectional differences among firms pre- and post-introduction of regulation to stop the practice of selective disclosure showed that small firms lost 17% of analyst following, while big firms increased it by 7%. The regulation caused a reallocation of information-producing resources. This penalized smaller firms, which experienced higher cost of capital. (Gomes, Gorton, & Madureira, 2004) *No effect* • Comparison of new stock issues in 1923–1928 and 1949–1955 suggested that mandatory disclosure requirements adopted in 1934 had no important effects on the quality of new securities sold to the public. (Stigler, 1964) • Analysis of share prices before and after the 1934 Securities Act suggested that mandated disclosure had no measurable effects on the share prices or on investor risk. (Benston, 1973)	*Effective* • Analysis of stock prices on regional exchanges before and after mandatory disclosure found that variance of returns lessened substantially after disclosure was required, suggesting that investor risk was reduced even though mean returns did not change. (Simon, 1989) • Study of financial analysts' data suggested that more informative disclosure policies decreased the dispersion among analyst forecasts, leading to greater accuracy in forecasting. (Lang & Lundholm, 1996) • Analysis of 1990 annual reports suggested that greater disclosure was associated with lower cost of equity capital. (Botosan, 1997) • Literature review concluded that financial disclosure created incentives for improved corporate governance, informing executive compensation, contract management, and shareholder and board monitoring. (Bushman & Smith, 2001) • Analysis of the impact of the 1964 disclosure requirements on the over-the-counter (OTC) market showed dramatic reduction in stock volatility. However, disclosure had no impact on stock returns and stock price synchronicity. (Ferrell, 2003)

92

- Firms that were newly required to make disclosures under the 1964 Securities Act Amendments for stocks traded over the counter (OTC) had cumulative excess returns of 13% in period prior to passage versus 6–9% for firms that already had comparable disclosure requirements in the same period. (Greenstone, Oyer, & Vissing-Jorgensen, 2004)
- Analysis of cost of equity capital in 40 countries found that in countries with stronger disclosure requirements, regulations, and enforcement mechanisms, firms had lower cost of capital. (Hail & Leuz, 2006)

Effective

- Mandatory disclosure led to average increase in restaurant hygiene quality of 5.3% (based on point score), whereas voluntary disclosure increased it by 3.9%. The improvement of hygiene quality was reflected in a reduction of the number of hospitalizations for food-related illnesses. Restaurants under mandated disclosure also improved physical structure of buildings (longer-term investment effects). (Jin & Leslie, 2003)
- Los Angeles County restaurant hygiene grade cards were associated with a 13.1% decrease in hospitalizations owing to food-borne diseases in 1998 (a year after the introduction of grade cards). The decrease in hospitalizations persisted in 1999 and 2000. (Simon et al., 2005)
- Although chain-affiliated restaurants tended to have higher hygiene quality because of reputational incentives, the introduction of grade cards improved hygiene at franchised units in the chain, which tended to have lower hygiene than company-owned units. (Jin & Leslie, 2006)

Restaurant Hygiene Disclosure

Effect

- Mandatory grade cards increased restaurants' revenue by 3.3%; voluntary disclosure generated a 2.6% increase. For mandatory disclosure, authors found a 5.7% increase in revenue for A-grade restaurants, a 0.7% increase for B-grade, and a 1% decrease for C-grade. In the case of voluntary disclosure, A-grade revenues increased by 3.3%; difference for B and C grades not significant from A grade. The reduced impact on revenues in the case of voluntary disclosure might have had two causes: consumers might have been fully informed about the system, or they might have assumed that no grade card posted meant that the restaurant did not undergo an inspection. (Jin & Leslie, 2003)

(continued)

Table 4.6 (*continued*)

Disclosure System	Key Studies: Effect/ No Effect	Key Studies: Effectiveness
Mortgage Lending Disclosure	*Effect* • Federal Reserve study used HMDA data to evaluate the existence of mortgage discrimination. When minority and white applicants with similar financial characteristics were compared, rejection rates of minorities were 7–8 percentage points higher. Race proved to be an important explanatory factor in mortgage lending decisions both for institutions with the largest number of loans to minorities (5% of institutions accounted for 50% of applications) and for remaining institutions. (Munnell et al., 1996)	*Effective* • The higher the percentage of mortgage originations for low- and moderate-income individuals in a given year, the greater the probability that the institution acquired another bank the following year. The authors found that moving from the 25th to the 75th percentile of the distribution of CRA lending was associated with a 0.8 percentage point increase in the likelihood of making an acquisition in the following year. (Bostic et al., 2002) • From 1993 to 2000 the number of home purchase loans made to black borrowers increased by 94%, to Hispanics by 140%, and to other minority borrowers by 92%. Minority borrowers represented 25% of total home purchase lending in 2000, as opposed to 17% in 1993. Home purchase loans to lower-income borrowers (with incomes less than 80% of MSA median income) and/or lower-income communities increased by 77% (571,000 loans) from 1993 to 2000. The study attributed part of the increase to the expansion of government-backed lending, especially loans insured by the Federal Housing Administration (FHA). In 2000 minorities represented 40% of home purchase mortgages insured by FHA, as opposed to 22% in 1993. (Joint Center for Housing Studies, Harvard University, 2002)

Moderately effective

- Research found impact of CRA and HMDA difficult to quantify. Especially in 1990s these regulations might have increased access to mortgage credit for low-income/minority families, since banks introduced new mortgage programs. Furthermore, lenders were sensitive to the distribution of their loan portfolios. Finally, Congress empowered the Dept. of Housing and Urban Development to create new affordable housing goals for Fannie Mae and Freddie Mac. However, most of the increase in lending to minorities happened for banks that were not subject to CRA. But since authors found that changes in family characteristics do not explain the increase, they concluded this should be attributed to fair lending policies, good economic cycle, and low interest rates. (Bostic & Surette, 2001)

Moderately effective

- Survey data suggested consumers using labels focused on products' fat content. Owing to variety of factors, consumers reduced intake of calories from fat from 41.1% during 1977–1978 to 33.6% in 1995 but did not reduce caloric intake overall. Fat-modified products gained significant market share 1991–1995, both before and after mandatory labeling was introduced. (Derby & Levy, 2001).

Nutritional Labeling

Effect

- Survey data suggested label use increased after mandatory labeling, but 70% of adults wanted labels that were easier to understand. (Kristal et al., 1998)
- Purchase and survey data suggested that producers anticipated consumer responses by adding "positive" nutrients without reducing "negative" nutrients in base brands and reducing "negative" nutrients without adding "positive" nutrients in brand extensions when labels were introduced, creating a highly segmented market. (Moorman, 1998)

(continued)

95

Table 4.6 (continued)

Disclosure System	Key Studies: Effect/ No Effect	Key Studies: Effectiveness
Nutritional Labeling (*cont.*)	• Questionnaires on nutritional label use showed that lower-income individuals were less likely to read labels. Education and importance placed on nutrition were also positively correlated to label use. People who received their information from media (TV, radio, books) were less likely to use labels. (Nayga, Lipinski, & Savur, 1998) • Analysis of label and scanner data suggested that sales of highest-fat salad dressings declined after mandatory labeling was introduced. (Mathios, 2000)	• Label use had a positive effect in improving diet quality, ranging from 3.5 to 6.1 points in the Healthy Eating Index range. Higher income and education were associated with increased label use. Males, older individuals and those who reside in non-metro areas were less likely to use labels. (Kim, Nayga, & Capps, 2001) • Research found statistical evidence that nutritional labeling led to decreases in body weight and the probability of obesity among non-Hispanic white women, comparing those who reported using labels and those who did not before and after NLEA passage. Decrease in body weight equated to a monetary benefit between $63 and $166 billion over 20-year period. (Variyam & Cawley, 2006)
Toxic Releases Disclosure	*Effect* • There were 134 mentions of TRI-related stories by journalists for 1989; media focused on firms accounting for larger share of pollution. Investors' reaction to the publication of TRI information caused an average loss of $4.1 million in stock market value on day 0. The effect of the information was more dramatic for firms that had also received media coverage of their releases, with average abnormal returns of –$6.2 million on day 0. (Hamilton, 1995)	*Moderately effective* • In 1988–1999 reported releases dropped by more than 50%, harmful chemicals releases declined even more, and recycling improved (since 1991 recycling increased by 12%). But the rate of decline slowed down after the first 5 years of reporting. From 1988 to 1993 total releases decreased by 37%, an average of 7% per year. From 1993 to 1998 total releases fell by 10%,

- Of a sample of 40 firms with highest press coverage and highest abnormal returns, 32 reduced their TRI/$ revenue, 8 firms increased emissions. Firms also reduced their TRI/$ revenue ranking in their industry. Average firm in sample reduced emissions by 1.84 pounds per thousand $, whereas an industry-weighted sample of other firms reduced by 0.17 pounds. The top 40 in terms of abnormal return were compared to the 40 largest emitters (only 11 firms were among the top 40 and in the 40 largest emitters). It was found that top 40 reduced TRI emissions more than 40 worst polluters. (Konar & Cohen, 1997)

- Steep declines in TRI emissions were observed between 1987 and 1988. Since 1988 emissions have declined more moderately. Off-site transfers declined until 1990 but increased significantly from 1991, when off-site transfers started to include recycling and energy recovery. Stock market analysis showed that abnormal returns were not significant in days −1 and 0 of the event study, in any of the years. The average abnormal returns were negative and statistically significant in day 1 from 1990 to 1994. They were not significant in 1989. Over a 0–5-day window, abnormal returns were significant only in 1992 and 1994. (Khanna, Quimio, & Bojilova, 1998)

average of 2% per year. Reduction is not a national phenomenon but rather a media/industry/facility-specific phenomenon. TRI emissions decreased, but toxic waste increased. Air releases decreased dramatically (−61%). Surface water releases were down by 66% overall, but the amount varied significantly year by year. Land disposal of toxic chemicals increased because of higher costs of recycling. Facilities with large amount of emissions have been more successful at reducing them. There were large variations by industries, with significant reductions from chemical manufacturers and increases in food and primary metal sector. New industries (reporting for the first time in 1998) increased their releases by 5% (with metal mining and electric utilities driving the increase). (Graham & Miller, 2001)

- Emissions beyond 1-mile circle around property had no effect on property values. Property values increased within the 1-mile distance as a result of TRI info release; results suggested that perceptions were even more favorable for risks within 0.5 miles. (Oberholzer-Gee & Mitsunari, 2002)

(continued)

Table 4.6 (*continued*)

Disclosure System	Key Studies: Effect/ No Effect	Key Studies: Effectiveness
Toxic Releases Disclosure (*cont.*)	• Reductions in emissions and transfers between 1990 and 1996 were 1.5 to 2.2 times greater than the general TRI trend and 1.3 to 19 times greater than for other companies in their same industry sector. Facilities that received negative press reduced emissions more than other facilities. For example, one facility reduced emissions of a chemical cited in the press by 86%, and overall facility emissions by 64%, whereas emissions at other facilities owned by the same company stayed the same. Hazardous substances released declined from 7,800 in 1994 to 5,400 in 1999. A study of 4 states with similar industry composition found that releases had declined by 60% from their peak year (1992). Episodic releases of TRI chemicals from manufacturers and releases of substances above reportable quantities declined by 68% from their peak year (1990). (EPA, 2000) • TRI releases fell by 78.37% from 1988 to 1995. Differences in TRI emissions attributable to variation in stringency of state regulations of TRI emissions showed that states with additional regulations (but no numeric goals) cleaned up more than states that had no additional TRI-type regulations (i.e., states that had only federal-level regulation). However, states with stringent regulations, with numeric goals for reduction of TRI, did not reduce emissions more rapidly. Evidence was inconclusive on the impact of state regulations on TRI abatement. (Bui, 2002).	*Ineffective* • Plants that emitted TRI-listed substances were in lower-income communities. Declines in emissions were not uniform across locations. Larger reductions occurred in higher-value regions and in regions with higher initial releases. Economic impact (measured as change in housing values) of initial TRI information was exceedingly low. Even in case of chemicals with strong link to cancer and other diseases, impact was very low. Impact was not significant beyond the zip code where the plant was located, for emissions traveling through air or water. (Bui & Mayer, 2003)

98

(continued)

- TRI disclosures had a positive impact on companies' willingness to disclose environmental information in their 10Ks. Number of companies providing environmental disclosure in 10Ks increased from 99 in 1985 to 110 in 1990. Also, the extensiveness of disclosures improved. Companies with worse environmental performance (measured by size-adjusted level of TRI emissions) increased the provision of environmental information more than others. Companies that received negative media coverage may have increased disclosure, but TRI variable alone remained significant. (Patten, 2002)

- Research on pollutant emissions by subsidiaries found that they have significantly higher emission rates than other facilities. Because parent firms were not liable for pollution generated by their subsidiaries, the latter received less corporate pressure to reduce pollution. (Grant & Jones, 2004)

- Analysis of house sales showed that releases of TRI pollutants had negative and statistically significant impact on property values. More expensive properties were especially impacted, indicating that environmental attributes are subject to a wealth effect. (Decker, Nielsen, & Sindt, 2005)

Table 4.6 (*continued*)

Disclosure System	Key Studies: Effect/No Effect	Key Studies: Effectiveness
Workplace Hazards Disclosure	*Effect* • Joint labor-management training proved effective in improving workers' understanding of safety information. Participants in the special training program perceived the training as helpful; that perception grew over time. Workers responded that they had changed work practices: they read labels, were more aware of dangers, avoided hazardous areas, and used protective equipment. 54% of supervisors had changed their own practices in response to the training program. 30% of workers reported that working conditions had improved following the training. The program also increased the level of concern and responsiveness of managers and unions. Joint labor-management training program had positive impact on employees' behavior. More interactive training (delivery to smaller groups was key factor for success. (Robins et al., 1990) • Evaluation of 150 material safety data sheets (MSDS) showed 83% of MSDS provided specific chemical names for all the listed ingredients. Of 134 MSDS with identifiable chemical components, 37% reported accurate health effects; 47% were inaccurate and 16% partially accurate. 76% of MSDS had accurate first-aid information; 47% of MSDS had accurate information for personal protective measures; 22% had inaccurate information on this topic. 47% had accurate info on exposure limits; 16% had inaccurate values. Only 11% of reviewed MSDS were accurate in all the 4 dimensions. 51% of MSDS were partially accurate in all 4 areas. (Kolp, Williams, & Burtan, 1995)	*Moderately effective* • Study found that almost 70% of small employers reported little difficulty with MSDS preparation and accessibility, but 80% had problems in complying with training requirements. 56% of employers reported a "great" or "very great" improvement in the availability of information and 30% of employers reported switching to less hazardous chemicals. (GAO, 1992a) • For 91 tested workers, 2/3 of info in MSDS was comprehended. 80% of surveyed workers had seen an MSDS before survey; only 45% had seen it during training. 2/3 requested information on the chemicals with which they worked; 2/3 of these workers found MSDS they received in response difficult to comprehend. 80% of workers receiving chemical hazard information of any type reported changing behavior, and 50% reported MSDS were helpful in preventing or responding to emergency situation. Workers had trouble understanding difficult vocabulary, and layout of MSDS was confusing. Differences in educational level were an important factor impacting understanding; workers with college education scored higher. (Kolp et al., 1993) • According to 3 studies on the comprehensibility of MSDSs, workers understood 60% of the information reported. A 1990 study by the Printing Industries of America found that employees with 15+ years of education understood 66.2% of MSDS information. (OSHA, 1997)

- Evaluation of MSDS understanding gave mixed evidence. Out of a sample of 160 workers (95% of sample had undergone training on MSDS), 39% found MSDS difficult; 46% did not. 90% of workers said MSDS were satisfactory to very satisfactory in providing information. 3/4 of workers changed work habits following disclosure of MSDSs. But workers' frequency of usage was low: 1/3 used MSDS half/all of the time; the rest rarely to never used them. Workers reported easy access to MSDS. (Phillips et al., 1999).

Patient Safety Disclosure (NY, PA)	*Effect* • Survey of hospitals' CEOs in California and New York found report cards were generally rated as fair or good by hospitals, with respondents in large/high-volume hospitals more knowledgeable of cards. Hospitals with higher mortality rates were more critical of report cards. (Romano, Rainwater, & Antonius, 1999) • Analysis of the impact of report cards on cardiac surgery in New York and Pennsylvania showed evidence of selection behavior by providers, leading to an increase of procedures performed on healthier patients. Sorting among patients caused delays in the execution of surgery. Authors also found increased matching of patients with hospitals, with patients with more severe conditions being treated in higher-quality hospitals. (Dranove et al., 2003) *Effective* • Analysis of New York hospital data suggested that the dissemination of information on surgery outcomes resulted in an improvement of surgery results from 1989 to 1992. Authors found a decrease in the actual mortality rate and an increase in average patient severity of illness. (Hannan et al., 1994) • Improvements in certain heart surgery procedures in New York attributed to changes adopted by hospitals in response to disclosure. Especially hospitals identified as very poor performers improved after disclosure, while mediocre or below-average hospitals did not respond as strongly. Managed-care companies and patients did not use reported data. (Chassin, 2002) • Analysis of Medicare data from 1994 to 1999 showed that in regions with public reporting on certain heart procedures – including Pennsylvania and New York – risk-adjusted mortality rates were lower than in the rest of the country. (Hannan et al., 2003)

(continued)

Table 4.6 (*continued*)

Disclosure System	Key Studies: Effect/ No Effect	Key Studies: Effectiveness
Patient Safety Disclosure (NY, PA) (*cont.*)	• Research on the impact of the New York cardiac surgery reporting system found that, after the release of report cards in 1991, the gap between whites and black and Hispanic patients receiving surgery increased, but the difference declined over time, going to pre-reporting levels in a decade. Possible explanations were that physicians may have initially associated race with higher risk but later learned that race was not associated with outcomes, or they might have learned that reported information had limited impact on physician selection. (Werner, Asch, & Polsky, 2005) • Study of New York State data from 1989 to 2002 found hospital ratings reliably predicted risk-adjusted mortality rates. However, performance was not associated with changes in market share; changes in market share were similar for best performers and worst performers. Surgeons with poor performance ratings were more likely to leave practice in the state within 2 years from data publication. (Jha & Epstein, 2006) *No effect* • Evaluation of New York's report cards found predictive accuracy of the disclosure model low and internal inconsistencies in data. Mortality rates might be imperfect metric. (Green & Wintfeld, 1995)	• Analysis of 1991–1999 data from a cross-sectional time series for specific New York hospitals suggested that the state's Cardiac Surgery Reporting System led to fewer relatively healthy patients seeking treatment at poor-performing hospitals and to subsequent improvements in those hospitals' performance (i.e., a lower rate of risk-adjusted mortality). High-performing hospitals did not increase in patient volume or improve in performance. (Cutler, Huckman, & Landrum, 2004) *Moderately effective* • Hospitals and physicians with better reported outcomes showed higher growth in market share in some geographical areas. Correlation was stronger for surgeons than for hospitals, but it tended to decline over time. (Mukamel & Mushlin, 1998) • Statistical analysis of the probability of a contract between individual cardiac surgeons in New York State and managed-care organizations in 1998 (1993–1995 data) in relation to surgeon's risk-adjusted mortality rates suggested that local market conditions may be significant variables. Downstate, lower surgeon mortality rates were associated with an increased probability of a contract. Upstate, the association was weaker. (Mukamel et al., 2002)

(continued)

- Study found no movement of patients away from hospitals with high mortality rates, nor did patients move to hospitals with low rates (Chassin, Hannan, & DeBuono, 1996)

- Survey of cardiologists' and surgeons' opinions on Pennsylvania report cards found large awareness of disclosure system among physicians; however, fewer than 10% discussed report cards with more than 10% of their patients. Physicians criticized report cards for absence of quality indicators other than mortality, inadequate risk adjustment, and data unreliability. Cardiologists reported increased difficulties in finding surgeons to treat severely ill patients. Majority of surgeons confirmed they were less willing to operate on such patients. (Schneider & Epstein, 1996)

- Study of New York report cards found no evidence that provider profiling limited procedure access for elderly or increased out-of-state transfers. (Peterson et al., 1998)

- Patient survey found that 20% of respondents were aware of Pennsylvania's report cards, but only 12% knew about them before surgery. Fewer than 1% knew the correct rating of their surgeon or hospital and reported that information had a moderate or major impact on their selection of provider. (Schneider & Epstein, 1998)

- Analysis of empirical evidence on impact of hospital performance data suggested that consumers and purchasers rarely searched out the information and did not understand or trust it. Reporting had small, although increasing, impact on their decision making. Small portion of physicians and larger portion of hospitals used the data. (Marshall et al., 2000)

Table 4.6 *(continued)*

Disclosure System	Key Studies: Effect/ No Effect	Key Studies: Effectiveness
Patient Safety Disclosure (NY, PA) *(cont.)*	• Literature review found little evidence of report cards' impact on patients' choice of provider or health plan, perhaps owing to inability of providers to respond rapidly to shifts in demand, information already incorporated in consumers' choices, and problems with report cards' quality and credibility. (Mukamel & Mushlin, 2001)	
Plant Closing, Mass Layoff Disclosure	*No effect* • Comparison of Displaced Worker Surveys conducted in 1988, 1990, and 1992 (WARN was implemented in 1989) showed little impact of WARN in workers' notification. Both before and after disclosure was required, there was very limited formal notice (with less than 15% of displaced workers receiving notice). Authors observed a decline in workers receiving informal notice, balanced by an increase in the number of workers receiving no notice at all. Workers displaced because of plant shutdown were more likely to receive notice than workers displaced by layoffs. Overall, WARN legislation did not seem to have affected workers' notification trends. Results could not be attributed to employers' ignorance, because they often deliberately chose certain firm sizes to avoid coverage by WARN,	*Ineffective* • Analysis of Displaced Worker Surveys showed limited impact of WARN in reducing unemployment. Comparison of escape rates from unemployment for notified and nonnotified workers showed that escape rate is higher for notified workers who immediately transitioned from one job to the other (0 days unemployed). This could be explained by the fact that notified workers had benefited from an additional period to search for new jobs. However, considering that on-the-job search was less productive than off-the-job and correcting for this difference, the escape rates for notified and nonnotified workers became similar. Notified workers conducted less intensive search in notification period than nonnotified workers did after leaving their jobs. (Addison & Blackburn, 1997)

104

with some firms seeking legal advice before deciding to comply. Limited impact was also attributed to the fact that firms with fewer than 100 employees (35% of workforce at time of study) were not required to comply. (Addison & Blackburn, 1994)

- WARN's limited impact arose from absence of enforcement mechanisms other than lawsuits by workers. (Levin-Waldman, 1998)

- GAO assessment of WARN's implementation found that in 2001 there were 1.75 million job losses through extended mass layoffs. In that year, employers provided notice for an estimated 36% of mass layoffs or closures that qualified for WARN (717 out of 1,974). Employers provided notice for 46% of plant closures and 26% of mass layoffs. Remaining ones were subject to WARN, but notice was not provided. 2/3 of notices provided were on time. Employers had problems applying WARN because of difficulties in calculating the layoff threshold, and courts applied WARN provisions inconsistently, which created confusion. Educational materials by DOL were not widely available. (GAO, 2003b)

FIVE

What Makes Transparency Sustainable?

We have seen this pattern repeatedly: Enron and WorldCom accounting scandals trigger Sarbanes-Oxley reporting reforms. The chemical catastrophe in Bhopal, India triggers toxic pollution reporting in the United States. A rash of deaths from microbes in drinking water triggers a national water safety disclosure. A wave of SUV-related deaths triggers a rollover rating system.

Transparency systems are often tacked together in times of crisis. They emerge out of high-stakes political debates driven by newly perceived needs for public action. As a result, they often begin as half-baked compromises, missing crucial elements and suffering from flawed design. After the crisis passes from the headlines, the transparency system is typically neglected and necessary improvements go unaddressed.

It is not particularly surprising that transparency systems fail, for two reasons. First, transparency typically imposes costs on a small group of information disclosers in the hope of generating benefits for a large and dispersed class of information users. Since the stakes are higher for the potential disclosers, they dominate the political processes that shape transparency systems over time. Second, transparency conflicts with other core values – the need to protect trade secrets and personal privacy, for example – that can tip the balance toward keeping information confidential. Under these circumstances, it is remarkable that some relatively robust targeted transparency systems actually emerge from legislative deliberations and survive.

In fact, many targeted transparency systems that are flawed in the beginning manage to improve over time and ultimately deliver the public benefits that policymakers hoped for. This chapter investigates why some transparency policies gain accuracy, scope, and use over time, becoming, in our terms, *sustainable*, while others degenerate into costly exercises in paper pushing or excuses for avoiding real action.

CRISIS DRIVES FINANCIAL DISCLOSURE IMPROVEMENTS

The accounting scandals at Enron, Tyco, WorldCom, and other large corporations that rocked capital markets in 2001–2002 demonstrate that the system of corporate financial disclosure in the United States – the nation's most respected and most mature targeted transparency system – is far from perfect. Yet few would dispute that corporate financial disclosure has improved markedly in scope, accuracy, and usefulness during the seven decades since its adoption. Improvement has not followed a smooth and continuous path, however. Instead, it has advanced by fits and starts, driven by the push and pull of conflicting investor and corporate interests. Crises like the collapse of conglomerates in the 1960s, bribes and illegal campaign contributions in the 1970s, and corporate accounting scandals have spurred episodic reforms. A look at the checkered history of financial disclosure rules suggests how transparency policies can become sustainable.

Improvements in financial disclosure have followed a common scenario: Changes in markets produce new business practices, accompanied by creative accounting methods that obscure risks to investors. Then sudden revelations or market reversals direct public attention to the new practices, producing a crisis of confidence. To restore public trust, government agencies, institutional investors, and members of Congress demand more accurate and complete information, and reformers seize the moment to make permanent changes in the system. As a result, the scope of transparency becomes broader, information becomes more accurate, and the number of users increases.

In the 1960s, for example, the scope of disclosure was broadened when a sudden collapse in conglomerate stock prices after an unprecedented wave of mergers created pressures for better information. Between 1962 and 1969, 22 percent of *Fortune* 500 companies were acquired in mergers, during which the value of the combined companies was often inflated by creative accounting methods. Conglomerates like Gulf and Western and Ling-Temco-Vought produced instant earnings growth by using accounting techniques that obscured the full cost of mergers. In addition, the profitability of specific product lines, previously reflected in the accounts of separate companies, became hidden after mergers.

By the end of the decade, government agencies, members of Congress, increasingly powerful institutional investors, leading authorities on accounting, and the media were all calling for broadened disclosure rules. The Federal Trade Commission (FTC), charged with enforcing anti-trust laws, called conglomerate accounting a "tool of deception" and urged the Securities and Exchange Commission (SEC) to outlaw it. Newsweeklies decried "profits without honor."[1] In this crisis atmosphere, pressure from the FTC and other regulators, institutional investors, and financial analysts proved stronger than opposition by some large accounting firms and conglomerate interests. Congress responded in 1968 with the Williams Act, which required disclosure of cash tender offers that would change ownership of more than 10 percent of company stock. This law was strengthened two years later by lowering the reporting threshold to 5 percent. In addition, the SEC required companies to disclose product-line data.[2]

Over time, the accuracy of disclosed information also improved, though slowly. Congress gave the SEC authority to establish uniform accounting standards in 1934. But for the next forty years companies continued to exercise broad discretion in the way they reported assets and liabilities to the public, and the SEC left accounting professionals broad discretion to interpret government reporting rules. Until 1963, companies were not even required to disclose the accounting methods they employed.[3]

In 1969–1970, however, as the speculative fever of the "go-go years" gave way to rapid decline in stock values and the Dow Jones average fell 35 percent, investors began to flee the market. To restore public trust in the transparency system, the Accounting Principles Board, an outdated instrument of accounting industry self-governance, was replaced by the Financial Accounting Standards Board (FASB). The new board had broader representation and funding, a larger professional staff, and a better system of accountability.[4]

New crises brought further improvements. In the late 1970s, congressional investigations raised questions about FASB's domination by big business. In response, the board opened its meetings, began accepting public comment on proposals, started publishing its schedules and technical decisions, framed industry-specific accounting standards, began to analyze economic consequences of proposed actions, and eliminated a requirement that a majority of its members be chosen from the accounting profession.[5]

Finally, users of accounting information increased as capital markets expanded domestically and internationally. Institutional investors became increasingly important players in public markets. Pension funds poured billions of dollars into stock markets, and with those investments came greater scrutiny of the practices and value of public companies. The demand for financial information was further increased by the growth in the number of financial advisers, media commentators, and, later, Web-based advisers who sought to help individual investors – and themselves – make money by providing assistance on the complexities of Wall Street. In the 1990s, increases in individual investing and the rise of online investing led the SEC to adopt "plain English" disclosure rules, which required prospectuses to be written in short, clear sentences using nontechnical vocabulary and featuring graphic aids.[6] In September 2006, the SEC announced that the agency was adopting a dynamic real-time electronic filing and search system that would make it easier for individual investors to analyze companies' financial data without expert advisers.[7]

Viewed from a cost/benefit perspective, the history of financial disclosure is a surprising one. The disclosure rules impose large costs on individual firms, some of which have much to gain from concealing or misrepresenting various aspects of their finances. At the same time, the benefits to investors and other users of such information are very broadly diffused. Under the circumstances, one might predict that mandated disclosure requirements would be weak and would erode over time, especially when disclosers possess significant political power. Yet the history of financial disclosure is one of episodic but steady improvement. What factors explain its growing strength?

SUSTAINABLE POLICIES

Transparency policies tend to evolve over time. Often, they degenerate, for reasons we have discussed. Sometimes, however, they become more effective, as illustrated by the positive response of financial disclosure to changing markets, technology, public priorities, and company executives' discovery of loopholes.

Although it is difficult to find consistent ways to measure the dynamics of transparency across the diverse range of policies that are the focus of this book, we define a sustainable system as one that improves over time along three important dimensions:

- expanding *scope* of information relative to the scope of the problem addressed;
- increasing *accuracy and quality* of information; and
- increasing *use* of information by consumers, investors, employees, political activists, voters, residents, and/or government officials.

The transparency policies we have studied exhibit a range of improvement along these dimensions. Some policies, like corporate financial disclosure, mortgage lending disclosure, and school performance report cards, have improved in all three dimensions. Other policies, like toxic chemical disclosure, nutritional labeling, and campaign finance disclosure, have improved in some dimensions but not others. Still other policies, such as labor union finances disclosure and workplace hazards reporting, have improved little since they were enacted.

For reasons described in Chapter 4, policies that improve along all three dimensions may still be ineffective. For example, the terrorist threat reporting system has improved somewhat in accuracy since its creation in 2002. Yet that system has so far produced only marginal changes in the targeted behavior of individual users, although it has had a more significant impact on first responders and other government agencies with security responsibilities. Sustained improvement is, therefore, a necessary but not sufficient condition for the success of transparency policies.

THE POLITICS OF DISCLOSURE

From a political perspective, the creation of effective, sustainable transparency policies is hard to achieve for two reasons. First, as we have noted, transparency policies are usually produced by the convergence of unusual and short-lived circumstances. They are created in moments of crisis or scandal that throw open the arenas of narrow group politics and private deal making to broader public scrutiny. Such crises reveal flaws in existing regulatory arrangements that allow political entrepreneurs to gain sufficient support for their disclosure remedies to translate them into laws and regulations. But the dependence of disclosure requirements upon momentary public attention also makes them vulnerable. As crisis fades, so does support.

The second reason that transparency laws tend to degrade over time arises from the distribution of disclosure costs and benefits. As we have noted, transparency typically imposes costs upon a small group of disclosers in the hope of generating benefits for a large group of dispersed users. For example, nutritional labeling requirements direct food processing companies to reveal product information to millions of food consumers. In *The Politics of Regulation*, James Q. Wilson suggested that such conditions of concentrated costs and dispersed benefits allow targeted parties to capture regulatory systems and turn them to their advantage. When industry is the target, industry associations and organizations make collective political action easier still. As a general matter, then, those who suffer the costs of mandatory disclosure policies usually enjoy a substantial political advantage over those who benefit from them. As Wilson noted, "Since the incentive to organize is strong for opponents of the policy but weak for the beneficiaries, and since the political system provides many points at which opposition can be registered, it may seem astonishing that regulation of this sort is ever passed."[8]

The history of targeted transparency includes many stories of powerful disclosers using their political clout to limit the scope of disclosure systems. Take, for example, the case of toxic pollution reporting. This disclosure requirement represented a small part of a legislated emergency response system for chemical accidents enacted by Congress. The requirement was supported by key senators, by right-to-know groups, and by some environmental organizations but was opposed by the Reagan administration's federal Environmental Protection Agency and by manufacturers who regarded it as burdensome.

The political compromise these warring groups reached created a narrowly defined system, limiting the number of chemicals to be reported and the companies required to report. The law did not require reporting of overall chemical use and permitted companies to estimate toxic pollution using a variety of techniques that could be changed without notice. Finally, the law required reporting only of total pounds of releases and did not require manufacturers to assess exposure or toxicity risks.

Similarly, in the case of nutritional labeling, political compromise produced a disclosure system limited in scope and too complex for many users to understand. Responding to industry pressure, Congress provided that fast-food outlets, restaurants, grocery delicatessens, and small retailers did not have to label products they packaged, even though the convenience foods offered by such places were often particularly high in harmful fats.[9] Pressured by groups such as the American Beef Cattlemen's Association, Congress also did not require labeling for fresh meats, poultry, and seafood, even though red meats were among the most significant sources of fats linked to heart disease and cancer. Congress and the FDA also opted for a system of quantitative labeling that did not include color coding, graphics, or other simple messages to alert shoppers to foods high in fat, sodium, and other nutrients linked to chronic diseases. And after an extraordinary lobbying effort by health-food stores and the supplement industry, Congress placed herbal remedies and other dietary supplements on a separate, and ultimately less restrictive, track – even though little was known about their benefits and risks.

Of course, many proposed disclosure systems never get off the ground at all, even if they address extremely serious risks. An urgent call by the prestigious Institute of Medicine in 1999 for a new disclosure system for medical mistakes in hospitals, the eighth largest cause of accidental deaths in the United States, met insurmountable political obstacles. Key groups representing doctors and hospitals lobbied strenuously against public disclosure.

HUMBLE BEGINNINGS: PROSPECTS FOR
SUSTAINABLE TRANSPARENCY

As we have seen, political pressures often lead to the creation of weak transparency policies. But over time some policies do improve. Policies that evolve so as to transform the typical imbalance between concentrated costs and diffuse benefits can change the political dynamic in the direction of sustainability. How does that happen?

First, transparency systems improve when some of their target organizations champion more accurate, complete, and useful disclosure. There are several factors that may push disclosers to press for improvements in transparency over time. Of particular importance, competitive, political, and social factors may convince some that improved transparency will give them advantages over other disclosers. Disclosers' divergent interests in providing full rather than partial disclosure can create a dynamic that fractures the political coalition opposing transparency.

Second, dispersed users of information may form political coalitions that press effectively for better disclosure. New crises often coalesce users' interests in a national debate and force reexamination and improvement of disclosure. Permanent user coalitions, represented by consumer or public health groups, for example, can exert continuing pressure for improvement to gain perceived economic or political benefits. Such groups are often formed or strengthened in the wake of crises. Finally, because of their personal stake in the issue, entrepreneurial politicians may choose to continue to act on the behalf of information users in hopes of achieving political benefits.

In the absence of either divergent interests among disclosers or the emergence of organized user groups, transparency policies tend to remain trapped in James Q. Wilson's political dead end of dispersed benefits and concentrated costs and have poor prospects for improvement over time. If those conditions remain unchanged, policies will be underutilized, implemented weakly, and subject to gradual erosion. But even these targeted transparency policies can improve – and therefore become sustainable – when conditions change in ways that undermine the common interests that concentrated costs impose on disclosers or create mechanisms that allow interest groups to integrate the diffused benefits to users.

One way of depicting the sustainability prospects of specific targeted transparency systems is shown in Figure 5.1. The axes in this figure represent two possible sources of political support: (1) the extent to which disclosers reap benefits from the transparency policy (the vertical axis) and (2) the extent to which user groups champion the policy (the horizontal

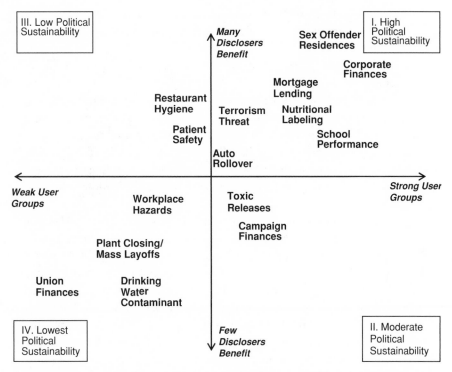

Figure 5.1. Sources of Political Support and Policy Sustainability for Transparency Policies

axis). Figure 5.1 plots the fifteen U.S. targeted transparency policies we have studied along both dimensions.

The two axes divide the space into four regions. Policies in the upper-right region (high political sustainability) enjoy political support from two sources: user interest groups and subsets of disclosers who benefit from disclosure. Because diverse coalitions that cut across discloser and user boundaries frequently support these policies, they will, as a general rule, reliably improve over time by expanding their scope, enhancing the quality of information they provide, and enlarging the base of users.

Federal requirements for nutritional labeling of packaged foods fall into this region because some food manufacturers have come to support the disclosure policy, both to avoid having to disclose under multiple state standards and also because uniform labeling opens new marketing channels for healthier foods. These motivations have created common ground between some food producers and public health and consumer advocates. Similarly, under the mortgage lending disclosure system, some urban banks have become quite adept at serving high-risk borrowers and now are recognized as leaders in the fair-lending arena by regulators and the general public. These banks not only accept mortgage lending disclosure as part of their regulatory environment but have occasionally offered public support for the policy.

The lower-right-hand region (moderate political sustainability) is characterized by politically organized user groups and a near absence of disclosers who benefit from transparency. In this region, interest groups of users and disclosers oppose one another politically. The result is usually a fitful pattern in which disclosure requirements advance and retreat according to momentary political advantages occasioned by issue visibility, friendly or hostile officials, and crises of legitimacy.

Federal campaign contribution disclosure rules exemplify the policies in this quadrant. Few disclosers (predominantly incumbents in Congress) have any incentive to press for improvement in the system absent political crises. Instead they share a strong common interest in limiting disclosure. But a wide array of groups representing particular political interests (from the National Rifle Association, right-to-life groups, and the Christian Coalition on the right to the AFL-CIO, Handgun Control Inc., and the Sierra Club on the left) have an interest in improving disclosure. The resulting conflict has led to infrequent but occasionally significant shifts in disclosure rules, usually triggered by some new scandal.

The upper-left region (low political sustainability) mirrors the lower-right. Transparency policies here benefit some of those compelled to disclose information, but organized groups of users who support the policies are lacking. Policies with these underlying political dynamics are unlikely to be sustainable.

As we have discussed, a potential disclosure policy for hospital mistakes emerged as a viable proposal briefly in this quadrant after release of an Institute of Medicine report in 1999 documenting the significant extent of medical errors in the United States.

Major purchasers of medical services, including companies like General Electric and General Motors, had strong incentives to reduce errors. They could have become advocates for a federal and state medical mistakes disclosure system. However, within months, conflicting interests brought about a political stalemate. The apparent consensus for national action splintered into conflicts among the groups representing disclosers (doctors and hospitals), which generally opposed disclosure, and a more diverse and fractured group representing users (public health advocates, state interests, insurers, employers, consumers, and trial lawyers). When the debate got down to specifics, the American Medical Association and the American Hospital Association opposed the kind of hospital-by-hospital disclosure of serious errors that would be meaningful to consumers. They feared liability, embarrassment, and public misunderstanding, and expressed doubts that any disclosure system could adjust adequately for differences in patient populations. Large employers, potentially powerful advocates of a disclosure requirement, instead chose to create their own advocacy groups for changing hospital practices.[10] The temporary alliance of users was not cohesive enough to overcome opposition from potential disclosers.[11]

As this story illustrates, transparency policies in this quadrant will usually be unable to develop in a sustained fashion. In part, that is because disclosers who benefit from transparency policies generally do so only after they have accepted disclosure as part of their operating environment and developed new skills and strategies in response. Significant incentives for disclosers to support transparency do not materialize until a viable system is in place or seems inevitable. The lower-left quadrant (lowest political sustainability) is where transparency policies have the poorest prospects, since they are supported neither by organized users nor by factions of disclosers. Though policies in this region may be created by effective political entrepreneurs following a crisis or scandal, the underlying politics will make it difficult for them to improve over time. Absent changes by either users or disclosers, these policies will be underutilized, implemented weakly, and subject to gradual erosion.

TWO ILLUSTRATIONS

Two cases help illustrate the political dynamics that can lead to improvement or stagnation of transparency policies. Mandatory disclosure of the current addresses of sex offenders ("Megan's Laws") appear in the upper-right-hand quadrant of Figure 5.1. They have proven sustainable – although they remain highly controversial. By contrast, disclosure of unions' internal financial and governance information has languished for most of the past forty years in the lower-left-hand quadrant.

State-level policies that require disclosure of information to the public about the current residences of released sex offenders typically operate in a political environment that pushes them toward continual increases in the quantity, quality, and scope of information. Often created in the wake of highly publicized and particularly heinous sexual assaults committed by ex-offenders, they are created in a context where politicians have strong incentives to push for disclosure of detailed personal information. Police departments, which retain control over this information, have limited incentives to restrict its disclosure, since they act more as the agents of users (the public) than of the true disclosers (the ex-offenders themselves). Groups that champion the interests of the unusual disclosers, such as the American Civil Liberties Union or prisoners' rights groups, usually have relatively little political influence and can therefore exercise only weak countervailing pressure. Meanwhile, information users – often residents of communities where ex-offenders are believed to be living – have strong incentives to organize and press for greater disclosure.[12]

In Washington State, one of the first to approve a sex offender community notification law, the political crisis arose from a series of highly publicized sexual assault cases in the late 1980s. The first case involved the abduction, rape, and murder of a young Seattle businesswoman in 1988. The killer, Gene Raymond Kane, had been on work release for two months after completing a thirteen-year sentence for attacking two women. The resulting public outrage was so intense that Governor Booth Gardner was forced to act quickly. To "channel the citizens' outrage into a more measured, reasonable process," he convened a task force charged with developing proposals on how the state could better protect communities from predatory sex offenders. To underscore the bipartisan nature of the issue and to satisfy critics in both parties, Governor Gardner, a Democrat, appointed Norm Maleng, the Republican who had challenged him in the previous gubernatorial race, to head the task force. After a series of public hearings at which 151 victims testified, David Boerner, a University of Puget Sound law professor, drafted the bill that was approved by the state legislature in January 1990.[13]

The same dynamic has driven steady expansion in the accuracy and scope of the policy from 1993 to 2005:[14]

1993: Police initiate "community notification meetings" to provide information to communities in which sex offenders live.

1994: The state legislature amends the law to require local law enforcement officials to notify the public at least fourteen days prior to an offender's release into a community.[15]

1997: The state legislature again amends the law, creating more objective and standardized "risk-level" factors to determine whether ex-offenders should be included in the disclosure system.[16] A separate amendment expands it to include kidnappers.[17]

1999: The law is strengthened again to require ex-offenders to notify the county sheriff within fourteen days of becoming homeless or transient, or changing county location.[18]

2001: The law is strengthened to require county sheriffs to publish Level III sex offender notices in local newspapers and to require newspapers to publish this information when an offender moves into a new community. A separate bill requires Level III offenders to provide written notice to landlords prior to entering rental agreements.[19]

2002: The law is amended to require hotel and motel owners to notify all other guests if they are lodging a Level III sex offender.[20]

2005: The law is amended to require ex-offenders who attend or plan to attend an educational institution to notify the sheriff within ten days of enrolling or prior to arrival at the school, which triggers notification of the school principal and staff.[21]

The public demand for additional information and the positive incentives facing police and state governments have led to passage of similar laws in every state and the District of Columbia over the past decade.[22] What is more, the pattern of benefits and costs facing users and disclosers continues to drive many of these systems to improve in the quantity, quality, and scope of information released.

The story of union financial reporting illustrates a very different political dynamic. The Labor Management Reporting and Disclosure Act requires unions to reveal to their members information regarding financial practices and governance procedures.[23] Its goal: to use transparency to reduce corruption in union activities. The law was enacted in 1959 in response to public outrage about charges of corruption in some of the nation's most powerful unions (in particular the International Brotherhood of Teamsters), revealed in Senate hearings. A number of rising politicians, including John F. Kennedy and his brother Robert Kennedy, built their political reputations around the issue. However, legislative compromise produced a disclosure requirement that was relatively narrow in scope and that placed significant barriers in the way of use of the information by rank-and-file union members.

The disclosure law required each level of a union with governance responsibility to provide separate disclosure of financial activity (revenues and expenses) at that level. This disaggregated reporting made it difficult for users examining reports from union locals to locate information regarding related activity at regional and national levels. The law also focused narrowly on each union's balance sheet (such as loan activity, officer salary, and line-item disbursements) rather than on programmatic expenditures (like political action, organizing, and member servicing) of more direct interest to members.[24]

Neither disclosers (the unions themselves) nor users (primarily union members) had much incentive or opportunity to support or seek to strengthen the reporting policy. There was little incentive for unions to promote financial disclosure beyond that required by their own by-laws and constitutions, and many union leaders regarded the law as part of a conservative and business backlash against the labor movement. At the same time, very few unions had strong internal political units that could act on behalf of union members to push for broader or more easily accessible financial data.

Until 2000, when information became available on the Internet, union members seeking data under the disclosure law had to visit a reading room at the Labor Department in Washington, D.C., travel to a regional office of the department, or make a request by mail and pay a per-page charge. Since the typical LM-2 form (the reporting document filed by the union) runs well over a hundred pages, it might cost fifteen dollars or more to purchase. A user who wanted reports from several different reporting levels of the union might pay much more. But these out-of-pocket expenses were relatively small compared to the investment of time and energy needed to interpret the documents once they were obtained. High user search costs made the system moribund for decades, with few calls from union members for strengthening or expansion of its disclosure requirements.

In 2003, the Bush administration undertook the first major change of union financial reporting when the secretary of labor, Elaine Chao, used her authority under the disclosure policy to require far greater detail in reporting, a move toward programmatic reporting, and broader coverage of the law (for example, by expanding reporting requirements to smaller unions).[25] The Bush reforms were supported by nonunion business interests rather than by union members or union officers and were perceived by some as aiming to thwart unionization efforts, rather than to promote the interests of users. In fact, even some of the individuals and groups that had long fought for greater internal union democracy and disclosure opposed the Bush administration changes.[26]

Thus, in contrast to Megan's Laws like those in Washington State, union financial reporting lacked strong support from its inception, and the relative benefits and costs to users and disclosers have changed little over time. It remains to be seen whether recent attempts to strengthen and expand the disclosure system will last.[27]

SHIFTING CONDITIONS DRIVE CHANGES IN SUSTAINABILITY

As we have seen, the sustainability of targeted transparency systems is shaped by political conditions at the time of legislative enactment and at later legislative moments when an established system is revised. However, the scope, accuracy, and use of information may also change as a result of *shifts* in the relationship between costs and benefits to users and disclosers owing to changes in such elements as market structure, the strength of intermediary organizations, and information technology. Such shifts in discloser or user benefits and costs can affect the larger political environment, and thus strengthen or weaken disclosure.

Changing Costs and Benefits for Disclosers

Typically, disclosers' costs increase with the amount, scope, and level of detail of information they provide to users. For example, firms providing financial information incur costs in gathering, processing, and releasing that information that rise with the stringency of disclosure requirements. The more information required and the more frequently reports must be created, the higher the costs. The average incremental costs of disclosure requirements under the Sarbanes-Oxley accounting reform law were originally estimated by the SEC to be ninety thousand dollars, but more recent estimates put the number at many multiples above that.[28]

In one sense, the costs of disclosure arguably have fallen for many disclosers as a result of advances in information technology that reduce the costs of gathering, processing, and storing data. If technology were the only driver of the costs of disclosure, these advances might lower the threshold for information a typical discloser might be willing to provide. However, disclosers face still more significant costs associated with competitive or political risks arising from reporting – for example, the risk of a company revealing strategic information useful to competitors or a politician exposing herself in the thick of an election to potential embarrassment because of a particular campaign donor. Providing more detailed information may also open the discloser to greater pressure from certain user groups to adopt costly changes in policies.

The potential benefits of disclosure to target organizations may also change substantially following the introduction of a new transparency requirement. In particular, organizations may gain "first mover" advantages from providing more information than competitors and then attempting to raise the bar of voluntary or mandated disclosure for others. For example, a firm may gain investors from being more forthcoming about financial returns once others are required to disclose some financial information. Although the benefits of complete disclosure must still be balanced against the competitive downside of providing too much detailed knowledge, some firms may conclude that transparency represents a net gain.

The SEC's decision in early 2006 to require full disclosure of executive pay, including pensions, illustrates how changes in the benefits and costs of disclosure can lead to improvement.[29] Consumer advocates, labor unions, and shareholder advocates have long called for greater transparency in executive compensation to little effect. However, recent controversial cases involving exceedingly high-compensation executives (e.g., Richard Grasso, former chairman of the New York Stock Exchange, who received an estimated $187 million pay package)[30] brought investor and financial community calls for greater transparency, including appeals from former Federal Reserve Chairman Alan Greenspan and legendary investor Warren Buffett.[31]

As a result, the benefits of increased disclosure of CEO compensation packages began to shift for individual companies. Coca Cola, Inc., an early mover, announced in 2002 that it would voluntarily list executive stock options as an expense item in its future accounting statements, a reform advocated by many critics of the current reporting system. Although this move lowered Coca Cola's reported profitability, it also gave the company a comparative advantage with investors increasingly worried about the accuracy and completeness of corporate financial statements, and a political stake in pushing for wider disclosure. Other companies followed suit, providing investors with detailed accounts of their compensation practices voluntarily, in part to quell growing concern about the negative consequences of excessive compensation on profitability but also to gain a competitive leg up on growing demands for mandatory disclosure. Thus, an increasingly divided discloser community led to a more politically conducive environment for increasing disclosure.[32]

We have seen similar dynamics in other targeted transparency cases. Several of the largest food companies pushed for expansion of nutritional labeling to other sectors not covered by requirements. Corporations in the forefront of toxic use reduction and the pollution prevention effort pushed successfully for expansion of toxic pollution reporting to industrial sectors exempted under the original act. Even in Los Angeles, eating and drinking associations that originally opposed restaurant hygiene reporting have recently fought efforts by certain ethnic restaurant organizations to exempt themselves from parts of the grading system because of their different standards and methods of food preparation.[33]

Changing Costs and Benefits for Users

As we saw earlier, using new information is often costly and yields benefits only when it improves the decisions made by consumers and other information users. As a result, users will push for further improvement in disclosure systems only if their perceived benefits from the information provided outweigh their costs. The key drivers of benefits and costs for information users are the following:

- User benefits tend to rise as more information is provided. However, there is a limit beyond which users receive little additional benefit from additional information.
- User costs may rise, fall, or stay the same as more information is provided.
- Because the benefits of information flow to more individuals than just the direct consumers of information (the "public good" aspect of information), users may tend to underconsume disclosed data *unless* third-party agents act for groups of users in collecting, interpreting, and disseminating information.

Users, like disclosers, will balance the perceived benefits and costs of information. If the benefits of information rise over time (for example, if consumers become more aware of risks and more eager to learn how to avoid them) or the costs of acquiring the information fall (for example, as Internet access has become widely available), the demand for more detailed, more accurate, and broader information is likely to increase.

There is a close link between the degree to which disclosed information is embedded in users' decision routines and the demand for better information, as illustrated by restaurant hygiene, auto rollover, and nutritional labeling systems. In all three cases, the costs of obtaining information for users are quite low. And because many users value the information, not only is it embedded in their decisions, but it also provides a basis for demanding further disclosure improvements. By contrast, there are fewer demands for improvement where information is not embedded in user decisions or where active intermediaries who pool user interests are lacking.

Understanding the benefits and costs to information disclosers and users makes it possible to anticipate whether a particular targeted transparency system will tend to improve over time. Where users do not value the information provided and fail to incorporate it in their decisions, there is little reason to expect demands for improvement. But where information is embedded in user decisions, we expect users (or their representatives) to push for more and better information. During crises that reveal the limitations of the existing transparency policy, these pressures provide political opportunities for the expansion of disclosure requirements.

The Importance of Intermediaries

Organizations of those who benefit from information provide an important source of political support for transparency policies. The larger the perceived benefits to specific, well-organized groups or coalitions of potential users, the more likely it is that users' interests will be reflected in the initial structure of transparency policies. But if the potential users are an undefined "public interest" that has not coalesced into organized groups, users' impact on policy improvement is likely to be far more limited.[34] This is the case with school performance report card policies, where the intended beneficiaries – parents of students – are a highly diffuse and relatively unorganized group.

Sometimes disclosure policies begin without deep or well-organized political backing but gain such backing when advocacy groups or associations of users come to recognize how transparency can advance their own agendas. The emergence of such political intermediaries can then underwrite the continuous improvement of transparency regulation by shifting the regulatory politics from Wilson's entrepreneurial mode (concentrated costs, disbursed benefits) to a more evenly matched interest-group contest between organized users and disclosers.[35]

There are many examples of political interest groups that have found that transparency policies create tools they can use to advance their causes. For example, urban community organizations have used the information provided by mortgage lending disclosure to publicize the extent of discriminatory lending. This information has helped them build public opposition to these bank practices, forge alliances with bank regulators, identify and embarrass discriminatory lenders, and negotiate with specific lending institutions to improve credit access for previously excluded groups. Broad-based community reinvestment task forces in Washington State, Rhode Island, New Jersey, and Michigan have forged partnerships among community organizations, lending institutions, and state and local governments to address problems of access to credit.[36]

Other types of intermediaries, such as investigative reporters and financial analysts, have also used mortgage lending information to document pervasive patterns of discriminatory lending and the exodus of banks from minority neighborhoods. In 1988, for example, two reporters for the *Atlanta Journal-Constitution* reported on widespread redlining in *The Color of Money*, a series of articles that received national attention.[37] In 1992, a rigorous study conducted by the Boston Federal Reserve concluded that race had a strong influence on lending decisions.[38] The report received broad media coverage, confronting banks with discrimination allegations from a particularly authoritative source. All these uses of lending information by organizations that represent users' interests have made such organizations into champions of the disclosure policy and advocates of its improvement.

Similarly, transparency policies have strengthened the political stature of environmental organizations with respect to corporations, public health advocates with respect to food producers, and proponents of campaign finance reform with respect to candidates and donors. When transparency requirements alter the political terrain in ways that favor particular interest groups, they can create users who are organized and motivated and have resources to defend the disclosure policies and press for improvements.

In some cases, particular industry-segment users may favor transparency as an economic weapon against disclosers in another industry segment. Corporate financial disclosure illustrates this dynamic. In that case, investors as a class have a strong financial interest in obtaining accurate information about companies where they may buy stock. They are thus natural supporters of strong and continuously improving financial disclosure. Large pension funds, mutual funds, and other institutional investors, increasingly prominent investor groups, have become powerful advocates of financial disclosure. Similarly, industry associations representing major manufacturers that use hazardous chemicals in production and fear potential liability from their use have been the primary advocates for improvement of workplace chemical hazard reporting.[39]

User intermediaries can also reduce the costs of information acquisition and interpretation. Unlike other goods and services, information has a value that does not diminish when it is consumed by additional parties. Economists refer to this as *non-rival consumption*, one of two prerequisites for a public good. (The second is a relatively high cost for excluding other users from consumption once the good has been produced. With the recent explosion of information technology, especially the Internet, this second prerequisite is becoming increasingly applicable to information as well.)

Non-rival consumption means that the information provided to users by disclosers will tend to be underconsumed from a social perspective. Why? Because individuals who use the information may not realize that others might also benefit from the same information or from its effects on decision making. These ancillary benefits are referred to as *spillover effects*.

Imagine a worker who has obtained information about hazardous chemicals at her workplace through the disclosure process. Her awareness of the increased health risks she faces will inform her subsequent decisions, including assessment of her personal risk/cost equation: If she plans to have a baby, should she request a transfer to another facility before becoming pregnant? If she does, will she face the risk of losing her job or her seniority? How should the economic and health factors be balanced? Our hypothetical worker has clearly benefited from the information she has obtained. But she may not consider that other women in her workplace could also benefit from the same information. If she does not take this wider set of beneficiaries into account (by sharing the data, for example), her incentive to invest in acquiring this information will be too low from a social point of view.

In such situations, an organized group can help by serving as an agent for users. For example, a labor union or an employee health counselor might produce a special booklet or conduct an informational meeting for workers in their childbearing years to discuss the potential dangers of exposure to hazardous chemicals during pregnancy. In fact, labor unions have been shown to substantially increase workers' exercise of rights provided under labor statutes.[40]

The greater the spillover effects, the more important an organized group may be. In some instances, the spillovers from information are limited. For example, the spillover benefits from nutritional data on a food package are likely to be small, since not all consumers will find the information relevant to their health status and objectives. User intermediaries are less important in such cases. (An exception might arise if there is a subset of consumers who have special needs requiring additional, specialized information, such as those with food allergies. We discuss this case later.)

An important factor in the role of user intermediaries is the alignment of their interests with those of the individuals they represent. The more fully such groups' incentives mirror those of individual users, the more likely it is that the groups will be able to correct the problems posed by the non-rival character of information. Unions, for example, operate under political incentives as well as statutory requirements that push them toward considering the interests of workers. The politics of union organizations impel their leaders to consider the interests of the median voter in setting union policies, and the "duty-of-fair representation" requirement arising from labor law penalizes union officials who fail to represent both members and nonmembers covered by collective bargaining agreements.[41]

In some cases, however, user representatives' interests are not aligned with those of individual users. Once again, financial disclosure offers a clear example. Some institutional investors – pension fund managers, for example – have incentives to use the information they collect for the benefit of all their clients. But this may not be the case with some investment advisers. For example, stockbrokers who earn commissions from the sale of shares sometimes face incentives to withhold negative information about a company from their clients.[42]

User intermediaries can also help reduce information costs. In many arenas, especially as Internet use becomes more pervasive, the costs of collecting information are low, but processing and disseminating that information can be expensive. For example, anyone can log on to the Web site of the Federal Election Commission (FEC) to download information about financial contributions to congressional candidates.[43] But it takes time to learn how to use the Web site, how to specify the correct reporting period, and how to aggregate contributions into relevant categories (for example, money donated by anti–gun-control organizations). What is more, disclosers have gamed the system by donating under multiple organizational names, intentionally confusing users. As a result, the time and costs of gathering and analyzing contribution data are substantial.[44]

In this situation, organizations can help by applying their expertise to the tasks of gathering and analyzing information and reporting it in easy-to-grasp form to concerned users. For example, a pro–gun-control organization might publicize a simple, annotated list of the congressional candidates who have received the largest donations from anti–gun-control groups. In parallel fashion, advocacy groups in other areas from consumer rights to the environment are mining FEC data and translating it into a format that users find easy to digest.

Even where the costs of aggregating information are not substantial, interpreting the data so that users can incorporate them into their individual decisions may be costly or complicated. In many areas of risk-related disclosure systems, such as toxic pollution or drinking water safety reporting, translating complicated information into comprehensible formats is essential. There is also significant misuse of information because of hidden complexities – for example, in the interpretation of school report card data.[45] In response, a variety of parent and community groups in different states have created Web sites that allow parents to compare their children's schools with other schools with similar characteristics. These groups turn disclosed data into the kind of information parents can use in making location decisions or in seeking greater involvement in the schools.[46]

To sum up, targeted transparency policies are often born in crisis, usually as political compromises reflecting the relative power of organized representatives of potential disclosers and weak coalitions of potential users. Improving such policies over time is similarly hampered by the distribution of political power. Yet new market conditions and corporate strategies can alter the benefits and costs for disclosers, empowering some interests and threatening others, thereby rearranging the political environment that surrounds transparency systems and occasionally opening opportunities for improvement. Improvement also depends on the growth of user constituencies and intermediaries that stand to benefit from greater access to more accurate and complete information. One requirement for transparency effectiveness, therefore, is that the dynamics of the system favor sustainability.

To this point, our analysis has focused almost entirely on transparency systems within the United States. Now we expand the discussion with a look at attempts to use targeted transparency as a strategy for furthering international priorities.

SIX

International Transparency

Transparency policies have the potential to reduce risks and improve public services in the United States, although they must overcome many obstacles to do so, as we have seen. But can targeted transparency reduce risks and improve services that cross national boundaries? That is a more difficult question.

Assessing three important cross-border transparency policies, we find preliminary evidence that such policies can help further nations' shared agendas, even when no overarching treaty guides international action. At best, targeted transparency provides a form of governance without government.

In some ways, international transparency policies work like domestic policies. The analytical framework we have developed to assess the effectiveness of domestic policies can also assess the effectiveness of international policies. The effectiveness of international policies, like that of domestic policies, depends heavily on whether policies are user-centered and improve over time. But international policies also confront two unique challenges. First, they must earn legitimacy. Second, they must become embedded not only in the decision routines of information users and disclosers but also in national laws, regulations, and enforcement practices of participating nations.

Whether targeted transparency can become a useful tool of international governance is a question with new urgency. Markets are integrating rapidly, while governance remains fragmented, defined by traditional national geographical boundaries. National governments have increasing difficulty framing rules for markets and for collective action unilaterally.

At the same time, the failure of national transparency systems can have dire international consequences, as two recent examples illustrate.

In 2001–2002, the sudden collapse of Enron, WorldCom, and other respected U.S. companies destroyed the savings of investors not only in the

United States but around the world. The failure of U.S. financial accounting rules to keep up with market changes increased risks to investors –
without regard to national boundaries. Reforms became an international
effort.

In 2003, the outbreak of a virulent infectious disease known as Severe
Acute Respiratory Syndrome (SARS) spread from a few villages in China
to thirty countries in six months. National transparency failed as Chinese
officials delayed reporting of provincial outbreaks. Late and incomplete
information created international panic. In the end, SARS killed more than
700 people and caused an estimated $40 billion in economic losses.

Of course, the growing interdependence of nations has increased calls
for strengthened international institutions. Yet formal treaties and multinational agreements remain relatively rare, and efforts to reform the United
Nations, the World Bank, and other international institutions proceed
slowly. As the need for cross-border governance increases, transparency
policies provide one pragmatic means of pursuing shared priorities.

This chapter represents a first step toward assessing targeted transparency
as a tool of international governance. It asks three questions:

- How do international targeted transparency policies work?
- Why are such policies emerging now?
- What factors contribute to their effectiveness?

Our analysis is based on examination of three international cases chosen for the diversity of their origins and goals, their relative maturity, and
their potentially broad impact. We first examine in detail the evolution of
international corporate financial reporting. We do so because our analysis
of domestic cases suggests that transparency policies are likely to be most
mature in the financial sector. International corporate financial reporting
grew out of thirty years of private-sector efforts by an informal committee of
accountants to harmonize disclosure rules across major securities markets.
The committee's aims were to reduce investor risks and improve corporate
governance. By 2005, those private efforts had evolved into public mandates
as the committee gradually adopted rules for participation and procedural
fairness, and as national governments in major securities markets endorsed
its standards.

We then analyze two international transparency cases of current importance – one concerning public health and the other concerning food safety –
for comparison. International infectious disease surveillance, the first case,
has long aimed to reduce deaths and illnesses by limiting the spread of diseases from one nation to another. A moribund system was re-created and

broadened when the SARS epidemic of 2003 revealed the urgent need for rapid and accurate international reporting.

By contrast, the labeling of genetically modified foods, the second case, represents, so far, a costly and unsuccessful international transparency effort. Nations participating in international food markets have failed to agree about whether genetic modification of grains presents safety risks that warrant public disclosure and what form that disclosure should take when consumer preferences vary widely and science remains uncertain.

HOW DO INTERNATIONAL TRANSPARENCY POLICIES WORK?

Transparency is a widely acclaimed value in international governance. Targeted transparency, however, has a specific meaning. As we have seen, targeted transparency means the government-mandated disclosure by corporations or other private or public organizations of standardized, comparable, and disaggregated information regarding specific products or practices to a broad audience in order to further a defined public purpose.

These policies differ from more familiar forms of international transparency. Their specific regulatory purpose distinguishes such policies from broad efforts by the United Nations, World Bank, national governments, and other institutions toward more transparency in decision making. Their reliance on the accountability and permanence of public mandates distinguishes them from the many efforts by private organizations to create international transparency systems that will, for example, reduce public corruption or improve environmental protection or labor standards.[1]

Targeted transparency policies' reliance on information itself as a regulatory tool distinguishes these policies from the more familiar form of regulatory disclosure – standard setting and compliance transparency. Standard setting and compliance transparency rely on information as an input to the framing and enforcement of government rules.[2]

At the outset, we find that international targeted transparency policies share the architectural elements of domestic policies, discussed at length in Chapter 3. Different as they are, international accounting, infectious disease surveillance, and labeling of genetically modified foods all feature the same architectural elements: a defined policy purpose; specified discloser targets; a defined scope of information; a designated information structure and vehicle; and an enforcement mechanism.

International transparency systems also work in essentially the same way as domestic systems, following the action cycle described in Chapter 4. Disclosure of factual information creates incentives for consumers and citizens to change their choices. Those changed choices in turn create incentives for corporations or other disclosers to align their practices more closely with public objectives.

Scores of international targeted transparency systems have emerged in recent years. Besides the three we study in this chapter, prominent examples include food-ingredient, country-of-origin, and nutritional labeling coordinated by the United Nations' Codex Alimentarius; stringent auto safety and fuel-economy disclosure adopted by Europe, China, Japan, and other nations; labeling of tobacco products under the Framework Convention on Tobacco Control; the labeling of hazardous chemicals under UN guidance; and the European Union's cross-border reporting requirements for toxic pollution.[3]

Scholars and commentators have begun to acknowledge the importance of international targeted transparency in their recent work. In *Global Public Policy: Governing Without Government?* Wolfgang H. Reinicke suggests that "applying strict principles of disclosure-based regulation is one important way to allow public sector and other non-state actors to review industry activity on a regular and timely basis."[4] In *Why Globalization Works*, Martin Wolf suggests that "[t]he flow of reliable *information* and the ability to *trust* are the life-blood of markets. . . . Regulators can help by certifying the quality of a company's processes or products, their financial soundness or whatever else may be relevant."[5] And in *A New World Order*, Anne-Marie Slaughter suggests optimistically that

regulation by information . . . allows regulators to move away from traditional command-and-control methods and instead provide individuals and corporations with the information and ideas they need to figure out how to improve their own performance against benchmarked standards. This approach is gaining popularity in the United States, is increasingly prevalent in the European Union, and is being tried at the United Nations.[6]

WHY NOW?

Even as markets have integrated rapidly over the last two decades, governance remains problematic.[7] No nation advocates ceding broad sovereignty to a world government. And even limited international rules, taxes, subsidies, and other conventional forms of public intervention often have proven politically difficult to create and enforce. In such circumstances, a question arises: can international transparency policies offer a relatively light-handed pragmatic means of protecting investors, improving the safety of products, minimizing the spread of diseases, and improving cross-boundary services such as transportation?

The emergence of international transparency policies has been driven by three long-term trends that suggest their lasting importance. First, in a political change, national governments in the world's largest markets have eliminated quotas and reduced tariffs, foreign exchange controls, interest rate ceilings, securities regulation, and other barriers to international trade and investment.[8] Second, in an economic change, shipping and travel costs have plummeted, helping to expand international trade and tourism.[9] Third, in a technological change, rapid advances in computing power and the Internet have dramatically lowered the costs of international business transactions and increased the potential power of transparency.[10]

These changes have transformed the character as well as increased the volume of international business. As the debate in the United States over outsourcing suggests, it has become increasingly cost-effective for firms to locate workers and facilities in many countries. At the same time, investors are seeking higher returns outside their home countries. In 1980, global cross-border purchases of stocks, bonds, and derivatives amounted to about $49 billion. By 1990, that figure had almost quintupled to $237 billion. By 2000, it had nearly quintupled again, to $1.06 trillion.[11] By the mid-1990s, more than 45,000 transnational corporations with 280,000 foreign affiliates accounted for about a third of the world's output.[12]

Such market integration has not been truly global, of course. Business transactions remain more geographically limited than frequent references to "globalization" might suggest.[13] As of 2003, about 90 percent of all capital moving across borders still flowed among the industrialized countries of Europe, North America, Japan, and Australia. Virtually all of the remaining 10 percent involved a group of high-growth developing countries known as emerging markets: China, India, and the rest of industrializing Asia, along with the larger Latin American economies such as Brazil, Mexico, and Venezuela. This 90/10 split in capital flows between industrialized and emerging market countries has been constant since at least the 1970s.[14]

Securities markets have remained even more concentrated. Almost half of the globe's corporate market value is held in the New York Stock Exchange and Nasdaq. Adding a handful of others – the Tokyo, London, Euronext, and German exchanges – accounts for about three-quarters of the world's publicly traded corporate value.[15] Investors also continue to display a significant "home bias" in their purchase of stocks. In 2000, portfolios around the world were still made up almost entirely of domestic stocks. United States investors held 89 percent U.S. stocks, Japanese investors held 92 percent Japanese stocks, and United Kingdom investors held 78 percent U.K. stocks.[16]

As a final cautionary note on inflated predictions of globalization, history teaches that unanticipated future events may slow or reverse the process of market integration. Periods of rapid economic growth have generally coincided with periods of rapid market integration. But those times have been interspersed with periods of slower growth and less integration. Contemporary observers often point to the years from 1870 to 1914 as a time of rapid integration of capital markets, technological innovation that reduced transportation and communication costs, growing international trade, and population migration. But this integration slowed with the outbreak of World War I.[17] Recent backlashes against globalization in both industrialized and developing nations and new barriers erected to the movement of goods and people as part of antiterrorism measures indicate that countervailing forces remain important.

Nonetheless, the demand for international systems of problem solving is likely to continue to grow. As more products, services, manufacturing operations, financial transactions, and people cross borders, conflicts over how to protect investors, assure the safety of cars, food, and medicines, reduce environmental risks, and protect public health will also increase.

In response to such market integration, as well as new scientific findings and periodic crises, governments have begun to adopt cross-border transparency policies. When domestic securities markets cratered during the Asian financial crisis of the mid-1990s, banking and securities regulators concluded that more transparency would help avoid future surprises. When scientists concluded that a range of events from melting glaciers in the Arctic to droughts in Africa could be traced to global warming, pressure increased for nations and corporations to disclose the climate-altering emission of greenhouse gases. When improved monitoring suggested that mercury and other toxic pollutants could travel long distances, policymakers began to design transparency measures for cross-border toxic pollution. When terrorism fears called attention to nations' porous borders, officials worked toward new international tracking and disclosure systems for shipping containers, air travel, microbes, and immigrants.

By our definition, an international transparency policy is effective if it creates lasting changes in the products or practices of target organizations that advance the shared priorities of the sponsoring nations. Empirical studies are needed to definitively measure the effectiveness of specific international policies, but so far few such studies have been published. The three policies we have studied offer suggestive insights about the potential for international transparency.

International corporate financial reporting provides an example of a transparency policy that has gained strength by becoming increasingly user- and discloser-centered and that appears likely to prove effective.

Infectious disease reporting provides a different model. Ad hoc responses to the SARS epidemic revived a moribund public health transparency measure and set a new course for international reporting.

By contrast, efforts to address public concerns about food safety by labeling genetically modified foods remind us about the limits of transparency in international public policy. To date, such labeling has failed to serve the needs of consumers or to keep pace with changing science and markets.

FROM PRIVATE COMMITTEE TO PUBLIC MANDATE: INTERNATIONAL CORPORATE FINANCIAL REPORTING

The newly emerging system of international corporate financial reporting illustrates how a private group of experts can create a transparency policy that grows into a public mandate. But it also illustrates how difficult it can be for such policies to gain legitimacy.

The idea that companies that seek public investors in more than one country should report their finances in a uniform way emerged in the 1970s in response to growing confusion about conflicting national accounting requirements. Exponential increases in cross-border investment left companies, regulators, and investors struggling with an outdated patchwork of variable national rules. The accounting profession, with its international perspective, long professional tradition, technical expertise, and quasi-public role, had the strongest and most enduring interest in harmonizing national standards.

As early as 1973, Henry Benson, the head of the Coopers Brothers accounting firm in Britain (later Pricewaterhouse Coopers), brought together leading accountants from nine countries to form the International Accounting Standards Committee (IASC) to issue proposed international rules for financial disclosure. Although the group operated independently, it was technically a committee of the International Federation of Accountants, a membership organization of accounting associations that promoted improvements in standards, auditing practices, ethics, and education in many countries.[18]

By 2005, this small private effort had grown into a robust public mandate. Approximately a hundred nations, including the twenty-five countries of the European Union, had authorized companies to use international standards in addition to or instead of national disclosure rules. Most leading stock exchanges, including those in the U.K., Japan, France, Germany, and Austria, accepted financial reports based on international standards. Although the United States still required foreign companies to reconcile their accounting with U.S. rules when they sold stock on U.S. exchanges, American regulators had issued qualified statements that they too planned to accept international standards by 2007. Most significant of all, the European Union *required* the use of such standards by all companies listing in member countries as of January 1, 2005.[19]

As we have discussed, transparency policies must be user- and discloser-centered to be effective, embedding new information in decision routines. By 2006, there were signs that international accounting standards were becoming embedded in the choices of international investors and that firms were paying attention. International accounting standards appeared quite likely to be effective in furthering their stated purposes, at least to some degree. Those purposes included improving market efficiencies by lowering the cost of capital, minimizing hidden risks to investors, reducing market volatility, and improving corporate governance.

What accounts for the apparent success of international financial reporting? Transparency effectiveness is always improbable. Especially in the international arena, one would expect that the political deck would be stacked against rigorous reporting. Multinational companies have both the motivation and the resources to fight demands for transparency, while national governments are committed to established traditions that could be expected to outweigh shared interests. By contrast, those who benefit from transparency – whether investors, consumers, or employees – remain separated by language, location, and cultural traditions. They would not be expected to either sustain interest or provide resources to maintain and improve transparency systems. Those dynamics could produce a "race to the bottom" in which a least common denominator of disclosure prevailed.[20] Why did rigorous international standards prevail instead?

Our analysis suggests that five factors have contributed to the success of the new international accounting standards. With the exception of competition among national regulators, these factors track those that contribute to the success of domestic transparency standards:

- a costly information problem
- competition among national regulators to influence international standards
- support from multinational corporations
- the influence of established groups representing investors' interests
- crises that highlighted the need for international standards.

We consider each of these factors in turn.

A Growing Information Problem Creates Costly Confusion

Rigorous international reporting standards gained support because they addressed a growing information problem. The problem was that companies headquartered in different countries added up their profits and losses in different ways.

Beginning in the 1930s, the United States had produced voluminous, specific accounting rules that reflected a considerable tolerance of risk, focused on the needs of public shareholders, were independent of tax calculations, and allowed companies relatively little discretion. Seventy years later, those rules exceeded a hundred thousand pages in length. By contrast, France, Germany, Japan, and other civil-law countries had produced less voluminous, less specific accounting rules that reflected a relatively risk-averse approach to business, focused on the needs of banks and other creditors, combined investor and taxation data, and allowed companies considerable discretion in their application.

Regulators Compete to Control International Transparency

At the same time, international organizations and regulators in dominant markets competed to control the terms of international accounting. The United Nations, the European Commission, the United States, and a group of international accountants oriented toward U.S. and U.K. traditions each maneuvered for three decades to gain international recognition of international accounting standards that reflected their unique political and economic interests.

However, by the mid-1990s, both U.S. and European regulators had concluded that other nations would not accept their systems of financial reporting as the international standard, and the UN had dropped out of the competition. Instead, U.S. and European authorities focused their efforts on competing to influence the financial reporting standards being drafted by the private-sector IASC. Making a qualified commitment to allow reporting on U.S. exchanges using such standards by 2007, U.S. regulators lobbied successfully to gain the United States a position as a nonvoting member of the IASC board and to participate in board discussions, comment on drafts, and provide research and technical assistance to the committee.[21]

Meanwhile, European Commission officials attempted to gain leverage by warning that each standard would be subject to European Union (EU) endorsement to assure that it furthered European public interest, was understandable, and presented no conflict with European accounting principles.

In 2002, the commission formally required most publicly traded companies headquartered in the EU to adopt the private-sector-created international accounting standards by 2005.[22] Adoption of a single set of accounting rules represented an important step toward creating a single European market, and the commission preferred IASC rules to increasing dominance by the United States as international standard setter.

The IASC responded by strengthening its own status as an expert body while providing procedures to structure nations' participation in standard setting. In 2002, the committee reorganized as the International Accounting Standards Board (IASB). The board's guidelines provided for published agendas, open meetings, notice and comment concerning rule making, and other due process requirements. By 2005, the new board had issued a virtually complete set of accounting standards.[23]

Multinational Companies Embrace Transparency

Some multinational corporations also found reasons to favor rigorous international disclosure. As securities markets integrated, such companies increasingly listed on more than one country's stock exchange. Such cross-listing created new reporting costs. At least as important, it created new credibility costs when national rules produced different balance sheets. In an often-cited example, Daimler-Benz, the first German company to adopt U.S. disclosure rules, reported 1993 profits of $102 million using German accounting standards but net losses of nearly $579 million under U.S. rules.[24] "[I]n the end nobody knew whether the company was making a profit or suffering a loss," noted Karel van Hulle, accounting administrator for the European Commission.[25] To avoid such confusion, many multinational firms advocated one set of international standards.

Influential Groups Represent Users' Interests

Meanwhile, a number of well-established groups representing the interests of dispersed investors began to call for more rigorous disclosure policies. Each group had its own reasons for doing so. Institutional investors supported rigorous accounting rules in order to strengthen their market positions. In the United States and Europe, pension funds, mutual funds, and other institutional investors favored international standards so they could diversify abroad without having to expend resources on interpreting financial standards created in accordance with multiple policies. By 2002, a McKinsey survey reported that 90 percent of large institutional investors favored an international financial accounting system.[26]

Major stock exchanges in mature markets also favored international accounting standards as a way of reducing barriers to foreign listings, which represented an important growth opportunity for them. From 1990 to 2003, for example, the proportion of New York Stock Exchange companies based outside the United States grew from one in fifteen to one in six.[27] The New York Stock Exchange's 1994 adoption of "The world puts its stock in us" as its motto reflected both a new reality and the exchange's strategy for future growth.

Accounting firms themselves led the effort to create international standards. Although they worked for disclosing corporations, accounting firms prospered only if they also served the interests of information users. Multiple conflicting corporate balance sheets not only confused investors but also raised doubts about the credibility of accounts and accountants. Therefore, as we have noted, the big accounting firms began working through the International Federation of Accountants (IFAC) to promote auditing, ethics, and education reforms to strengthen the administration of international standards, and international accounting firms provided the bulk of the funding for the International Accounting Standards Committee from the 1970s on.[28]

Crises Add Momentum for Rigorous Reporting

Finally, crises such as the Asian financial collapse of the mid-1990s mobilized pro-disclosure interests by highlighting the need for greater international transparency. Crises demonstrated the growing volatility and interdependence of national economies, the ineffectiveness of conventional stabilizing measures, and the high cost to be paid in economic decline and human suffering for inaccurate and incomplete financial information.[29] In fact, corporate accounting flaws did not play a central role in the Asian crisis. Nonetheless, the economic destabilization that accompanied the crisis spurred moves toward improvements in both government and corporate disclosure systems that were endorsed by the International Monetary Fund (IMF), the G-7, and U.S. and European regulators.[30]

The U.S. accounting scandals in 2001–2002 demonstrated that U.S. accounting rules failed to provide full disclosure of potential risks to investors. Humbled U.S. officials suggested they might even drop the requirement that non-U.S. companies follow U.S. reporting rules. "If we think the international approach is better or equal, we will propose moving" in that direction, conceded Robert Herz, chairman of the Financial Accounting Standards Board.[31]

Countervailing Pressures Reduce Harmonization

While the confluence of all these factors created a situation in which a rigorous international transparency system rapidly gained momentum, countervailing pressures slowed harmonization. As proposals for new accounting standards became more specific, national interests began to diverge. In 2004–2005, for example, a dispute about how to account for derivative financial instruments erupted into accusations by French bankers and European regulators that international standards lacked accountability and were too oriented toward U.S. disclosure traditions. National regulators, including those representing the EU and the United States, announced that they would review international standards one at a time, reject those that conflicted with national laws, and continue to treat the others as supplementary to national rules.[32] In addition, it remained uncertain how much the fact that disclosure rules were based on the immediate needs of current dominant markets would limit the rules' future adaptability to reporting needs in China, Vietnam, and other emerging markets that did not share Anglo-American traditions.

Variable national capacities created additional roadblocks to international standards. Many countries and companies simply lacked the talent and resources to adopt sophisticated new accounting rules. National enforcement authority and practices varied widely even among major industrialized countries. In February 2003, the *Economist* reported that "Europe's systems for ensuring the accuracy of company accounts look full of holes." Auditors faced few restrictions on their non-audit work (creating potential conflicts of interest), and most securities regulators lacked authority to investigate flawed reporting. In six EU countries, the European Federation of Accountants concluded that there was no enforcement of accounting rules at all.[33]

U.S. and European regulators as well as international accounting organizations initiated efforts to educate, train, and monitor regulators and accountants in less-advanced countries.[34] Still, the variability of national practices continued to pose a challenge to the effectiveness of international standards.

In addition, some disclosing corporations opposed more rigorous financial transparency. Companies with concentrated ownership and limited need for outside capital had little to gain and sometimes much to lose from stricter disclosure. They benefited from keeping information secret from competitors, avoiding litigation, and maintaining tightly controlled systems of corporate governance.[35] Smaller stock exchanges, too, might suffer from great uniformity if companies sought greater liquidity by listing on larger exchanges abroad.[36]

In addition, domestic crises provoked some government actions that raised, rather than lowered, barriers to international capital flows. New rules adopted in the wake of the corporate scandals of 2001–2002, for example, increased requirements associated with listing on U.S. exchanges.

Legitimacy Issues Undermine Transparency Efforts

More important, the effectiveness of international standards was also threatened by continuing doubts about their legitimacy. To be effective, international targeted transparency policies had to be accepted as legitimate by information disclosers, users, and officials of national governments. Could a policy that emerged from a private-sector group gain acceptance as a public mandate? Anne-Marie Slaughter notes that it is problematic for private actors to uphold the public trust, since "corporate and civic actors may be driven by profits and passions, respectively."[37]

Initially, international standards followed what Robert Keohane and Joseph Nye have called the "club model" of legitimacy, in which self-appointed experts bargain over public issues. In Keohane's analysis, this model has become less and less tenable in international governance. He suggests that there are three core elements of legitimacy: *accountability*, *participation*, and *deliberation*. Accountability depends on the adequacy of chains of delegation between international institutions, national governments, and national mechanisms that allow national publics to monitor international institutions. Participation is facilitated by processes such as public agendas and open meetings. Deliberation benefits from the free flow of information and from inclusion of diverse groups and interpretation by objective third parties.[38] In Keohane's view, network-based disclosure systems such as international financial accounting are particularly prone to "democratic deficits," since their links to accountable democratic processes may be weak or indirect and their procedures for due process and other aspects of administrative fairness may not be well developed.[39]

When examined through the lens of Keohane's analysis, the emerging system of international financial accounting illustrates some of the conflicts that must be resolved if an international transparency system is to achieve legitimacy. The reformed IASB remained a private-sector deliberative body that relied on existing national regulators and enforcement mechanisms to carry out disclosure requirements. Decision making was designed to provide insulation from national politics, with a governing board of accounting experts who explicitly did *not* represent national constituencies. The board consisted of twelve members in 2006: three from the United States, two from the U.K., and one each from Germany, France, Sweden, South Africa, Canada, Australia, and Japan.[40]

The board members, in turn, were selected by an International Accounting Standards Committee Foundation (IASCF), which exercised general oversight. Its nineteen-member self-perpetuating board of trustees was designed to be "representative of the world's capital markets and a diversity of geographical and professional backgrounds" as well as "financially knowledgeable." Foundation trustees served three-year terms, with a limit of two terms and with a chair elected by the trustees.[41]

In other ways, however, the international accounting system was structured to promote legitimacy. Under 2002 rules, IASB meetings were required to be public. Ten of twelve board members served full-time, and board members were limited to two five-year terms. The board and affiliated organizations employed a professional staff, and their deliberations were supplemented by the International Financial Reporting Interpretations Committee and the geographically diverse Standards Advisory Council. (In 2006, the Standards Advisory Council consisted of four members from North America, fourteen Europeans, two Africans, nine from the Asia-Pacific region, three Latin Americans, and an Israeli, as well as seven representatives of international organizations.)[42]

Linkages to public and private networks also promoted legitimacy. A network of national securities regulators, the International Organization of Securities Commissions (IOSCO), brought together regulatory agencies from over a hundred countries to cooperate on financial regulation, including accounting oversight, and to support the board as international standard setter.[43] The International Federation of Accountants (IFAC), a membership organization of international accountants, led the effort to create international standards and worked to improve domestic and international accounting practices.[44]

Nonetheless, acceptance of international accounting standards by governments, investors, and companies was not assured in 2006. Debates continued concerning "fair-value" versus "historical-cost" accounting, the use of complex rules versus simpler principles, and the dynamics of enforcement. European representatives expressed growing impatience with what they considered to be the Anglo-American tilt of proposed rules, which they argued could increase the volatility of earnings reports and substantially change profit and loss statements. A spokesman for the EU noted, "We are in favour of convergence, but convergence somewhere in the middle of the Atlantic as opposed to somewhere on Staten Island."[45]

Are International Accounting Standards Effective?

Researchers have begun to examine the impact of international accounting standards. They have found initial evidence that standards are sustainable along the dimensions discussed in detail in Chapter 5. They have confirmed that international accounting standards are more rigorous than many national accounting systems. They require higher-quality disclosure (better measurement, more information, timelier reporting) than national accounting systems outside of the United States and U.K.[46]

Researchers have suggested that comparability of financial information across markets is an important factor in encouraging international investment. A 2003 study by investigators at Harvard and the University of Pennsylvania found that U.S. institutional investors invested more heavily in foreign firms whose financial statements and accounting methods conformed fairly closely to rigorous disclosure rules.[47] Other inquiries have found that international standards help to reduce information imbalances between companies and investors at least as well as U.S. standards.[48] Firms that engage in more rigorous disclosure than required in their home country seem to experience lower bid-ask spreads, higher trading volume, and lower share price volatility. (The bid-ask spread is the difference between the price at which market makers will purchase shares – the bid price – and the price at which they will sell – the ask price.)[49]

Lessons to date from the evolving system of international financial accounting suggest that targeted transparency policies may be effective in reducing risks, even if they originate in private networks and outside the recognized bounds of international governance. A small voluntary disclosure system grew into a user-oriented and improving public mandate because it addressed serious information gaps, benefited from the advocacy of groups that represented the needs of dispersed information users, and tapped into the core interests of national regulators and some disclosing companies. But differing national interests, traditions, and capacities may limit harmonization in practice, creating an illusion of international uniformity that masks variable reporting.

IMPROVING A MORIBUND SYSTEM: INTERNATIONAL DISEASE REPORTING

International transparency policies need to improve over time for the same reasons as national policies – because political compromises almost always produce initial systems that are weak and incomplete, because organizations that stand to lose from greater openness game the system, and because policies must keep pace with changing markets, changing science, and changing public priorities. Continuing improvement is particularly difficult to achieve in international transparency systems since consensus among nations often requires overcoming dominant national interests, as illustrated by the next case – international reporting of infectious diseases.

Disease reporting represented one of the earliest international efforts to employ transparency as a policy tool. Starting in the mid-nineteenth century, nations joined forces to control the spread of infectious disease and reduce resulting interruptions in trade and travel. Transparency in the form of rapid reporting of disease outbreaks was recognized as critical to preventing the spread of deaths and illnesses. Beginning in 1951, the World Health Organization (WHO), an arm of the United Nations governed by a World Health Assembly (now representing 192 member governments),[50] required governments to disclose cases of specified infectious diseases within set time periods. The organization also mandated specific public health activities at ports and airports, as well as trade and travel restrictions.[51]

But by the mid-1990s, this policy was languishing. The reporting system covered only three diseases – plague, cholera, and yellow fever – and had never been updated to deal with devastating new threats, including the spread of AIDS. Also, the WHO's surveillance system relied on reporting by national governments that often ignored even the narrow reporting requirements. As David Fidler of Indiana University notes, "WHO member states routinely violated their . . . obligations to report outbreaks of diseases subject to the Regulations" out of fear of economic repercussions.[52] Such failures reflected the fact that countries had different incentives to report or withhold information. Reporting failures were tolerated in part because U.S. and European officials turned their attention elsewhere as vaccines and antibiotics minimized common infectious diseases.

In the 1970s and 1980s, however, a resurgence of infectious diseases and the AIDS epidemic reawakened U.S. and European governments' concern about disease spread and highlighted the failings of the WHO system. Finally, in 1995, the World Health Assembly directed the WHO to revise the failed government-centered reporting system, a slow and difficult process.[53]

Meanwhile, networks of public and private groups began to use the capabilities of information technology and the Internet to put new reporting mechanisms into practice. In 2000, WHO officials joined with other public and private groups to legitimize one of those efforts – the creation of the Global Outbreak Alert and Response Network to pool public and private sources for rapid identification and confirmation of and response to international outbreaks of disease.[54]

However, it was a public health crisis – the sudden spread of SARS in 2002–2003 – that truly brought disease reporting into the information age. Tragically, the disease spread quickly while information flowed slowly. Starting with a small outbreak in China's Guangdong Province in November 2002, SARS reached thirty countries in six months, killing an estimated 774 people. Thanks to the speed of international travel, it spread to five countries within twenty-four hours from one infected individual in a Hong Kong hotel.[55]

Transparency failures helped promote the spread of the disease. It took four months for the Chinese government to acknowledge the SARS outbreak and for the WHO to respond with a global alert (March 12, 2003),[56] despite much earlier reporting by ordinary citizens in millions of cell phone and Internet messages and by the private ProMED-mail system.[57] The lack of timely, accurate information not only contributed to deaths and serious illnesses but also fueled public fears that resulted in huge economic costs, estimated at $40 billion.[58]

Once the outbreak was confirmed, however, the WHO and public health authorities around the world responded quickly and creatively with new transparency measures. They cobbled together informal networks that enabled them to communicate directly with the public through daily Web updates, satellite broadcasts, and news conferences. Through the nascent Global Response Network, sixty teams of medical personnel moved to control the disease in affected areas while a network of eleven infectious disease laboratories in nine countries worked on causes and diagnosis, linked by a secure Web site and daily conference calls. Within a month, collaborating researchers were able to identify the disease's cause. Even without formal authorization from its members to do so, the WHO recommended against nonessential travel to Hong Kong, Guangdong Province, Beijing, and Toronto, Canada. U.S. and Canadian authorities issued broader warnings against unnecessary travel to China, Singapore, Hanoi, and Hong Kong.[59]

Meanwhile, the Chinese government, much criticized for its initial transparency failures, worked to catch up. China declared a nationwide war on SARS in April 2003, apologized for not informing the public more quickly about the outbreak, pledged accurate and timely reporting in the future, created a public hotline, and replaced the national health minister and Beijing's mayor for their roles in the cover-up. Chinese officials shut down government offices, schools, and universities in affected areas and instituted quarantines to prevent public gatherings and stop travel.[60]

By July 2003, the epidemic was under control. After the fact, WHO members renewed their commitment to revise International Health Regulations, acknowledged the legitimacy of the WHO's impromptu travel advisories, and endorsed the legitimacy of using nongovernmental sources of information for surveillance.[61]

A WHO report concluded that the SARS crisis showed how failure to disclose outbreaks could lead to "loss of credibility in the eyes of the international community, escalating negative domestic economic impact, damage to health and economics of neighboring countries, and a very real risk that outbreaks within the country's own territory can spiral out of control."[62]

On the positive side, the crisis played a central role in improving international transparency to reduce public health risks. The SARS outbreak spurred action by national governments that stood to benefit from timely reporting and demonstrated that attempts to hide information about outbreaks could carry a high price in reputational damage and in the promotion of public fears that cycled out of control in the absence of reliable information. Crisis also mobilized powerful intermediaries such as public health authorities, hospitals, and private information networks, as well as ordinary citizens themselves, to improve both public disclosure and specialized information-sharing networks.

Finally, SARS provided an early demonstration of the power of information technology to transform international transparency systems. Electronic networks of ordinary citizens in China were the first to express concern that a new disease was spreading and suggest that the government was covering up the full extent of public health risks. David Fidler notes that "[i]nformation provided by non-state actors provided the catalyst for WHO and other countries to intensify pressure on the Chinese government."[63] In effect, the users of information also became its sources, pooling their fragments of knowledge to map the spread of a deadly disease.

Legitimacy remains a difficult issue for international disease monitoring. Such monitoring traditionally was anchored in a formal agreement among nations, which created more legitimacy than characterized the private efforts to establish international financial accounting standards, for example. But informal practice, driven by immediate crisis, departed from formal agreement terms. As we have seen, WHO officials had to rely on nongovernmental information during the SARS crisis and issue advisories without authorization from its governing World Health Assembly. In response to that crisis, the WHO issued new international health regulations in May 2005, which are scheduled to enter into force in 2007.[64]

Whether and how quickly the WHO and national authorities will integrate new transparency mechanisms into international disease surveillance also remains to be seen. Where resources and talent are scarce and other priorities pressing, as in many developing countries, progress depends not only on political will but also on how much assistance nations with advanced medical capacity are willing to offer.

In addition the evolution of international infectious disease surveillance shows how crisis and the Internet can help to improve the sustainability of targeted transparency. Crisis can tip the political balance in favor of more rigorous disclosure by coalescing the interests of diverse information users around the world. The Internet, in turn, can lower the costs of sharing information, make it easier to customize data, provide instantaneous communication, and empower information users. Whether these opportunities lead to lasting improvements in targeted transparency systems depends on the will and energy of policymakers in each case.

THE LIMITS OF INTERNATIONAL TRANSPARENCY: LABELING GENETICALLY MODIFIED FOODS

International efforts to resolve how and whether to label foods made from genetically modified crops have so far made little progress. With nations' core interests deeply divided, a European labeling regime that remained costly and did not meet consumers' needs, an ingredient-segregation process prone to errors, and no constituency powerful enough to improve the system, this targeted transparency effort remained ineffective in 2006.

Safety and environmental issues concerning genetically modified (GM) foods spread from the United States to Europe and developing countries beginning in the mid-1990s. Initially, GM corn, soy, and other crops provided resistance to pests, pesticides, or herbicides, or provided extra vitamins, proteins, or other nutrients. In the future, GM plants promised drought resistance and immunity to or treatments for specific diseases. However, the creation of new allergens and environmental effects remained a concern.[65]

Primed by earlier food scares that were unrelated to genetic modification, the European public responded to the sudden introduction of GM foods in 1996 and 1997 with fear. The EU regulated genetically modified crops as a novel health and environmental issue. Employing a precautionary principle of approving foods only when scientific evidence proved them safe, the EU required thorough review and risk assessment for each field trial and product introduction. In the United States, by contrast, government officials decided to approve GM crops on a case-by-case basis, using conventional safety criteria.

In the late 1990s, European Union member states placed a de facto moratorium on importing bulk shipments of products that might contain unapproved GM organisms, and they required labels on packaged foods containing GM corn or soy. The United States rapidly increased production of GM crops.

The European ban proved extremely costly for developing countries, many of whose farmers relied on European markets for their crops. Zambia, Zimbabwe, Mozambique, and Malawi rejected U.S. food aid in 2002 because shipments contained genetically modified corn, despite near-famine conditions. The corn was meant for famine-relief consumption, not planting. But African officials feared that some of it might find its way into farmers' fields and threaten their access to European markets.

In 2004, the EU adopted an exacting system for labeling and tracking GM foods and animal feed. In principle, labeling was not an unreasonable approach to resolving this international puzzle. Europe, the United States, and developing countries shared an interest in promoting efficient food markets, yet the attitudes of their publics and governments toward GM food differed widely. Why not use labeling to promote informed choice without imposing any explicit restrictions on these foods?

In practice, however, differences in nations' fundamental views of whether risks warranted public action and in the economic interests of importing and exporting nations led to a costly stalemate over labeling. Responding to its voters' acceptance of GM crops and its farmers' economic interests in planting them, the United States did not require labeling. In voluntary guidelines, the Food and Drug Administration (FDA) recommended that any labels that companies did employ feature statements that products were (or were not) genetically engineered or were (or were not) made using biotechnology, rather than statements that products were "GM free," since some degree of contamination was unavoidable.[66] In an unrelated regulatory change, the United States introduced rules to standardize labeling of organic foods, a growing portion of the U.S. food market. Those rules included a requirement that foods labeled organic could not contain genetically modified ingredients.[67]

The high costs of tracking and labeling created an economic disincentive to plant GM crops for farmers who sold to European importers. In effect, labeling prevented many farmers in developing countries from planting such crops, since few had the capacity to segregate crops and maintain an audit trail. Nor did managers of grain elevators, railroad cars, processing facilities, and food manufacturing plants in developing countries have the capacity to

Figure 6.1.　European No-GMO Label. Photo by David Weil, June 2005

build separate facilities for conventional and GM grains. Even U.S. officials estimated that crop segregation and tracking requirements to export GM crops to Europe might increase food production costs by 10 to 30 percent.[68]

Labeling was also of questionable value in communicating with a fearful public. There were many different genetic modification processes. Each had different potential environmental and health consequences. Simply labeling foods as genetically modified did not provide consumers with any factual information about variable health or environmental risks of specific GM ingredients. See Figure 6.1 for an example of labels.

In addition, EU officials admitted that creating products with absolutely no GM ingredients was simply infeasible. That meant that consumers who wanted to avoid consumption of genetically modified corn or soy could not do so. In Europe, regulators wrote the rules so that "GM-free" products could contain 0.9 per cent of genetically modified corn or soy.[69]

The European public wanted the facts but did not get them. A careful study of public perceptions about GM crops in five European countries, sponsored by the European Commission and conducted in 1998–2000, found that European consumers were neither categorically supportive of nor opposed to genetic modification. Instead, they wanted to know about specific risks, benefits, and uncertainties – precisely the kind of detail that labeling did *not* provide. Furthermore, with memories of reassurances about mad cow disease still fresh, Europeans were generally distrustful of any messages from authorities – corporate promises of benefits or government reassurances about safety.[70] Labeling simply for the presence or absence of genetic modification, therefore, could feed public fears without fostering informed choices.

Legitimacy remained an issue as well. Many of the European Union member countries continued a de facto ban on the import of GM grains as of 2006, despite the European Commission's efforts to replace the ban with the new labeling system. Meanwhile, the United States and exporting companies challenged the EU's ban in the World Trade Organization (WTO) as an unauthorized restraint of trade. In February, 2006, the WTO ruled that the ban was not based on scientific evidence, raising questions about whether member states would capitulate, accept fines, or appeal. The WTO issued a final decision on September 29, 2006.[71]

Persistent scientific uncertainties meant that polarized debate about the safety and environmental effects of GM crops was likely to continue. In the United States, the National Research Council remained supportive of the benefits of GM crops but also emphasized the importance of assessing each product individually because of potential risks from allergens, contamination of other plants, or damage to insects or animals. Meanwhile, the Research Directorate General of the EU, as well as French and British authorities, acknowledged that no human health or environmental problems have yet been associated with GM crops, but they also cautioned about potential long-term risks. The truth was that a great deal still was not known about the effects of genetic modification of foods.

As of 2006, a transparency system that labeled genetically modified foods seemed unlikely to prove sustainable or effective. The central problems remained disagreements among nations about whether there was a safety problem that called for mandated disclosure and the conflicting economic interests of importing and exporting nations. Tracking and labeling were not yet embedded even in the practices of the member nations of the European Union. There appeared to be little inclination by nations outside Europe to adopt similar rules. At least in its early years, GM labeling failed to improve public safety or market efficiency, its two intended purposes.

These three cases suggest how important it is for designers of international transparency policies to start by asking how people make choices and how new information might inform and improve those choices. International financial reporting gained strength because it responded to the information needs of investors, analysts, competitors, and disclosing companies. Infectious disease surveillance gained strength because it employed computer power and the Internet to respond to an urgent need for information about the spread of SARS.

However, these cases also suggest that the conditions for effective international transparency are even more demanding than those for effective domestic policies. The most difficult challenge remains that of gaining legitimacy. Only those policies that are authorized by treaties or other formal agreements among governments gain legitimacy easily. International policies with weak or indirect links to democratic processes create a "democratic deficit," meaning that they lack strong links to democratically accountable decision processes.[72] Both the small private-sector effort that produced international financial reporting and the ad hoc responses by public health authorities to the SARS crisis raised legitimacy issues that have not yet been fully resolved.

One remedy would be for national governments to reach an informal consensus concerning appropriate participation and accountability measures for international transparency systems. Such a consensus could provide a baseline from which designers of new policies could improvise. Over time, such a consensus might produce increasing convergence concerning due process, equal protection, and other administrative principles.[73]

Designers of international transparency policies also face special hurdles in embedding requirements in national decision making. Virtually all international transparency policies rely on actions by national governments for implementation, enforcement, maintenance, and repair. Ultimately, their effectiveness depends on mobilizing national rule-making and enforcement authority. Policymakers therefore struggle to establish standardized disclosure rules while tailoring reporting requirements to fit the priorities and traditions of participating nations, with their diverse cultural backgrounds, educational patterns, and social and economic priorities. An understanding of variable national will and capacities, and a commitment to provide capacity-strengthening assistance is therefore central to the success of international transparency systems.

Where national variations persist, effectiveness will depend on making those variations themselves transparent. Pragmatic partial harmonization may be a workable compromise if policymakers create transparency concerning national differences. In the case of international financial reporting, each nation will determine over time what degree of harmonization with international accounting standards makes sense politically and economically. Those with strong interests in convergence of accounting rules might join in a limited network of countries that commit to high-quality, strictly comparable, rigorously enforced disclosure standards. Others might accept some but not all standards or adopt standards on paper that are not fully put into practice. Individual companies might also find reasons to follow international standards with varying degrees of rigor. Such mixed reporting will not provide full comparability. The more variations are transparent, however, the more investors can still discern relative risks.

Competition among transparency regimes might even provide benefits. It could create incentives for countries to continue to experiment in order to improve their measures, perhaps creating a further "race to the top" among nations and companies vying for the highest standards of transparency.

Our analysis of three international cases suggests that, for the most part, the structure, workings, and effectiveness of international policies parallel those of national policies. That is significant because it means that national and international transparency systems represent variations on a single governance theme. It also means that designers of national and international transparency systems can learn a great deal from one another to the benefit of both.

SEVEN

Toward Collaborative Transparency

The brief but serious SARS pandemic of 2003 showed how crisis can revive a moribund international transparency policy. The response to this new and sometimes fatal disease also provided an intriguing glimpse into the future by suggesting how communication technologies can transform the way transparency systems work.

As noted earlier, emails, cell phone calls, and Internet chatroom messages from health-care workers and villagers in China's Guangdong Province in late 2002 and early 2003 first spread the word that people were falling ill from a mysterious respiratory illness. As the Chinese government continued to deny the existence of such an illness, private electronic trackers of infectious diseases, such as ProMED-mail, picked up the electronic traffic and warned that the outbreak might be caused by a previously unknown virus that attacked the respiratory system.[1]

Officially, the United Nations' World Health Organization (WHO) could not act on this information. Under its rules, which could only be changed by a vote of its 192 member nations, the WHO was supposed to respond only to government alerts. However, spurred by messages from ordinary citizens and private aggregators of data, the WHO continued to press the Chinese government for information. Confronted with de facto public knowledge, the government finally acknowledged the outbreak. In response, the WHO issued a global alert on March 12, 2003, and a travel advisory on March 15.

But by then it was already too late. SARS had infected travelers. It would spread to thirty countries in six months, killing 774 people and causing an estimated $40 billion in economic losses.[2] After the epidemic was over, the WHO's member nations changed its rules to allow the organization to respond to citizen messages as well as government alerts.

It is not too far-fetched to contend that the SARS public health crisis resulted mainly from a failure of transparency. Heeding those early messages

151

from villagers and local authorities in Guangdong Province might have averted a worldwide pandemic.

This glimpse of a technology-enabled future revealed that the ordinary citizens who have traditionally been the users of information could become also its sources. Villagers shared fragments of experience. Collectively, those fragments formed a compelling mosaic of a rapidly spreading infectious disease and ultimately spurred international action. In effect, geographically dispersed individuals collectively created their own transparency system using new communication technology. That system in turn changed the character of international infectious disease reporting.

INNOVATION AT THE EDGE

It is now commonplace to note that the Internet, personal computers, cell phones, remote sensing, advanced bar coding, and other leaps in information and communication technology have revolutionized the ways in which people generate and share knowledge. Transparency systems have by no means escaped these changes. To the contrary, a new generation of technology-enabled collaborative transparency is emerging as entrepreneurs, activists, regulators, and citizens invent new ways to collect, process, and distribute information.

It is still too early to predict the precise forms that third-generation transparency will take. But we can discern some of the common characteristics of such systems, suggest how they work, and consider some of the benefits they might create and some of the dangers they will face.

The next generation of transparency will likely differ from second-generation targeted transparency in two important ways. First, third-generation transparency, enabled by information and communication technologies, will empower information users themselves to provide and pool much of the essential data. By contrast, recall that second-generation systems rely upon regulators and/or self-reporting by disclosers.

Second, the methods through which users gain access to data – the "front ends" of "user interfaces" of third-generation transparency – will become much more interactive and customized, and they will be revised at a much faster pace. Users gain access to second-generation transparency systems through signage, labels, printed reports, and sometimes Web pages. Often, these channels are difficult to change in response to user feedback, new sources of data, and the changing shape of policy problems. Early experiences indicate that a hallmark of third-generation transparency systems will be that entrepreneurs – from the civic, private, and governmental sectors – will compete with one another to develop ever more effective human interfaces. In an analogy to consumer electronics, if gaining access to second-generation transparency data is like programming a 1980s-era VCR, gaining access to third-generation data may be more like rotating the ubiquitous iPod click wheel.

We call these third-generation systems "collaborative" policies because – in contrast to first- or second-generation transparency – we anticipate that they will result from closer collaboration between the designers of transparency policies and their users. They will also facilitate the collaborative production and use of information by users themselves. Though we discuss many examples of Internet-enabled information search and collaboration in this chapter, none of these qualify as full-blown third-generation collaborative transparency systems. Today, third-generation transparency is evolving piecemeal at the edges of second-generation policies.

Third-generation systems share the fundamental features of their predecessors even as they are deeply transformed by new technologies and the social practices that accompany them (features not shared with second-generation policies are italicized):

- disclosure of factual information from target organizations *and from technology-facilitated pooled experience of information users*
- concerning specific products and practices
- in standardized, disaggregated, comparable formats
- *employing interactivity, data customization, and other capabilities of information technology*
- in order to further a policy purpose *with government playing a key role as convener and facilitator.*

As transformative as they can be, communication and information technologies will not, however, allow transparency policies to escape the political, economic, and regulatory dynamics that govern second-generation targeted disclosure systems.

Collaborative transparency policies work in essentially the same way as second-generation targeted transparency policies, with information technology contributing to each step of the "action cycle" described in Chapter 4. Information users perceive and understand new information (some of which is provided through their own efforts) and incorporate new information in their everyday choices. Target organizations note users' changed choices and, in turn, alter products and practices in ways that reduce risks or improve performance. Likewise, the political sustainability of collaborative policies is still powerfully affected by the degree to which targeted organizations have differing interests in information disclosure and by the engagement of key users and user intermediaries in political processes, as we discussed in Chapter 5.

Collaborative transparency policies, however, promise to alter the dynamics of sustainability and effectiveness described in the preceding chapters. We explore these transformations by first reviewing how information technology expands the capacities of users, disclosers, and the government. We then analyze examples in environmental protection, public health, auto safety, and school performance in which information technologies have already enhanced second-generation policies. Next, we consider several major challenges that third-generation systems will face. Finally, we offer some preliminary ideas about how third-generation transparency changes the roles of information users, disclosing organizations, and government.

It is worth recalling that the three generations of transparency policies remain complementary. Just as targeted transparency did not replace or lessen the importance of right-to-know measures, collaborative transparency does not replace targeted measures. Instead, many hybrid transparency systems are likely to flourish.

TECHNOLOGY EXPANDS CAPACITIES OF USERS, DISCLOSERS, AND GOVERNMENT

Even though technology-driven change is still in its early stages and has not yet produced full third-generation transparency systems, it is rapidly transforming the capacities of individuals and groups to collect, process, and share information. Such change is also raising expectations about when, where, and how fast information people use in daily life will be provided and shared. Along the way, such advances are altering the roles of citizens, businesses, and government.[3]

Information Users Develop New Skills and Habits

For citizens and consumers, new opportunities to gather and share information instantly, customize it to serve specific needs, and work interactively with others are changing the way people decide where to live and work, select one product over another, choose schools or airlines, and decide how to participate in public life.

Many individuals have become accustomed to actively seeking out electronically provided information in order to find everything from apartments and dates to candidates to support for public office.

A survey conducted by the Pew Internet and American Life project in June 2004 found that the 107 million Americans who used search engines conducted about 3.9 billion Internet searches a month, about half from home and half from work. Forty-four percent reported that they urgently needed the information they were seeking, and most people (87 percent) reported that they found the information they were looking for most of the time. Half of American adults searched for health information.[4] Seventy-five million Americans sought political information on the Internet during the 2004 campaign.[5] In surveys in 2004 and 2005 the Pew Project found that 60 million Americans had turned to the Internet for help with major life decisions, up from 45 million in 2002 surveys. People sought help with major investments, job changes, illnesses, and voting choices.

Electronic fact-finding did not take place in a vacuum, however. It interacted with established social networks. The Internet helped people tap their acquaintances for advice, find experts, and provide information to compare options.[6] Aggressive seekers circulated newly discovered information around the world – without the need for intermediaries such as researchers, journalists, interest groups, or government officials. Barry Wellman has termed such technologically enhanced decision-making "networked individualism."[7]

In addition to new social habits of information search, millions of individuals are becoming accustomed to providing information to each other through the new communication technologies rather than relying on professionals. In their earliest incarnations, information technologies provided mechanisms for user collaboration around issues of common interest (for example, a large user group on the precursor to the Web was designed for Honda owners to share their experiences) and for the exchange of medical information.[8]

The communicative infrastructure of the World Wide Web itself made it even easier for ordinary individuals to become information providers and so engendered new habits of social and public information pooling. Hundreds of thousands of threaded discussions on corporate, organizational, and individual Web pages allow users to share information on everything from consumer electronics to diseases that they suffer from to the latest political intrigue or corporate disaster.[9] Millions of bloggers around the world share their thoughts about life in Baghdad, presidential politics, the latest computer designs, and nearly every other conceivable subject for a worldwide virtual audience. Wikis allow anyone to contribute to collaborative Web entries. Wikipedia, the online collaborative encyclopedia, has nearly 4 million pages of entries.[10]

On Web pages like epinions.com, babycenter.com, hotornot.com, and countless other commercial sites, users review products and services for the benefit of others, becoming active participants in the construction of specialized knowledge.[11] But active customers not only critique products, they also design them. Dell invites purchasers to design their own computers and then delivers them in days. Levi's invites customers to design their own jeans, using computer-created images for exact measurements. Nike's Times Square billboard invites passersby to use their cell phones on the spot to customize and order the shoes shown in digital splendor above. Eric Von Hippel, scholar of innovation at MIT's Sloan School, has argued that communities of "lead users" who modify products to improve them and suit them to particular needs are proliferating and becoming a major force in cutting-edge design. In one survey, for example, 22 percent of surgeons customized surgical equipment to suit their needs. In the consumer realm, 38 percent of "extreme" sports aficionados and 20 percent of mountain bikers report that they develop or modify products for their own use.[12] Customers also tailor services to suit their specific preferences and needs. Fidelity.com, for example, has created online tools that help clients design their own retirement investment plans.

Users' growing technological sophistication and accompanying expectations are not confined to commercial transactions and the search for the best-fitting pair of jeans or running shoes, however. Information-empowered users have begun to transform public debate and policy outcomes. Photos taken by individual soldiers in the American-run Abu Ghraib prison in Iraq and posted on the Web created an international debate about torturing prisoners of war in 2004. Reports by thousands of cell phone– and Internet-empowered citizens alerted authorities to the seriousness of the disaster caused by hurricane Katrina in 2005 and the failure of government relief efforts.

Businesses Gain New Challengers and Choices

Information technology is also changing the capacities of companies and other organizations to run operations efficiently, ascertain customers' preferences, and design and market products effectively. Plummeting communication costs and new communication options, along with shrinking trade barriers and transportation costs, are creating new and specialized competitors to many traditional businesses.

In *Blown to Bits*, Philip Evans and Thomas S. Wurster remind readers that "[e]very business is an information business."[13] "[B]usiness units, industries, supply chains, customer relationships, organizational structure . . . are held together by a 'glue,' and that glue is essentially information. The glue gets dissolved by new technologies." As a result, "evolving technological capabilities for sharing and using information can transform business definitions, industry definitions, and competitive advantage. . . . [T]he most stable of industries, the most focused of business models, and the strongest of brands can be blown to bits by new information technology."[14]

Some of the most visible signs of these changes are the sudden growth of Web competitors such as Amazon.com and Netflix.com, the outsourcing of specialized tasks to locations where they can be most efficiently performed, and the growth of new kinds of partnerships that form business networks.

Advances in information technology open new competitive strategies that provide business opportunities even as they create strategic risks and business rivals. In response to the new products and techniques of their competitors, companies are disaggregating operations into specialized units – sometimes in different cities or countries – and partnering with others.

Many of these changes benefit customers. Companies create products at lower cost. They also gain new capacity to avoid accidents, to improve product and service quality, and to discern when customers' preferences change. Pressed by large employers like General Motors and General Electric to reduce medication errors, some hospitals require doctors to enter prescriptions on handheld devices that check for accurate dosages and drug interactions. Striving to keep up with new trends, some supermarkets monitor customers' precise preferences by tracking purchases each time they shop. Wal-Mart used predictive technology to analyze the data it had collected from its 100 million customers and then to stock seven times the usual amount of Poptarts in addition to flashlights, bottled water, and beer during the 2004 hurricane season.[15]

Technology advances also increase companies' incentives as well as their capacities to meet customers' needs. As competitors move in, companies must fight harder to keep the customers they have and gain new ones. At the same time, customers have new choices and better information that makes them more willing to change their purchasing habits. Fewer are held captive by brands or shortages.[16]

Governments Adopt Information Technologies

Governments, too, gain new capacities through advances in information and communication technology. Agencies share information electronically, making possible more collaborative decisions based on richer data and

providing more comprehensive public information. The U.S. Environmental Protection Agency combines pollution, health, and enforcement
data from nearly a million regulated facilities on its Envirofacts and
EnviroMapper Web site.[17] An online Information Network of Public Health
Officials aims to provide reliable information to state, local, federal, and
private-sector representatives as well as to the public.

Governments employ technology to improve compliance and enforcement. Authorities track student loans, procurement processes, and tax payments electronically, reducing opportunities for fraud.

Most filings by public companies to the federal Securities and Exchange
Commission (SEC) are done electronically through the SEC's EDGAR system. Most labor unions now file required financial reporting documents via
an electronic system provided by the U. S. Department of Labor.[18]

Some government Web sites combine information from many different
agencies and sources for targeted audiences. For example, Business.gov aims
to provide one-stop shopping for businesses seeking answers to questions
about government regulation. At all levels, governments are integrating
information technology to provide constituent services, foster communication, and augment civic participation.[19]

FOUR EMERGING POLICIES

The application of information technologies to disclosure problems has
already enhanced second-generation policies in at least four policy areas:
environmental protection, public health, auto safety, and school performance. Although not full-blown "third-generation" systems, these cases
provide insight into how the drivers of effectiveness and the political dynamics underlying sustainability are altered by the collaborative opportunities
provided by new technologies.

User-Centered Transparency to Improve Environmental Disclosure

Scorecard (www.scorecard.org), an online transparency system that has
sprung up at the edge of the toxic pollution disclosure policy, illustrates
the potential for technology to make transparency more user-centered.
Although Congress required companies to disclose annually amounts of
toxic pollution at each facility beginning in 1986, such reporting has provided only a partial picture of toxic pollution in the United States.

Reporting of the quantities of toxic chemicals released by tens of thousands of factories in the United States each year represented a complex
political compromise. Congress required disclosure of some toxic chemicals

but not others, and pollution from some sources but not others. Busy with other priorities, regulators at the federal Environmental Protection Agency, charged with carrying out the disclosure mandate, focused on a simple outcome: total pounds of emissions by each factory of each chemical. They decided against providing interpretations that would have offered users more meaningful information about toxicity, exposure, and resulting health risks, despite the urging of the chemical industry to do so.[20]

Regulators viewed their job as getting the data in and getting them out. They collected company reports, added up the numbers, and issued annual summaries. They did not develop an enforcement strategy to assure that required reporting took place and was accurate. In the early years of the program, Congress's investigative General Accounting Office suggested that more than a third of covered facilities failed to report at all.

Recognizing these problems, Bill Pease, a community organizer trained in toxicology, grafted onto the government disclosure system a more user-centered search format. Working at the School of Public Health at the University of California, Berkeley, in the early 1990s, Pease was deluged with requests from people to explain the newly disclosed government data on toxic pollution. He teamed up with Philip Greenspun, a graduate student in computer science at MIT, and David Abercromby, an expert in complex data systems, and developed Scorecard. The initial cost was $1.5 million, with funding from the Clarence E. Heller Foundation in San Francisco.

Launched in 1998, Scorecard customized toxic pollution data by zip code, translated complex results into maps and graphics, added toxicity and exposure information, layered data in various forms for those who want simplicity or complexity, ranked polluters, and provided ways for those who visit Scorecard's site to express their views or to email their representatives in Congress or regulators in the executive branch of the federal government.

Scorecard was not perfect. The data it provided were not as customized as they appeared; in response to zip-code inquiries about pollution, the site offered only countywide data. Its risk-scoring system and other interpretive data were controversial, partly because of the organization's assumed leanings (it was administered for many years under the auspices of Environmental Defense, an environmental advocacy group). Furthermore, Scorecard relied upon data generated by federal reporting requirements and so inherited the limitations of those regulations. It did not cover facilities that are exempted from legal disclosure requirements, nor could it publicize chemicals that were not on regulators' lists of toxics.

Nonetheless, Scorecard created a richer, more complete, more user-centered source of information, making it easier for community residents to embed data about local toxic pollution into their choices of where to live, work, and go to school. Scorecard also reduced the chances that data would be misinterpreted by providing users with the means to translate technical chemical release information into terms relevant to their decisions.

Scorecard also changed the dynamics of toxic pollution disclosure by overcoming some of the political obstacles to improving the accuracy, scope, and timeliness of data. Information could be added and updated without appealing to government regulators or to Congress, and data from many sources could be combined and accessed. Other entrepreneurial Web sites also reported on toxic pollution, notably RTKnet (http://www.rtknet.org). Federal regulators responded to Scorecard's growing impact by making the government's Envirofacts Web site (http://www.envirofacts.gov) more user-friendly and by adopting similar formats. The Chemical Manufacturers Association, which represented some of the largest disclosing companies, also launched its own Web site (http://www.americanchemistry.com/s_acc/index.asp) to highlight factories' contributions to job creation, taxes, and quality products, as well as their improving environmental and safety performance. Improvements in transparency therefore arose from competition among alternative information platforms.

In the future, technology might even overcome Scorecard's main limitation – its dependence on the partial pollution data that government requires companies to place in the public domain. As sensor technology improves, high school students, community residents, or automated devices might take daily toxic pollution readings at locations near factories and record them on collaborative Web sites featuring user-friendly graphics, much like weather reports.[21]

Online Polling and Hospital Ranking to Improve Medical Care

Examples of emerging online public health transparency systems illustrate how users can become disclosers of information that helps patients make choices. The politics surrounding patient-care disclosure make it difficult to require hospitals or doctors to report medical mistakes or other indications of treatment quality, but individual experience, pooled electronically in a structured way can create new collective knowledge. Several examples show how such systems might combine the efforts of patients, health-care providers, and government:

- In recent years, the federal government and private groups have combined forces to create an annual survey that allows patients to assess the quality and convenience of their health plans. Patients report their experience. Health-care plan managers monitor the results. The federal government's Agency for Healthcare Research and Quality plays a facilitating role by establishing consistent standards and formats for the survey.[22]

- The California Health Care Foundation, an independent research organization, gives California hospitals star ratings based on patient surveys. Patients report on coordination of care, safe medical practices, information and education, and other criteria (calhospitals.org).

- Public health wikis (from the Hawaiian word for "quickly") represent another way to create collaborative knowledge. Wikis are usually open narratives created and continuously expanded, corrected, and updated by users. Fluwikie.com, for example, is a collaborative site created in June 2005 by a freelance writer from Falls Church, Virginia, to gather and share information about the spread of avian flu. Wikipedia, the collaborative online encyclopedia, offers detailed articles on avian flu and on many other specific diseases (along with a vast array of non-medical topics).[23] In the long run, however, wikis could be reframed as structured transparency systems to facilitate collaborate information on emergent public health problems.

- Many online efforts rank hospitals' quality of care. These systems, most of which do not yet include patient input, illustrate how customized responses to specific questions can reduce users' search costs and make complex data comprehensible. Such ranking systems have been gaining ground in response to employers' demands for better means of guiding their employees to quality care.

- The federal Department of Health and Human Services ranks hospitals on the basis of Medicare and Medicaid data (hospitalcompare.hhs.gov). The Joint Commission on Accreditation of Healthcare Organizations (JCAHO) has begun to offer user-friendly online hospital rankings for treatment of heart attacks, pneumonia, and other specific diseases, searchable by hospital name or location. Rankings are based on JCAHO surveys and data submitted by hospitals in response to government and commission requirements. A check means hospital performance is on a par with that of other accredited institutions. A minus means performance is below others', and a plus means performance is above other hospitals'.[24] Many other public and private ranking systems have sprung up in recent years. In one notable effort, Massachusetts's largest health insurers have created online hospital ranking sites that allow patients to customize data according to their needs and priorities.[25]

Technology-enhanced public health transparency systems hold great promise for pooling individual experience to indicate strengths and weaknesses of hospitals, health plans, insurers, and doctors. They also hold promise for customizing information to meet diverse users' needs and for making complex data more comprehensible. In principle, such systems could create new incentives to improve transparency over time since they draw on major users' (e.g., companies providing health care for their employees) common interests in improvement in their new role as disclosers.

Collaborative Transparency to Improve Auto Safety

The federal government is also beginning to play a facilitating role in developing new knowledge to improve auto safety. In response to a spate of deaths and injuries from a combination of tire blowouts and SUV rollovers in 2002, described in Chapter 1, Congress created a new role for government in generating information: A collaborative early-warning system gathers data on consumer complaints, warranty claims, and field reports from auto company employees and dealers to inform car owners of possible safety problems. Consumers contribute information about safety problems from their own experience. Automakers act as intermediaries, aggregating data and submitting them quarterly to the government. The government acts as *facilitator*, requiring the disclosure of information, providing standardized metrics, and taking responsibility for enforcement. Automakers are required to report "communication of any kind made by a consumer" by email, telephone, letter, or other means.[26] Legislators thus created a second-generation rollover rating system and the seeds of a third-generation collaborative early-warning system at the same time.

Collaborative transparency that aims to improve auto safety holds particular promise because large numbers of users reporting on their experience with a limited number of car models are likely to create useful standardized knowledge. Such knowledge could save lives and prevent injuries by calling attention to safety defects more quickly than traditional government information gathering can produce results. Experience has shown that industry reporting often lags far behind incidents that could reveal design defects or other safety problems. Such transparency could create more accurate, complete information that is, in turn, more likely than individual complaints to be noticed by auto companies, whose actions can reduce safety risks. Like public health collaborative systems, auto safety collaborative systems create incentives to improve transparency over time, since information users themselves are the sources of information.

Collaborative Transparency to Improve School Performance

Many second-generation transparency systems aim to improve public services. Could technology-enhanced collaborative transparency help to resolve a particularly contentious national issue concerning such services: how to provide accurate, up-to-date information about the performance of public schools and encourage their improvement?

A third-generation transparency system for elementary school ratings might combine the government-mandated school report cards that already exist with the active efforts of parents and students at two levels. First, technology could enable parents and students to contribute their own experiences of schools, facilities, courses, and personnel (as they already do for college faculty on Web sites like http://www.ratemyprofessors.com). These experiences and views could be integrated into the overall rating of a school along with such standardized metrics as test scores, funding levels, and class size.

Second, all centrally designed school report card systems incorporate judgments, implicit or explicit, regarding educational outcomes that schools ought to pursue (college preparation, vocational training, civic understanding, or cultural competence, for example). They also incorporate judgments about the validity of various predictors of those outcomes (such as test scores, graduation rates, and college admission statistics). These goals and metrics may fit well with the values and preferences of some parents and communities but not with those of others. A third-generation transparency program could give parents and students a greater role in determining the goals and metrics by which school performance is measured. This could happen collectively, as user-driven discussions inject new priorities and educational goals not captured by second-generation report cards. It could also happen individually, as third-generation systems enable parents and students to select schools, classes, and teachers to suit their diverse aims and tastes.

Thus, collaborative transparency policies that pool users' experiences can make available a wide range of information, even information that governments or corporate interests might seek to suppress. They can provide information in ways that are more dynamic and responsive to the needs of users than those depending on centralized, government-directed second-generation efforts. Finally, third-generation transparency has the potential to serve a much broader and more diverse range of aims and preferences than second-generation transparency systems.

CHALLENGES TO COLLABORATIVE TRANSPARENCY

A technologically enhanced third generation of collaborative transparency also faces distinctive dangers. Experience has already shown that information technology, a neutral tool, can magnify intentional or accidental information distortions, spread deception, create sudden public scares, or serve as an instrument of manipulation. Two recent incidents are illustrative.

The week after the terrorist attacks of September 11, 2001, thousands of Internet messages warned people in Boston to stay home on September 22. They reported that Arab customers in a Boston bar were overheard to say that there would be a lot of bloodshed in Boston on that date. Many who passed along the message did it simply as a curiosity. Nonetheless, the result was a groundless public scare.[27]

Three years later, as word of the devastation of the South Asian tsunami spread in December 2004, rumormongering blogs suggested that the earthquake that caused it was related to atmospheric contamination by atomic testing, air pollution, or bombing in Iraq. All three ideas were false, of course, but the Web acted as an echo chamber.[28]

Cascades of false or distorted information spreading across the Web or via cell phones move much faster than public efforts to correct false rumors. Cass Sunstein describes this phenomenon in *Republic.com*:

New technologies, emphatically including the Internet, are dramatically increasing people's abilities to hear echoes of their own voices and to wall themselves off from others. An important result is the existence of cyber cascades – processes of information exchange in which a certain fact or point of view becomes widespread, simply because so many people seem to believe it.[29]

Even collaborative systems can be manipulated via technology. In 2005, a mini-scandal erupted in the book publishing industry when it was disclosed that Amazon.com had been recommending particular books not on the basis of objective data or a collaborative filtering algorithm but instead because of fees paid by the publisher. Because this relationship had not been disclosed, the recommendations had the undeserved credibility of a disinterested third-party endorsement.[30]

In early 2006, the collaborative and widely read virtual encyclopedia Wikipedia was criticized for allowing to stand for 132 days an entry that implied that a seventy-eight-year-old respected former federal official, John Seigenthaler, was involved in the 1968 assassination of Robert F. Kennedy. By the time it was removed, the groundless entry had spread to several other respected Web sites.[31] Research suggested that Wikipedia generally was no more error-prone than the *Encyclopedia Britannica*.[32] Nonetheless, the incident demonstrated how easily false and damaging information can gain credence on the Internet.

A corollary to the problem of the Internet as echo chamber is the potentially greater difficulty of sharing critical public information efficiently. Ironically, the technological wonders of the information age may create new barriers to sharing information broadly about risks and service flaws. If clusters of individuals and organizations seek out and share specialized knowledge on diverse Web sites as broader media (e.g., network nightly news programs) lose audience, it may become more difficult to build the common knowledge base that makes transparency policies meaningful.

Another danger is that organizations and individuals with narrow political or commercial interests may be able to game information systems in new ways. An irony of the information age: the Internet, which is transforming access to information, is also characterized by a new opacity concerning information's sources and reliability. Those who contribute information can do so without identifying themselves or their sponsoring organizations, or taking responsibility for what they are saying. In 2000, for example, a phony earnings report for Lucent Technologies, typical of Internet scams directed at companies' stock prices, caused its stock to lose $7 billion of value.[33]

Thus, the transparency benefits associated with advancing technology are by no means automatic. They depend heavily on the willingness of information users, disclosers, and government officials to assume new responsibilities. Rapid advances in technology do not appear to change the core factors that influence the effectiveness and sustainability of transparency policies as instruments of governance. Such advances do, however, change the ways in which information users, disclosers, and government officials create and respond to new knowledge. A new generation of technology-driven collaborative transparency can reduce search costs, enrich and broaden public information, customize data to meet users' disparate needs, and reduce political bottlenecks that have often kept second-generation transparency systems from being accurate, up-to-date, or complete. Embedding new information in the decision routines of users and target organizations remains the crucial challenge for transparency effectiveness. Concentrating dispersed users' interests in a continuing way remains the crucial challenge for transparency sustainability. Technology-enhanced transparency holds promise to assist with both.

NEW ROLES FOR USERS, DISCLOSERS, AND GOVERNMENT

Sustainable and effective third-generation transparency requires new roles for information users, target organizations, and government itself:

- Information users become more active, initiating searches for customized information and often becoming information disclosers themselves, empowered by technology to pool their experiences concerning experiences, risks, problems, and new data.
- Corporations and other target organizations respond to customers' changing capacities and expectations by employing more interactive processes and customized information both to attract new business and to track and respond to customers' preferences and public concerns.
- Governments increasingly play a facilitating, rather than controlling, role in transparency systems by supporting the new capacities of ordinary citizens to access and respond to public information. Public officials construct technology-enabled systems to discern public preferences and to further citizens' efforts to pool information about risks and public services. But their role as the principal "convener" of those systems remains essential.

As the four examples of incipient third-generation systems imply, technological leaps create the capacity for information users to originate, share, and patrol the accuracy of information they need. Many of the information asymmetries that create public risks or impair services can be solved by people pooling their experience. Others, where risks and performance problems cannot be discerned from experience, can be solved by better sensors, structured expert knowledge, and users' demands for better information from companies. At best, new public knowledge creates new incentives to reduce risks and improve services.

We have discussed the potential for better toxic pollution reporting, rating the quality of medical care, earlier auto safety alerts, and enriched school performance reports. Other opportunities abound. Restaurant goers could share information about suspected food poisoning, which now goes largely unreported, thereby augmenting less frequent public health inspections that underlie second-generation restaurant hygiene disclosure systems. City residents using simple test kits could pool information about daily levels of contaminants in drinking water. Company employees and customers could pool information about products' manufacturing defects and safety hazards. Residents of dangerous neighborhoods could collaboratively map the "no go" zones and strategize about how to make them safer.

Third-generation transparency to reduce risks and improve services therefore requires the kind of vigilant and active users that, as we have noted, have already become commonplace on commercial Web sites, blogs, and other emerging daily Web-based applications. These users will create the collaborative knowledge essential to the success of the next generation of transparency systems.

Consumers already expect a larger voice in the products they buy and the services they use. The companies and organizations that provide those products and services must listen and respond in new ways. Even in these early days of information technology, leading corporate executives and organizational managers are making fundamental changes in the way they approach relations with their customers, driven by new challenges to their businesses and by customers' changing expectations.

"We used to think we were just taking care of the consumer buying Tide," A. G. Lafley, chief executive officer of Procter & Gamble, told the *Wall Street Journal*'s Alan Murray in 2006. But "this consumer is also a citizen, is also a member of the community," and may care about animal testing or global warming.[34]

With the increase in technological capabilities, companies use advanced bar-coding and sales data to ascertain the habits of their customers and respond quickly to new concerns about risk or service quality. Food companies introduced lines of "low carb" and "trans-fat free" foods almost immediately when research and media attention focused on links to obesity and heart disease.

Retailers are beginning to use technology to deliver customized product information directly to their customers at the time and place when they make choices. Stop & Shop, a grocery retailer with 336 stores, experimented with electronic "shopping buddies" that track purchases, offer promotions, and allow customers to place deli orders as they navigate the other aisles of the store.[35] If shoppers had frequented Stop & Shop in the past, the shopping buddy already knew their preferences and would provide customized advice about items they might want to add to their lists. In 2004, Albertsons, another large grocery retailer, created wi-fi environments in its stores and introduced "shop 'n' scan" devices that customized promotions on the basis of information gathered from customers.[36] Other retailers have brought the Internet into their stores. For example, GNC, the health supplement retailer, provides Internet kiosks in its stores so that shoppers can compare the effectiveness and safety of dietary supplements.[37]

It is only a small step from store-controlled information through shopping buddies, or limited access to the Web, to customer-controlled assessments of products' risks and benefits accessible in stores through cell phones or other handheld devices that link bar codes and Web sites that offer risk data, product by product. Dara O'Rourke, a U.C. Berkeley professor, is developing a prototype of such a system.[38]

Thus, early commercial applications suggest how technology might offer shoppers customized, current, reliable information about risks and benefits of products and services wherever and whenever they most need it. Web sites designed for cell phones or other portable devices could provide customized answers to questions about information that is excluded from product labels, airline safety and on-time records, hospital and doctor ratings, and other product- and service-related data. Interactive sites could begin with government-provided data and build in customer ratings and recommendations.

Third-generation collaborative transparency depends on government participation for the same three reasons as second-generation targeted transparency. First, only government can mandate that private organizations and public agencies disclose information, can specify user-friendly formats, and can assure access when and where users need it. Such intervention is needed when users, even marshaling their new information-pooling power, cannot obtain information to ascertain performance problems or risk. Second, only government can legislate measures to assure the longevity of transparency as political winds shift. Finally, only government can create fully accountable transparency, backed by the imprimatur of democratically elected representatives.

To foster successful collaborative transparency systems, however, government must learn to work with a lighter touch – more collaboratively and less hierarchically. Whereas government mandates both the form and the content of disclosed information in second-generation transparency, two hallmarks of third-generation transparency are that users control – in distributed and evolutionary ways – many decisions about the sorts of information to be pooled and the manner of its disclosure. Many of these efforts – as the commercial examples in this chapter show – occur outside the penumbra of legal regulation.

When there are important public purposes and values at stake, however, the active hand of government must continue to define boundaries and set minimal reporting requirements to provide the foundation for the subsequent efforts of users and volunteers. Government can, for example, mandate disclosure of key unobtainable facts, provide standard definitions and formats, offer new scientific findings, sponsor research to fill information gaps that users worry most about, assure that disclosing organizations display risk data when and where it is most helpful to users, and patrol the boundaries of user-managed systems to minimize distortion and gaming by parties with narrow political or economic interests.

LOOKING AHEAD: COMPLEMENTARY GENERATIONS OF TRANSPARENCY

Three generations of transparency policies represent historic stages in the evolution of public access to information. Each has a place in the future of democratic governance.

First-generation right-to-know provisions allow citizens and groups to pry information out of governments that would often rather keep it secret. Preserving and expanding public access to government information remains a political struggle.

Second-generation transparency policies represent legislators' efforts to reduce risks and improve services by judging what information people need to make better choices that will in turn improve products and practices. Targeted transparency remains critical to provide information that people cannot gain from experience, such as the nutrients or allergens in food, the character and degree of air and water pollution, or the profits and losses of publicly traded companies.

Third-generation transparency will allow citizens to initiate transparency systems and to use deeply textured and varied information that is responsive to their diverse needs.

Working in combination, these three generations of transparency can, when carefully designed, deployed, and maintained, help citizens more successfully navigate the myriad economic, political, and social decisions they face in modern life. At their best, public transparency systems embody a kind of virtual partnership in which the authority of government empowers citizens to act with greater wisdom and confidence in an increasingly complex world.

EIGHT

Targeted Transparency in the Information Age

In November and December 2004, surgeons at Duke University's respected hospitals operated on thirty-eight hundred patients with instruments mistakenly cleaned in hydraulic fluid. The fluid had been drained from elevators and placed in containers that became mixed up with cleaning supplies.[1]

Shocking? Yes. But unprecedented? Unfortunately, no. Six years earlier, the national Institute of Medicine had informed the American public that medical mistakes were common, even at good hospitals, and that they were often deadly. According to the institute report, every year at least forty-four thousand Americans died and nearly a million were injured by mistakes in hospitals – not counting those killed or injured by mistakes in clinics or doctors' offices. That made such errors the eighth leading cause of death in the United States, surpassing auto accidents, breast cancer, and AIDS – and the only major source of accidental fatalities not reported to the public. Even patients and their families often were not informed about mistakes when they occurred.[2]

The institute's committee recommended immediate action to reduce medical mistakes by 50 percent in five years. But what policies would encourage hospitals to take steps to minimize such risks? New national rules probably wouldn't help because mistakes, their causes, and their settings were so variable. Instead, the committee recommended a new transparency system. Their report urged Congress and state governments to require hospitals to publicly disclose errors that caused death or serious injury. Disclosure would empower patients to choose safer hospitals. Patients' changed choices would create new incentives for hospital managers to reduce errors.

However, six years after the institute's urgent call for transparency, virtually all information about deaths and injuries from medical errors remained locked in hospital files – if it was collected at all. The few states that mandated disclosures concerning physician and hospital quality restricted that information to a narrow set of outcomes or did not make information available when and where patients needed it. New York and Pennsylvania laws, for example, required disclosure only of events related to cardiac bypass surgery.[3]

Why had the institute's proposal failed to gain traction? The short answer is that it was swamped by conflicting political interests. Congress and the states failed to act after groups representing doctors and hospitals, including the American Medical Association and the American Hospital Association, formed a coalition to defeat transparency proposals. Doctors argued that error reports should remain confidential because public reporting could drive physicians to hide their mistakes in order to avoid liability. Hospital executives agreed that confidential reporting would be more productive than public disclosure. And large companies like General Motors and General Electric that funded health care for millions of employees and retirees preferred to negotiate directly with health-care providers to improve staffing and technology.[4]

Disclosure of medical mistakes became contentious precisely because legislators and representatives of hospitals, doctors, and consumer groups all recognized that new facts could have enormous power in the hands of millions of patients making everyday health-care choices. In effect, those choices would create new social policy by telling managers of hospitals what level of safety the public expected.

Consumer and public health groups that favored public reporting couldn't compete with the antidisclosure lobbying effort. In the end, federal and state policymakers gave lip service to health-care transparency but failed to follow through. The proposed law never made it out of committee.

TWO POSSIBLE FUTURES

As this account illustrates, the story of governance by transparency often becomes one of missed opportunity. In this instance narrow political interests overwhelmed efforts to create greater accountability by doctors and hospitals, even when the risks involved tens of thousands of needless deaths and more than a million needless injuries.

This failure suggests one possible future for governance by transparency. If information the public needs remains hidden or distorted owing to politics or poor planning, a promising instrument of public policy becomes a tragic disappointment.

We are drowning in information. Many people in the United States have access to more than a hundred cable television channels, spend hours each week sending and receiving emails and instant messages, and are besieged by radio, television, and Web advertisements.

Yet millions of dollars are lost and hundreds of thousands of needless deaths, injuries, or illnesses occur each year because needed, knowable facts remain hidden from public view. Without information that is essential for informed choices, people invest in stocks with undisclosed risks, check into hospitals with bad safety records, drink contaminated tap water, mishandle workplace chemicals they don't realize are dangerous, and travel to places where unreported and deadly infectious diseases threaten their health. Inside a small circle, corporate executives, scientists, or government officials have access to the critical facts. But members of the public are left out.

As we have seen, political dynamics often produce gerrymandered transparency – nutritional labeling with exceptions carved out for fast-food stores and full-service restaurants, toxic pollution reporting with exceptions made for neighborhood businesses that release some of the most dangerous toxins. In the United States, a nation that prides itself on openness, secrecy remains a closely guarded privilege.

In other instances, failed transparency results from poor planning or execution. Poor design of drinking water contaminant disclosure fails to provide comparable measures. Lack of enforcement leaves the accuracy of toxic pollution reports uncertain.

Failed transparency wastes not only lives but also resources. Companies, school systems, health-care providers, and other organizations spend millions of dollars compiling and disseminating information that is useless, out of date, or unintelligible.

Failed transparency also undermines trust in public and private institutions. City dwellers who learn to disregard government alerts may fail to heed accurate warnings about the next terrorist attack. Investors who are discouraged about ineffective accounting reforms may desert the stock market. Patients who are uncertain about the risk of medical errors may wait too long to check into the hospital. More needless losses result.

But another future is possible. Targeted transparency policies could gain effectiveness through better understanding, design, and advances in information technology. Private and public groups could develop better practices for transparency systems that would minimize failures. Growing public awareness of the promise and pitfalls of such policies could create new vigilance and political dynamics that favor transparency.

In today's complex world, legislated transparency could become a powerful tool for improving the choices people make. As consumers, people make nuanced trade-offs among price, quality, and risks, often balancing conflicting preferences. As citizens, people make nuanced trade-offs among conflicting values and among short- and long-term priorities. We want hospitals that are safe, convenient, universally accessible, equipped with all the latest technology, and affordable. We want cars that are safe, cheap, fuel-efficient, nonpolluting, and powerful. The goods we purchase, the schools where we enroll our children, and the votes we cast reflect complex balancing acts to reconcile contradictory desires amid bewildering information.

Technology and transparency could work together to empower people making everyday choices:

- Consumers seeking safe toys or healthy foods could zap a product's bar code with their cell phones to see an instant map of risks and benefits and a comparison to similar products.
- Car buyers could create a checklist of their preferences for safety, performance, price, and fuel economy, and visit a Web site to see immediately which models came closest to meeting their needs, on the basis of objective data as well as the comments of other buyers.
- Community residents could conduct daily air pollution and tap water purity tests with handheld devices and share the information they gathered via user-friendly graphics like those of weather forecasts.
- Voters, advocacy groups, and members of the media could readily check frequently updated charts showing how campaign contributions to legislators from particular lobbying groups or wealthy donors correlate with voting records.
- And patients could check the relative quality of care provided and medical errors committed by particular hospital departments, clinics, or doctors, and share their personal experiences with others.

In this final chapter, we will examine how the choices of policymakers, information users, and target organizations will determine the future of targeted transparency. We first summarize our insights into the types of policy problems that targeted transparency can and cannot address. We then explore some design features that are critical for the success of transparency policies.

WHEN TRANSPARENCY WON'T WORK

A theme of this book has been that the availability of more information does not always produce markets that are more efficient or fair, or collective action that advances public priorities. Transparency policies are likely to be effective when the new information they generate can be easily embedded into the routines of information users and when information disclosers, in turn, embed users' changed choices in their decision making in ways that advance public aims. As we saw in Chapter 4, corporate financial disclosure, nutritional labeling, mortgage lending disclosure, and restaurant hygiene grading succeeded in becoming doubly embedded transparency systems.

In other cases, even well-designed and well-supported transparency is unlikely to be effective. Sometimes it is difficult to embed policy-relevant information into users' routines because they have few real choices. At other times, the goals and actions of users are incongruous with those of policymakers. Or it can be difficult to bring disclosers' actions in line with policy goals.

Thus, targeted transparency policies work best when six characteristics mark the underlying problem:

- *A bridgeable information gap contributes substantially to risks or public service failures.* Clarity about the nature of the information gap, its relationship to the problem to be addressed, and how to fill the gap helps to increase the chances of policy success. At our present state of technology, no amount of information could prevent an asteroid collision with the earth, but deaths and injuries from earthquakes could be reduced if we had information about exactly when and where they would occur – not yet a scientifically solvable problem. International labeling of genetically modified foods is problematic in part because nations can't agree about whether genetic engineering creates a public safety problem – is there an information gap that merits government intervention?
- *The policy problem lends itself to consensus metrics.* Transparency is unlikely to work if people disagree about how to measure improvement. Parents, teachers, government officials, and students disagree about appropriate metrics of public school performance (test scores versus more complex measures, for example). Lack of consensus about metrics impairs the credibility of transparency.
- *Communication is practical.* Some problems are too complex or multi-faceted to make public communication of risks or performance problems practical. The effectiveness of workplace hazard transparency was hampered by the complexity of risk exposure information. Toxic pollution reporting still lacks a simple metric that incorporates toxicity levels and exposure, important components for assessing risk.

- *Information users have the will, capacity, and cognitive tools to improve their choices.* Information that bears on risk but that consumers or citizens do not value is not a good candidate for targeted transparency. Cities could publicize pedestrian injuries in jaywalking accidents, but lifelong jaywalkers would probably ignore the data. Governments could rank cities by the likelihood of natural disasters, but most residents would find it hard to pick up and move. The U.S. government does report the relative safefy of airlines, but many people will still systematically exaggerate the risk of traveling on the airline that had the latest major accident.[5]
- *Information disclosers have the capacity to reduce risks or improve performance.* Transparency policies are unlikely to work when target organizations are unable to improve their practices. The ability of manufacturers to reduce toxic pollution is limited by the availability of substitute materials that create less-hazardous wastes. The ability of food companies to remove harmful fats from processed foods depends on viable substitutes. The ability of automakers to reduce rollovers depends on the feasibility of safer designs.
- *Variable results are acceptable.* Finally, targeted transparency is desirable only when it is acceptable to reduce risks or improve services for some people but not others. Consider the problem of reducing lead in gasoline. Congress might have required labeling of leaded gas, giving gas-station managers and drivers a purchase choice. Instead, legislators concluded that leaving some communities exposed to more lead than others was untenable, since lead can cause serious neurological damage in children. As a result, they chose to impose a national ban on leaded gasoline rather than leave the outcome to be determined by transparency-assisted market forces.

Chapter 3 discussed two other forms of government intervention – standards-based and market-based interventions – that are widely used in many of the areas of social policy reviewed throughout this book. As we have pointed out, different types of policy problems fit different methods of intervention. Take the myriad problems arising under the general heading "environmental pollution." Chemicals that pose significant health risks given even minimal levels of exposure (like mercury or lead) lend themselves to traditional standards-based interventions because they call for uniform performance outcomes across all regulated parties (i.e., strict enforcement of minimum exposure levels). In those cases, it makes sense to use intervention tools that directly order a change in the behavior of companies to achieve these clear outcomes, without recourse to the complexities of targeted transparency.

Now consider the case of interventions to limit greenhouse gases associated with global warming. The need to achieve overall pollution reduction has become increasingly clear, but the costs of greenhouse gas reduction vary considerably across companies (and nations). Accordingly, achieving variable levels of reduction may be appropriate – with largest reductions for companies or countries facing the lowest marginal cost of greenhouse gas reductions and lower reductions for those facing higher marginal costs. But global warming arises from what is often described as the "tragedy of the commons" – that is, the overuse of a collective good – and not fundamentally from an information asymmetry problem. As a result, the problem lends itself more to incentive-based interventions like tradable pollution allowances than to targeted transparency.

Finally, return to the problem of controlling pollution releases at a local level, particularly where there is a range of potentially acceptable policy outcomes, arising either from scientific uncertainties or from a desire by policymakers to balance pollution-related risk reduction against other social risks or community values (like employment or economic development). Such a case is particularly well suited to targeted transparency given the desirability of achieving different reduction levels across varied localities, the need to balance different public interests against one another, and the centrality of redressing information asymmetries between the companies discharging chemicals and the communities affected by them to arrive at more socially desirable levels of risk exposure.[6]

We do not see targeted transparency, then, as a replacement for other forms of public intervention. Instead, it represents an increasingly important, but complementary, mechanism of public governance that can be used to further public priorities. When policy problems are marked by the six characteristics described above, targeted transparency is a viable means of approaching them. However, even then, designing effective policies presents formidable challenges.

CRAFTING EFFECTIVE POLICIES

Even in circumstances where targeted transparency is feasible, policies must be carefully crafted with a clear understanding of the needs and limitations of their many audiences. Once launched, they also require frequent tune-ups to adapt to changing times. We suggest ten principles for the design of effective transparency policies:

- *Provide information that is easy for ordinary citizens to use.* The most important condition for transparency effectiveness is that new information become embedded in the decision routines of information users. Therefore, once transparency is chosen as a way to address a policy problem, the first step is to understand how diverse groups of customers, employees, voters, or other intended users make decisions. Taking account of the culture, education, and priorities of these diverse audiences becomes critical. Designers can then tailor transparency systems to provide new facts at the time, in the place, and in the format that will be convenient for most people.
- *Strengthen user groups.* Targeted transparency systems are likely to be more sustainable when advocacy groups, analysts, entrepreneurial politicians, or other representatives of user interests have incentives to maintain and improve them. Policymakers can design systems to formally recognize the ongoing roles of user groups. Institutional investors, stock exchanges, stock analysts, and other organizations have formal roles in maintaining the integrity of the financial disclosure system. Health insurance companies and major employers have incentives to improve and disseminate quality-of-care data.[7] Labor unions and health and safety committees have roles in interpreting and disseminating information on workplace risks. Transparency systems can also create watchdog roles for user groups. The Community Reinvestment Act, for example, provides incentives for community groups to monitor and improve banks' mortgage lending disclosures. Policymakers may also encourage continuing oversight by user groups by requiring opportunities for public participation (including Web-based user-rating and information-input systems) and advisory council or audit functions.
- *Help disclosers understand users' changed choices.* Transparency policies fail if companies are unable to discern customers' changed choices and the reasons for those changes. Advances in information technology are rapidly improving disclosers' capacities to track customer, employer, investor, or voter responses. Where disclosers' capacity to discern changed choices remains weak, it is sometimes possible to design transparency policies that improve their attention to the impact of newly disclosed data. Requirements that chief executives certify the accuracy of reported data (included in Sarbanes-Oxley accounting

reforms and toxic chemical reporting, for example) increase the likelihood that executives will track their impact.

- *Design for discloser benefits.* When some disclosers perceive benefits from improved transparency, systems are more likely to prove sustainable. Policymakers can seek to generate information that harnesses and amplifies economic, political, and regulatory incentives that already exist in disclosers' environments. Companies and other disclosing organizations may seek to improve disclosure for competitive reasons (for example, to raise entry barriers for other firms), to ward off more stringent federal regulation, to avoid the headaches that come with variable state disclosure requirements, or to reduce reputational risks. Thus, food companies aimed to avoid a patchwork of state actions and to gain profits from healthier products when they supported nutritional labeling requirements in 1990. Chemical companies aimed to avoid stricter pollution rules and reputational damage, and also to gain competitive edge, when they drastically reduced toxic pollution in response to new disclosure requirements and sought to broaden requirements to include other disclosers. As technology allows users themselves to become disclosers of infectious disease outbreaks, drinking water contamination, or concentrations of toxic pollutants, target organizations have new incentives to improve metrics.

- *Design metrics for accuracy and comparability.* Corporate accounting standards, restaurant hygiene grades, and nutritional labeling succeed in part because they feature metrics that are reasonably well matched to policy objectives and allow users to compare products or services easily. Policies for disclosure of workplace hazards and drinking water contaminants, by contrast, feature confusing metrics that skew incentives and fail to provide comparable results. Achieving comparability can involve difficult trade-offs, since simplification may erase important nuances and standardization may ignore or discourage innovation. Corporate financial reporting and nutritional labeling provide interesting examples of balancing comparability with data complexity.

- *Design for comprehension.* Policies are most effective when they match information content and formats to users' levels of attention and comprehension. If information users are likely to be rushed, simple distinctions, grades, stars, bar or pie charts, or other relatively straightforward metrics – with back-up facts available – may work well. Web sites can provide quick answers while also allowing more interested users to delve further into the facts. Policymakers can draw on research insights concerning cognitive distortions (discussed in Chapter 2) to design transparency systems that build in probabilities, limit information search costs, and minimize the impact of other cognitive problems.[8]

- *Incorporate analysis and feedback.* Transparency systems can grow rigid with age, resulting in a tyranny of outdated benchmarks. Generously funded requirements for periodic analysis, feedback, and policy revision can help keep such systems supple and promote adaptation to changing circumstances. For example, in recommending a disclosure system for medical errors, the Institute of Medicine also recommended a new and well-funded federal Center for Patient Safety to initiate and coordinate research and to continuously assess the disclosure system and adjust it accordingly.[9]

- *Impose sanctions.* Corporations and other organizations usually have many reasons to minimize or distort required disclosure. Organizations almost always resist revealing information about public risks they create or flaws in services they provide. Information can be costly to produce and even more costly in reputational damage. As a result, substantial fines or other penalties for nonreporting and misreporting are an essential element of successful systems.

- *Strengthen enforcement.* Sanctions are not enough, however. Legal penalties must be accompanied by rigorous enforcement to raise the costs of not disclosing or disclosing inaccurately. The fact that there is thus far no systematic mechanism for auditing toxic pollution data provided by companies means that no one knows for sure how accurate or complete those data are. Some systems include provisions for institutional watchdogs. The confessed crimes of lobbyist Jack Abramoff in 2006 led to proposals in Congress for the creation of an audit board for campaign finance disclosures, for example.[10] And some proposals create watchdogs to watch the watchdogs. Federal law requires accounting firms to audit corporate financial disclosures. Recent accounting reforms created a public oversight board to monitor the practices of those accounting firms.[11]

- *Leverage other regulatory systems.* When targeted transparency by itself is insufficient to generate effective outcomes, transparency can be designed to work in tandem with other government policies. Los Angeles County's restaurant hygiene grading would not work without a health inspection system that provides the basis for letter grades. Mortgage lending reporting generates information that allows community organizations to identify discrimination practices by local banks, while the Community Reinvestment Act powerfully embeds that information into the strategies of users and disclosers. As noted earlier, this suggests that targeted transparency should be considered a complement and not a replacement for other forms of public intervention.

THE ROAD AHEAD

The future of targeted transparency remains uncertain. Political controversies about specific transparency policies fill the news. Some controversies suggest that a constructive learning process is under way, while others signal continuing transparency failures.

Spirited debate continues over how to improve corporate financial disclosure in the wake of accounting scandals, including battles over reporting of stock options, special entities, and executive pay. The European Union has required its twenty-five member nations to adopt a single set of corporate financial reporting standards even as doubts persist about whether those nations have the capacity to implement the edict.

Food labeling issues remain contentious. Democrats in the U.S. Congress led a long and ultimately successful fight to clarify labeling of allergens like peanuts and shellfish on packaged foods after reports of several consumer deaths. A twenty-year struggle to include harmful trans fats on nutritional labels ended with a new disclosure rule effective in 2007.

In 2006, the Food and Drug Administration announced the first major revision of prescription drug labeling in thirty years. New labels were designed to highlight major risks of side effects and drug interactions.

In 2005, federal regulators concluded an acrimonious debate about how to more accurately report auto fuel economy with a new system that was expected to reduce previous ratings by as much as 20 percent.

On the other side of the ledger, the George W. Bush administration was widely criticized for its hard-to-understand color-coded terrorist threat warning system, which fell into disuse.

Even as national concern grew about the public health risks from obesity, Congress buried proposals to require fast-food stores and restaurants to report on calories and nutrients.

The Bush administration proposed backtracking on toxic chemical disclosure by reducing the scope and frequency of reporting for some firms.

In 2003, inadequate reporting contributed to more than seven hundred deaths from the SARS epidemic and pointed to the failure of the international infectious disease surveillance system.

As a nation, we continue to test the proposition that government can legislate transparency to reduce risks and improve public services. Effective transparency is far from assured in our public policies and institutions. As we have seen, transparency systems begin as imperfect compromises and must evolve to keep pace with changing markets, advancing science and technology, and new political priorities. Yet improving them is no simple matter. New facts alter the competitive playing field and change benefits and costs for disclosers. They empower some interests and threaten others, rearranging the political environments surrounding transparency systems.

To illustrate the promise of targeted transparency, let us return once more to the dynamics of financial disclosure. Despite its flaws, financial disclosure has improved markedly in scope and accuracy since the 1930s. Until the 1970s, the SEC didn't even require uniform accounting standards. After the 1960s rash of hostile takeovers and conglomerate mergers, regulators called both for advance notice of plans to buy large blocks of stock and more detailed accounting of earnings. When illegal campaign contributions and falsification of corporate records created public alarm, additional checks encouraged management oversight. These improvements, imperfect though they were, reflected a common interest in improving the system's integrity. Despite criticisms of their costs, many analysts regard changes enacted in the Sarbanes-Oxley law as the latest step forward.

The larger insights provided by financial disclosure apply to myriad targeted transparency systems. At their best, such systems represent a promising form of information-age governance. However, the benefits of targeted transparency are not automatic. Transparency is likely to work best when it is part of a disciplined process that sets priorities, assesses probable impacts of alternative or complementary government measures, minimizes unintended consequences, and generates feedback, analysis, and system improvement over time.

We have argued for fundamental changes in ideas about transparency policies. We advocate beginning the design of any new system by analyzing what information users want and their decision-making habits. More broadly, we call for a new understanding of the democratic mantra of "access to information" so that it means more than simply placing data in the public domain. Instead, it means requiring the provision of content that is useful, customized, and interactive.

Despite the heralded arrival of the information age, we are only beginning to grasp the ways in which public policies can harness information to reduce serious risks and improve important services. There have so far been few crosscutting studies of transparency effectiveness. Likewise, there has so far been little work comparing transparency policies with other regulatory tools. Despite a generation of new research, relatively little is known about how people make choices when confronted with new facts or about how to design systems to communicate effectively with diverse audiences.

Whether the broad innovation of targeted transparency increases trust in public and private institutions or erodes that trust will depend on both a greater understanding of how transparency really works and the political will to translate that understanding into action.

APPENDIX

Eighteen Major Cases

This book is based on an analysis of fifteen major U.S. and three international transparency policies. This Appendix provides a summary of the legislative history, purpose, provisions, politics, and dynamics of each of these policies. We have categorized U.S. cases by two broad policy objectives: reducing risks to the public and improving the quality and fairness of critical services. The three international policies are described in the final portion of this Appendix.

Further detail on each of these cases and links to related materials are available at the Transparency Policy Project Web site: http://www.transparencypolicy.net/.

TARGETED TRANSPARENCY IN THE UNITED STATES

Reducing Risks to the Public

Disclosing Corporate Finances to Reduce Risks to Investors

Created as a response to crisis, the United States' system of corporate financial disclosure was cobbled together in 1933 and 1934 as a pragmatic compromise. Millions of Americans were left holding worthless securities when the stock market crashed in October 1929. By 1932, the value of stocks listed on the New York Stock Exchange had fallen by 83 percent. Congressional hearings revealed patterns of inflated earnings, insider trading, and secret deals by J. P. Morgan, National City, and other banks, hidden practices that contributed to the precipitous decline of public confidence in securities markets. Echoing Louis D. Brandeis's declaration that "sunlight is . . . the best disinfectant," Franklin D. Roosevelt, the nation's newly elected president, championed legislation to expose financial practices to public scrutiny.[1]

The Securities and Exchange Acts of 1933 and 1934 required that publicly traded companies disclose information about their finances in standardized form in quarterly and annual reports. Congress also authorized the newly created Securities and Exchange Commission (SEC) to issue uniform accounting standards for company financial disclosures. To gain support for a workable compromise, the disclosure requirements excluded banks, railroads, and many companies. Felix Frankfurter, Roosevelt's senior adviser on the legislation, called the Securities Act a "modest first installment" in protecting the public from hidden risks.[2]

Later crises strengthened disclosure requirements.[3] In the 1960s, the scope of disclosure was broadened when an unprecedented wave of conglomerate mergers followed by a sudden collapse of their stock prices created pressures for better information. Congress responded in 1968 with the Williams Act, which required disclosure of cash tender offers that would change ownership of more than 10 percent of company stock; Congress strengthened the law two years later by lowering the threshold for reporting to 5 percent and adding disclosure of product-line data.[4]

In 1969 and 1970, the Accounting Principles Board, an outdated instrument of accounting industry self-government, was replaced with the current Financial Accounting Standards Board (FASB) as one way to improve investors' confidence in the disclosure system. The new private-sector board had authority to set accounting standards and featured broader representation and funding, a larger professional staff, and a better system of accountability. Over time, the board substantially tightened accounting standards.[5]

In the late 1970s, congressional investigations raised new questions about FASB's domination by big business. In response the board opened meetings, allowed public comment on proposals, provided weekly publication of schedules and decisions on technical issues, framed industry-specific accounting standards, analyzed economic consequences of proposed actions, and eliminated a requirement that a majority of its members be chosen from the accounting profession.[6]

Over the years, other crises broadened the scope of disclosure and improved the accuracy and use of information. In 1970, for example, after 160 brokerages failed, Congress required new disclosures from broker-dealers concerning their management and financial stability.[7] In 1977, Congress broadened transparency in response to publicity about bribes and illegal campaign contributions by corporate executives.[8] Lapses in management in some of the nation's largest corporations led the SEC to issue rules in 1978 and 1979 that required new disclosures concerning the independence of board members, board committee oversight of company operations, and failure of directors to attend meetings.[9] In the 1990s, increases in individual investing and the rise of online investing led the SEC to adopt "plain English" disclosure rules, which required prospectuses filed with the agency to be written in short, clear sentences using nontechnical vocabulary and featuring graphic aids.[10]

The sudden collapse of Enron Inc. in December 2001 once again created a crisis-response scenario that generated pressures to improve corporate financial reporting. Shareholders lost their savings and employees lost retirement funds when the nation's largest energy trader filed for bankruptcy.

Enron's collapse pointed to systemic problems with the United States' most trusted public disclosure system. The SEC charged executives of Waste Management, World-Com, Adelphia Communications, Tyco International, Dynergy, Safety-Kleen Corp., and other large companies with a variety of offenses related to withholding information from the public. Executives of Enron, WorldCom, and other large companies were indicted for fraud and other offenses. Ten large investment firms settled with the SEC, the New York State attorney general, and other regulators for permitting improper influence of their research analysts by their investment banking interests. Arthur Andersen, Enron's auditor, was charged with obstruction of justice for destroying auditing documents, a blow to the firm's reputation that drove it out of business. Evidence of collaboration by accounting firms that also earned huge consulting fees, stock boosting by analysts, and inadequate oversight by company boards, as well as a declining stock market, once again called into question the integrity of the corporate financial disclosure system.[11]

The systemic problem was that the disclosure system had failed to keep pace with changing markets. After the fact, Congress's General Accounting Office (GAO) concluded that

changes in the business environment, such as the growth in information technology, new types of relationships between companies, and the increasing use of complex business transactions and financial instruments, constantly threaten the relevance of financial statements and pose a formidable challenge to standard setters.... Enron's failure ... raised ... issues ... such as the need for additional transparency, clarity, more timely information, and risk-oriented financial reporting.[12]

By 2002, another round of disclosure reform was under way. Public companies, accounting firms, stock exchanges, analysts, and other participants in securities markets all made voluntary changes. On July 30, 2002, President George W. Bush signed into law the most far-reaching reforms of financial disclosure since the 1930s. The Sarbanes-Oxley Act, sponsored by Senator Paul Sarbanes (D-Md.), senior Democrat on the Senate Banking Committee, and Representative Mike Oxley (R-Ohio), chair of the House Financial Services Panel, created a new agency charged with watching over the accounting watchdogs. The private, nonprofit Public Company Accounting Oversight Board, consisting of five members appointed by the president and a staff of five hundred, was authorized to establish auditing standards, monitor accounting firms' practices, and fine them for improprieties.

The law also limited consulting services that auditors could offer to corporate clients and required rotation of partners assigned to corporations every five years. It established new criminal penalties, including twenty-five-year jail terms for securities fraud and twenty-year terms for destroying records. It required chief executives and financial officers to certify financial reports and required that material changes in financial condition be disclosed immediately in plain English. It also established a restitution fund for wronged shareholders. In what would become the law's most controversial provision – because of its high cost, as its requirements were translated into new demands on companies by outside auditors – section 404 held managers responsible for maintaining adequate internal controls over financial reporting.[13]

In other disclosure reforms, the SEC required public companies to file annual and quarterly reports more quickly (generally annual reports within sixty rather than ninety days after the end of the year and quarterly reports within thirty-five rather than forty-five days after the end of the quarter). New disclosure rules also required expensing of stock options, fuller financial disclosure by mutual funds, and more information about executive pay.[14]

The accounting scandals of 2001 and 2002 also led to new ideas about making financial reporting more useful to investors. A forum convened by the GAO in December 2002 noted that the model of financial reporting had not changed since the 1970s and was "driven by the supply side ... accountants, regulators, and corporate management and boards of directors."[15] The GAO suggested layering reporting to give users the information they needed and encouraging "demand-side," user-centered disclosure reforms.[16]

In an interesting complementary effort to improve the capacity of information users to understand financial information, Congress also approved the Financial Literacy and

Education Improvement Act, which created a commission to develop a national strategy to promote financial literacy. The new law responded to research that suggested that many Americans lacked the knowledge needed to make informed financial judgments.[17]

In 2006, the reform of the corporate financial disclosure system remained a work in progress. The costs of more rigorous disclosure, especially to small businesses, and the reach of reforms to companies headquartered in other countries were among the many controversial political issues. It remained to be seen whether recent legislative cures in fact would reduce underreporting and misreporting by companies and prove cost-effective in the long run.

Disclosing Chemical Hazards to Reduce Workplace Health and Safety Risks

A National Institute for Occupational Safety and Health survey conducted in 1972 found that "approximately 25 million U.S. workers, or one in four, [were] potentially exposed to one or more of . . . nearly 8000 hazards" and that 40 to 50 million Americans, amounting to over 20 percent of the population, may have been exposed to hazardous chemicals.[18] Often neither employers nor employees were aware of the presence of hazardous substances in the workplace. Lack of knowledge hampered diagnosis and treatment when workers became ill from chemical exposure.

Responding to this problem in the 1970s, unions, public interest groups, and state legislators promoted the idea of a workers' "right-to-know" about chemical exposures and associated dangers.[19] The federal Occupational Safety and Health Administration (OSHA) had issued standards specifying limits on levels of benzene, lead, and some other extremely toxic chemicals, but promulgating separate standards for hundreds of thousands of hazardous chemical products seemed impractical. Instead, labor and other public interest groups pressed for an approach based on greater transparency.

In 1981, the Carter administration proposed a disclosure requirement that would have applied "to virtually all businesses that used hazardous substances."[20] The Reagan administration, however, proved more hostile to greater transparency, prompting unions to shift their lobbying efforts from the federal to the state level. As a result, many states – including New Jersey, Pennsylvania, and Illinois – adopted their own right-to-know laws by the mid 1980s.[21] At that point, industry groups supported adoption of a uniform federal standard as an alternative to variable state right-to-know laws, and the federal hazard communication standard was adopted in 1983. The Reagan administration narrowed the initial rule to require only manufacturing firms to disclose chemical information.[22] OSHA argued that manufacturing amounted to 32 percent of total employment and accounted for more than 50 percent of illnesses caused by exposure to chemicals.[23]

The requirement created a two-part chain of disclosure. First, chemical manufacturers and importers evaluated the hazardousness of the substances they produced or imported and disclosed that information to employers who purchased their products. Second, employers made the information available to workers who handled hazardous substances. Manufacturers and importers attached to containers of hazardous chemicals descriptive labels listing the identity of the substance, a hazard warning, and the company's name and address. Chemical manufacturers also provided employers with material safety data sheets that contained more extensive information about chemical identity, physical and chemical characteristics, physical and health hazards, precautions, and emergency measures. Finally, in plants where workers were exposed to hazardous substances, employers were required to provide the data sheets and train employees in accessing chemical information, protecting themselves from risk, and responding to emergencies.

Many labor and consumer groups were unsatisfied with the disclosure system's limited scope, however. Soon after its approval, United Steelworkers of America, AFL-CIO-CLC, and Public Citizen attacked the standard's narrow scope and preemption of sometimes stronger state right-to-know laws. Rejecting the Reagan administration's rationale for limiting disclosure to manufacturing firms, the U.S. Court of Appeals in 1985 directed the secretary of labor to extend disclosure to all sectors. In 1987, a new court ruling confirmed that all industries where employees were potentially exposed to hazardous chemicals had to comply with the disclosure requirements. By 2004, OSHA estimated that over 30 million American workers were exposed to hazardous chemicals in their workplaces and that the hazardous chemical reporting system affected around 3 million workplaces and 650,000 chemical substances.[24]

Over time, chemical manufacturers improved their disclosure of chemical hazards. Manufacturers responded to employers' requests for additional chemical information and sought to limit their potential liability for willfully hiding information on dangerous chemicals.[25] A 1992 study by the GAO found that 56 percent of surveyed employers reported "great" or "very great" improvement in the availability of information, and 30 percent said they substituted less-hazardous chemicals because of the information they received.[26]

Material safety data sheets became a routine method of conveying product information about both hazardous and nonhazardous chemicals. Many firms now post on the Internet data sheets for all their products, and a number of Web sites offer searchable databases. Some manufacturers use disclosure as a competitive tool, offering their customers more information than OSHA requires, including guidance on how to comply with disclosure requirements, training materials, and experts to assist customers.[27]

Manufacturers and employers also improved the quality of the reported information. Responding to criticism about the quality of material safety data sheets, the Chemical Manufacturers Association convened a committee to develop guidelines for the preparation of such sheets. Their effort contributed to the adoption of a voluntary industry standard for these sheets in 1993, which was subsequently endorsed by OSHA.

Despite progress of this kind and several OSHA guidelines aimed at improving disclosure, chemical hazard disclosure ranked second in the list of the ten most violated OSHA standards in 2005, accounting for over 8 percent of all violations.[28]

The extent to which workers comprehend disclosed information about chemical hazards and take protective measures in response also remains unclear. Surveys have shown that employees are generally able to understand only around 60 percent of information in chemical data sheets,[29] with more-educated workers doing significantly better than those who are less educated.[30] Even in cases where workers understand safety information, surveys suggest that they often make only limited use of it.[31] It is also interesting to note that all documented cases suggesting that training and information disclosure have a positive impact on workers' behavior involve unionized firms where labor organizations may have played an intermediary training or information-disseminating role.[32]

At the international level, OSHA played an important role in the development of an international format for chemical classification and labeling, leading to the United

Nations' adoption of a globally harmonized standard in 2002.[33] That standard, scheduled for implementation by 2008, had not yet been adopted in 2006 by OSHA for use in the United States, however.

Disclosing Toxic Releases to Reduce Pollution

Following a tragic accident at a pesticide plant in Bhopal, India, in 1984, in which deadly gas killed more than two thousand people in surrounding areas and injured more than a hundred thousand, the U.S. Congress required manufacturers that produced or used large quantities of a selected list of toxic chemicals to report annually on quantities of their release into the air or water or onto land, chemical by chemical and factory by factory. The company disclosures were assembled by the federal Environmental Protection Agency (EPA) in a Toxics Release Inventory (TRI). The Bhopal disaster provided the immediate impetus for toxic pollution disclosure. But the idea that the public had a right to know about toxic pollution in communities was also rooted in a decade of work by labor and community groups aimed at disclosing workplace and community hazards.[34]

The new requirement represented a hastily constructed political compromise tacked onto a larger legislative effort to provide an emergency response system for chemical accidents. Disclosure was supported by key senators – Robert Stafford (R-Vt.), Frank Lautenberg (D-N.J.), and Lloyd Bentsen (D-Tex.) – and by right-to-know and environmental groups. However, manufacturers sought successfully to narrow its scope by limiting the chemicals to be reported and the manufacturers required to report, excluding reporting of toxic chemical use (as opposed to release into the environment), and allowing companies to estimate releases using a variety of techniques that could be changed without notice. The EPA initially saw the disclosure system as a burdensome paperwork requirement.

Over time, however, toxic pollution disclosure provided an important bridge between traditional right-to-know measures and newer targeted transparency systems. When disclosure caused some large companies to make voluntary, immediate, and drastic reductions in toxic pollution, federal officials began to refer to the requirement as one of the nation's most successful environmental regulations. By the late 1990s, the disclosure system was credited with reducing toxic releases by nearly half in little more than a decade.[35]

The dynamics of toxic pollution disclosure reflected shifting political priorities. In the 1990s, the Clinton administration substantially strengthened disclosure by increasing the number of chemicals covered, lowering thresholds for reporting of particularly hazardous chemicals, and requiring federal facilities, power plants, and mining operations to report.[36] However, the George W. Bush administration asked for cutbacks in reporting in 2006. The administration proposed relieving nearly four thousand companies from detailed reporting and suggested reducing reporting to every other year as a cost-cutting measure.[37]

Weaknesses in the disclosure system persisted. Disclosure metrics (releases in pounds) did not help citizens assess toxicity or exposure and therefore could not create incentives to reduce risks efficiently.[38] In addition, companies used different estimating techniques, data accuracy remained uncertain, and, despite advances in information technology that made near real-time reporting feasible, timeliness of disclosure remained a serious problem. Factory-by-factory toxic pollution for calendar year 2004 was not reported to the public until April 12, 2006.[39]

Disclosing Nutritional Information to Reduce Disease

The Nutrition Labeling and Education Act of 1990 (NLEA) required food processors to label products with amounts of key nutrients as a public health measure.[40] Chronic diseases such as heart ailments, cancer, and diabetes were the largest causes of preventable deaths in the United States, killing more than 1.5 million people each year. Scientists agreed that the single most important factor in preventing and minimizing the effects of such diseases was improved diet. Before Congress acted, however, consumers had no way to assess the healthfulness of most packaged foods. Supporters of the law hoped that it would create new incentives for Americans to eat healthier foods and for manufacturers to market healthier products.[41]

Consumer groups combined with organizations such as the American Cancer Society and the American Heart Association to promote nutritional labeling as a public health measure rather than simply a right-to-know cause. Entrepreneurial members of Congress, led by Representative Henry Waxman (D-Calif.) and Senator Howard Metzenbaum (D-Ohio), pressed for the new labeling law. The food industry supported disclosure both as preferable to conflicting state requirements and as a means to reap profits from marketing healthy products.

The new law required food processors to label in standardized formats amounts in each serving of total fat, saturated fat, cholesterol, sodium, total carbohydrates, complex carbohydrates, sugars, dietary fiber, and total protein, in the context of amounts recommended for consumption as part of a daily diet. Companies also had to list total calories and calories from fat in each serving. Serving sizes were standardized to conform to amounts customarily consumed. Products that were not labeled accurately and completely could be deemed misbranded by the federal Food and Drug Administration and removed from the market. In 1994, when the law took effect, interested shoppers could compare nutrients in virtually every can, bottle, or package of processed food for the first time. The law was appropriately heralded as the most important change in national food policy in fifty years.[42]

However, Congress also gerrymandered the labeling requirement to satisfy powerful interests, exempting nearly half of consumers' food purchases. Fast-food outlets, full-service restaurants, fresh meats and seafood, deli items, and dietary supplements all escaped labeling.[43]

Nutritional labeling did improve over time – but only slowly and sporadically. Often labeling failed to keep pace with new science. Scientists had known since the 1970s that trans fatty acids were the most health-threatening fats, for example. The FDA, however, did not require their listing on food labels until 2006.[44] Major food allergens, too, were not clearly labeled until 2006.[45] And labels continued to group together all carbohydrates despite evidence that complex carbohydrates were healthier than simple carbohydrates. In a particularly serious limitation, the risks and benefits of dietary supplements remained largely undisclosed.

Disclosing Medical Mistakes to Reduce Deaths and Injuries

Despite an urgent call by the prestigious Institute of Medicine in 1999 for a new disclosure system to reduce medical mistakes in hospitals, federal moves to increase transparency have been slow and contentious, and state reporting requirements have proven difficult to sustain.[46]

In its 1999 report, the institute, an arm of the congressionally chartered National Academy of Sciences, concluded that between 44,000 and 98,000 patients died in the United States annually as a result of hospital errors.[47] In addition, as many as 938,000 hospital patients were injured each year by such errors. High rates of error were costly not only in deaths and injuries but also in loss of trust by patients in the health-care system, loss of morale by health-care professionals, loss of productivity by the workers who were their victims, and in many other ways. In economic terms alone, estimated national costs of preventable hospital errors resulting in injury or death totaled between $17 and $29 billion a year.[48]

Instead of new rules or stiff penalties for doctors, the institute called on Congress and state governments to require standardized public disclosure by health-care organizations of incidents where mistakes resulted in death or serious injury. Public disclosure would hold providers accountable for serious errors, create incentives to reduce them, and inform patients' hospital choices. The report also recommended that Congress take action to encourage voluntary and confidential reporting by doctors, nurses, and other health-care workers of less serious errors and near misses.[49]

Response was immediate. President Bill Clinton announced that he favored national action to reduce medical errors by 50 percent in five years, as the institute's panel had recommended. National news reports featured the institute's troubling findings about the frequency of medical mistakes and officials' commitments to take action. Weeks after the report was released, a poll taken by the Kaiser Family Foundation found that an astonishing 51 percent of respondents were aware of it.

However, conflicting interests created a political stalemate that blocked disclosure. The apparent consensus for national action splintered into battles among groups representing doctors and hospitals, public health advocates, state officials, consumer groups, and trial lawyers. When the debate got down to specifics, the American Medical Association and the American Hospital Association opposed the kind of hospital-by-hospital disclosure of serious errors that would be meaningful to consumers, although the American Nurses Association and a variety of consumer groups supported such transparency. Organizations representing health-care providers argued that information about errors should have broad protection from discovery in lawsuits. On that issue they were opposed by the American Trial Lawyers Association, which sought to narrow such confidentiality. Agreement on legislation remained elusive.[50]

These unsuccessful efforts to institute a national hospital-specific reporting system came in the wake of some limited reporting initiatives by a few states in the early 1990s. Most state hospital-specific public reporting systems reported patient outcomes (mortality rates, for example) rather than medical mistakes and focused on narrow subsets of medical procedures rather than on the comprehensive system proposed by the Institute of Medicine report. Among the strongest state systems were New York's Cardiac Surgery Reporting System, adopted in 1989, which provided both hospital- and doctor-level information on patient outcomes for that procedure,[51] and Pennsylvania's requirement in 1992, which provided information regarding mortality, morbidity, and other patient treatment outcomes related to coronary artery bypass surgery.[52]

However, as of 2006, most state and federal efforts continued to focus on confidential reporting or on reporting that aggregated hospital data, rather than on public disclosure of facility-specific information about medical mistakes that could help patients make informed choices and bring public pressure to bear on hospital safety. In 2005 Congress approved the Patient Safety and Quality Improvement Act, which provided a framework for voluntary reporting of medical errors by hospitals to state data centers but also established strong confidentiality requirements.[53] Twenty-three states collected data on medical errors, but virtually all required that information remain confidential. An exception was Minnesota, which required in 2002 that medical errors be reported to the public, hospital by hospital.[54] Periodic audits suggested that even confidential reporting was often late or inaccurate.[55]

More-general quality-of-care rating systems fared better. By 2006, the federal Department of Health and Human Services as well as the Joint Commission on Accreditation of Healthcare Organizations had nascent systems that ranked hospitals on the basis of Medicaid and Medicare data and surveys.[56]

Disclosing Sex Offenders' Residences to Improve Public Safety

In response to public outrage following the rape and murder of a seven-year-old girl named Megan Kanka by a released sex offender, New Jersey approved legislation in 1994 requiring disclosure of the places of residence of released sex offenders. Two years later, the federal Megan's Law was enacted. It required that all states release information to the public about known convicted sex offenders. States were given considerable discretion in how information would be provided, how frequently it would be updated, and how detailed it would be. The federal law amended an earlier statute that required states to maintain registries of released sex offenders.[57]

By 2006, all fifty states and the District of Columbia had created some form of sex offender registry and had provided for community notification of offenders' places of residence.[58] Notification methods varied widely from state to state, from active communication by police via door-to-door visits, mailings, and community meetings, to notice via hotlines or Web sites.[59] The constitutionality of state laws in Connecticut and Alaska was upheld by the Supreme Court in 2003 after lower courts struck them down as violations of due process and on other grounds.[60]

Washington State's sex offender registration and notification system, the state system that we have analyzed for this book, predates both federal statutes. The state's 1990 Community Protection Act was based on a finding that "sex offenders pose a high risk of engaging in sex offenses even after being released from incarceration"[61] and aimed to provide notice about the current residence of released sex offenders as a means of reducing risks to individuals and the community.[62]

In order to provide "necessary and relevant information" to the public, the law required that any adult or juvenile convicted of any sex or kidnapping offense register with the county sheriff's department within twenty-four hours of release or thirty days of becoming a new state resident.[63] Offenders were required to provide their name, address, date and place of birth, place of employment, information about the crime, a photograph, and other personal data.[64] Those convicted of Class A felonies remained on the list throughout their lives, while those convicted of lesser crimes remained on the list for ten or fifteen years. Failure to register or provide accurate information was deemed a class C felony or gross misdemeanor, depending on the severity of the original crime.[65]

Community notification was provided through mailings, direct notification by the police, and the Internet. Washington was one of the first states to provide an Internet-based system for searching and locating individuals on the registry, which includes photographs of offenders.[66] Members of the public are given essentially unlimited access to personal information on offenders, including their conviction records. The state's Web site does caution that "[t]he information . . . should not be used in any manner to injure, harass, or commit a criminal act against any individual named in the registry, or residing at the reported address. Any such action could subject you to criminal prosecution."[67]

Washington's sex offender disclosure system has become more rigorous over time. The law has been amended to allow police to disclose relevant information to public and private schools, child and family day care centers, and businesses and other organizations that primarily serve children and community groups. State officials have increased the amount of information required and tightened the timeliness of submission and requirements for updating changes in residence. As of March 31, 2006, 18,943 sex and kidnapping offenders were listed on the Washington public registry. The state does not estimate compliance rates. Parents for Megan's Law, a national organization that monitors state-level Megan's Laws, estimates that about one-quarter of sex offenders nationally fail to comply with state registration requirements.[68]

Disclosing Contaminants to Improve Drinking Water Safety

Under the Safe Drinking Water Act of 1974,[69] the federal EPA set maximum safe contaminant levels for drinking water and required water systems to notify customers of violations.[70] However, in practice such notification often did not take place.[71] Public attention focused on the health risks associated with contaminated water in 1993 after the largest outbreak of waterborne disease on record in the United States. In Milwaukee, Wisconsin four hundred thousand people became sick, forty-four hundred were hospitalized, and more than fifty died from drinking water contaminated with a microbe called cryptosporidium.[72]

In response, Congress in 1996 amended the federal Safe Drinking Water Act to require that water suppliers, starting in October 1999, provide customers with annual reports on contamination. The annual reports included information on the source of tap water, contaminants found in the water, sources of contamination, and violations of EPA maximum contaminant levels. Their purpose was to allow consumers to make better choices concerning their use of tap water and to encourage water utilities to be more vigilant in minimizing contaminants.[73]

The Milwaukee incident was not the only driver of greater transparency. Americans were losing confidence in their public water supplies. Surveys in the late 1990s found that only three-quarters of Americans regularly drank tap water, and 65 percent increasingly used bottled water or filtered water at the tap.[74] Experts suggested that drinking water contaminants were responsible for as many as one-third of nine hundred thousand "stomach flu" illnesses each year.[75]

Contamination levels varied widely with seasons, rainfall, and waste discharges. Sometimes chemicals and microbes entered systems as water flowed to homes through century-old pipes.[76] The EPA stated in 2004 that 27 of the 834 water systems serving more than fifty thousand people had exceeded federal safety standards for lead at least once since 2000.[77] The water system serving the nation's capital had failed to comply with sampling requirements and had failed to report to consumers that more than 10 percent of tap water samples since 2000 exceeded federal lead levels.[78]

Transparency requirements proved too weak to help residents assess risks or compare the safety of different water systems, however. They did not require consistent protocols, units of measurement, or formats for reporting contaminants. In 2003, an analysis of drinking water reports in nineteen cities by the National Resources Defense Council found that some cities buried or omitted information about health effects of contamination or warnings to consumers with compromised immune systems, all omitted information about specific polluters, fewer than half offered reports in languages other than English, and many made sweeping and inaccurate claims about water safety despite violations of federal contaminant levels.[79]

As of 2006, the drinking water contaminant disclosure system appeared to be unsustainable. Reports had improved little over the years in scope, quality, or use. Interestingly, new emphasis on homeland security raised the possibility of requiring more timely monitoring (and perhaps disclosure). In 2004, experts convened by the federal Government Accountability Office ranked "near real-time monitoring technologies" to detect contaminants as the highest priority in improving drinking water security.[80] Two years earlier, the National Academy of Sciences rated improved monitoring technologies as one of four top security priorities for drinking water supplies.[81]

Disclosing Restaurant Hygiene to Protect Public Health

On November 16, 1997, the CBS affiliate in Los Angeles, KCBS, broadcast the first of a three-part series regarding restaurant hygiene. Using the increasingly popular "hidden camera" technique, the local news exposé took viewers behind the scenes into a number of restaurant kitchens.[82] The series revealed a smorgasbord of unsanitary practices that – according to the series – were common in restaurants throughout Los Angeles County, despite the presence of an aggressive restaurant hygiene monitoring system maintained by the county. The anecdotal evidence in Los Angeles, however, was indicative of a more widespread problem. Food-borne diseases cause an estimated 325,000 hospitalizations and 5,000 deaths each year in the United States. The Centers for Disease Control (CDC) estimates that nearly 50 percent of food-borne disease outbreaks are connected to restaurants or other commercial food outlets.[83]

The public outcry arising from the investigative series led the Los Angeles County Board of Supervisors to legislate transparency to inform the public about hygiene conditions in all restaurants in the region. They unanimously adopted a disclosure requirement on December 16, 1997 (one month after the series was aired), which went into effect on January 16, 1998. The county ordinance requires public posting of restaurant hygiene grades (A, B, or C) based on Los Angeles County Department of Health Services (DHS) inspections. By making these grades public, the Board of Supervisors sought to reduce the effects of food-borne diseases by putting competitive pressure on public eating establishments with poor hygiene practices.[84] Not surprisingly, the requirement was opposed by the California Restaurant Association (a statewide trade group), as well as by many local restaurant associations. Although the transparency requirement was adopted at the county level, individual cities within the county were not required to adopt the ordinance (all but ten had chosen to do so by the end of 2005).[85]

The system builds directly on the health inspections conducted regularly by the DHS. Health inspections cover a range of very specific practices, including food temperatures, kitchen and serving area handling and preparation practices, equipment cleaning and employee sanitary practices, and surveillance of vermin.[86] Each violation receives one or more points. Cumulative points are then deducted from a starting score of 100. A score from 90 to 100 points receives an A, 80 to 89 a B, and 70 to 79 a C.[87] Cumulative scores below 70 require immediate remediation by the restaurant owner, which may include suspension of the owner's public health permit and closing of the restaurant.[88]

The transparency system requires restaurants to post the letter grade arising from the most recent inspection on the front window.[89] A searchable Web-based system includes inspection grades, numeric scores on which the grades were based, and a listing of specific violations found on the last inspection. Restaurants receive two or three unannounced inspections and one reinspection, upon request, per year. Thus, although the posting of grade cards entails relatively small costs, the system relies on a large number of inspections (about seventy-five thousand in 2003) and therefore means a sizable enforcement budget for the DHS.

The introduction of the new transparency system led to fairly rapid and significant changes in the overall grade distribution in county restaurants (as noted, the grading system existed before the disclosure requirement). When the program began, 58 percent of restaurants received an A grade, a number that grew to 83 percent by 2003. The incentives to improve are significant. Jin and Leslie report that after grade posting became required, restaurants receiving an A grade experienced revenue increases of 5.7 percent (other factors held constant); B grade restaurants had increases of 0.7 percent; and those with a C grade had declines in revenue of 1 percent.[90] The introduction of grades also improved hygiene at franchised units in chain restaurants, whereas franchised units tended to have lower hygiene than company-owned restaurants.[91]

More important, studies found significant decreases in food-borne-illness hospitalizations, ranging from 13 percent (Simon et al., 2005) to 20 percent (Jin and Leslie, 2003).

The system is not without its problems. There is some evidence that inspectors have become more lenient over time.[92] There is no systemic evidence of corruption in grading, although the economic incentives for it are significant, given the high stakes involved in restaurant grades.[93] Some critics of the system have argued that it is incompatible with the standard food preparation practices of certain ethnic groups who therefore face an unfair disadvantage from the grading system.[94]

Several other cities in the United States have similar restaurant hygiene disclosure systems.[95] While eight states had introduced legislation requiring posting grade cards, as of 2005 only Tennessee and North Carolina had statewide systems.[96]

Disclosing Rollover Propensities to Improve Auto Safety

In 2000, a series of widely reported traffic fatalities associated with rollovers of popular sport utility vehicles (SUVs) drew national attention. These incidents, which also involved sudden tread separation in certain lines of Firestone tires, highlighted a more general public safety problem. SUVs were more likely than sedans or station wagons to roll over, and some SUVs were much more likely to roll over than others.[97]

Improving public understanding of the propensity of vehicles to roll over was important because rollover accidents remained the most deadly auto accidents in the United States and were increasing. Rollovers accounted for less than 4 percent of all auto accidents but accounted for about a third of driver and passenger fatalities (61 percent of SUV fatalities and 22 percent of passenger-car fatalities). From 1991 to 2001 the number of drivers and passengers killed in all automobile accidents in the United States increased by 4 percent, while deaths in rollover accidents increased by 10 percent. Light-truck (including SUV) rollover fatalities increased 43 percent, whereas passenger-car rollover fatalities declined 15 percent.[98]

Improving public understanding of rollover risks was also important because federal rules did not set any minimum safety standards for new-model rollover performance, as they did for front and side impact crashworthiness. The auto industry had successfully opposed such a standard for two decades.[99]

In response to the Firestone/SUV accidents, Congress approved a new targeted transparency system aimed at informing car buyers' choices and providing incentives for manufacturers to design vehicles less prone to rollovers. The Transportation Recall Enhancement, Accountability, and Documentation (TREAD) Act of 2000 required public disclosure of the rollover propensity of each new-model car and SUV as measured by government tests.[100]

Regulators required rollover ratings to be presented in a simple five-star format that paralleled the existing star rating systems for front and side impact crashworthiness.[101] A five-star vehicle had a 10 per cent or less chance of rolling over while a one-star vehicle had a 40 percent or more chance of rolling over.[102]

The new law and regulations added other disclosure requirements. They required tire pressure monitoring sensors by 2004, automakers' disclosure of information on customer complaints and other early indications of safety defects,[103] and new labels to make it easier for car owners to see if their tires had been recalled.[104]

Disclosure improved over time. The TREAD Act included an innovative provision that required that the government's initial mathematical modeling of rollover propensity be replaced with a road test that would more accurately mimic real-world driving conditions; Congress also directed the National Academy of Sciences to study possible tests quickly and required regulators to consider the academy's recommendations.[105] As a result, officials instituted a more accurate test in 2004 that combined modeling with driving maneuvers.[106] In 2005, Congress further increased consumer access to rollover information by requiring that rollover ratings be posted on new-car stickers in auto showrooms.[107]

Early evidence suggested that auto rollover disclosure helped to inform consumers and encourage safer new-model design. Five years after the requirement was introduced, only one model (the Ford Explorer Sport Trac) received as few as two stars, while twenty-four models earned four-star ratings.[108] Congress's Government Accountability Office concluded that ratings were "successful in encouraging manufacturers to make safer vehicles and providing information to consumers."[109] Manufacturers used ratings as a marketing tool in television and print ads.[110]

Interestingly, this targeted transparency system also helped to change the politics of auto safety regulation. By encouraging manufacturers to accelerate introduction of new stabilizing technology, the rollover rating system reduced industry opposition to a minimum safety standard for rollovers. In 2005, Congress directed regulators to issue such a standard.[111]

However, as of 2006, the rollover rating system still had significant weaknesses. The system relied on government rather than manufacturer tests. As a result of budget and logistical constraints, not all new-model cars were tested, and some test results were not available until late in the model year.[112] Ratings also did not allow consumers to compare the safety of specific models across weight classes.[113] In addition, backup data for star ratings remained difficult to access. Consumers had to delve into the government's docket management system or research and development Web page, or visit a National Crash Analysis Center in Washington, D.C.[114]

Rollover star ratings themselves remained controversial, as did the longer-established star ratings for crashworthiness in front and side impacts. The Transportation Research Board, as well as consumer groups and auto insurance associations, charged that star ratings gave consumers a falsely positive impression of safety, since one-star vehicles could have a 40 percent chance of rolling over, and that ratings diminished in usefulness when most vehicles earned four or five stars.[115]

Disclosing Terrorism Threats to Improve Public Safety

Six months after the attacks of September 11, 2001, the Bush administration created a color-coded ranking system to inform the public about terrorist threats. The system's stated purpose was "to provide a comprehensive and effective means of disseminating information regarding the risk of terrorist acts to Federal, State, and local authorities and to the American people" in order "to inform and facilitate decisions appropriate to different levels of government and to private citizens at home and at work." The aim was to minimize attacks and their consequences. The system was designed to be flexible and information-based. It provided a framework for communicating the severity of national, local, or sector-specific threats as well as their likely character and timing.[116]

The alert system established five color-coded levels of terrorist threat: green – low; blue – guarded; yellow – elevated; orange – high; red – severe. The presidential directive clearly contemplated that alerts would be accompanied by factual information.[117]

The directive also made it clear that information was intended to create incentives for action. Each level of alert was meant to trigger threat-specific protective measures by government agencies, private organizations, and individuals. The directive provided that threat levels would reflect both the probability and the gravity of attack and would be reviewed at regular intervals to see if they should be adjusted. The level set was to be based on the degree to which a threat was credible, corroborated, imminent, and grave.[118]

The system provided flexibility. Threat levels could be set for specific geographical areas or for specific industries or facilities. The system provided for case-by-case judgments about whether threat levels would be announced publicly or communicated in a more limited way to emergency officials and other selected audiences. The stated intent was to "share as much information regarding the threat as possible, consistent with the safety of the Nation."[119]

Once the Department of Homeland Security (DHS) was created in March 2003, the secretary of homeland security was charged with responsibility for setting threat levels, with the advice of the Homeland Security Council.[120] Within the department, the warning system was administered by an undersecretary for information analysis and infrastructure protection.

As of early 2006, the terrorist threat warning level had been raised and lowered seven times, each time from yellow (elevated) to orange (high) and back again. The system generally produced warnings that proved too vague to provide government officials, business managers, or ordinary citizens with incentives to take appropriate protective actions.

However, alerts were increasingly specific. On August 2, 2004, the Department of Homeland Security issued a warning concerning three particular facilities: the Prudential building in Newark, New Jersey, and the headquarters of the World Bank and International Monetary Fund in Washington, D.C. On July 7, 2005, when several bombs were detonated in the London subway system, DHS raised the threat level from yellow to orange for mass transit only, though noting that the government had "no specific, credible information" to suggest that an attack in the United States was imminent.[121]

The system worked differently for different audiences. When a decision was made to change the threat level, department officials notified federal, state, and local agencies electronically or by phone and also called chief executives of major corporations, using a secure connection maintained by the Business Roundtable.[122]

DHS also developed channels for communicating threat information without raising the overall threat level. The department issued threat advisories or less urgent information bulletins for specific locales or sectors. Access to these communications was often restricted, however, leaving the public uninformed. Officials explained that such information was shared on a need-to-know basis, since it was often derived from classified sources. A GAO review of a sample of secret threat advisories in 2004 concluded that they contained "actionable information about threats targeting critical national networks, infrastructures, or key assets such as transit systems."[123]

In practice, however, the terrorist threat warning system remained problematic. Several in-depth evaluations and surveys found that rankings were little used by its intended audiences. The Gilmore Commission, a broad-based congressional commission charged with continuing oversight of domestic responses to terrorism, concluded in 2003 that "[t]he Homeland Security Warning System has become largely marginalized." On occasion, governors and mayors declined to elevate threat levels or take other federally recommended actions. Public and private groups expressed frustration at the lack of information about the character and location of threats. The commission recommended the creation of a regional alert system featuring specific guidance, as well as training local officials for responses to each threat level.[124]

A report by the nonpartisan Congressional Research Service in 2003 concluded that threat alerts were so vague that the public "might begin to question the authenticity" of threats and therefore ignore them. The report noted that the government "has never explained the sources and quality of the intelligence upon which the threat levels were based."[125]

Government officials have rarely received information specific enough to act upon. A survey by the General Accounting Office in 2004 found that sixteen of twenty-four federal agencies had received information about elevated threat levels from the media before they received it from homeland security officials.[126] One of the potential strengths of the alert system was that it was constructed to work synergistically with regulatory requirements. Each federal department was required to come up with its own protective measures appropriate to each threat level and to take those actions each time the threat level was raised. However, federal agencies surveyed by the GAO reported that changes from yellow to orange had minimal impact on their practices, since they maintained high levels of security at all times.[127]

State officials, too, reported that they received much of their information about changed threat levels through the media and got little specific information from the government. The GAO survey found that fifteen of forty states learned about threat level changes from the media before they heard from federal officials in at least one instance. State and local officials reported that learning about threats at the same time as the public could carry heavy political costs. State officials also noted that they received conflicting advice from different federal authorities about what actions to take.[128]

The most serious failing of the transparency system has been its lack of meaningful information and guidance. Local officials, always on the front lines in preparing for and responding to disasters, need accurate, specific, and timely information. A report by the minority staff of the Senate Governmental Affairs Committee concluded in 2003 that two years after the attacks on the World Trade Center and the Pentagon, state and local officials had too little information to respond to terrorist attacks. The report noted that effective communication channels still had not been established with state and local officials, so states and localities had no effective way of communicating with one another or of learning from the successes or mistakes of others.[129] A June 2004 report by the nonpartisan GAO echoed these themes. It suggested that warnings would be more effective if they were more specific and action-oriented; communicated through multiple methods; included timely notification; and featured specific information on the nature, location, and timing of threats as well as guidance on actions to take in response to threats.[130]

The public remained confused. Information accompanying increases in the threat level often has been vague or irrelevant to the daily activities of most Americans. Most state governments and many local governments have developed their own alert systems which are not necessarily consistent with the federal system. The administration has also sent mixed messages to the public concerning what actions to take. In raising the threat level to orange on September 10, 2002, for example, Secretary Ridge told people to "continue with your plans" but "be wary and be mindful."[131] In June 2003, Ridge acknowledged that the system needed improvement. "We worry about the credibility of the system . . . we want to continue to refine it, because we understand it has caused a kind of anxiety."[132]

Members of Congress from both parties expressed growing impatience with vague and conflicting messages. After the government raised the threat level to orange over the 2003 Christmas holidays and told citizens to be vigilant but continue their daily routines, Christopher Shays (R-Conn.) asked: "Why would the department tell people to do everything they would normally do? . . . We're at high risk." Christopher Cox (R-Calif.), chairman of the House Select Committee on Homeland Security, noted that vague warnings could also cause too much action, citing evidence that groups had canceled field trips and other activities.[133] Senator Frank R. Lautenberg (D-N.J.) noted that "the system may be doing more harm than good."[134]

Public confusion was reflected in polls. A Hart-Teeter poll sponsored by the Council for Excellence in Government in March 2004 found that 73 percent of those polled were anxious or concerned about terrorism and 34 percent had looked for information about what to do in the event of an attack, but only one person in five was aware of state or local preparedness plans.[135] Earlier Fox News polls found that 78 percent of those responding did not know or said they were not sure what the current threat level was and that 90 percent responded to recent elevation of the threat level by going about their lives as usual.[136] A *New York Times* poll in October 2004 found that nearly two-thirds of those responding did not have emergency kits prepared and more than two-thirds did not have communication plans.

Philip Zimbardo, the president of the American Psychological Association, suggested that the terrorist threat system had turned the United States into a nation of "worriers, not warriors," by "forcing citizens to ride an emotional roller coaster without providing any clear instructions on how to soothe their jitters." He noted that a large body of research suggested that effective safety measures required a credible source, information about the particular event that created a threat, and information about specific actions citizens could take to reduce risks.[137]

Improving the Quality and Fairness of Critical Services and Processes

Disclosing Union Finances to Minimize Corruption

In the 1950s, about one-third of the U.S. workforce in the private sector was unionized (as compared to 8 percent in 2005), and unions represented the majority of workers in steel and auto manufacturing, trucking, construction, food processing, and other industries central to the economy. Union leaders like John L. Lewis, Walter Reuther, George Meany, and Jimmy Hoffa were well-known national figures. The considerable economic and political influence exercised by labor unions provoked concern in the business community and in Congress.[138]

In 1957, congressional hearings chaired by Senator John L. McClellan (D-Ark.) focused on one source of concern: bribery, fraud, and other forms of racketeering in parts of the labor movement. The two-year, high-profile, and often sensational Senate investigations revealed corruption in a number of major labor organizations and resulted in calls for government intervention in union governance.[139] In this crisis atmosphere, Congress debated different methods to improve standards of democracy, fiscal responsibility, and transparency in private-sector labor organizations.

Political compromise produced the Labor Management Reporting and Disclosure Act (LMRDA), which created standards for democratic governance and required unions to periodically reveal detailed information regarding financial practices and governance procedures.[140] Disclosure requirements were relatively narrow in scope, focusing on union balance sheets, loan activities, officer salaries, and line-item disbursements (e.g., for employee salary and benefits, administrative expenses, and rent and operating expenses) rather than on programmatic expenditures at the national and local union level.[141] A division of the U.S. Department of Labor, the Office of Labor Management Services (OLMS), was created to enforce the law, including its disclosure provisions.[142] The penalties associated with failing to provide timely and accurate reports were significant. From the start, disclosure imposed substantial costs on union officers but offered few benefits to them, creating incentives for officers to provide minimal information.[143]

For most of the disclosure requirement's history, it was difficult and costly for union members to gain access to the information that was ostensibly made public.[144] They had to go to a reading room at the Labor Department in Washington, D.C., or to a regional office, or make a request by mail, paying a per-page charge.[145] Even then, information remained fragmented. Regional offices carried only records relating to union affiliates in their geographical area.[146] Most union members were unaware that the information existed, and even for those who learned about it, reporting forms proved technical and difficult to interpret.[147]

These high costs to individual information users created a potential role for intermediaries. But, as of 2006, it remained uncommon to find formal groups within unions that could act independently of incumbent officers and were capable of playing an intermediary role. Employers, too, rarely used the information from the disclosure system to discredit unions – they had more effective tools at hand. The decline of union strength beginning in the early 1980s also made many in the labor movement reluctant to "air dirty laundry" in public for fear of providing ammunition to antiunion employers and damaging public support for the labor movement.[148]

With high costs to information disclosers and users, and few intermediaries available to lower user costs, it is not surprising that the scope, accuracy, and use of this disclosure system did not improve much in forty years. The only significant expansion in scope occurred with the passage of legislation that created similar access to union financial information for federal government workers and the addition of reporting requirements for financial institutions that made loans to unions.[149]

Accuracy or timeliness of the disclosed information improved little. The financial categories and definitions remained the same, as did the level of required financial detail.[150] And despite strong enforcement provisions, the annual delinquency rate in filing reports was 25 percent, the GAO found in 2000. The likelihood of a recordkeeping inspection was small, and most penalties were directed toward unions that intentionally failed to file or that falsified reports.[151]

Overall use of information by rank-and-file union members remained minimal. Contrary to Congress's expectation that information would be used by union members, most users over the past three decades have been business groups, antiunion consultants, or academics.[152] In 1999, a typical year prior to the creation of Internet-based access, the Labor Department responded to only eight thousand disclosure requests from all sources (out of 13 million union members who were covered by the transparency policy).

The costs of disclosing and particularly of using information, however, fell substantially when Congress appropriated funds in fiscal years 1998 and 1999 to develop and implement electronic filing and dissemination of reports. Over the following three years, the Labor Department developed systems for both filing and accessing disclosure forms via the Internet.[153] As of 2006, unions could file forms electronically, and users could view and print all union financial reports from the year 2000 to the present, search records by a variety of criteria, and request copies from earlier periods via the Department of Labor's Internet Public Disclosure Room (http://www.union-reports.dol.gov).

The most significant changes to union financial reporting requirements since 1959 came with the election of George W. Bush in 2000. From 2001 to 2006 the Bush administration dramatically increased funding to the Labor Department office that administers the disclosure system (while reducing budgets in much of the rest of the Labor Department), expanding the number of full-time equivalent staff from 290 in FY 2001 to 384 in its proposed FY 2006 budget, and raising overall funding from $30.5 million in FY 2001 to $48.8 million in its proposed FY 2006 budget.[154] The administration cited improving the accuracy and timeliness of union reporting as one of the strategic priorities for this division.

More important, the Bush administration used its authority to issue regulations to alter a variety of reporting requirements.[155] These included expanding reporting for smaller labor unions; requiring electronic filing; and changing the way that financial information is provided by, for example, requiring that unions disclose information on all services purchased for five thousand dollars or more.[156] The new regulations also required reporting of financial information on a programmatic – as well as a line-item – basis (e.g., providing information on the amount of money spent for representation, organizing, and other major union activities).[157] Individual unions and the AFL-CIO opposed many of these changes, arguing that they would substantially increase the costs faced by labor organizations with little additional benefit to union members. They ultimately lost these legal challenges in 2005.[158]

Disclosing Campaign Contributions to Reduce Corruption

Public disclosure of campaign contributions to congressional and presidential candidates represents one of the United States' earliest, most sustainable, and most perennially controversial targeted transparency systems.

From the beginning, the primary purpose of campaign finance disclosure was to reduce corruption in government. In *Buckley v. Valeo*, the 1976 Supreme Court decision that upheld the constitutionality of federal disclosure requirements, the Court concluded that disclosure reduced corruption in three ways. First, it provided the electorate with information about where money came from and how it was spent, in order to aid voters in evaluating those running for office, including alerting voters "to the interests to which a candidate is most likely to be responsive." Second, disclosure helped to "deter actual corruption and avoid the appearance of corruption by exposing large contributions and expenditures to the light of publicity." Such exposure "may discourage those who would use money for improper purposes either before or after the election," because "a public armed with information about a candidate's most generous supporters is better able to detect any post-election special favors that may be given in return." Third, the Court said, reporting was "an essential means of gathering data to detect violations of contribution limits."[159] Disclosure worked in tandem with a rule-based regulatory system that limited amounts and sources of contributions.

The use of transparency to reduce campaign finance corruption began early and improved in response to episodes of perceived abuses. The first campaign finance disclosure law, the Publicity Act of 1910,[160] was championed by President Theodore Roosevelt and progressive reformers as an antidote to the influence of big business in politics. Roosevelt pressed for disclosure after his opponent in the 1904 election accused him of accepting corporate gifts intended to buy influence in the administration. Civic organizations such as the National Publicity Law Organization kept pressure on Congress until the law was passed.[161]

Today's national system of campaign finance disclosure dates from the Federal Election Campaign Act (FECA) of 1971, which was enacted in response to the perceived ineffectiveness of earlier laws and the growing influence of money in politics. FECA required candidates for national office to disclose contributions of one hundred dollars or more in quarterly reports. In election years, contributions of five thousand dollars or more had to be reported within forty-eight hours and disclosed to the public forty-eight hours after reporting. The law also limited contributions and media expenditures.[162] Allegations of corruption in the 1972 presidential election, including the Watergate scandal, led Congress to expand disclosure requirements in 1974 and to create an independent bipartisan Federal Election Commission (FEC) that received disclosed information and made it available to the public.[163] Later amendments aimed to broaden disclosure and make it more efficient. Reforms required reporting by "527" nonprofit organizations that promoted candidates but were not campaign committees and focused reporting on committees that raised substantial amounts of funds.[164]

In 2002, Congress again tightened spending limits and strengthened disclosure. The main purpose of the McCain-Feingold law (officially, the Bipartisan Campaign Reform Act) was to close loopholes that allowed candidates and their supporters to use "soft money" to circumvent campaign spending limitations. Soft money refers to funds used to finance issue ads that promote particular candidates. As part of the effort to regulate "soft money," Congress required organizations that sponsored candidate-specific issue ads to disclose the names of contributors and spending on such ads. Anyone who "knowingly and willfully" violated disclosure provisions could face a maximum penalty of five years in prison.[165] In *McConnell v. Federal Election Commission*, decided in 2003, the Supreme Court again upheld the constitutionality of disclosure requirements as an important means of informing voters, reducing corruption, and enforcing spending limits.[166]

Campaign finance disclosure remains widely supported in concept but perennially debated in its specifics. Over the years, the system has gained diverse users and the support of many candidates. The press, advocacy groups, political consultants, groups concerned with expanding public information, and other intermediaries often repackage the disclosed data and provide their own interpretations for the public. Federal enforcement authorities use the data to ferret out violations of spending limits. Candidates use the data to gather information about their opponents and sometimes have a reputational interest in disclosing campaign finance information beyond what is required by federal law. In the 2000 and 2004 elections presidential candidates disclosed all their contributions on campaign Web sites.[167]

The Internet is fundamentally changing the dynamics of campaigning and of campaign finance disclosure. By 2006, candidates used the Internet to raise money, convene virtual town meetings, collect signatures, reach organizers, and customize email messages to supporters. The campaigns of George W. Bush and John Kerry in 2004 raised $100 million on the Internet, mostly in small donations. Howard Dean, former governor of Vermont, built much of his 2004 presidential campaign on the Internet. Advocacy groups used the Internet to convene online primaries and mobilize supporters and resources. Ordinary citizens used the Internet to share facts, express their views about candidates, and provide contributions.[168]

In 2006, Congress and regulators were still struggling to integrate into federal campaign laws changes in campaigning brought about by the Internet. "The rise of the Internet . . . changes the fundamentals of political speech," Trevor Potter and Kirk L. Jowers concluded in an early analysis of election law and the Internet. By making it possible to reach large audiences with rich and customized information at little or no cost, the Internet challenges the premise of election law that controlling and disclosing funding controls corruption. "With no cost of communication, current law has nothing to measure . . . [and] the entire mechanism for disclosing political expenditures . . . is thrown into question."[169] The Internet has also created new ways to spread false or misleading information. Sham Web sites proliferated during the 2004 campaign, and both Republicans and Democrats routinely set up sites to post negative information about opponents.[170]

In the 1990s and early 2000s, new requirements also employed the Internet and computer technology to provide more timely campaign finance information. In the 1970s, committees made paper or microfilm filings to the FEC, which could be accessed by the public only at FEC headquarters. In the early years of the Internet, the FEC allowed information to be downloaded for a fee. By 2006, most information was required to be filed electronically and was available on the FEC Web site within forty-eight hours free of charge.[171]

More difficult questions concerned whether and how to regulate campaign activities on the Internet. In March 2006, the FEC provided some answers by ruling unanimously that most political communication on the Internet was not covered by campaign finance laws. Only paid political Internet ads were covered by such laws.[172] Exempting most political communication on the Internet from regulation was "an important step in protecting grass roots and online politics," commission chairman Michael E. Toner told the *New York Times*.[173]

Contentious issues continued to surround campaign finance disclosure. A report by the Senate Committee on Government Affairs in 1996 described widespread and systematic evasion of disclosure requirements.[174] The FEC's restricted budget raised continuing questions about the commission's capacity to monitor and enforce disclosure requirements. Finally, the growth of the Internet raised new issues concerning the appropriate balancing of the public interest in disclosure against the public interest in protecting freedom of expression.

Disclosing Lending Practices to Reduce Discrimination

The Home Mortgage Disclosure Act (HMDA), initially enacted in 1975 and substantially expanded in 1989,[175] required banks to disclose detailed information about their mortgage lending. The law aimed to curb discrimination in such lending to create more equal opportunity to access credit. The disclosure requirement compelled banks, savings and loan associations, and other lending institutions to report annually the amounts and geographical distribution of their mortgage applications, origins, and purchases disaggregated by race, gender, annual income, and other characteristics. The data, collected and disclosed by the Federal Financial Institutions Examination Council, were made available to the public and to financial regulators to determine if lenders were serving the housing needs of the communities where they were located.[176] The Examination Council was an interagency body that included the Federal Reserve System, the Federal Deposit Insurance Corporation, and other agencies. In 2004, as many as 33.6 million loan records were reported by nearly nine thousand financial institutions.[177]

Mortgage lending disclosure was part of Congress's response to activists' calls, in the later stages of the civil rights movement of the 1960s and 1970s, for greater economic equality. It followed congressional action in 1968 to bar racial discrimination in housing sales or rentals; a settlement negotiated by the Department of Justice to end racial discrimination in the appraisal profession; and approval of the federal Equal Credit Opportunity Act in 1974, which outlawed racial and ethnic discrimination in lending.[178] Community-based organizations pressed for disclosure requirements to aid their local campaigns to end lending discrimination. One of the most prominent figures in this debate was Gale Cincotta, a Chicago-based leader of the fair housing and community reinvestment movement, who founded National People's Action and the National Training and Information Center, two of the local organizations that documented the retreat of banks from inner-city neighborhoods in the 1960s and 1970s and pressed for more equitable lending. She and other activists found an ally in Senate Banking Committee chair William Proxmire (D-Wis.). In 1975, Proxmire sponsored a bill requiring disclosure of lending practices.[179] Despite opposition from the banking industry, the requirement was ultimately approved by a narrow margin in both the Senate (47–45) and the House (177–147).[180]

Under initial disclosure requirements, banks were required to report minimal data about the geographic location of home loan approvals and purchases. Additional legislation expanded and refined these disclosure requirements. In 1977, Congress approved the Community Reinvestment Act (CRA), which required lending institutions to meet the credit needs of the communities in which they operated and linked community lending records to approval of merger applications.[181] In 1980, Congress approved the Housing and Community Development Act, which directed the Federal Financial Institutions Examination Council to serve as a central clearinghouse for mortgage lending data.[182] Finally, in response to the savings and loan crisis of the 1980s, Congress approved in 1989 the Federal Financial Institutions Reform, Recovery, and Enforcement Act (FIRREA),[183] which sought to stabilize and provide new oversight for the savings and loan industry. Community reinvestment groups lobbied successfully to include improvements in disclosure, such as reporting of applications as well as loans; reporting of the race, sex, and income of borrowers and applicants; and reporting by a broader range of mortgage lenders.[184]

As Congress expanded the scope and depth of this transparency system, it gained wider use. Advocacy groups used mortgage lending data to document constraints on credit in their communities and to negotiate new mechanisms for low-income lending with individual banks. Broad-based community reinvestment task forces in Washington, Rhode Island, New Jersey, and Michigan forged partnerships among community organizations, lending institutions, and state and local governments to address access problems. Investigative reporters, financial analysts, and intermediaries used the information to document pervasive patterns of discriminatory lending and the exodus of banks from low-income neighborhoods. In 1988, for example, the *Atlanta Journal-Constitution* reported on widespread redlining in that city in "The Color of Money," a series of articles that received extensive national attention.[185]

In 1992, the Boston Federal Reserve conducted a rigorous study that concluded that race had a strong influence in lending decisions.[186] The study received broad media coverage, confronting banks with discrimination allegations from a particularly authoritative source.

As they responded to a wave of requests for bank mergers in the late 1980s and 1990s, federal regulators also employed mortgage lending data in deciding whether to grant approvals. The banking industry was shaken in 1989 when the Federal Reserve Bank first exercised this power by denying a merger request from Continental Illinois National Bank and Trust Company of Chicago on the ground that the bank had not met its community reinvestment requirements. Advocacy groups that tracked the performance of particular banks often petitioned regulators to turn down merger requests if their performance indicated unfair lending practices.

This shift in the competitive environment led many more banks to improve lending practices in the 1990s.[187] The competitive shift resulted in part from mortgage lending disclosure and the requirements of the Community Reinvestment Act, as well as from the proliferation of sophisticated community organizations that had developed the expertise to understand bank lending patterns and negotiate with financial institutions. More banks developed products, divisions, and methods to compete in low-income markets, and bankers acknowledged that disclosure and community reinvestment requirements had proven less burdensome than expected.[188]

The accuracy and scope of disclosed lending data also continued to improve. Disclosure became more frequent, data quality increased, more financial institutions were required to report, and data were collected and distributed electronically.[189]

After the successes of the 1990s, community organizations and regulators turned their attention to predatory lending, a practice in which vulnerable minorities were offered higher-interest mortgages and less-favorable terms than other borrowers.[190] In 2002, mortgage lending disclosure rules were amended to require banks to disclose not only the disposition of loan applications but also mortgage prices. Beginning in 2004, lenders were required to report data on loan pricing for loan originations in which the annual percentage rate exceeded the yield of comparable Treasury securities by a specified amount. These new data allowed intermediaries such as the National Community Reinvestment Coalition and the Association of Community Organizations for Reform Now to document disparities in access to credit and press for measures to address predatory lending.[191] Regulators used the expanded information to enforce fair lending laws. In 2005, the Federal Reserve incorporated these new data into their statistical strategies for identifying potentially discriminatory institutions that warranted closer regulatory scrutiny.[192]

Disclosing Plant Closings and Layoffs to Reduce Community Disruptions

Concerned over the economic impacts of intensifying global competition in the manufacturing sector and facing political fallout from a growing number of high-profile plant closings and mass layoffs, Congress debated a variety of proposals in the late 1970s and early 1980s. Policy options ranged from restrictions on employer rights to close major facilities to industry-based policies to improve competitiveness and major modifications of the unemployment insurance system.[193]

In 1988, political compromise led to a more modest targeted transparency approach: the Worker Adjustment and Retraining Notification Act (WARN).[194] This law sought to protect affected parties from the effects of major employment loss by requiring covered employers to provide advance notice of plant closings or large-scale layoffs to affected workers and local communities.[195] The aim of the new disclosure requirement was to improve post-layoff and plant closing outcomes for displaced workers as well as to provide communities facing significant economic impacts with time to find alternative solutions or make adjustments for the impending closings.

Even this modest, disclosure-based response to economic restructuring involved significant political compromises. Opponents of advance notice argued that it would restrict the capital mobility that was increasingly important given international competition from countries like Japan and South Korea. In so doing, it would further widen labor productivity gaps with the rest of the world, making U.S. companies less competitive. Further, critics of advance notice argued that it would lead customers, suppliers, and capital markets to overreact, making already weakened companies less able to recover and expand. If advance notice was to be required, they argued, it should be provided a relatively short time before plant closing. It should also exempt wide classes of employers whose decisions to reduce employment reflected the normal ebb and flow of production, rather than more profound, long-term reductions in employment.[196]

The resulting disclosure requirements reflected these concerns. Covered employers were required to provide affected employees with only sixty days notice of a closing.

Although virtually all workers at covered employers – hourly, salaried, and managerial workers – were entitled to notice, employer coverage was quite restricted. Private and not-for-profit employers were covered if they had one hundred or more workers, but employees were excluded from that count if they had worked for fewer than six months in the past year or fewer than twenty hours per week on average. That meant that a large number of small businesses were not required to provide advance notice of layoffs or closings.

The definition of plant closing and mass layoff also left many potential company decisions involving large employment cuts outside the targeted transparency system's disclosure requirement. A covered employer was required to provide advance notice if an impending shutdown would lead to a loss of 50 or more workers in a thirty-day period. Mass layoff was defined narrowly as reducing employment at any site of 500 or more workers or laying off 50–499 workers if that number represented at least a third of the workforce.[197] In addition, covered employers were not required to provide advance notice for a variety of "unforeseeable" business reasons, for natural disasters, or where it could be shown that even the sixty-day disclosure would cause irreparable harm to the business's viability.[198]

The law did not provide an extensive apparatus for implementation. Unlike most federal workplace policies, the advance notice requirement did not vest a particular division of the U.S. Department of Labor with authority to investigate or enforce the law. Enforcement was provided instead through lawsuits lodged in federal courts by workers, their representatives (if any), and/or local governments. An employer found in violation of the disclosure requirement could be required to pay the affected workers back pay and benefits for the period when notice was not provided (up to sixty days). Employers were also subject to civil penalties of up to five hundred dollars for each day of violation. Companies were left with considerable discretion concerning the means by which they would notify workers and communities. The law did not provide a notification format or indicate through whom (union officers or other representatives) workers would be contacted or the "local community" informed.[199]

The combination of restrictive employer coverage and the rather narrow definition of plant closings and mass layoffs has meant that a relatively small percentage of layoffs has been covered by the disclosure policy's requirements. In an early study of the requirement's impact, Ehrenburg and Jakubson concluded that although compliance with the policy was high, "WARN does not affect a substantial proportion of permanently laid off workers."[200] That conclusion was still valid in 2006, given the large percentage of the workforce employed in workplaces with fewer than a hundred workers and the fact that the vast majority of employment reductions (even in large workplaces) do not fall within the narrow definitions of employment loss described in the regulation.[201]

Disclosure provisions for plant closings and layoffs have not changed substantially since their initial approval, although several recent events have led Congress to consider expanding or modifying disclosure. Following the terrorist attacks on the United States in 2001, Congress held hearings about the significant employment dislocations associated with those attacks – particularly in the hotel and hospitality industries – which led some in Congress to call for expanding the reach of the disclosure policy.[202] In 2004, high-profile instances of "offshoring" work to India and China led the Senate to consider expanding the transparency rules' definition of employment loss.[203] As of 2006, however, neither of these efforts had led to changes in the law.

Disclosing School Performance to Improve Public Education

Many states enacted school report card requirements in the mid-1980s as concern about the inadequacies of public education mounted.[204] In 1983 *A Nation at Risk*, a report commissioned by President Ronald Reagan's secretary of education, Terrell Bell, warned that American public education often was mediocre compared to that of other countries.[205] In a study of students' performance in twenty-two countries, U.S. students placed twelfth. SAT scores, too, had declined in the 1960s and early 1970s. Press coverage of discipline and drug problems also suggested the need for better school accountability. Education was the largest single item in most state budgets, and candidates featured education issues prominently in state election campaigns in the 1980s.

State and local officials saw school report cards as one way to provide parents with greater choice and to put pressure on school administrators to improve performance. Report cards could work in tandem with other novel approaches that states were experimenting with – vouchers to pay for private schools, charter schools, and performance contracting, a form of financing that allowed schools to design educational programs and secure resources in exchange for agreements to achieve certain performance outcomes. Report cards could reward schools for meeting their performance targets.[206]

In an effort to spread the innovative practices of a few states, Congress required in 1994 that all states establish school performance standards and test students to assess whether they met these standards.[207] Congress also required educational agencies receiving funding under Title I of the Elementary and Secondary Education Act to "publicize and disseminate to teachers and other staff, parents, students, and the community" the results of annual performance reviews.[208]

The content, presentation, and means of disseminating information in school report cards continued to vary widely from state to state, however. According to a national study by *Education Week* in 1999, only thirty-six states published regular report cards on individual schools.[209] Most presented information on schools' past test scores and on state averages. Reporting on other aspects of performance – school safety, class size, and faculty qualifications – was less common. Only a quarter of the states with report cards presented information that allowed comparisons among test scores of schools with similar student demographics. Some states distributed school report cards to students, while most made them available on the Internet.

One major problem was the lack of consensus about the kinds of data that school report cards should contain to measure performance. Surveys conducted in 1998 found that parents and educators sometimes had quite different views regarding important content, and that existing school report cards did not always contain information that both regarded as very important. Educators were more likely to want demographic and disaggregated data, while some parents were concerned that such data would be divisive. Only about a third of those polled thought that schools should be judged principally on student achievement on standardized tests. Most regarded indicators of teacher quality and school climate as among the critical data to include.[210]

In addition, some early research suggested that surprisingly few parents and educators made use of report card information. Research by Public Agenda conducted in 1999 found that only 52 percent of teachers and 31 percent of parents had seen a school report card.[211]

In 2001, the George W. Bush administration championed the No Child Left Behind Act as a centerpiece of public eduction reform. Among other provisions, the law required school districts that received federal assistance for disadvantaged students under Title I of the Elementary and Secondary Education Act to publish report cards for each of its schools.[212]

The new federal requirements demanded disclosure of more information than was commonly published by districts at that time. School report cards had to disclose students' achievement on state tests and disaggregate test scores by race, disability status, and English proficiency. They also had to disclose teacher qualifications and show trends in achievement, dropout rates, graduation rates, and percentages of students not tested.[213]

The quality of school report cards has increased substantially since the enactment of the No Child Left Behind law, although report cards still fall short of full compliance.[214] By 2004, all fifty states provided school report cards and forty-four states disaggregated student achievement data by race and disability as required by 2001 law. However, only fourteen states disaggregated graduation data and provided information regarding the number and percentage of "highly qualified" teachers as required by the law.

At the same time, multiple federal and state reporting requirements created confusion. In 2004, nineteen states had more than one report card per school and sixteen states created special report cards to comply with the requirements of the No Child Left Behind law.[215]

One careful study of state-level student performance in 2004 found that the incentives and sanctions associated with accountability systems in education reform had a significant and positive impact on test scores but that school report cards alone had no independent statistically significant effect.[216] In 2006, it was still too early to determine whether school report cards would improve over time and whether they would create incentives for better public education.

TARGETED TRANSPARENCY IN THE INTERNATIONAL CONTEXT

Harmonizing Disclosure of Corporate Finances to Reduce Risks to Investors

International rules for corporate financial disclosure evolved slowly in the 1990s as rapid integration of securities markets made compliance with widely varying national rules both costly and confusing for companies and regulators. By 2006, a limited effort by a small group of international accountants to write disclosure rules for companies that sold stock in more than one country had become an unusual instrument of international governance. No treaty or international agreement provided a framework for financial disclosure rules. Instead, private efforts became public law by means of a slow process of government endorsement.

An important date was January 1, 2005, when the European Union (EU) required more than seven thousand public companies headquartered in its twenty-five member countries to follow the financial disclosure rules established by the private International Accounting Standards Board (IASB).[217] Officials of the Bush administration announced that the United States, too, might hand over to the board as early as 2007 financial reporting rule making for foreign listings.[218] Russia, South Africa, Australia, Taiwan, Hong Kong, and India also had plans to adopt the rules made by the international board.

However, the seemingly technical task of harmonizing accounting standards produced difficult political issues from the start, because what financial information was disclosed and how it was disclosed could change markets. Reporting requirements could alter the projects firms chose to undertake, how they compensated employees, how well firms fared against competitors, and how effectively they attracted investors. Traditionally, national financial disclosure rules varied so widely that a substantial profit under one country's rules could be a substantial loss under another's.

International standards developed gradually over a generation. In 1973, a committee of private-sector accountants from nine countries formed the International Accounting Standards Committee and began issuing proposed international accounting standards. The committee, one of several competing efforts in the 1970s and 1980s, initially skirted thorny political issues by proposing standards that left companies and national regulators wide latitude in interpretation.[219]

In the 1990s and early 2000s, rapidly integrating markets and international financial crises increased companies', stock exchanges', and national regulators' interest in more rigorous international disclosure rules. The Asian financial crisis of the mid-1990s created calls for greater corporate transparency, even though corporate reporting flaws were not among its main causes. Accounting scandals in the United States and Europe in 2001–2004 alerted international investors to hidden risks and highlighted major weaknesses in national disclosure rules.

Company executives, stock exchange managers, accountants, investors, and other market participants each had somewhat different reasons for supporting harmonization of corporate financial reporting. Multinational companies, seeking to diversify their shareholder base and lower their cost of capital by listing on stock exchanges outside their home countries, found duplicate reporting not only burdensome but also sometimes embarrassing. Managers of large stock exchanges, seeking to gain listings from foreign companies, found their national reporting rules created a competitive disadvantage. The accounting profession, dominated by five international firms through most of the 1990s, feared that conflicting statements of profits and losses under different national rules could impair accountants' credibility. Investors, seeking higher returns in foreign markets, found variable results a new source of uncertainty.

In order to gain public legitimacy, the harmonization effort started by a small committee of accountants – the IASB – reformed its structure and improved procedural fairness in 2000 and 2001. The board's new structure emphasized expertise rather than national representation, paralleled that of the U.S. and British accounting standard setters, and was dominated by members from countries with Anglo-American accounting traditions.[220] The reformed board consisted of twelve full-time and two part-time members who served a maximum of two five-year terms and were appointed for their technical expertise as auditors, preparers, and users of financial statements. To coordinate the board's rule making with that of national standard setters, seven board members were given formal liaison responsibilities with specific countries, the United States, Britain, France, Germany, Japan, Canada, and Australia, giving those countries an elite status. The board also drew on the expertise of a geographically diverse advisory council and interpretations committee. By early 2005, the board had issued forty-one accounting standards, including controversial requirements for expensing of stock options and accounting for derivatives.[221]

The board aimed to produce international standards "under principles of transparency, open meetings, and full due process."[222] Board meetings were open to the public. Agendas of board and committee meetings were posted in advance on the board's Web site, and summaries of decisions were posted afterward. Draft standards and interpretations were subject to public notice and comment (usually 120 days for standards and 60 days for interpretations), and sometimes to public hearings. The publication of final standards included a discussion of their rationale, responses to comments, and the board's dissenting opinions. The board also published an annual report. The board and affiliated organizations, headquartered in London, employed about sixty people, including board members, and had an annual budget of about $18 million, provided through contributions from accounting firms (including $1 million from each of the four largest international firms), corporations, central banks, and international organizations.[223]

As in the United States and Britain, a self-perpetuating oversight group, the International Accounting Standards Committee Foundation (IASCF), was intended to provide a buffer from political pressures and assure efficient operation. Its trustees chose board members, appointed the board chair, raised operating funds, and reviewed the board's constitution and procedures every five years. Its constitution provided that its twenty-two-member self-perpetuating "financially knowledgeable" board of trustees be "representative of the world's capital markets and a diversity of geographical and professional backgrounds." It called for six representatives from North America, six from Europe, four from the Asia/Pacific region, and others without geographical designation.[224] The foundation's first chair was Paul Volcker, former head of the United States' Federal Reserve Board.

Informal public and private networks also supported the board's work. The EU encouraged the creation of a private-sector technical group (the European Financial Reporting Advisory Group, EFRAG) and formed the Committee of European Securities Regulators (CSER), which quickly established guidelines for member states' enforcement bodies, including independence and authority to monitor and correct accounts. To reduce the chances that each nation would in effect create its own standards through different interpretations, CESR also established a database of nations' enforcement decisions and urged national regulators to follow precedents as they were established.[225] The International Federation of Accountants (IFAC) proposed a peer review system for periodically and randomly reviewing the accounts of multinational companies and issued a new standardized audit report form to improve the comparability of accounts.[226] In May of 2004 the SEC and CESR announced that they were increasing their collaborative efforts in order to improve communication about regulatory risks between Europe and the United States and to promote convergence in future securities regulation.[227]

Enforcement of accounting standards, however, was left to national regulators. The board remained a private membership organization with no authority to compel nations or companies to adopt its disclosure rules. The public character of its authority rested solely on the endorsement of its processes and standards first and foremost by national governments and then by complex networks of national politicians, regulators, accounting firms, stock exchanges, companies, investors, and other market participants. Enforcement practices varied widely among nations that represented major markets.[228]

In 2006, the development of international corporate financial accounting standards appeared to be sustainable. Standards had improved markedly over time in scope, accuracy, and use. However, it was not yet clear what degree of harmonization the international board would achieve, whether a critical mass of nations and companies would continue to support the board's efforts, and how well standards would be enforced by national regulators. Standards for financial derivatives, stock options, and other complex instruments remained controversial. Nations' capacities to administer and enforce international disclosure rules varied widely, raising the possibility that standards would be accepted on paper but ignored in practice. EU companies complained that standards were costly and confusing: "The standards have been criticized by businesses of all sizes for making accounts unreadable and irrelevant," the *Financial Times* reported in March 2006.[229] In addition, the board's funding remained uncertain. The "big four" accounting firms continued to provide a third of funding, raising charges of undue influence, while other contributions were ad hoc.

Political realities suggested that gradual partial harmonization of standards and practices over a period of years was as much as could be expected. Whether such harmonization would reduce or increase hidden risks to investors remained to be seen.

Disclosing International Infectious Disease Outbreaks to Protect Public Health

From the mid-nineteenth century on, nations sought to create international practices to control the spread of infectious disease. International surveillance – the rapid reporting of disease outbreaks – was early recognized as a key to preventing deaths and illnesses. After several devastating cholera epidemics in the early 1800s, many nations negotiated international sanitary conventions that sought to harmonize variable national surveillance and quarantine laws.

Since 1951, the International Health Regulations of the World Health Organization (WHO) have governed international surveillance of infectious diseases among member countries. An arm of the United Nations, the WHO is governed by a World Health Assembly composed of representatives of the WHO member governments. International Health Regulations require member governments to inform the WHO about cases of specified infectious diseases within set time periods. Traditionally, national governments have controlled the flow of information on which disease surveillance is based. Regulations also specify public health activities at ports and airports and set procedures for trade and travel restrictions, including limits on those restrictions. Their stated purpose is to minimize the international spread of disease with minimal interference with trade and travel.[230]

By the 1970s, however, the WHO surveillance system was moribund. Only plague, cholera, and yellow fever were subject to international reporting rules and member states routinely violated even those reporting obligations. In practice, member governments' incentives to protect national reputation and economic stability often outweighed incentives to join in international efforts to report disease outbreaks. At the same time, vaccines and antibiotics minimized some common infectious diseases in the United States and Europe, easing political pressure for effective surveillance.[231]

But in the 1980s, the AIDS epidemic as well as the spread of other infectious diseases highlighted the failure of existing international regulations and reawakened international interest in more effective surveillance. In the United States, the national Institute of Medicine identified fifty-four infectious diseases that were on the rise owing to a combination of increased travel and trade, germs' adaptability, and a lack of public health measures.[232]

In 1995, the World Health Assembly directed the World Health Organization to revise the failed government-centered surveillance rules. But reaching agreement on new surveillance rules proved to be a slow process. New International Health Regulations were not adopted until 2005.[233] Meanwhile, the WHO cooperated with private groups to create informal networks to share information. The Global Outbreak Alert and

Response Network was designed to pool public and private information for response to international outbreaks. In 2001, the four-year-old network was officially endorsed by the World Health Assembly.[234]

However, it was the rapid spread of SARS (Severe Acute Respiratory Syndrome) in 2002 and 2003 that sparked the revival of the international system of infectious disease reporting. The disease first appeared in China's Guangdong Province in November 2002, spread to thirty countries in six months, and killed more than seven hundred people. Public fears fed by a paucity of reliable information contributed to large economic costs – estimated at $40 billion.[235]

Significantly, initial information about the SARS outbreak did not come from government reports. It came from millions of cell phone and Internet messages in Guangdong Province and elsewhere in late 2002, as well as from information provided by private reporting systems such as ProMED-mail. It was these on-the-ground reports from ordinary citizens and local health workers that spurred the WHO to make inquiries of the Chinese government, which, in turn, led the Chinese government to acknowledge the outbreak and led the WHO to issue a global alert on March 12 and a travel advisory on March 15, 2003.[236]

The new capabilities of information technology not only marshaled far-flung resources to identify the source and character of the disease but also helped to combine the scientific expertise of many nations to bring the epidemic under control. Public health authorities in many countries cobbled together informal networks to respond with unprecedented speed. The WHO coordinated sixty teams of medical personnel to help control the disease in affected areas and a network of eleven infectious disease laboratories in nine countries, linked through a secure Web site and daily conference calls, to work on the disease's causes and diagnosis. These networks made new scientific information available to researchers around the world and hastened collaborative progress on diagnosis and treatment. Researchers were able to identify the cause of SARS within a month. By July 2003, the five-month epidemic had ended.[237]

In retrospect, it was clear that the SARS epidemic coupled with advances in communication technology signaled the end of government control of the flow of information about disease outbreaks. Even in the absence of an international legal obligation, China was pressured into reporting the spread of SARS by masses of local data provided by villagers and aggregated by private electronic surveillance systems. In May 2003 the World Health Assembly acknowledged the legitimacy of the crisis-driven de facto changes in the international reporting system. In an important change, the assembly asked the WHO to continue using nongovernmental sources of information for surveillance. The WHO concluded that the SARS crisis demonstrated that government attempts to hide information carried a very high price – "loss of credibility in the eyes of the international community, escalating negative domestic economic impact, damage to health and economics of neighboring countries, and a very real risk that outbreaks within the country's own territory can spiral out of control"[238]

Labeling Genetically Modified Foods to Protect Health and the Environment
Controversies concerning the safety and environmental effects of genetically modified food crops created extraordinary political conflict and market disruptions in the United States, Europe, and developing countries during the 1990s and early 2000s. Early genetic modification of crops, introduced commercially in the mid-1990s, created corn, soy, and

other grains, fruits, and vegetables that were resistant to pests or pesticides or enhanced to produce extra vitamins, proteins, or other nutrients. Genetic modification differed from conventional crossbreeding by altering plants at the molecular level, sometimes by combining the DNA of different species. In the pipeline were bioengineered plants that promised drought resistance or immunity to or treatments for specific diseases. However, new benefits were accompanied by questions concerning the possible introduction of allergens when DNA from different species was combined; the long-term environmental effects of pest-resistant crops on beneficial insects, birds, and animals; and the possible creation of "superweeds" or other pesticide-resistant plants or insects from inadvertent crossbreeding between conventional and bioengineered plants.[239]

The EU and the United States took different approaches to the introduction of genetically modified food crops in the mid-1990s. The EU regulated genetically modified crops as a novel health and environmental issue, requiring thorough review and risk assessment for each field trial and product introduction.[240] The United States regulated genetically modified crops as a variation on familiar health and safety concerns, allowing many field trials and introductions to take place without government permits.[241]

After an informal six-year ban on imports of genetically modified crops, Europe adopted a mandatory labeling regime in 2004.[242] After welcoming genetically modified crops, the United States adopted guidelines for voluntary labeling.[243] As of 2005, however, labeling had not improved the efficiency of international markets or public safety, and both its effectiveness and its sustainability were in doubt.

The European public responded to the sudden introduction of genetically modified foods by the American Monsanto Corporation in 1996 and 1997 with demonstrations and boycotts. Inflammatory headlines warned of the dangers of "frankenfoods"; Green Party representatives cautioned about environmental risks; respected consumer organizations called for product labeling or withdrawal; and Prince Charles, Paul McCartney, and other well-known figures echoed public skepticism about the safety of such foods. Already frightened by risks associated with mad cow disease (risks that initially were downplayed by public officials), an incident of dioxin-contaminated Belgian food, and the spread of hoof-and-mouth disease (none of which had anything to do with genetic modification), European consumers were distrustful of government and commercial assurances of food safety.

In contrast, the American public barely noticed the introduction of genetically modified foods. Antiregulatory sentiment ran high in the United States in the mid-1990s, following gains by conservatives in the midterm elections of 1994. Experts in government and the private sector debated safeguards and determined that no new regulatory system was needed for genetically modified foods. Risks could be considered product by product – just like risks associated with other advancing food technologies. Interestingly, the U.S. food industry favored a mandatory safety assessment for genetically modified foods, although the industry opposed mandatory labeling.[244]

In 1998, European Union member states instituted an informal ban on the import of bulk shipments of products that might contain genetically modified organisms, stopped approving genetically modified foods, and required labels on packaged foods already on the market that contained genetically modified corn or soy. In the United States, farmers rapidly increased production of genetically modified crops so that nearly 40 percent of corn acreage and more than 70 percent of soybean acreage was planted with crops engineered to increase resistance to pests or herbicides. Planting such genetically modified seeds had benefits for farmers. It could reduce significantly costs associated with plowing and purchase of pesticides.

In the late 1990s, however, European protests spread to the United States and other countries. In 1999, protests by a variety of activist organizations led national farm associations in the United States to warn their members about the economic risks of planting genetically modified crops. Companies such as Frito-Lay and Nestle banned such crops from their products in the United States as well as in Europe. Gerber and H. J. Heinz removed genetically modified ingredients from baby food. Domestic incidents also triggered alarm. When Starlink, a variety of genetically modified corn approved only for animal feed in the United States, was found in taco shells in fast-food restaurants in 2002, it raised the specter of possible allergens. After ten years of commercialization, virtually all the production of genetically modified crops remained concentrated in only four countries – the United States, Canada, Argentina, and Brazil.

International disagreement took the highest toll in Africa. Zambia, Zimbabwe, Mozambique, and Malawi rejected U.S. food aid in 2002 because shipments contained genetically modified corn, even though those countries were threatened with famine conditions and genetically modified corn had been distributed without controversy in Zambia for six years. African nations could not risk losing the European market for their crops if the seed found its way into farmers' fields. The United States remained the world's largest exporter of agricultural products. But Europe, one of the world's two largest importers (along with Japan), had more influence over market rules.

Scientific uncertainty continued to leave room for polarized debate. In the United States, the National Research Council remained supportive of the benefits of genetic engineering of crops but also emphasized the importance of assessing each product individually for potential risks from allergens, contamination of other plants, or damage to insects or animals. The Research Directorate General of the EU, as well as French and British authorities, acknowledged that no human health or environmental problems had yet been observed but also cautioned about long-term risks. All agreed that there was a great deal that was not yet known about the effects of genetic modification of foods.

Labeling of genetically modified foods was not an unreasonable approach to promoting more efficient markets, improving consumer choice, and creating incentives for minimizing the risks of genetic modification – goals that Europe, the United States, and developing countries shared. In the past, governments had often employed food labeling to promote public health and inform consumer choice when individual preferences differed. Europe and the United States already specified the labeling of ingredients, allergens, and nutrients in packaged foods.

In 2004, the EU did replace its informal moratorium with an exacting system of labeling and tracking genetically modified foods and animal feed. Some allowance was made for accidental contamination on the grounds that some mixing of crops was inevitable. Foods that contained less than 0.9 percent of genetically modified substances did not have to be labeled.[245] In order to implement the labeling regime, the EU required that the characteristics, shipping, and sale of genetically modified food ingredients be tracked from planting to incorporation in products. Tracking was essential in order to verify labeling and facilitate recalls. Genetically modified seeds also had to be labeled and tracked. In effect, genetically modified crops had to be segregated at each step of production and distribution – from farm to fork. The European Commission approved one variety of Bt corn for human consumption (but not planting) in May 2004, the first biotech product to gain approval since 1998. The commission also approved a variety of genetically modified maize in 2006.

After the Starlink contamination incident in 2002, the United States also proposed voluntary guidelines for companies to use if they wanted to inform consumers that their products did or did not contain genetically modified ingredients. The FDA recommended that labels feature statements that products were (or were not) genetically engineered or were made (or not made) using biotechnology, rather than statements that products were "GMO free," since some degree of contamination seemed unavoidable.[246] In an unrelated regulatory change, the United States also introduced rules to standardize labeling of "organic" foods, a growing portion of the U.S. food market. Those rules included a requirement that foods labeled organic could not contain genetically modified ingredients.[247]

As of 2006, however, the labeling of genetically modified foods appeared unlikely to prove sustainable or effective as a public health measure or as a means of increasing market efficiency by informing consumer choice, for two reasons. First, frequent incidents of contamination between genetically modified and conventional crops, as well as acknowledgement that some contamination was inevitable, raised doubts about whether accurate labeling was technically feasible. Second, the underlying complexity and uncertainty of safety and environmental issues concerning genetic modification made it difficult to communicate accurately with consumers by means of labels. "GMOs fall into the class of risk situations characterized by both low certainty and low consensus," David Winickoff and his coauthors suggested in an analysis of these food wars.[248] In such situations, labels that warn but do not inform tend to inflame public fears rather than improve public knowledge.

Labeling of genetically modified foods by the European Union also had extreme unintended consequences. In effect, it continued to preclude farmers in developing countries from planting genetically modified crops. Seemingly simple labeling required farmers, distributors, and food companies to segregate genetically modified crops at every step. Farmers, grain elevators, railroad cars, processing facilities, and food manufacturing plants needed separate facilities and processes for conventional and genetically modified fruits, vegetables, and grains. In the United States, officials estimated that crop segregation and tracking requirements might increase food production costs by 10 to 30 percent.[249]

In the absence of any more appropriate international forum, the continuing battle over the labeling of genetically modified foods took the form of a trade dispute, with the World Trade Organization (WTO) acting as arbiter. In February 2006 the WTO ruled that the EU's informal ban against imports of genetically modified foods represented an unlawful restraint of trade (although the EU had by then technically lifted the ban).[250] EU officials countered that the WTO ruling would not influence their policies.

Notes

Preface

1. *The 9/11 Commission Report: Final Report of the National Commission on Terrorist Attacks upon the United States*, pp. 13–14, http://www.gpoaccess.gov/911/pdf/ fullreport.pdf (site accessed May 1, 2006).
2. http://www.whitehouse.gov/news/releases/2002/03/20020312-11.html (site accessed May 1, 2006).
3. Graham, 2001.
4. Fung, Graham, and Weil, 2002.
5. Fung et al., 2004; Weil et al., 2006.

Chapter 1. Governance by Transparency

1. Hearing Before the Senate Commerce, Science and Transportation Committee, 106th Cong., 1041 (2000) (statement of Masatoshi Ono, Chief Executive Officer, Bridgestone/Firestone).
2. These accidents and their causes received sustained national media coverage in 2000 and 2001. Major articles in the *New York Times* include Keith Bradsher, "Tire Deaths Are Linked to Rollovers," August 15, 2000, p. 1; Keith Bradsher and Matthew L. Wald, "More Indications Hazards of Tires Were Long Known," September 7, 2000, p. 1; Keith Bradsher, "Congress Appears Ready to Tackle Rollover Problem," September 21, 2000, p. C1. Other sources include Joann Muller and Nicole St. Pierre, "Ford vs. Firestone: A Corporate Whodunit," *Business Week*, June 11, 2006, p. 46; "Automobiles. Firestone Tires. The Firestorm Continues," *Consumer Reports*, November 2000, p. 9.
3. http://www.nhtsa.dot.gov/cars/rules/rulings/UpgradeTire/Econ/TireUpgradeI. html (site accessed May 6, 2006).
4. Hearing on the Reauthorization of the National Highway and Transportation Safety Act, 108th Cong., 9, 13 (2004) (statement of Rep. Schakowsky, ex-officio, Subcommittee on Commerce, Trade and Consumer Protection, Committee on Energy and Commerce).

5. Transportation Recall Enhancement, Accountability, and Documentation (TREAD) Act, Pub. L. 106–414, November 1, 2000, 114 Stat. 1800 (codified at 49 U.S.C. §30170 (2000)).

6. Safe, Accountable, Flexible, Efficient Transportation Equity Act: A Legacy for Users (SAFETEA-LU), Pub. L. 109–59, August 10, 2005, 119 Stat. 1144 (codified in scattered sections of 18 U.S.C.A., 23 U.S.C.A., and 49 U.S.C.A).

7. Final Policy Statement, 68 Fed. Reg. 59250–59304 (October 14, 2003) (to be codified at 49 C.F.R. pt. 575); see also National Health Traffic Safety Administration, 2005.

8. Federal Motor Vehicle Safety Standards: Tire Pressure Monitoring Systems; Controls and Displays, 66 Fed. Reg. 38982 (proposed July 26, 2001) (to be codified in 49 C.F.R. pt. 571).

9. Reporting of Information and Documents About Potential Defects, 66 Fed. Reg. 66190 (proposed December 21, 2001) (to be codified at subpart C 49 C.F.R. pt. 579).

10. Tire Safety Information, 66 Fed. Reg. 65536 (proposed December 19, 2001) (to be codified at 49 C.F.R. pts. 567, 571, 574, and 575).

11. New-model rollover ratings are listed by the National Highway Traffic Safety Administration at http://www.safercar.com.

12. Congress directed officials to issue a minimum performance standard for rollovers by 2009. Safe, Accountable, Flexible, Efficient Transportation Equity Act, Pub. L. 109–59.

13. Brandeis, 1932, p. 92.

14. Securities Act of 1933, May 27, 1933, ch. 38, Title I, 48 Stat. 74 (codified at 15 U.S.C. §77 (2000)); Securities and Exchange Act of 1934, June 6, 1934, ch. 404, 48 Stat. 881 (codified at 15 U.S.C. §78 (2000 and Supp. II 2002)).

15. Safe Drinking Water Act Amendments of 1996, Pub. L. 104–182, August 6, 1996, 110 Stat. 1613 (codified at 42 U.S.C. §300g–j and 33 U.S.C. §1263 (2000)). See also Graham, 2002a, p. 8.

16. For a summary of shortcomings of consumer contaminant reports see Natural Resources Defense Council, 2003, http://www.nrdc.org/water/drinking/uscities/contents.asp (site accessed February 3, 2006).

17. For an overview of the Washington, D.C., incident, see Congressional Research Service, 2005.

18. Statement of EPA administrator Stephen L. Johnson, June 8, 2005, concerning drinking water as top EPA priority.

19. U.S. Geological Survey, Drinking Water Initiative, http://pubs.usgs.gov/fs/FS-047–97/FS-047–97.pdf (site accessed February 3, 2006).

20. The National Environmental Education & Training Foundation 1999 Safe Drinking Water Report Card Summary, http://www.neetf.org/pubs/watersummary.doc (site accessed May 15, 2006).

21. Other trends may also support the growing impact of targeted transparency as mainstream policy, though their influence is harder to document. For example, as consumer choices are multiplying and brand loyalty is decreasing, it makes sense that increasingly well-educated consumers would demand better factual information on which to base more complex decisions.

22. See, for example, Evans and Wurster, 1997, p. 74.

23. http://www.scorecard.org (site accessed April 28, 2006); see also http://www.epa.gov/enviro/html/ef_feedback.html (site accessed April 28, 2006).

24. See, for example, Federal Aviation Administration Data and Statistics, http://www.faa.gov/data_statistics and http://www.faa.gov/data_statistics/accident_incident (sites accessed April 28, 2006); Bureau of Transportation Statistics, http://www.transtats.bts.gov/OT_Delay/OT_DelayCause1.asp (site accessed April 28, 2006); National Transportation Safety Board, Aviation Database, http://www.ntsb.gov/ntsb/query.asp (site accessed April 28, 2006).

25. Some, but not all, transparency policies will benefit from future leaps in information technology, depending upon when and where users need information to make their decisions. For example, for many customers, the provision of crashworthiness ratings directly on new-car stickers may provide all the information they need for their purchase decisions. These consumers would gain little from technological enrichment via the Internet.

26. Over the last three decades, the public's confidence in policymakers has plummeted. Polled in 1966, about 40% of respondents indicated that they had "a great deal" of confidence in leaders of the executive branch and Congress. Twelve years later, in 1978, only 14% expressed such confidence in the executive branch and 9% in Congress. Confidence rose to 20% for Congress and 17% for the executive branch in 1988 but fell once again to around 14% for both institutions by 1996. These results are taken from Nye, Zelikow, and King, 1997, p. 207.

Chapter 2. An Unlikely Policy Innovation

1. We discuss in depth the obstacles to transparency in Chapters 4 and 5.

2. The procedure for conducting the search for final federal regulations was as follows. We searched the online Federal Register database for the period January 1, 1996, to December 31, 2005, using the nine keywords/phrases that are most associated with the use of information disclosure in regulations: labeling and warning, information disclosure, labeling and disclosure, mandatory disclosure, voluntary disclosure, hazard information, transparency, right-to-know, and report card. To avoid double counting and focus only on regulations that actually were promulgated, we narrowed our initial search to interim rules *or* final rules; search results related to notices, proposed rules, or any other return that did not explicitly result in an interim or final rule were not counted. Using this search procedure, a total of 3,502 cases were identified using the nine general search terms. We then reviewed the resulting set of rules, eliminating those that (1) did not represent final rules; (2) did not fit our specific definition of targeted transparency (e.g., disclosures that are intended only to provide the public with information on administrative processes, or disclosure laws that are solely forms of public warnings); (3) represented final rules that had only a minor disclosure component (e.g., a small disclosure requirement that was wedded to a more conventional standard-based regulation); or (4) represented final rules that provided information solely to the government as a means to sharpen enforcement efforts. Thus, our tally of 133 policies includes only those final rules whose central regulatory mechanism was information disclosure. The

following are our year-by-year tabulations of final targeted transparency rules from the survey:

Targeted	1996	1997	1998	1999	2000	2001	2002	2003	2004	2005
Transparency Final Regulations	20	14	14	8	14	6	13	28	12	4

Information about specific final regulations that make up the survey is available on request from the authors.

3. J. Madison, letter to W. T. Barry, August 4, 1822, in Madison, 1910, p. 103.
4. Mill, 1861, Chapter 6, section 1.
5. Weber, 1946, pp. 233–234.
6. Moynihan, 1998, p. 59.
7. Altshuler, 1997, p. 39.
8. The Supreme Court Historical Society, History of the Court: The Jay Court, http://www.supremecourthistory.org.
9. Administrative Procedure Act, June 11, 1946, ch. 324, 60 Stat. 237 (codified at 5 §U.S.C. 551 *et seq.* (2000)).
10. U.S. Department of Justice, 2000, p. 6.
11. The Freedom of Information Act, Pub. L. 89–487, July 4, 1966, 80 Stat. 250 (codified as amended at 5 U.S.C. §552(b) 2000)).
12. Freedom of Information Act, Pub. L. 89–487, at §552(a)(2) (2000). See also H.R. Rep. 104–795, at 11–13 (1996), *as reprinted in* 1996 U.S.C.C.A.N. 3454–3456.
13. Federal Election Campaign Act of 1971, Pub. L. 92–225, Title III, §301, February 7, 1972, 86 Stat. 11 (codified at 2 U.S.C. 431 *et seq.* (2000 & Supp. III 2003)); amended by Federal Election Campaign Act of 1974, Pub. L. 93–443, Title II, §§201(a), 208(c)(1), October 15, 1974, 88 Stat. 1272, 1286 (26 U.S.C. §§9031–9042 (2000 & Supp. III 2003)); amended by Federal Elections Campaign Act Amendments of 1976, Pub. L. 94–283, Title I, §§102, 115(d),(h), May 11, 1976, 90 Stat. 478, 495, 496 (2000 & Supp. III 2003); Federal Election Campaign Act Amendments of 1979, Pub. L. 96–187, Title I, §101, January 8, 1980, 93 Stat. 1339 (codified at 2 U.S.C. §431 *et seq.* (2000 & Supp. III 2003)); amended by Tax Reform Act of 1986, Pub. L. 99–514, §2, October 22, 1986, 100 Stat. 2095; Pub. L. 106–346, §101(a) [Title V, §502(b)], October 23, 2000, 114 Stat. 1356, 1356A-49; McCain-Feingold Campaign Finance Reform Act (Bipartisan Campaign Reform Act of 2002), Pub. L. 107–155, Title I, §§101(b), 103(b)(1), Title II, §211, Title III, §304(c), March 27, 2002, 116 Stat. 85, 87, 92, 100 (to be codified at 2 U.S.C. §441 *et seq.*).
14. Federal Advisory Committee Act, Pub. L. 92–463, October 6, 1972, 86 Stat. 770 (codified at 5 U.S.C. App. 2, §1 *et seq.* (2000)).
15. Government in the Sunshine Act, Pub. L. 94–409, September 13, 1976, 90 Stat. 1241 (codified at 5 U.S.C §552b (2000)). This public law is also known as the Open Meetings Act.
16. Strauss et al., 9th ed., 1995, pp. 909–916. See also H.R. Rep. 104–795, at 13–14 (1996), *reprinted in* 1996 U.S.C.C.A.N. 3448, 3456–3457.
17. For an account of these events, see Graham, 2002b, p. 38.

18. Graham, 2002b, p. 38.
19. Information requests increased substantially in the late 1990s and early 2000s after the enactment of E-FOIA in 1996. The GAO reported that 25 agencies surveyed logged 119 percent more requests in FY 1999 than in 1998. General Accounting Office, 2001. In a later report the GAO found that agency requests increased by 71 percent from 2002 to 2004. Government Accountability Office, 2005.
20. Pure Food and Drug Act, June 30, 1906, ch. 3915, 34 Stat. 768; Insecticide Act, April 26, 1910, ch. 191, 36 Stat. 331. See also Comprehensive Smokeless Tobacco Health Education Act of 1996, Pub. L. 99–252 §3, February 27, 1996, 100 Stat. 30 (codified at 15 U.S.C. §4402 (2000)); Alcoholic Beverage Labeling Act of 1988, c. 816, Title I, as added Pub. L. 100–690, Title VIII, §8001(a)(3), November 8, 1988, 102 Stat. 4518 (codified at 27 U.S.C. §213 *et seq.* (2000)); Public Health Cigarette Smoking Act, Pub. L. 91–222, §2, April 1, 1970, 84 Stat. 88 (codified at 15 U.S.C. §1333 (2000)).
21. U.S. financial disclosure laws drew on much earlier English laws. In 1844 the Companies Act required British companies to disclose to the public their assets and liabilities. For an intriguing article on the history of financial disclosure, see Frankfurter, 1933. The 1933 Securities Act required that investors receive financial and other significant information concerning securities being offered for public sale and prohibited fraudulent practices in the sale of securities. Securities Act of 1933, May 27, 1933, ch. 38, Title I, 48 Stat. 74 (codified at 15 U.S.C. §77 (2000)). The 1934 Securities Exchange Act created the Securities and Exchange Commission (SEC) to regulate the securities industry. Securities and Exchange Act of 1934, June 6, 1934, ch. 404, 48 Stat. 881 (codified at 15 U.S.C. §78 (2000 & Supp. II. 2002)).
22. Safe Drinking Water and Toxic Enforcement Act, Cal. Health & Safety Code §225249.5 *et seq.* (West 1999) (added by Initiative Measure November 4, 1986, and effective January 1, 1987).
23. Occupational Safety and Health Administration's Hazard Communication Standard, 29 C.F.R. §1910.1200 (2005). For a discussion on the development of right-to-know in connection with health and safety risks, see Hadden, 1989, p. 20; Ashford and Caldart, 1985, pp. 383–401; Baram, 1984.
24. For a detailed account of the development of the disclosure system for toxic pollution, see Graham, 2002a, pp. 21–61.
25. See, for example, Grossman, 1989, pp. 461–483; Grossman and Hart, 1980, pp. 323–334; Milgrom, 1981, pp. 380–391.
26. See Tietenberg, 1998, and Tietenberg and Wheeler, 2001, for a discussion of this problem of the Coasian framework in regard to environmental policy.
27. The classic presentation of this view can be found in Hayek, 1945, pp. 519–530.
28. Stiglitz, 2000, provides a complete but readable overview of this literature.
29. The work of Mancur Olson famously shows that private parties, even with coordinated activities, have difficulty overcoming the problem of providing public goods like information. See Olson, 1971.
30. Akerloff, 1970, pp. 488–500.
31. Stiglitz, 2000, p. 1470.
32. See March and Simon, 1958, for the classic discussion of bounded rationality in organizations.

33. See generally Kahneman and Tversky, 2000.
34. Fischoff, 2002.
35. Cass Sunstein and others call this cognitive outcome "probability neglect" (see Sunstein, 2005). See, for example, Rottenstreich and Hsee, 2001, pp. 185–188.
36. Hogarth and Kunreuther, 1995, pp. 15–36.
37. For example, see Thaler, 1991.
38. Sunstein, 2005, p. 123.

Chapter 3. Designing Transparency Policies

1. This early history is drawn from Commons and Andrews, 1916 (quotation from p. 158).
2. Commons and Andrews, 1916, p. 256.
3. Occupational Safety and Health Administration's Hazard Communication Standard, 29 C.F.R. §1910.1200 (2005).
4. See, for example, Viscusi, 1979, pp. 134–143, in regard to the voluntary incentives for providing information on workplace hazards.
5. See, for example, Zeckhauser and Marks, 1996, pp. 32–34.
6. Child Safety Protection Act, Pub. L. 103–267, June 16, 1994, 108 Stat. 722 (codified at §15 U.S.C. 1278 (2000) and 15 U.S.C. §§6001–06 (2000)).
7. Upon voting to issue implementation instructions for the act in February 1995, Ann Brown, chairman of the Consumer Product Safety Commission, noted: "The CSPA and the toy labeling regulation approved by the Commission assure uniform, consistent, prominent and conspicuous warning labels on certain toys and games, marbles, balloons, and balls intended for children at least 3 but under 6 years. These warning labels will provide parents and others who purchase marbles, balls, balloons, and toys and games containing small parts for children 3 years and older, with information, at the point of purchase, that informs them of the risk of choking or suffocation that these products present to children under the age of three years." Press Release, Statement of Chairman Ann Brown, Toy Labeling and Choking, February 15, 1995, http://mbd2.com/Articles/95083.htm (site accessed April 29, 2006).
8. Gormley and Weimer, who have extensively studied organizational report cards, define them as "a regular effort by an organization to collect data on two or more *other* organizations, transform the data into information relevant to assessing performance, and transmit the information to some audience external to the organizations themselves." Gormley and Weimer, 1999, p. 3 (emphasis in original).
9. The classic description of the link between public goods and location is Tiebout, 1956.
10. See Ehrenberg and Jakubson, 1990, for a discussion of the problems arising from voluntary disclosure of plant closing decisions.
11. See Graham, 2002a, pp. 31–35, for a discussion of these exemptions.
12. In September 2005, the federal EPA proposed three changes, each of which would dramatically cut information available to the public on toxic pollution. The agency proposed that it (1) reduce annual reporting to every other year; (2) allow companies to release ten times as much pollution before being required

to report the details of how much toxic pollution was produced and where it went; and (3) permit facilities to withhold information on low-level production of persistent bio-accumulative toxins (PBTs), including lead and mercury, which are dangerous even in very small quantities because they are toxic, persist in the environment, and build up in people's bodies. Toxics Release Inventory Burden Reduction, 70 Fed. Reg. 57822 (proposed October 4, 2005) (to be codified at 40 C.F.R. pt. 372). See also Mark Hammond, "EPA Update," *GATF World*, February 1, 2006, 18(1), 2006 WLNR 4533381 (noting that the exemptions could benefit the printing industry); Bruce Geiselman, "States Ask EPA to Reconsider TRI Changes," *Waste News*, January 31, 2006, 11(21), 14 (stating that the National Association of Manufacturers endorsed the Bush administration's proposals).

13. The legislation states that it is "predicated upon the principle of public disclosure, that timely and complete disclosure of receipts and expenditures would result in the exercise of prudence by candidates and their committees and that excessive expenditures would incur the displeasure of the electorate who would or could demonstrate indignation at the polls." Federal Election Campaign Act, Pub. L. 92–225, February 7, 1972, 86 Stat. 3 (codified at scattered sections in 2 U.S.C.); Federal Election Campaign Amendments of 1974, Pub. L. 93–443, October 15, 1974, 88 Stat. 1263 (codified at 26 U.S.C. §§9031–9042 (2000)); S. Rep. 92–96 (1971), *as reprinted in* 1972 U.S.C.C.A.N. 1773, 1776.

14. In particular, finding a group to deal with the public goods nature of information collection and interpretation raises a classic "collective action" problem where no parties capture all of the benefits of acting as agents and all parties therefore have lowered incentives to play those roles (Olson, 1971).

15. Some analysts (e.g., Coglianese and Nash, 2004) have argued that this represents one of the principal benefits of toxic release reporting and related interventions: if firms are forced to recognize for the first time the amount of pollutants they have been discharging, managers are more likely to find ways to reduce those releases than if the releases go unmeasured.

16. De Marchi and Hamilton, 2006, find considerable differences in reported levels of chemical release reductions for two major chemicals, lead and benzene, when comparing toxic release reports from the disclosure system and EPA direct monitoring data. They show that while disclosure reports indicated that average air emissions of benzene fell by 84% between 1988–1990 and 1998–2000, actual EPA monitoring data indicated reductions of only 56%. Similarly, disclosure reports indicated reductions of 45% in air emissions of lead versus 24% based on EPA monitoring data over the same period. The study found smaller discrepancies between disclosure-based and EPA monitoring data for three other chemicals. See De Marchi and Hamilton, 2006, Table 1 and pp. 63–65.

17. Schwartz, 2004, Chapter 3, has a useful overview of the cognitive literature regarding choosing and making decisions.

18. These findings are reported in Degeorge, Patel, and Zeckhauser, 1999.

19. The Bipartisan Campaign Reform Act of 2002, Pub. L. 107–155, March 27, 2002, 116 Stat. 81 (codified at 2 U.S.C.A. §438, 441, and 36 U.S.C.A. §510 (West 2005)). The law providing for the penalty of five years in prison can be found at 2 U.S.C.A. §437j.

20. Worker Adjustment and Retraining Notification Act, Pub. L. 100–379, August 4, 1988, 102 Stat. 890 (codified at 29 U.S.C. §§2101–2109 (2000)). See also H. Conf. Rep. 100–576, at 1046 (1998), *as reprinted in* 1988 U.S.C.C.A.N. 1547, 2079.
21. Under the disclosure law in Washington State, for example, failing to register or maintain an accurate record of current location is a class C felony if the original crime for which the individual was convicted was a felony sex offense or, if other than a felony conviction, a gross misdemeanor. Wash. Rev. Code Ann. §9A.44.130(10)(a),(b).
22. Hamilton reports that the EPA increased the number of inspections in the years immediately following passage of the law in 1987, going from 153 in 1988 to 768 in 1989. Inspections remained relatively high under the elder Bush administration and only began to fall in the mid-1990s as the Clinton administration faced increasing congressional opposition to regulatory policies. On the general issue of enforcement under the toxic releases act, see Hamilton, 2005, pp. 191–198.
23. De Marchi and Hamilton's 2006 estimate of the gap between reported and actual air emissions of toxic chemicals is an example of this problem.
24. See Masters, Atkin, and Florkowski, 1989, pp. 720–722; see also General Accounting Office, 1999, and General Accounting Office, 2000.
25. The number of full-time equivalent staff increased from 290 in FY 2001 to 384 in the Bush administration's proposed FY 2006 budget. Similarly, overall funding rose from $30.5 million in FY 2001 to $48.8 million in its proposed FY 2006 budget. This increase contrasted with budget reductions in the many other programs administered by the department. See Office of Management and Budget, Executive Office of the President, Budget of the United States Government, Fiscal Year 2001 (2000), and Office of Management and Budget, Executive Office of the President, Budget of the United States Government, Fiscal Year 2006 (2005).
26. See generally Bardach and Kagan, 1982; Ayers and Braithwaite, 1992; Sparrow, 1994; Gunningham and Grabosky, 1998; Sparrow, 2000.
27. For example, Coglianese, Nash, and Olmstead, 2003, and Stavins, 2004, see the data provided by many disclosure-based systems as important inputs for market- or incentive-based approaches, but not a separate class of regulatory tools. Gunningham and Grabosky, 1998, Chapter 2, describe information instruments as a counterpart to education-based regulatory instruments.
28. Tietenberg, 1998, examines a range of environmental transparency policies. Viscusi and Magat, 1987; Sunstein, 1993; and Zeckhauser and Marks, 1996, focus specifically on risk communication aspects of a variety of disclosure policies. Weiss and Gruber, 1984, and Gormley and Weimer, 1999, focus on a subset of policies that deal with organizational effectiveness.
29. See, for example, De León, 1999, pp. 87–88; Alman, 2001, pp. 379 and 382; Norton, 2001, pp. 1443 and 1468.
30. See Becker, 1968, for a discussion of how the probabilities of detection and penalty translate into an economic calculus regarding whether or not to comply with laws.
31. See CAIR SO_2 Trading Program General Provisions, 40 C.F.R. pt. 96, subpt. AAA (2005).

32. Ellerman et al., 2000.
33. Clean Air Act Amendment of 1970, Pub. L. 91–604, December 31, 1970, 84 Stat. 1676 (codified as amended in scattered sections of 42 U.S.C.); see also 42 U.S.C. §7479(C)(3) (2000) (defining the term "best available control technology"); see also Anderson, 2004, pp. 81 and 86 (noting that the Clean Air Act Amendment of 1977 required coal-fired power plants to have scrubbers installed on their smokestacks).
34. OSHA standards are codified within Title 29 of the C.F.R. and can be searched through the Occupational Safety and Health Administration's Web site at http://www.osha.gov/pls/oshaweb/owasrch.search_form?p_doc_type=STANDARDS &p_toc_level=0&p_keyvalue= (site accessed May 20, 2006). See also Occupational Safety and Health Administration Web site (describing its mission), http://www.osha.gov/oshinfo/mission.html (site accessed May 20, 2006).

Chapter 4. What Makes Transparency Work?

1. Los Angeles County Ordinance 97-0071 §2, 1997, http://municipalcodes. lexisnexis.com/codes/lacounty/ (site accessed April 29, 2006); County of Los Angeles Department of Health Services, Public Health Programs and Services, Environmental Health, Posting Requirements Advisory Bulletin: Retail Food Establishments, http://search.ladhs.org/images/nrfood.htm (site accessed April 29, 2006).
2. Jin and Leslie, 2003; Simon et al., 2005.
3. The full list of eighteen targeted transparency policies and an overview of each can be found in Chapter 1, Table 1.1. The Appendix provides a detailed description of the legislative history, purpose, provisions, and dynamics of each policy.
4. Because relatively few researchers have recognized the need to evaluate transparency policies rigorously, the available literature on which we draw is quite variable. Some researchers have undertaken direct analyses of specific user and/or discloser responses to new information. Others have focused on one step in the action cycle, such as discloser compliance with information requirements, user understanding of new information, or responses by investors, consumers, or others. The relative paucity of studies of some important transparency systems indicates the continuing prevalence of the assumption that such systems always produce net benefits.
5. Kahneman, Slovic, and Tversky, 1982; Samuelson and Zeckhauser, 1988; Kahneman and Tversky, 2000; Sunstein, 2005.
6. The action cycle helps place in context research on the impact of organizational report cards (Gormley and Weimer, 1999), as well as related research on regulation through information disclosure (for example, Sunstein, 1993; Kleindorfer and Orts, 1998; Mitchell, 1998; Tietenberg, 1998; Sage, 1999). Gormley and Weimer focus on the validity of report card metrics and the accessibility of that information to users. Their evaluative criteria pertain to the utility of report cards to users (based on characteristics such as relevance and comprehensibility) and disclosers (particularly regarding report card functionality). By

contrast, our approach focuses on users and disclosers (rather than information itself) and how disclosed information and resulting behavioral responses fit into their decision-making processes. We therefore place a greater emphasis on the context – for example, what does the user want, what are his/her choices and options, what are the costs of gaining the information? – than upon the construction of the report card per se. A related idea is described in Zeckhauser and Marks, 1996, who refer to the interaction of users and disclosers as the consumer and manufacturer effect: "Consumers increase their demand for products possessing the newly posted characteristic and sellers increase their production of such products" (p. 33).

7. Simon, 1997, is the seminal treatment of this issue. See also Payne, Bettman, and Johnson, 1993, for a full discussion of information seeking and its impact on decision making.

8. The ability of companies and organizations to shape preferences is the subject of a rich theoretical and empirical literature. See, for example, Carpenter and Nakamoto, 1989, and Mantel and Kardes, 1999.

9. Fagotto and Fung, 2003.

10. Weil, 2002.

11. The literature indicates that socioeconomic and educational factors affect user comprehension of disclosed information. For example, education and income affect users' comprehension of nutritional labeling (Mathios, 2000; Derby and Levy, 2001), workplace hazards (Occupational Safety and Health Administration, 1991; Kolp et al., 1993), and patient safety (Mukamel et al., 2004).

12. Occupational Safety and Health Administration, 1997; see also Kolp et al., 1993; Phillips et al., 1999.

13. Robins et al., 1990.

14. See, for example, Hammit and Graham, 1999.

15. County of Los Angeles, Department of Health Services, Retail Food Inspection Guide, Document No. H-3046, 2000, http://lapublichealth.org/eh/rfig/rfigfiles/documents2/rfigprnt.PDF (site accessed April 29, 2006).

16. The stated purpose of the advisory system is to "inform and facilitate decisions appropriate to different levels of government and to private citizens at home and at work." Homeland Security Presidential Directive 3 (HSPD-3), March 12, 2002, as amended by Homeland Security Presidential Directive 5 (HSPD-5), February 28, 2003. The system arguably provides more useful information to federal, state, and local government officials than to ordinary citizens because each threat level is intended to trigger threat-specific protective measures by governments.

17. See "Citizen Guidance on the Homeland Security Advisory System," http://www.dhs.gov/interweb/assetlibrary/CitizenGuidanceHSAS2.pdf (site accessed July 26, 2005).

18. Bui and Mayer, 2003.

19. See, for example, Scorecard.org, rtknet.org, and envirofacts.gov.

20. Home Mortgage Disclosure Act of 1975, Pub. L. 94–299, Title III, December 31, 1975, 89 Stat. 1125 (codified at 12 U.S.C. §2801 *et seq.* (2000)), amended by Financial Institutions, Reform, Recovery and Enforcement Act of 1989,

Pub. L. 101–73, August 9, 1989, 103 Stat. 183 (codified in scattered sections of 12 U.S.C.).

21. Munnell et al., 1996.

22. The National Community Reinvestment Coalition, for example, represents local community reinvestment organizations that try to attract capital to underserved communities. See http://www.ncrc.org (site accessed February 16, 2006).

23. In 1994, 51 percent of consumers were "very" or "extremely" concerned about reducing fat in diet, but the proportion fell to 31 percent by 2006. See Melanie Warner and Julie Bosman, "Another Fad Hits the Wall: Marketers Start to Emphasize Good Fats over Bad Fats," *New York Times*, February 11, 2006, p. B1.

24. Polinsky and Shavell, 2000.

25. Graham, 2002a, pp. 40–45.

26. Fisher, Raman, and McClelland, 2000. Even highly motivated retailers that have long used sophisticated analyses of point-of-sale information, such as Wal-Mart or Best Buy, have had difficulty until very recently in determining whether changes in sales arise from pricing, advertising, or specific product characteristics. New retail forecasting software and the falling costs of computing have made more subtle analysis of trends feasible.

27. Gompers, 1995; Degeorge, Patel, and Zeckhauser, 1999.

28. For example, Stephen Marshall, a Maine resident, tracked down and killed two registered sex offenders (and then took his own life). One had been convicted of raping a child and the other of sex with a minor (when he was nineteen and his girlfriend was fifteen). Marshall had looked up details about the two victims as well as thirty-two other listed offenders on the state's online registry prior to his attack. See Libby Lewis, "Murders Put Focus on Sex-Offender Registry Policies," *All Things Considered* (National Public Radio), broadcast April 21, 2006; John Ellement and Suzanne Smalley, "Sex Crime Disclosure Questioned," *Boston Globe*, April 18, 2006, p. A1.

29. See Graham and Miller, 2005, and Hamilton, 2005, Chapter 6. For a related discussion regarding strategic discloser behavior under Massachusetts' Toxics Use Reduction Act, see Bennear, 2005.

30. Committee on Appropriate Test Use, 1999; Meier, 2000.

31. Dranove et al., 2003.

32. Kahneman and Tversky, 1996; Kahneman, 2003.

33. Graham, 2002a, pp. 40–45. Regarding the choice of metrics under toxic pollution reporting, see Hamilton, 2005, Chapter 2. More generally, see Hamilton and Viscusi, 1999, regarding the choice of metrics used to inform the public about environmental risks.

34. Occupational Safety and Health Administration, 1991; Viscusi, 1991; Kolp et al., 1993; Mathios, 2000.

35. The capacity to undertake such ongoing improvement will, in turn, be affected by the factors related to sustainability discussed in Chapter 5.

36. For research questioning the need for mandatory information disclosure, see Stigler, 1964; Benston, 1973.

37. Simon, 1989; Botosan, 1997.

38. Bushman and Smith, 2001; Ferrell, 2003; Bushee and Leuz, 2004; Greenstone, Oyer, and Vissing-Jorgensen, 2004.

39. For a discussion on financial disclosure and the cost of capital, see Botosan, 1997. Lang and Lundholm, 1996, analyze how more informative disclosure policies decrease dispersion among analysts' forecasts.
40. Ball, 2001; Bushman and Smith, 2001; Healy and Palepu, 2001.
41. Leuz and Verrecchia, 2000; Hail and Leuz, 2005.
42. Gelos and Wei, 2002.
43. Fielding et al., 1999.
44. Jin and Leslie, 2003.
45. Jin and Leslie, 2006.
46. Jin and Leslie, 2003.
47. Simon et al., 2005.
48. Joint Center for Housing Studies, Harvard University, 2002.
49. Schafer and Ladd, 1981; Munnell et al., 1996.
50. Bostic et al., 2002.
51. Bostic and Surette, 2001; Joint Center for Housing Studies, Harvard University, 2002.
52. Economic Research Service, United States Department of Agriculture, CPI, Prices and Expenditures: Foodservice as a Share of Food Expenditures, Table 12: "Food Away from Home as a Share of Food Expenditures," http://www.ers.usda.gov/Briefing/CPIFoodAndExpenditures/Data/table12.htm (site accessed May 8, 2006).
53. Nayga, Lipinski, and Savur, 1998; Mathios, 2000; Derby and Levy, 2001.
54. Garretson and Burton, 2000; Derby and Levy, 2001.
55. Moorman, 1998.
56. Derby and Levy, 2001.
57. Kim, Nayga, and Capps, 2001; Variyam and Cawley, 2006.
58. Graham, 2002a; Graham and Miller, 2005.
59. Graham, 2002a.
60. De Marchi and Hamilton, 2006.
61. Graham and Miller, 2001; Bui, 2002.
62. Hamilton, 1995; Konar and Cohen, 1997.
63. Patten, 2002.
64. Bui and Mayer, 2003; Oberholzer-Gee and Mitsunari, 2003; Decker, Nielsen, and Sindt, 2005.
65. General Accounting Office, 1992a.
66. Kolp, Williams, and Burtan, 1995.
67. Occupational Safety and Health Administration, 1997.
68. Phillips et al., 1999.
69. Fagotto and Fung, 2003; Weil, 2005.
70. General Accounting Office, 1992a.
71. Arnett, 1992.
72. For reasons we describe, some studies suggest that New York's system is moderately effective.
73. Graham, 2002a.
74. Jha and Epstein, 2006.
75. Green and Wintfeld, 1995.
76. Schneider and Epstein, 1996.

77. Schneider and Epstein, 1998.
78. Hannan et al., 1994.
79. Cutler, Huckman, and Landrum, 2004.
80. Chassin, 2002.
81. Chassin, 2002; Jha and Epstein, 2006.
82. Werner, Asch, and Polsky, 2005.
83. Hannan et al., 2003.
84. Dranove et al., 2003.
85. Mukamel et al., 2002.
86. General Accounting Office, 2003b.
87. U.S. Department of Labor, 1986; Gerhart, 1987.
88. Addison and Blackburn, 1994 and 1997; Levin-Waldman, 1998.
89. Addison and Blackburn, 1997.

Chapter 5. What Makes Transparency Sustainable?

1. Seligman, 1995, pp. 418–431 (quotation from *Newsweek* at 431).
2. Seligman, 1995, pp. 431–437.
3. Homer Kripke concluded: "Accounting was Congress' most important charge to the [SEC] and represented the Commission's greatest opportunity to be of use to the investor . . . and it is the one problem which the SEC chose to turn over to the technicians while it sat on its own hands for 40 years." Kripke, 1985, p. 62. See also Previts and Merino, 1998, pp. 271–276.
4. Pacter, 1985, pp. 6–10. See also Seligman, 1995, pp. 452–466 and 554.
5. Pacter, 1985, pp. 10–18; Seligman, 1995, pp. 555–557.
6. Commission chairman Arthur Levitt emphasized the importance of constant vigilance to produce clear and accurate information. Without continual oversight, "the competitive juices of corporate America are such that they will stay close to the line, and some of them will go over the line." Levitt is quoted in Floyd Norris, "Levitt to Leave SEC Early; Bush to Pick 4," *New York Times*, December 21, 2000, p. C1.
7. SEC press release, "SEC to Rebuild Public Disclosure System to Make It Interactive," September 25, 2006, http://www.sec.gov/news/press/2006/2006-158.htm.
8. Wilson, 1980, p. 370.
9. Institute of Medicine, 1990, pp. 90–91 and 144–150.
10. See, for example, http://www.leapfrog.org.
11. This account is drawn from a longer case study in Graham, 2002a.
12. For example, Ida Ballasiotes, the mother of a slain businesswoman, began a grassroots citizen campaign to reform Washington State's laws on sex offenders. Along with the mother of another victim of crime by an ex-offender and organizations such as "Friends of Diane" and "Tennis Shoe Brigade," she marched on the state capitol and dumped thousands of tennis shoes to represent the vulnerability of children, women, and elders. Dorsett, 1998 (citing Barry Siegel, "Locking Up Sexual Predators," *Los Angeles Times*, May 10, 1990, p. A30).
13. For an account of the passage of the first legislation in Washington State, see Siegel, "Locking Up Sexual Predators," p. A1.

14. Bureau of Justice Statistics, U.S. Department of Justice, Office of Justice Programs, National Conference on Sex Offender Registries: Proceedings of a BJS/SEARCH conference, April 1998, NCJ-168965, http://www.ojp.usdoj.gov/bjs/pub/ascii/ncsor.txt (site accessed May 10, 2006). See also Ellen Liberman, "Megan's Law's Unintended Result: Hysteria," *Providence Journal-Bulletin*, October 17, 1999, p. 1A (dicussing, *inter alia*, Washington's "community notification meetings").

15. Law 1994, ch. 129, §1 (codified at Wash. Rev. Code Ann. §4.24.550 (2005 & West Supp. 2006)).

16. Law 1997, ch. 364, §1 (codified at Wash. Rev. Code Ann. §4.24.550 (2005 & West Supp. 2006)).

17. Law 1997, ch. 113, §2.

18. 1999 1st special session, ch. 6, §6(a) (codified at Wash. Rev. Code Ann. 9A.144.130(6)(c)).

19. Law 2001, ch. 283, §2, and Law 2001, ch. 169, §2 (codified at Wash. Rev. Code Ann. 4.24.550(4) (2005 & West Supp. 2006)).

20. Under the revised law, if an ex-offender obtains employment in either a public or a private institution of higher education, the ex-offender must, either within ten days of accepting the employment or by the first day of work at the institution, whichever is earlier, notify the sheriff of the county of the ex-offender's residence of his/her employment at the higher education institution. If the ex-offender's position at the same institution is terminated, the ex-offender must within ten days notify the sheriff of his/her residence of such termination. Law 2003 ch. 215, §1.

21. The sheriff is then required to notify the principal of the school, who is then required to notify various personnel at the school depending on the student's classification as a Level I, II, or III sex offender. Law 2005, ch. 380, §1. The 2005 law became effective September 1, 2006.

22. All fifty states currently have sex offender registration laws, and many of these laws require community notification. The most recent sex offender law was passed in Tennessee in 2004. Tennessee Sexual Offender and Violent Sex Offender Registration, Verification and Trading Act of 2004, T.C.A. §40-39–201 *et seq.*

23. Labor Management Reporting and Disclosure Act of 1959, Pub. L. 86–257, September 14, 1959, 73 Stat. 519 (codified at 29 U.S.C. §401 *et seq.* (2000)).

24. Concern about union finance reporting violating union officers' Fifth Amendment rights under the U.S. Constitution is discussed in Robb, 1961. The need for more detailed disclosure as a curb against corrupt practices by union officers (such as kickbacks or other forms of illegal payments from unions to other parties) is discussed in Goldwater, 1961. A more pessimistic view from the time concerning the prospects for improving internal union democracy through government intervention can be found in Petro, 1959.

25. See Labor Organization Annual Financial Reports, 68 Fed. Reg. 58374 (October 9, 2003) (to be codified at 29 C.F.R. pts. 403, 408). A similar executive order had been issued by George H. W. Bush at the close of his presidency, but the order was rescinded in the early days of the Clinton administration. See Exec. Order No. 12,800, 57 Fed. Reg. 12985 (April 13, 1992), as corrected 57 Fed. Reg. 13413

(April 16, 1992), revoked by Exec. Order. No. 12836, 58 Fed. Reg. 7045 (dated February 1, 1993, and published February 3, 1993).

26. For example, Ken Paff, the national organizer of the dissident Teamsters for a Democratic Union and a long-time advocate of union member rights, noted that although he looked forward to learning how much Teamsters president James Hoffa paid the union's law firm via information provided by the expanded disclosure regulations, he worried that the new requirements would pose significant burdens on small union locals: "The bulk of these forms are filed by local folks. . . . It's an enormous hassle for a small workers' organization. That's where the harassment is very serious." Jane M. Von Bergen, "Unions Adjust to Stricter Oversight," *Philadelphia Inquirer*, December 11, 2005.

27. Bergen, "Unions Adjust to Stricter Oversight." Bergen notes that the Department of Labor opened the new Division of International Union Audits in 2004 to review the information provided with the new reporting requirements.

28. See James Surowiecki, "Sarboxed In?" *New Yorker*, December 12, 2005, p. 46; see also "Final Rule: Management's Reports on Internal Control Over Financial Reporting and Certification of Disclosure in Exchange Act. Periodic Reports Securities and Exchange Commission" (Release Nos. 33–8238; 34–47986; IC-26068; File Nos. S7–40–02; S7–06–03) (effective August 14, 2004) (to be codified at 17 C.F.R. pts. 210, 228, 229, 240, 249, 270, and 274); speech by SEC Commissioner, Roel C. Campos: Remarks Before ASIC Summer School (by recorded DVD, February 13, 2006).

29. Executive Compensation and Related Party Disclosure (February 8, 2006) (Release Nos. 33–8655; 34–53185; IC-27218; File No. S7–03–06) (to be codified at 17 C.F.R. pts. 228, 229, 239, 240, 245, 249, and 274). See also Press Release, January 17, 2006, "SEC Votes to Propose Changes to Disclosure Requirements Concerning Executive Compensation and Related Matters," http://www.sec.gov/news/press/2006–10.htm (site accessed May 9, 2006).

30. Krysten Crawford, "Spitzer Seeks $100M from Grasso: N.Y. Attorney General Announces Sweeping Lawsuit Seeking Return of Some of $187M Pay Package," *CNN/Money.com*, May 24, 2004, http://money.cnn.com/2004/05/24/markets/spitzer_grasso/ (site accessed May 9, 2006).

31. See Jim McTague, "Cloud Hovers over Fed's Record on Transparency," *Barron's*, November 21, 2005, 85(47), 12; see also Warren Buffett, "Dividend Voodoo," *Washington Post*, May 20, 2003, p. A19, http://www.washingtonpost.com/ac2/wp-dyn/A13113-2003May19?language=printer (site accessed May 9, 2006); Donald Luskin, "Warren's World: It's as Whacky as Krugman's," *National Review Online*, May 21, 2003, http://www.nationalreview.com/nrof_luskin/truthsquad052103.asp (site accessed May 9, 2006).

32. Lucien Bebchuk, "How Much Does the Boss Make?" *Wall Street Journal*, January 18, 2006. See Bebchuk and Jackson, 2005, for studies of the consequences of inadequate disclosure of executive compensation on shareholder value. See also Gary Strauss and Barbara Hansen, "Companies Think They're Worth . . . ," *USA Today*, April 10, 2006, p. 1B (stating that disclosure of executive compensation not likely to curb other executives' compensation); contrast with Editorial, "Executive Envy," *Wall Street Journal Europe*, January 23, 2006, p. 11.

33. David Pierson, "Where 'A' Is Not on the Menu: Chinese Eateries in an L.A. County Enclave Struggle with Hygiene Ratings," *Los Angeles Times*, September 28, 2005, p. A1.
34. For a theoretical discussion of interest group politics, see Becker, 1983.
35. Wilson, 1980; Becker, 1983. Gunningham and Grabosky, 1998, pp. 94–122, have an extensive discussion of intermediaries under a variety of environmental policies.
36. See *Washington State Housing Finance Commission Legislative Report for 2005*, http://www.wshfc.org/admin/2005LegislativeReport.pdf; State of Rhode Island Housing Resources Commission, http://www.hrc.ri.gov/geninfo/index.shtml; New Jersey Housing Resource Center, http://www.njhousing.gov/njhrc/; Community Reinvestment Initiative, http://mcul.cusiteonline.com/Community_Reinvestment_Initiative/About_CRI/cri_taskforce_and_charge.php (sites accessed May 16, 2006).
37. Fishbein, 1995, pp. 345–346.
38. Alicia H. Munnell et al., *Mortgage Lending in Boston: Interpreting HMDA Data* (Boston: Federal Reserve Bank of Boston, 1992), p. 1.
39. Fagotto and Fung, 2003.
40. The role of unions and other workplace agents in dealing with the public goods aspects of regulation is discussed in Weil, 2005.
41. Freeman and Medoff, 1983.
42. For a recent discussion of this problem, see Gene Koretz, "Stock Analysts Shun Bad News; Good Reports Appear More Quickly," *Business Week*, May 11, 1998, p. 24 (stating that an adviser or analyst might be less likely to give bad news about a fund when it may possibly hurt its relationship with a client or potential client); see also Bodie and Clowes, 2003; Scherbina, 2005; and Shapiro, 2005.
43. http://www.fec.gov/disclosure.shtml (site accessed May 17, 2006).
44. Aron Pilhofer, "MBNA's Sudden Generosity: Coincidence or Quid Pro Quo?" *Campaign Finance Information Center*, Winter 2002, http://www.campaignfinance.org/tracker/winter02/MBNA.html (discussing the difficulty of finding information on the FEC Web site); Mark S. Sullivan, "Click to See Your Neighbor's Politics," *PC World*, August 10, 2004, http://www.pcworld.com/news/article/0,aid,117309,00.asp (sites accessed May 19, 2006).
45. Kane and Staiger, 2002.
46. See, for example, The School Report Express, http://www.homefair.com/sr_home.html; Northwest Regional Education Laboratory, http://www.nwrel.org/planning/reports/rptcards/; Education First: NC School Report Cards, http://www.ncreportcards.org/src/parents.jsp (sites accessed May 18, 2006).

Chapter 6. International Transparency

1. Transparency International (http://www.transparency.org) has constructed a respected system aimed at reducing public corruption. The Sustainable Forestry Initiative (http://www.sfi.org) represents a relatively mature private-sector effort to improve environmental protection. The Global Reporting Initiative

(http://www.globalreporting.org) is a broader effort to develop voluntary corporate reporting standards for environmental protection, human rights, labor
practices, and other goals.

2. For example, the 1979 Convention on Long-Range Transboundary Air Pollution
required that parties report their SO_2 emissions as a step toward framing and
enforcing agreements to reduce acid rain. The Barcelona Convention for Protection of the Mediterranean in 1976 required standardized monitoring of specific
pollutants as a prelude to multinational pollution regulation in 1980. During the
Cold War, members of NATO and the Warsaw Pact agreed to inform each other
of major military exercises near the East-West border to reduce the likelihood
that forces would be deployed. And parties to the Nuclear Non-proliferation
Treaty agreed to inspections of the equipment and materials they used in their
peaceful nuclear programs in order to provide assurance that none was used for
weapons.

3. Sebenius, 1984; Mitchell, 1994. See, for example, WHO Framework
Convention on Tobacco Control, http://www.who.int/tobacco/framework/
WHO_FCTC_english.pdf (site accessed May 21, 2006).

4. Reinicke, 1998, pp. 98–99.

5. Wolf, 2004, pp. 46–47 (emphasis in original).

6. Slaughter, 2004, pp. 24–25.

7. Wolfgang Reinicke has explored the influence of globalization on national and
international public policy in Reinicke, 1998. For a discussion of impacts on
national regulation, see, for example, pp. 65–68.

8. Sobel, 1994, p. 34; Reinicke, 1998, p. 15.

9. Levinson, 2006.

10. Bryant, 2003, p. 147.

11. IMF Balance of Payments Statistics, September 2003. Figures reported are total
portfolio investment liabilities.

12. Reinicke, 1998, p. 19.

13. Martin Wolf describes globalization as "a hideous word of obscure meaning."
Wolf, 2004, p. 13.

14. IMF Balance of Payments Statistics, September 2003. The proportion of total
financial liabilities going to twenty-one industrialized countries was 86.5% over
the period 1978–1985; 91.7% over 1986–1993; and 90.3% over 1994–2001. The
same figures for portfolio investment were 96.3%, 92.3%, and 92.8%. Emerging market countries received 11.5%, 7.7%, 8.7%, and 4.3%, 7.6%, and 6.3%,
respectively. The twenty-one industrialized countries are Australia, Austria,
Canada, Denmark, Finland, France, Germany, Great Britain, Greece, Iceland,
Ireland, Italy, Japan, Netherlands, New Zealand, Norway, Portugal, Spain, Sweden, Switzerland, and the United States. The seventeen emerging market countries in our data are Argentina, Brazil, Chile, China, Colombia, Indonesia, India,
Israel, Korea, Mexico, Malaysia, Pakistan, Philippines, Thailand, Turkey, Taiwan,
and Venezuela.

15. Market capitalization information from the New York Stock Exchange Web site,
http://www.NYSE.com (site accessed May 12, 2004).

16. Jeske, 2001. In the United States, this marked a significant diversification from
previous years: the percentage of domestic equities in U.S. portfolios was about

94 in 1992 and 98 in 1987. U.S. Federal Reserve, *Flow of Funds Accounts of the United States*, Table L.213, http://www.federalreserve.gov/releases/Z1/Current. For other industrialized countries, home bias has remained the same or even increased. Equity portfolios in the United Kingdom, Spain, and Italy were about as diversified in 1987 as they were in 2000; in Japan, Germany, and France they were significantly more diversified in 1987. Figures for 1987 are from Cooper and Kaplanis, 1994, pp. 45–60, Table 1.

17. See, for example, Reinicke, 1998, pp. 43–48, and Wolf, 2004, pp. 106–134, emphasizing differences between current trends and those of earlier periods.
18. Flower and Ebbers, 2002, pp. 220–237; Zeff, 2003, p. 880.
19. Regulation (EC) No. 1606/2002 of the European Parliament and of the Council of 19 July 2002, on the Application of International Accounting Standards, 2002 O.J. (L 243) 1–4.
20. Simmons, 2001, p. 590.
21. U.S. Securities and Exchange Commission, 1997, p. 15.
22. Regulation (EC) No. 1606/2002 of the European Parliament and of the Council of 19 July 2002, on the Application of International Accounting Standards.
23. These rules are available in print and can also be accessed online by IASB subscribers at http://shop.iasb.org.uk/onlineservices/onlinehome.asp?s=101298595&sc={8286D35B-D3AE-4E33-B679-D7D9ADB20CD5}&sd=239426964. One can purchase a subscription by visiting the IASB shop at http://www.iasb.org/resources/shop.asp.
24. Kung, 2002, pp. 458–459.
25. Van Hulle, 2004, p. 355.
26. McKinsey Global Investor Opinion Survey on Corporate Governance, July 2002, http://www.mckinsey.com/governance.
27. The growth in the number of non-U.S. listings on the NYSE from 1993 to 2004 can be seen at http://www.nyse.com/pdfs/nonussum040308.pdf. The total number of listings from 1980 to 2002 is available at http://www.nysedata.com/factbook/viewer_edition.asp?mode=table&key=76&category=4.
28. The financing of the International Accounting Standards Committee Foundation (IASCF) is described in the IASCF Annual Report, 2005. The "big four" accounting firms each contribute $1 million, out of an $18 million annual budget. The activities of IFAC are described at http://www.ifac.org.
29. Sources for this account of the Asian financial crisis include Stiglitz, 2002, and Blustein, 2003.
30. *G-22 Countries, Summary of Reports on the International Financial Architecture – The Working Group on Transparency and Accountability*, October 5, 1998; Declaration of G7 Finance Ministers and Central Bank Governors, October 30, 1998; Arthur Levitt, Speech to the American Council on Germany, October 7, 1999.
31. Cassell Bryan-Low, "Accounting's Global Rule Book," *Wall Street Journal*, November 28, 2003, p. C1.
32. U.S. Securities and Exchange Commission, 1997, p. 18. In 2001, the EC set up a procedure to review international standards one at a time, since "it is not possible politically, nor legally, to delegate accounting standard setting unconditionally

and irrevocably to a private organization over which the EU has no influence." Commission of the European Communities, 2001.

33. "Holier Than Thou," *Economist*, February 8, 2003, p. 69.
34. Ruder, 2001, pp. 14–18, examines U.S. and EC approaches to enforcing account-ing standards. See also International Accounting Standards Survey 2000 (David Cairns), http://www.cairns.co.uk/surveys.asp. Adrian Michaels, "US Watchdog Is Not Afraid to Take on Distant Targets," *Financial Times*, January 23, 2004, p. 24, discusses the SEC's efforts to intervene in cases involving foreign companies.
35. Turner, 2001, pp. 3–4.
36. Coffee, 2002, p. 1760, refers to some of this research, including Di Noia, 2001.
37. Slaughter, 2004, pp. 9–10.
38. Keohane, 2002, pp. 260–267.
39. Keohane, 2002, p. 36.
40. http://www.iasb.org/about/iasb_board.asp (site accessed May 3, 2006).
41. International Accounting Standards Committee Foundation Constitution, Arti-cles 6–7, July 2002, http://www.iasb.org/uploaded_files/documents/8_11_iascf-constitution.pdf. This structure mimicked that of the U.S. Financial Accounting Standards Board (FASB), the expert body that issues U.S. accounting standards and has been the object of fierce lobbying by large corporations, the Business Roundtable, and corporate trade associations. FASB reconsidered several stan-dards during the 1990s as a result of such lobbying, including accounting for stock options and intangibles and fair-value accounting of marketable securities. It remained to be seen whether the similar structure of the IASB would provide insulation from politics or encourage freelance lobbying by special interests.
42. http://www.iasb.org/about/sac_members.asp (site accessed May 3, 2006). The Standards Advisory Council also has three observers, one each from the Euro-pean Commission, the Financial Services Agency of Japan, and the U.S. Securities and Exchange Commission.
43. IASC Standards Assessment Report, 2000. Available at http://www.iosco.org/pubdocs/pdf/IOSCOPD109.pdf. A list of IOSCO members is available at http://www.iosco.org/lists.
44. http://www.ifac.org/Guidance (site accessed May 5, 2006).
45. Andrew Parker, "IASB Creates Advisory Group at EC's Request," *Financial Times*, February 3, 2004, p. 29.
46. Leuz and Verrecchia, 2000, pp. 97–98, address the question of whether interna-tional accounting standards require more and better disclosure than German standards and conclude, with reference to academic opinion and the business press, that it does.
47. Bradshaw, Bushee, and Miller, 2003.
48. Two studies by Christian Leuz of the University of Pennsylvania (one of them with colleague Robert Verrecchia) of German firms switching to international and U.S. standards did not find a difference between the effectiveness of the two sets of standards in reducing information asymmetry. Leuz, 2000; Leuz and Verrecchia, 2000, p. 111.
49. For a discussion of these proxies, see Leuz and Verrecchia, 2000, pp. 99–100.
50. http://www.who.int/governance/en/ (site accessed May 5, 2006).
51. Fidler, 2004, p. 34.

52. Fidler, 2004, p. 35.
53. See World Health Assembly, *Revision and Updating of the International Health Regulations*, WHA48.7, May 12, 1995. See also Revision Process of the International Health Regulations (IHR), http://www.who.int/csr/ihr/revision/en/index.html (site accessed May 21, 2006) (describing the process over the last eleven years).
54. Fidler, 2004, p. 66. See also *Global Outbreak Alert and Response Network – GOARN: Partnership in Outbreak Response*, http://www.who.int/csr/outbreaknetwork/goarnenglish.pdf; *Report on a WHO Meeting in Geneva, Switzerland, 26–28 April 2000: Global Outbreak Alert and Response*, http://www.who.int/csr/resources/publications/surveillance/whocdscsr2003.pdf (sites accessed May 5, 2006).
55. Institute of Medicine, 2003, p. 8; Fidler, 2004, pp. 74–80.
56. Press Release, "WHO Issues a Global Alert About Cases of Atypical Pneumonia: Cases of Severe Respiratory Illness May Spread to Hospital Staff," March 12, 2003, http://www.who.int/mediacentre/news/releases/2003/pr22/en/index.html (site accessed May 5, 2006).
57. ProMED-mail (http://www.promedmail.org) is an Internet-based warning system open to all sources of information, administered by the International Society of Infectious Diseases.
58. Institute of Medicine, 2003, p. 16 (noting the "lack of collaborative analysis" having allowed the virus to spread); Olsterholm, 2005, p. 28.
59. Fidler, 2004, p. 91.
60. Fidler, 2004, p. 102.
61. Fidler, 2004, pp. 103–104 and 135.
62. Institute of Medicine, 2003, p. 8.
63. Fidler, 2004, p. 116.
64. WHA58.4, http://www2a.cdc.gov/phlp/docs/58assembly.pdf (site accessed May 5, 2006). See also WHA58.3, http://www.who.int/csr/ihr/WHA58_3-en.pdf (resolution attached to the new IHR, also containing the new IHR) (site accessed May 6, 2006).
65. This discussion owes much to the work of Robert L. Paarlberg, who has written extensively about the politics of genetically modified food and its impact on developing countries. See Paarlberg, 2001. Other sources include Paarlberg, 2000, p. 24, and Paarlberg, 2003, p. 86. We are also grateful to Diahanna Post for her insights and helpful comments. See Post and Da Ros, 2003, and Post, 2005. A committee of the U.S. National Academy of Sciences examined these issues in depth. National Research Council, 2000.
66. http://www.cfsan.fda.gov/dms/biolabgu.html.
67. National Organic Program, 7 C.F.R. pt. 205 (2006).
68. Paarlberg, 2000, pp. 24 and 29.
69. http://europa.eu.int/comm/food/food/biotechnology/index_en.htm.
70. European Commission, *Final Report of the Public Perceptions of Agricultural Biotechnologies in Europe (PABE) Project*, 2002.
71. See WT/DS291 European Communities, *Measures Affecting the Approval and Marketing of Biotech Products*, http://www.wto.org/english/news_e/news06_e/291r_e.htm (site accessed October 11, 2006).

72. Many analysts have expressed concern that agreements among national regulators create a "democratic deficit" that undermines popular sovereignty. See, for
example, Reinicke, 1998, pp. 99–100, and Keohane, 2002, pp. 34–35.

73. See, for example, Kingsbury, Krisch, and Stewart, 2004, and http://www.iilj.org.

Chapter 7. Toward Collaborative Transparency

1. Institute of Medicine, 2003, pp. 4–6; Fidler, 2004, pp. 74–80. The Institute of
Medicine report also acknowledges the contribution to early reporting of the
Global Public Health Intelligence Network, administered by the Public Health
Agency of Canada.

2. Institute of Medicine, 2003, p. 107.

3. John Seely Brown, former president of the Palo Alto Research Center, suggests
in *The Social Life of Information* that this transformation has already occurred.
Brown, 2002.

4. Fox and Fallows, 2003, http://www.pewinternet.org/PPF/r/95/report_display.
asp.

5. Rainie et al., 2005, http://www.pewinternet.org/PPF/r/150/report_display.asp.

6. Boase et al., 2006, pp. 36–41, http://www.pewinternet.org/pdfs/PIP_Internet_
ties.pdf.

7. Boase et al., 2006, p. 56.

8. The first large-scale public system for bringing users together in peer-to-peer
information-pooling communication was the Usenet. Predating the public Web
by a decade, the Usenet is a system of distributed information sharing that
was invented by graduate students at the University of North Carolina and
Duke University in the early 1980s. The system is composed of geographically
dispersed "news servers" that carry queries, responses, articles, and ongoing
discussions posted by users. There are currently some hundred thousand such
discussion groups on the Usenet, more than a fifth of which are active even now.

9. The history of the Web itself provides insight into the central role of collaboration in its development. In November 1990, Tim Berners-Lee published
"WorldWideWeb: A Proposal for a Hypertext Project" as a suggestion for how
scientists at CERN, the European particle physics laboratory, might share information more easily with one another and with other scientists. Berners-Lee
developed all of the basic pieces for a contained Web by Christmas of that year.
His Web had two breakthrough features: it combined the earlier hypertext (point
and click links on a page) with the communication hardware and protocols of
the Internet and also made it much easier for individuals and organizations to
create Web servers and Web pages. In 1993, CERN announced that the Web
would be free for anyone to use. In that same year, Marc Andreessen at the
National Center for Supercomputing Applications released – free of charge –
the Mosaic World Wide Web Browser. Its straightforward user interface and
easy combination of text and graphics quickly made the Web the most popular
protocol used on the Internet. As a result, the Internet is synonymous with the
Web for most users. All contemporary browsers – Microsoft's Explorer, Mozilla's
FireFox, and Apple's Safari – are relatively minor and incremental evolutions of
Mosaic.

10. http://en.wikipedia.org/wiki/Wikipedia.
11. Information pooling itself is not new, of course. Markets and political processes have long pooled the judgments of many, whether the result is an agreed-upon price for a share of Microsoft stock, the viability of a new cola formula, or the winner of a presidential election. Long before the Internet was even imagined, Zagat and other guides produced restaurant and hotel ratings based on user contributions. But advances in information technology have taken such collaborative judgments to a new level of usefulness in everyday life, making it possible to draw on a much wider group of information providers, to customize results, and to keep information current.
12. Von Hippel, 2006.
13. Evans and Wurster, 2000, p. 9.
14. Evans and Wurster, 2000, pp. ix and 4.
15. Constance L. Hays, "What They Know About You," *New York Times*, November 14, 2004, p. C1.
16. Hagel and Brown, 2005, pp. 11–14.
17. http://www.epa.gov/enviro/. Also see Fountain, 2001, pp. 26–29.
18. The EDGAR system can be found at http://www.sec.gov/edgar.shtml; the Web site for the Office of Labor Management Services, the office in the U. S. Department of Labor that administers the union finances disclosure system, can be found at http://www.dol.gov/esa/olms_org.htm.
19. The expanding application of information technology to the work of local, state, and federal government has spawned a number of institutions that document and analyze different applications of "digital governance." See, for example, the National Center for Digital Government, based at the University of Massachusetts at Amherst's Center for Public Policy and Administration and funded by the National Science Foundation (http://www.umass.edu/digitalcenter); the Program on Networked Governance, based at Harvard's Kennedy School of Government (http://www.ksg.harvard.edu/netgov/html/index.htm); and the Center for Digital Government, which focuses on state and local government applications of information technology (http://www.centerdigitalgov.com).
20. For an in-depth discussion of the politics of toxic pollution disclosure and the development of Scorecard, see Graham, 2002a.
21. See O'Rourke and Macey, 2003.
22. https://www.cahps.ahrq.gov.
23. See, for example, http://en.wikipedia.org/wiki/AIDS; http://en.wikipedia.org/wiki/Avian_flu.
24. http://www.qualitycheck.org.
25. See, for example, http://www.partners.org; http://www.bcbsma.com.
26. 49 C.F.R. 579.4(c).
27. "Terror in America," *Patriot Ledger*, September 21, 2001, p. 11.
28. John Schwartz, "Myths Run Wild in Blog Tsunami Debate," *New York Times*, January 3, 2005, p. A9.
29. Sunstein, 2001, p. 49.
30. Nick Wingfield and Matthew Rose, "Amazon Puts a Price on Book Promotions – Retailer to Charge for Recommendations," *Wall Street Journal Asia*, February 8,

2001, p. N1; Nick Wingfield and Matthew Rose, "Amazon Plans to Charge Publishers Fee for Online Recommendations," *Wall Street Journal (Eastern Edition)*, February 7, 2001, p. B1.

31. See, for example, John Seigenthaler, "A False Wikipedia 'Biography,'" *USA Today*, November 30, 2005, p. A11.
32. Giles, 2005.
33. www.usdoj.gov/criminal/fraud/Internet.htm.
34. Alan Murray, "The CEO as Global Corporate Ambassador," *Wall Street Journal*, March 29, 2006, p. A2.
35. http://www.stopandshop.com/stores/shopping_buddy.htm.
36. http://www.albertsons.com/abs_investorinformation/companinfo/ annualreport_2004/imperative3.html.
37. http://www.gnc.com/corp/index.jsp?page=inTheStore.
38. Nathanael Johnson, "The Augmented Bar Code," *New York Times Magazine*, December 12, 2004, p. 54.

Chapter 8. Targeted Transparency in the Information Age

1. "Surgical Tools 'Washed' in Hydraulic Fluid," *Associated Press*, June 13, 2005, p. A15; see also Hydraulic Fluid Facts, Duke University Health System, http:// hydraulicfluidfacts.dukehealth.org/overview (site accessed May 6, 2006); Report on Instrument Sterilization, by Professor William A. Rutala, PhD, MPH, Director of the Statewide Program in Infection Control and Epidemiology at the UNC School of Medicine, http://hydraulicfluidfacts.dukehealth.org/ reports/index/Rutala_Report.pdf (site accessed May 6, 2006); RTI Analysis, by RTI International, http://hydraulicfluidfacts.dukehealth.org/reports/index/ RTI_Final_Report_6–24.pdf (site accessed May 6, 2006).
2. Institute of Medicine, 1999, pp. 22–42; see also Graham, 2002a, pp. 104–136.
3. 28 PA ADC §136.21 (West, Westlaw through May 2006); 10 NYCRR §709.14 (2005).
4. Graham, 2002a, pp. 106–107.
5. This problem also arises under state laws requiring disclosure of sex offenders' places of residence. Potential overreaction to risks posed to neighbors from released offenders can lead to a range of troubling outcomes, from local vigilantism to, in the extreme, murder (see Chapter 4). Linden and Rockoff, 2006, show that housing prices in the immediate vicinity of a listed sex offender decrease in value (by an average of $5,500) relative to comparable housing elsewhere. These results imply that homeowners perceive an increased risk from living near a released offender, although it is not clear whether this reaction represents a reasonable estimate of that risk.
6. In this example, the transparency policy provides the information necessary to strike the type of Coasian agreements between polluters and affected communities described in Chapter 2.
7. Milt Freudenheim, "To Find a Doctor, Mine the Data," *New York Times*, September 22, 2005, p. C1 (noting that Blue Cross Blue Shield, Wellpoint, Humana, United Healthcare, and Cigna all provide quality measures for health care). See the Web sites of Wellpoint, http://phx.corporate-ir.net/

phoenix.zhtml?c=130104&p=irol-govhighlights; United HealthCare, http://www.uhc.com/resources/; Blue Cross Blue Shield, http://bcbshealthissues.com/; Humana, information available at http://www.humana.com/members/home.asp (scroll down and choose "Transparency Tools"); and Cigna, http://www.cigna.com/index.html (sites accessed May 12, 2006).

8. Applying ideas from behavioral economics to public policy issues is gaining increasing interest. For example, in 2004, the Federal Reserve Board hosted a conference on the impact of ideas from behavioral economics (including the effects of cognitive biases on decision making) on a variety of critical policy areas such as health care, product safety, and environmental policy. See Thaler and Sunstein, 2003, for a related discussion of building default rules into public policy to adjust to systematic cognitive errors.

9. Institute of Medicine, 1999, pp. 67–73.

10. See Restoring Trust in Government Act, H.R. 4696, 109th Cong. (2006); Lobbying Accountability and Transparency Act, H.R. 4975, 109th Cong. (2006).

11. Financial Accounting Standards Board, http://www.fasb.org/ (site accessed May 6, 2006).

Appendix. Eighteen Major Cases

1. The Securities Act is codified at 15 U.S.C. §§78a *et seq*. For a detailed account of these events, see Seligman, 1995, pp. 41–42.

2. Quoted in Seligman, 1995, p. 71.

3. We discuss this evolution in detail in Chapter 5.

4. Seligman, 1995, pp. 431–437.

5. FASB was governed and financed by the new Financial Accounting Foundation, a non-profit organization whose trustees were nominated by five leading accounting organizations (though still elected by the board of the Association of International Certified Public Accountants, AICPA). Task forces drawn from a spectrum of interested groups as well as a broad-based advisory council gave FASB broader accountability. Unlike the previous board, its seven members held full-time positions and did not have other business affiliations. Soon after the board began operation, the SEC issued a policy statement recognizing its opinions as authoritative. Pacter, 1985, pp. 6–10. See also Seligman, 1995, pp. 452–466 and 554.

6. Pacter, 1985, pp. 10–18; Seligman, 1995, pp. 555–557.

7. One response was the Securities Investor Protection Act of 1970. It produced new SEC disclosure rules that required broker-dealers to give notice when new capital was insufficient or records were not current. Seligman, 1995, pp. 451–465.

8. The scandal led to the 1977 Corrupt Practices Act, which required companies to maintain new accounting controls to assure that transactions were authorized by management. This additional transparency was designed to discourage illegal transfers. Seligman, 1995, pp. 539–549.

9. Seligman, 1995, pp. 549–550.

10. See http://www.sec.gov/pdf/handbook.pdf. Commission chairman Arthur Levitt emphasized the importance of constant vigilance to produce clear and

accurate information. Floyd Norris, "Levitt to Leave SEC Early; Bush to Pick 4," *New York Times*, December 21, 2000, p. C1. See also Plain English Disclosure, 63 Fed. Reg. 6370, 6370 (February 6, 1998) (to be codified at 17 C.F.R. pts. 228, 229, 230, 239, and 274 (Release Nos. 33–7497; 34–39593; IC-23011; International Series No. 1113; File No. S7–3–97)).

11. Smith and Emshwiller, 2003, pp. 374–376.
12. General Accounting Office, 2002, p. 15.
13. Sarbanes-Oxley Act of 2002, Pub. L. 107–204, Title IV, §404, July 30, 2002, 116 Stat. 745 (codified at 15 U.S.C.A. §7201 *et seq.* (West 2005) and scattered sections of 18 U.S.C.). Section 404 is codified in 15 U.S.C.A. §7262 (West 2005). For a look at how the Sarbanes-Oxley Act has amended various sections of the Securities Exchange Act of 1933, see http://www.sec.gov/divisions/corpfin/33act/index1933.shtml (site accessed June 4, 2006).
14. See, for example, Executive Compensation, 17 C.F.R. §§228.402, 229.402 (2005).
15. General Accounting Office, 2003a, p. 13.
16. General Accounting Office, 2003a, pp. 16–17.
17. Financial Literacy and Education Improvement Act, 20 U.S.C. 9701–08.
18. Fagotto and Fung, 2003, p. 63.
19. For discussions of the development of right-to-know laws and regulations in connection with health and safety risks, see Baram, 1984; Ashford and Caldart, 1985; Hadden, 1989.
20. Schroeder and Shapiro, 1984.
21. Oleinick, Fodor, and Susselman, 1988, provide a timeline for the adoption of state right-to-know laws. By 1982 five states had worker right-to-know laws; the number increased by six new states in 1983 and eight in 1984; in 1985, twenty-seven states had worker right-to-know laws.
22. Hunter and Mason, 1996.
23. See Executive Summary of Hazard Communication in the 21st Century Workplace, http://www.osha.gov/dsg/hazcom/finalmsdsreport.html (site accessed June 10, 2006). The Hazard Communication final rule can be found at 48 Fed. Reg. 53280 (November 25, 1983) (codified at 29 C.F.R. §1910.1200 (2005)).
24. Occupational Safety and Health Administration, 2004.
25. Stillman and Wheeler, 1987.
26. General Accounting Office, 1992a.
27. Baram, 1996. According to the author, liability and market forces promote compliance with the hazard communication standard.
28. Tom Anschutz, "When OSHA Comes Calling," *Occupational Hazards*, March 2006, pp. 50–51.
29. See Occupational Safety and Health Administration, 1997.
30. Kolp et al., 1993.
31. Phillips et al., 1999.
32. Fagotto and Fung, 2003; Weil, 2005.
33. Occupational Safety and Health Administration, 2004.
34. The disclosure system was authorized by the Emergency Planning and Community Right-to-Know Act of 1986, 42 U.S.C. 11023(a). This account

draws on several detailed analyses of the Toxics Release Inventory, including Fung and O'Rourke, 2000; Case, 2001; Cohen, 2001; Graham and Miller, 2001; Karkkainen, 2001; Pedersen, 2001; Graham, 2002a; Hamilton, 2005.

35. Graham, 2002a, pp. 46–47.
36. Exec. Order 12,856, 3 C.F.R. 616 (1993); Exec. Order 12,969, 60 Fed. Reg. 40989 (August 8, 1995), revoked by Exec. Order 13,148, 65 Fed. Reg. 24595 (April 21, 2000) (set out as a note in 42 U.S.C. §4321 (2000)).
37. Toxics Release Inventory Burden Reduction, 70 Fed. Reg. 57822 (proposed October 4, 2005) (to be codified at 40 C.F.R. pt. 372).
38. In the late 1990s, the federal EPA did make available Risk-Screening Environmental Indicators software that allowed users to analyze risk in general terms using disclosed toxic chemical data, http://www.epa.gov/opptintr/rsei/index.html.
39. This account is drawn from a longer case study by Mary Graham: Graham, 2002a. For a summary of structural problems, see Graham, 2002a, pp. 47–49. For an empirical analysis of impact of disclosure, see Graham and Miller, 2005. On the issue of timeliness, see U.S. EPA, *2004 TRI Public Data Release*, April 12, 2006, http://www.epa.gov/tri/tridata/tri04/index.htm.
40. Nutrition Labeling and Education Act of 1990, Pub. L. 101–535, November 8, 1990, 104 Stat. 2353 (codified at 21 U.S.C. §343 *et seq.* (2000)).
41. This discussion is drawn from a longer case study in Graham, 2002a.
42. These provisions are set forth at 21 U.S.C. 343(q)(1) (2000). See also Statement on Signing the Nutrition Labeling and Education Act of 1990, 26 Weekly Comp. Pres. Docs 1795 (November 8, 1990).
43. See Graham, 2002a, pp. 81–101.
44. Food Labeling: Trans Fatty Acids in Nutrition Labeling, Nutrient Content Claims, and Health Claims, 28 C.F.R. §101.9 (2005).
45. Food Allergen Labeling and Consumer Protection Act of 2004, Pub. L. 108–282, Title II, August 2, 2004, 118 Stat. 905 (codified at 21 U.S.C.A. §374a (West 2005)).
46. This account is drawn from a longer case study in Graham, 2002a.
47. The Institute of Medicine defined errors as failures of planning or execution of a medical treatment. Errors were a subset of adverse events, defined as injuries attributable to medical management rather than to a patient's underlying condition. Errors were also referred to as preventable adverse events. Institute of Medicine, 1999, pp. 23–30.
48. Institute of Medicine, 1999, pp. 1–3.
49. Institute of Medicine, 1999, pp. 3–13.
50. Institute of Medicine, 1999, pp. 3–13.
51. 10 N.Y. Comp. R & Regs. §709.14 (2005).
52. 28 PA. Code §136.21 (West, Westlaw through May 2006).
53. Patient Safety and Quality Improvement Act of 2005, Pub. L. 109–41, July 29, 2005, 119 Stat. 424 (codified at 42 U.S.C.A. §299b21 *et seq.* (West, Westlaw through Pub. L. 109–169)).
54. The National Academy for State Health Care Policy publishes periodic summaries of state patient safety laws and practice, http://www.nashp.org/.

55. See, for example, Richard Perez-Pena, "Law to Rein in Hospital Errors Is Widely Abused, Audit Finds," *New York Times*, September 29, 2004.
56. http://www.hospitalcompare.hhs.gov; http://www.qualitycheck.org (sites accessed May 12, 2006).
57. The federal Megan's Law was preceded in 1994 by the Jacob Wetterling Crimes Against Children and Sexually Violent Offender Registration Act, which required states to establish registries for sex offenders and child molesters. The Wetterling Act also mandated more stringent registration requirements for the most dangerous offenders, designated as "sexually violent predators." States that fail to comply with the Wetterling Act risk losing 10 percent of federal anticrime funding. Jacob Wetterling Crimes Against Children and Sexually Violent Offender Registration Act, Pub. L. 103–322, Title XVII, Subtitle A, §170101, September 13, 1994, 108 Stat. 2038. See also Adkins, Huff, and Stageberg, 2000, p. 1.
58. See "Sex Offender Registration" (Westlaw 50 State Surveys: Surveys of Criminal Laws: Sex Offender Registration, 2006).
59. Logan, 2003.
60. In Alaska, the law had been ruled unconstitutional by the appellate courts because it punished *ex post facto* offenders who had been convicted before the state law was passed. Smith v. Doe, 538 U.S. 84 (2003). In the Connecticut case, one issue was whether disclosing offenders' data without proving that they remained dangerous represented a violation of the guarantee of due process. Connecticut Dept. of Public Safety v. Doe, 538 U.S. 1 (2003).
61. 1990 Wash. Legis. Serv., ch. 3, §117 (codified at Wash. Rev. Code Ann. §4.24.550 (2005 & West. Supp. 2006)).
62. "The legislature . . . finds that if the public is provided adequate notice and information, the community can develop constructive plans to prepare themselves and their children for the offender's release. A sufficient time period allows communities to meet law enforcement to discuss and prepare for the release, to establish block watches, to obtain information about the rights and responsibilities of the community and the offender, and to provide education and counseling to their children." 1994 Wash. Legis. Serv., ch. 129, §1 (codified at Wash. Rev. Code Ann. §4.24.550 (2005 & West Supp. 2006)).
63. The Washington Association of Sheriffs and Police Chiefs collects and maintains a statewide registry based on the information provided by individual county sheriff's offices.
64. Wash. Rev. Code Ann. §9A.44.130.
65. Wash. Rev. Code Ann. §9A.44.130(10)(a),(b).
66. The Web site can be found at http://ml.waspc.org.
67. See http://ml.waspc.org/index.aspx.
68. The organization provides a range of services including a helpline for communities on using registry information; advocacy at the local, state, and federal level; and education, counseling, and policy research. The site maintained by the organization, http://www.parentsformeganslaw.com, also provides links to all fifty state registries as well as an evaluation of the accessibility of information. It gave Washington state a grade of "C" for its registry on the basis of a nationwide review of information accessibility in 2005.

69. Safe Drinking Water Act of 1974, Pub. L. 93–523, July 1, 1974, c. 373, Title XIV, as added December 16, 1974, §2(a), 88 Stat. 1669 (codified at 42 U.S.C. §§300f *et seq.*).
70. 42 U.S.C. §300g-2(c)(1)–(3).
71. General Accounting Office, 1992b.
72. See, for example, MacKenzie et al., 1994; Environmental Protection Agency, 1999.
73. 42 U.S.C. §300g-2(c)(4). Regulations are codified at 40 C.F.R. §141.151 *et seq.*
74. National Environmental Education and Training Foundation, 1999.
75. Payment et al., 1991.
76. Natural Resources Defense Council, 2003, Chapter 1, p. 2.
77. Even small amounts of lead can cause neurological problems in children and high blood pressure in adults. The EPA findings are summarized in Congressional Research Service, 2005, p. 2.
78. Congressional Research Service, 2005, p. 5.
79. Natural Resources Defense Council, 2003, Chapter 3.
80. Government Accountability Office, 2004, p. 13.
81. National Research Council, 2002.
82. The series, by KCBS-TV newsman Joel Grover, aired November 16, 17, and 18, 1997, on the Channel 2 News in Los Angeles.
83. Hospitalizations and fatality estimates from Mead et al., 1999. CDC estimates, based on surveillance data from 1993 to 1997, reported in Centers for Disease Control and Prevention, Surveillance for Foodborne Disease Outbreaks – United States, 1993–1997, *Morbidity and Mortality Weekly Report*, vol. 49 (SS-1), 2000, pp. 22–26.
84. For a general description, see Simon et al., 2005, pp. 32–36. Los Angeles County Ordinance 97–0071 §2 (part), 1997. http://municipalcodes.lexisnexis.com/codes/lacounty/_DATA/TITLE08/Chapter_8_04_PUBLIC_HEALTH_LICENSE/8_04_225_Grading_and_letter_gr.html (site accessed June 3, 2006); see also County of Los Angeles Department of Health Services, Public Health Programs and Services, Environmental Health, *Posting Requirements Advisory Bulletin: Retail Food Establishments*, http://search.ladhs.org/images/nrfood.htm (site accessed April 29, 2006).
85. The cities that had not adopted grade cards in Los Angeles County as of 2005 were Avalon, Azusa, City of Industry, Hidden Hills, La Habra Heights, Montebello, Redondo Beach, San Marino, Sierra Madre, and Signal Hill. Restaurants in those cities were inspected and received grades from the county, but were not required to post them.
86. The DHS provides inspectors a detailed retail food inspection guide, broken into five sections. See County of Los Angeles, Department of Health Services, *Retail Food Inspection Guide*, H-3046 (May 2000). A subjective element (based on the inspectors' overall assessment of hygiene status) was eliminated from the survey in July 1997 to improve the objectivity of the guidelines.
87. The guidelines define an A as "[g]enerally superior in food handling practices and overall food facility maintenance"; a B as "[g]enerally good in food handling practices and overall food facility maintenance"; and a C as "[g]enerally acceptable in food handling practices and overall general food facility maintenance."

A score below 69 is associated with "[p]oor food handling practices and over-all general food facility maintenance." See County of Los Angeles, Department of Health Services, *Retail Food Inspection Guide*, "Understanding Your Grade," http://www.lapublichealth.org.

88. A total of 989 restaurants out of 24,000 received closure orders in Los Angeles County in 2002. Most were temporary. See Martin Miller, "Five Years into L.A. County's Grade-Posting Project, Most Restaurants Are Getting Top Marks," *Los Angeles Times*, July 28, 2003.

89. The ordinance specifically requires that the grade card be posted within five feet of the point of entry. If the numeric grade is below a C, the restaurant is required to post the numeric grade in its window.

90. See Jin and Leslie, 2005, for a summary of these results. Jin and Leslie find that these changes arise from a combination of "sorting" (customers switching from restaurants with low grades to those with higher grades) and improvement in the hygiene practices of restaurants with lower ratings. See Jin and Leslie, 2003 and 2005.

91. See Jin and Leslie, 2006.

92. Along with anecdotal evidence, Jin and Leslie, 2005, p. 100, report that the distribution of grades around the critical scores of 89 (the line between an A and B) and 79 (between a B and C) show a dramatic upward spike around the higher number, implying that inspectors may choose to bump up scores. If such activity occurs only at break points, this may imply only a mild form of grade inflation.

93. Miller, "Five Years into L.A. County's Grade-Posting Project, Most Restaurants Are Getting Top Marks."

94. David Pierson, "Where 'A' is Not on the Menu: Chinese Eateries in an L.A. County Enclave Struggle with Hygiene Ratings," *Los Angeles Times*, September 28, 2005.

95. An effort to replicate the Los Angeles County system in San Francisco faced fierce opposition when it was proposed in 2004. After a six-month battle, the San Francisco Board of Supervisors adopted a compromise measure requiring restaurants to post health inspection reports (but not summary grades), as well as merit symbols for those receiving high marks. See Suzanne Herel, "Health Ratings Win Approval," *San Francisco Chronicle*, May 12, 2004, p. B4. Efforts to adopt a similar system in San Bernardino County have also faced opposition from restaurant owners and restaurant associations. See Martin Hugo, "San Bernardino County Considers Grading Restaurants," *Los Angeles Times*, April 20, 2004, p. B5; see also Martin Hugo, "S.B. County Restaurants May Soon Get Health Ratings," *Los Angeles Times*, April 28, 2004, p. B3.

96. Based on a survey by the National Conference of State Legislators in 2005. North Carolina's system is called the "Know the Score" program and uses a grading system similar to the one employed in Los Angeles. See N.C. Gen. Stat. §130A-249 (2005). Tennessee's system also uses grade cards. See Tenn. Code Ann. §68–14–317 (2001). See also Pytka, 2005.

97. These accidents and their causes were extensively reported on by Keith Bradsher of the *New York Times* in 2000.

98. Government Accountability Office, 2005b, p. 31.

99. Federal regulators first proposed a rollover standard in 1973. For a detailed history of rollover regulation, see National Academies, 2002, pp. 9–13.

100. These goals are spelled out in Consumer Information Regulations; Rollover Prevention, 65 Fed. Reg. 34998–35024 (June 1, 2000) (codified at 49 C.F.R. pt. 575). See also Transportation Recall Enhancement, Accountability, and Documentation (TREAD) Act, Pub. L. 106–414, November 1, 2000, 114 Stat. 1800 (codified at 49 U.S.C. §30170) (2000)). In earlier rule makings, regulators established frontal crashworthiness ratings and side impact ratings for each new model.

101. For a detailed discussion of the development of the five-star rating, including reliance on focus groups, see National Academies, 2002, pp. 68–71. The government replaced numerical ratings with star ratings after a 1992 Senate and Conference Appropriations report asked that methods be improved for informing consumers of the comparative safety of new models. For ratings history, see Government Accountability Office, 2005b, pp. 10–12.

102. The final rule was published in 66 Fed. Reg. 3388–3437 (January 12, 2001).

103. 66 Fed. Reg. 66190 (proposed December 21, 2001) (codified at subpt. C 49 C.F.R. pt. 579).

104. 66 Fed. Reg. 65536 (proposed December 19, 2001) (to be codified at 49 C.F.R. pts. 567, 571, 574, and 575).

105. These requirements are set forth in 49 U.S.C. §30117(c).

106. Consumer Information; New Car Assessment Program; Rollover Resistance, 68 Fed. Reg. 59250 (October 14, 2003) (codified at 49 C.F.R. pt. 575). The dynamic rollover test complemented but did not replace the government's initial static test. The National Academies of Sciences' recommendations are set forth in National Academies, 2002.

107. Stars on Cars Act of 2005, S. 560, 109th Cong. (2005).

108. New-model rollover ratings are listed by the National Highway Traffic Safety Administration at http://www.safercar.com. In 2004, there were 4.3 million visits to the ratings Web site. Government Accountability Office, 2005b, p. 15.

109. Government Accountability Office, 2005b, p. 2.

110. Government Accountability Office, 2005b, p. 26.

111. Congress directed regulators to issue a minimum performance standard for rollovers by 2009. Safe, Accountable, Flexible, Efficient Transportation Equity Act: A Legacy for Users (SAFETEA-LU), Pub. L. 109–59, August 10, 2005, 119 Stat. 1144 (codified in scattered sections of 18 U.S.C.A., 23 U.S.C.A., and 49 U.S.C.A) (West, Westlaw through Pub. L. 109–169). See Federal Motor Vehicle Safety Standards; Roof Crush Resistance, 70 Fed. Reg. 49223 (proposed August 23, 2005) (to be codified at 49 C.F.R. pt. 571).

112. Government Accountability Office, 2005b, p. 36.

113. Government Accountability Office, 2005b, pp. 27–28.

114. Instructions for accessing backup crash test data are given at http://www.safercar.gov/pages/ResourcesLinksDCR.htm.

115. For a general critique of auto safety star ratings, see National Academies, 1996, pp. 65–73, and Government Accountability Office, 2005b, pp. 27–28.

116. Homeland Security Presidential Directive 3 (HSPD-3), March 12, 2002, http://www.fas.org/irp/offdocs/nspd/hspd-3.htm, as amended by Homeland Security Presidential Directive 5 (HSPD-5), February 28, 2003, http://www.fas.org/irp/offdocs/nspd/hspd-5.html and http://www.dhs.gov/dhspublic/display?content=4331 (sites accessed May 22, 2006).
117. Remarks by Governor Ridge at Announcement of Homeland Security Advisory System, March 12, 2002, http://www.whitehouse.gov/news/releases/2002/03/20020312-11.html (site accessed May 22, 2006).
118. Homeland Security Act of 2002, Pub. L. 107–296, Title II, Subtitle A, §201(d)(7), 116 Stat. 2135, 2146 (codified at 6 U.S.C. §§101 *et seq.* (Supp. III 2003)).
119. Homeland Security Presidential Directive 3 (HSPD-3), March 12, 2002.
120. Pub. L. 107–296, Title II, Subtitle A, Section 201(d)(7).
121. Alerts are summarized at http://www.dhs.gov/dhspublic/interapp/editorial/editorial_0844.xml.
122. Congressional Research Service, 2003, pp. 1–4.
123. General Accounting Office, 2004, p. 13.
124. Advisory Panel to Assess Domestic Response Capabilities for Terrorism Involving Weapons of Mass Destruction, 2003.
125. Congressional Research Service, 2003, pp. 4–5.
126. General Accounting Office, 2004, pp. 4–5 and 12–14.
127. General Accounting Office, 2004, p. 18.
128. General Accounting Office, 2004, p. 18.
129. Senate Governmental Affairs Committee, 2003.
130. General Accounting Office, 2004, p. 13.
131. Attorney General Ashcroft, Director Ridge Discuss Threat Level, September 10, 2002 (White House transcript).
132. Philip Shenon, "Threats and Responses: Domestic Security," *New York Times*, June 6, 2003, p. A15.
133. "Analysis: Congressional Hearings on Terror Alert System," *Morning Edition* (National Public Radio), broadcast February 5, 2004.
134. Philip Shenon, "Report Finds Threat Alerts in Color Code Baffle Public," *New York Times*, August 10, 2003, p. A18.
135. Council for Excellence in Government, from the Home Front to the Front Lines: America Speaks Out about Homeland Security (a Hart-Teeter poll, March 2004).
136. Fox News polls, July 2002 and February 2003.
137. Philip Zimbardo, "Phantom Menace," *Psychology Today*, June 2003, pp. 34–36.
138. One legislative reaction was passage of the Taft-Hartley Act of 1947, which set out sweeping amendments to the National Labor Relations Act. Among other features, the law described a new set of unfair labor practices for unions, including prohibitions against secondary boycotts and other forms of concerted activities by unions, as well as new employer rights to counter union organizing activities. Gross, 1981.
139. Newspapers and radio covered the hearings closely and a number of rising political figures of the day – including John F. Kennedy and Robert F. Kennedy – made

early reputations during the proceedings. See Robert Kennedy's 1960 account of the hearings, *The Enemy Within*.

140. Labor Management Reporting and Disclosure Act of 1959, Pub. L. 86–257, September 14, 1959, 73 Stat. 519 (codified at 29 U.S.C. §401 *et seq.* (2000)). Section 431(b) in Title 29 of the U.S. Code requires unions to file annual reports and sets forth information requirements. Section 438 of the same title provides for the secretary of labor to "have authority to issue, amend, and rescind rules and regulations prescribing the form and publication of reports required to be filed under this subchapter and such other reasonable rules and regulations (including rules prescribing reports concerning trusts in which a labor organization is interested) as he may find necessary to prevent the circumvention or evasion of such reporting requirements." The legislation was passed by a vote of 95–2 in the Senate and 352–52 in the House.

141. Concern about the LMRDA violating union officers' Fifth Amendment rights under the Constitution is discussed in Robb, 1961. A pessimistic view from the time concerning the prospects for improving internal union democracy through government intervention can be found in Petro, 1959.

142. The OLMS had a staff of 286 in fiscal year 1999, including an auditing staff of 5 and a total of 158 investigators. The GAO estimated that OLMS processed 2,435 reporting- and disclosure-related cases in that year, which required it to devote a little under 5 percent of its total time to these activities. See General Accounting Office, 2000, Appendix I, pp. 18–21.

143. If unions (or other parties required to file under LMRDA) willfully fail to file reports, knowingly make false statements or withhold information, or conceal or destroy materials, they face fines of up to a hundred thousand dollars and up to one year in prison. See Employment Standards Administration, Office of Labor-Management Standards, *Reports Required Under the LMRDA and the CSRA* (Washington, D.C.: U.S. Department of Labor, 2001).

144. The LMRDA requires each level of the union with governance responsibility to provide separate disclosure under the act, providing information regarding financial activity (revenues and expenses) only at that level of the union. This makes it a complicated matter for a user trying to examine reports of a local for information regarding related expenditures or revenues at regional and national levels.

145. See General Accounting Office, 2000, for a discussion of these costs.

146. For example, many union locals receive representation and administrative support from staff paid for by the international office of their union. These expenditures (the salaries of these individuals as well as associated expenses) show up in the accounts of the international, rather than local, union. Unions also deal with the flow of dues revenues to the various levels of the union in different ways. For example, in many unions, dues are paid to the local union, which then remits a portion of them to intermediate and national levels of the organization on the basis of per capita fees set out in union constitutions. Although the disclosure forms under the law allow one to analyze these flows, it requires significant understanding of union structures and accounting practices.

147. For critiques along these lines, see Masters, 1997.

148. For a classic discussion of the legal obstacles facing labor union representation under the National Labor Relations Act, see Weiler, 1983.

149. Unions representing U.S. Postal Service workers are covered by the LMRDA. Other federal workers became covered by comparable standards in the Civil Service Reform Act of 1978 and the Foreign Service Act of 1980. Civil Service Reform Act of 1978, Pub. L. 95–454, October 13, 1978, 92 Stat. 1111 (codified at 5 U.S.C. §§1101 *et seq.* (2000)); Foreign Service Act of 1980, Pub. L. 96–465, October 17, 1980, 94 Stat. 2071 (codified at 22 U.S.C. §§3901 *et seq.* (2000)).

150. Reporting requirements were reduced for small unions, in part because of requirements of the Paperwork Reduction Act. Rather than filling out the detailed Form LM-2, union entities with total annual receipts of less than two hundred thousand dollars were allowed to use the simplified Form LM-3 to report financial activities. Unions with annual receipts of less than ten thousand dollars of annual receipts were allowed to file the more abbreviated Form LM-4 (adopted in 1992 and put into effect in January 1994).

151. General Accounting Office, 2000. The report also cites other reasons why unions face minimal incentives for timely reporting (e.g., cases against union entities with receipts under five thousand dollars are not even initiated until they have been delinquent filers for three consecutive years). Further, in cases where unions provided deficient information, the agency used voluntary methods to handle 90% of the cases and took no action regarding the remaining cases.

152. Interviews with Hank Guzda, U.S. Department of Labor, Office of Labor/Management Services, April 1, 2002; David Geiss, Industrial Relations Specialist, U.S. Department of Labor, Office of Labor/Management Services, April 1, 2002.

153. See General Accounting Office, 1999.

154. See Office of Management and Budget, Exec. Office of the President, Budget of the United States Government, Fiscal Year 2001 (2000), and Office of Management and Budget, Exec. Office of the President, Budget of the United States Government, Fiscal Year 2006 (2005). The Department of Labor's budget for fiscal year 2006 can be found at http://www.dol.gov/_sec/budget2006/overview.pdf (site accessed June 4, 2006). Information regarding the Department of Labor's budget for fiscal year 2001 can be found at http://www.dol.gov/_sec/budget/budget01.htm (site accessed June 4, 2006). The budget of the U.S. government in its entirety can be accessed through http://www.gpoaccess.gov/usbudget/fy06/index.html for fiscal year 2006 and through http://www.gpoaccess.gov/usbudget/fy01/index.html for fiscal year 2001.

155. Similar changes to the LMRDA were introduced by President George H. W. Bush in 1992 but then rescinded by President Bill Clinton upon taking office in 1993. See Exec. Order No. 12,800, 57 Fed. Reg. 12985 (April 13, 1992), as corrected 57 Fed. Reg. 13413 (April 16, 1992), revoked by Exec. Order. No. 12836, 58 Fed. Reg. 7045 (dated February 1, 1993, and published February 3, 1993).

156. See Labor Organization Annual Financial Reports, 68 Fed. Reg. 58374 (October 9, 2003) (codified at 29 C.F.R. pts. 403, 408). This five-thousand-dollar figure

includes receipts and disbursements that total five thousand dollars or more, as well as payments to a single entity that total five thousand dollars or more in the reporting year, within certain specified categories as set out within the regulations.

157. See Labor Organization Annual Financial Reports, 68 Fed. Reg. 58374. The new reporting requirement became effective in 2004.

158. The changes in reporting requirements were upheld in the U.S. Court of Appeals decision, American Fed'n of Labor and Cong. of Indus. Org. v. Chao, 409 F.3d 377 (D.C. Cir. 2005).

159. Buckley v. Valeo, 424 U.S. 1 (1976), at 67.

160. Publicity Act of 1910, June 25, 1910, ch. 392, 36 Stat. 822 (repealed by Pub. L. 92–220, §2, Dec. 23, 1971, 85 Stat. 795.)

161. Anthony Corrado, "Money and Politics," in Corrado et al., 2005.

162. Pub. L. 92–225, February 7, 1972, 86 Stat. 3 (codified at scattered sections in 2 U.S.C.)

163. Federal Election Campaign Amendments of 1974, Pub. L. 93–443, October 15. 1974, 88 Stat. 1263 (codified at 26 U.S.C. §§9031–9042 (2000)). The FEC was established in §310 of Pub. L. 93–443, codified at 2 U.S.C. 437(C), and the powers of the commission are set forth in §311 of Pub. L. 93–443, codified at 2 U.S.C. 437(D).

164. Corrado, "Money and Politics," pp. 22–35; see also Press Release of Federal Election Commission, Campaign Finance Law Quick Reference for Reporters: Major Provisions of the Bipartisan Campaign Reform Act of 2002, http://www.fec.gov/press/bkgnd/bcra_overview.shtml (site accessed May 28, 2006).

165. The Bipartisan Campaign Reform Act of 2002, March 27, 2002, Pub. L. 107–155, 116 Stat. 81 (codified at 2 U.S.C.A. §438, 441, and 36 U.S.C.A. §510 (West 2005)). The provision providing for the penalty of five years in prison can be found at 2 U.S.C.A. §437j.

166. McConnell v. Federal Election Commission, 540 U.S. 93 (2003).

167. Trevor Potter, "Campaign Finance Disclosure Laws," in Corrado et al., 2005, pp. 148–149.

168. Potter, "Campaign Finance Disclosure Laws," pp. 123–160.

169. Trevor Potter and Kirk L. Jowers, "Election Law and the Internet," in Corrado et al., 2005, pp. 243–263.

170. Adam Nagourney, "Internet Injects Sweeping Change into U.S. Politics," *New York Times*, April 2, 2006, p. A1.

171. Electronic Filing of Reports by Political Committees, 65 Fed. Reg. 38415 (June 21, 2000) (codified at 11 C.F.R. §§100.19, 104.18, 101.1, 102.2, 104.5, 109.2, 114.10, 9003.1, and 9033.1 (2006)). 11 C.F.R. §104.18 specifically deals with electronic filing requirements pursuant to 2 U.S.C. §432(d) and 2 U.S.C. §434(a).

172. The full text of the FEC rules is available at http://www.fec.gov/law/law_rulemakings.shtml#internet05 (site accessed June 4, 2006). See also 71 Fed. Reg. 18589 (April 12, 2006) (to be codified at 11 C.F.R. pts. 100, 110, 114).

173. Adam Nagourney, "Agency Exempts Most of Internet from Campaign Spending Laws," *New York Times*, March 28, 2006, p. A15.

174. S. Rep. 105–167 (1998); see http://frwebgate.access.gpo.gov/cgi-bin/getdoc.cgi? dbname=105_cong_reports&docid=f:sr167p1.105.pdf or http://www.senate. gov~gov_affairs/sireport.htm (sites accessed May 12, 2006).

175. Home Mortgage Disclosure Act of 1975, Pub. L. 94–299, Title III, December 31, 1975, 89 Stat. 1125 (codified at 12 U.S.C. §2801 *et seq.* (2000)), amended by Financial Institutions, Reform, Recovery and Enforcement Act of 1989, Pub. L. 101–73, August 9, 1989, 103 Stat. 183 (codified in scattered sections of 12 U.S.C.).

176. See http://www.ffiec.gov/about.htm (site accessed May 24, 2006).

177. See http://www.ffiec.gov/hmda (site accessed June 8, 2006).

178. Legislative History, Pub. L. 94–200.

179. Proxmire also played a leading role in the enforcement of fair lending legislation. In 1988 he held public hearings in which he urged regulatory agencies to be more aggressive in assuring lending to low-income areas. In the late 1980s regulators started to deny banks' merger applications on the grounds of poor lending to local communities.

180. See 121 Cong. Rec. 34,581 (1975) (passage in the House) and 121 Cong. Rec. 27,623 (1975) (passage in the Senate.)

181. 12 U.S.C. §2901.

182. Housing and Community Development Act, Pub. L. 96–399, October 8, 1980, 94 Stat. 1614 (codified as amended at scattered sections of 12 U.S.C., 15 U.S.C., and 42 U.S.C.)

183. Financial Institutions, Reform, Recovery and Enforcement Act of 1989, Pub. L. 101–73, August 9, 1989, 103 Stat. 183 (codified in scattered sections of 12 U.S.C.). Following a wave of deregulation in the early 1980s, many savings and loans diversified their investments into unfamiliar areas. By 1987, hundreds of savings and loans had failed, the Federal Savings and Loan Insurance Corporation was insolvent, and losses amounted to more then $100 billion.

184. Community organizations argued that they represented neighborhoods that had not benefited from the bad loans that caused the savings and loan scandal and should not suffer the public costs of the bailout.

185. In 1989, Bill Dedman was awarded a Pulitzer Prize in investigative reporting for his series titled "The Color of Money," published in the *Atlanta Journal-Constitution* on May 1–4, 1988. The articles are available online at http://powerreporting.com/color/color_of_money.pdf (site accessed May 24, 2006).

186. Munnell et al., 1996, p. 25.

187. From 1977 to 1991, banks committed $8.8 billion in CRA agreements involving lending, investments, and other services to communities. From 1992 to 2000, banks committed more than $1.09 trillion. National Community Reinvestment Coalition, 2001.

188. A 2000 Federal Reserve Board study found that the vast majority of banks operated profitably in CRA-related loans. The study analyzed the performance and profitability of CRA-related lending and reported that nearly two-thirds of responding institutions agreed that CRA-related lending had opened new business opportunities and served as a tool to promote a good image of banks in the community. Board of Governors of the Federal Reserve System, 2000,

pp. 63–64. The study showed that CRA lending was overall profitable or marginally profitable and that performance of CRA lending activities in general did not differ from mortgage activities not related to CRA. Board of Governors of the Federal Reserve System, 2000, pp. 52, 58, 62–63, and 69.

189. These improvements were introduced through subsequent amendments of the Federal Reserve Board's Regulation C, which implements HMDA.

190. See Apgar and Calder, 2005.

191. See National Community Reinvestment Coalition, 2005, and Association of Community Organizations for Reform Now, 2005.

192. Avery, Canner, and Cook, 2005, pp. 344–394.

193. A number of books influential at the time proposed a spectrum of policy solutions. At one end of the policy spectrum, Bluestone and Harrison, 1983, and Magaziner and Reich, 1982, advocated comprehensive "industrial policies" to respond to the loss of U.S. manufacturing preeminence. On the other hand, books like McKenzie, 1982, argued that restructuring was a normal feature of an evolving economy and that government intervention through plant closing legislation could have deleterious effects on economic well-being.

194. Worker Adjustment and Retraining Notification Act, Pub. L. 100–379, August 4, 1988, 102 Stat. 890 (codified at 29 USC §§2101–2109 (2000)). The Department of Labor published final regulations on the law in 20 C.F.R. pt. 639 (2006).

195. Both Congress and state legislatures debated various forms of plant closing legislation from the late 1970s until the passage of WARN. When the legislation was finally passed, President Ronald Reagan chose not to either veto or sign it. For a legislative history, see U.S. House of Representatives, Committee on Education and Labor, Legislative History of S. 2527, *Worker Adjustment and Retraining Notification Act, Public Law 100–379*, 100th Cong., 2nd sess., serial no. 101-K (Washington, D.C.: GPO, 1990).

196. See Ehrenberg and Jakubson, 1990, pp. 39–46, for a discussion of these critiques.

197. The regulation provides a number of further refinements of these definitions relating to simultaneous employment reductions in multiple units of a company as well as to the length of the employment reductions.

198. See 29 U.S.C. §2102(b)(2)(A) ("unforeseeable" business reasons); 29 U.S.C. §2102(b)2)(B) (natural disasters); 29 U.S.C. §2102(b)(1); and 20 C.F.R. §639.9. Exemptions also apply in cases relating to transfers or reassignments of employees, sale of a business, or strikes and lockouts. See, for example, 29 U.S.C. §2103(1) (employees hired with understanding that such employment only for the duration of a project that has since been completed); and 29 U.S.C. §2103(2) (strikes or lockouts).

199. The notice must include the name and address of the employment site where the closing or layoff will occur, a statement regarding whether the action is permanent or temporary, the expected date of each worker's termination, the job titles of those affected, and the number of jobs that will be lost in each job classification. See 20 C.F.R. §639.7.

200. Ehrenberg and Jakubson, 1990, p. 44.

201. For a discussion of the limited impact of advanced notification on the universe of employment losses, see General Accounting Office, 2003b.

202. The U.S. Bureau of Labor Statistics estimated that for the eighteen-week period between September 11, 2001, and mid-January 2002, there were 430 "extended mass layoffs" directly or indirectly related to the attacks, involving more than 125,000 workers. See Levine, 2004.

203. In February 2004, the Jobs for America Act (S. 2090) was introduced to amend WARN by including offshoring in its definition of major employment events, as well as requiring collection of statistics on job loss arising from offshoring. Levine, 2004, p. CRS-2.

204. Performance-based accountability was initiated at the state level and was launched in the mid-1980s by the National Governors Association, headed by Bill Clinton, then governor of Arkansas. Many of the early systems were intended to provide schools with more flexibility in setting educational policies in exchange for accountability for resulting performance.

205. A detailed description of *A Nation at Risk* is offered in Kearns and Harvey, 2000. pp. 22–28.

206. Gormley and Weimer, 1999, p. 43.

207. Gorman, 2002, p. 40.

208. See Improving America's School's Act of 1994, Pub. L. 103–382, October 20, 1994, 108 Stat. 3518 (codified as amended at 20 U.S.C. §§6301 *et seq.* (2000)). This law reauthorized the Elementary and Secondary Education Act, Pub. L. 89–10, April 11, 1965, 79 Stat. 27 (codified as amended at 20 U.S.C. §§6301 *et seq.* (Supp. III 2003)). The 2001 No Child Left Behind Act requires the education agencies receiving funds under §1116 of Pub. L. 107–110 to "publicize and disseminate the results of the local annual review . . . to parents, teachers, principals, schools, and the community so that the teachers, principals, other staff, and schools can continually refine, in an instructionally useful manner, the program of instruction to help all children served under this part meet the challenging State student academic achievement standards established under section 1111(b)(1)." No Child Left Behind Act, Pub. L. 107–110, §1116(a)(1)(C). This section can be found in the United States Code at 20 U.S.C. §6316(a)(1)(C).

209. Lynn Olson, "Report Cards for Schools" *Education Week*, Vol. 18, No. 17, January 11, 1999.

210. Accountability for Public Schools: Developing School Report Cards, Findings of Group Research for Education Week, December 1998. Belden Russonello & Stewart, R/S/M, A-Plus Communications.

211. Public Agenda, 2000.

212. No Child Left Behind Act of 2001, Pub. L. 107–110, January 8, 2002, 115 Stat. 1421 (codified as amended at 20 U.S.C. §§6052 *et seq.*, §§1041 *et seq.*, §3427 (Supp. III 2003)). School report card requirements are contained in Title I, Part A, §1111.

213. Erin Fox, "Report Cards Provide More, or Less, Data," *Education Week*, Vol. 24, No. 15, December 8, 2004; Northwest Regional Educational Laboratory, 2002.

214. Fox, "Report Cards Provide More, or Less, Data."

215. Fox, "Report Cards Provide More, or Less, Data."

216. Hanushek and Raymond, 2004.

217. Sources for this account of adoption by policymakers in the European Union of international accounting standards include Flower and Ebbers, 2002, pp. 208–211 227; and Karel Van Hulle, 2004, pp. 349–375.

218. See, for example, Floyd Norris, "Europe Welcomes Accounting Plan; U.S. Remains a Bit Wary," *New York Times*, April 23, 2005, p. B3.

219. Flower and Ebbers, 2002; Zeff, 2003, p. 880.

220. Zeff, 2003. p. 886.

221. http://www.iasb.org/about/iasb_board.asp; Flower and Ebbers, 2002, pp. 252–261. The Standards Advisory Council in 2004 consisted of nine Americans, fourteen Western Europeans, two Japanese, two Africans, eight Asians, two Eastern Europeans, three Latin Americans, and an Israeli, as well as six representatives of international organizations. In 2006, the Standards Advisory Council membership had changed. It consisted of four members from North America, fourteen Europeans, two Africans, eight from the Asia-Pacific region, three Latin Americans, and an Israeli, as well as seven representatives of international organizations. The IASB's constitution, which was last revised in June 2005 and which became effective on July 1, 2005, provides that the Standard Advisory Council should be comprised of at least thirty members. See http://www.iasb.org/uploaded_files/documents/8_11_iascf-constitution.pdf. Information on the structure of the IASB is available on its Web site, at http://www.iasb.org/about/structure.asp (sites accessed May 23, 2006).

222. Testimony of David Tweedie, chairman of the International Accounting Standards Board, U.S. Senate, Committee on Banking, Housing and Urban Affairs, February 14, 2002.

223. *International Accounting Standards Committee Foundation Annual Report, 2003*, pp. 3, 16, 18, and 23, http://www.iasb.org/uploaded_files/documents/8_24_ar2003.pdf. In 2005, the IASB employed an average of sixty-seven employees including board members. *International Accounting Standards Committee Foundation Annual Report, 2005*, p. 26, http://www.iasb.org/uploaded_files/documents/10_845_IASCF2005-AnnualReports.pdf (site accessed May 23, 2006).

224. The 2005 International Accounting Standards Committee Foundation Constitution, Articles 6–7. See http://www.iasb.org/uploaded_files/documents/8_11_iascf-constitution.pdf (site accessed June 7, 2006).

225. Alexander Kern, "Establishing a European Securities Regulator: Is the European Union an Optimal Area for a Single Securities Regulator?" Working Paper No. 7, Carnegie Endowment for Research in Finance, 2002. See also CESR Web site, http://www.cesr-eu.org.

226. The activities of IFAC are described at www.ifac.org. See Benston et al., 2003, pp. 76–78.

227. Adrian Michaels and Andrew Parker, "Financial Regulators to Strengthen Collaboration," *Financial Times*, May 26, 2004, p. 33.

228. See, for example, Almar Latour and Kevin J. Delaney, "Toothless Watchdogs," *Wall Street Journal*, August 18, 2002, p. A1.

229. Barney Jopson, "IASB Faces Funding Headache," *Financial Times*, March 31, 2006, p. 16.

230. Constitution of the World Health Organization, July 22, 1946, 61 Stat. 2349, 14 U.N.T.S. 185 (also available at http://w3.whosea.org/aboutsearo/pdf/const.pdf and http://www.yale.edu/lawweb/avalon/decade/decad051.htm#1). See also Revision to the International Health Regulations 2005, A58/4, art. 2, May 16, 2005, http://www2a.cdc.gov/phlp/docs/58assembly.pdf (sites accessed May 23, 2006).

231. Fidler, 2004, p. 35.

232. Institute of Medicine, 1992.

233. World Health Assembly, Revision to the International Health Regulations 2005, WHA 58_3, May 23, 2005, http://www.who.int/csr/ihr/WHA58_3-en.pdf (site accessed May 23, 2006).

234. World Health Organization, 54th World Health Assembly, *Global Health Security – Epidemic Alert and Response*, A54/9, April 2, 2001.

235. Institute of Medicine, 2003, p. 16.

236. Institute of Medicine, 2003, p. 8; Fidler, 2004, pp. 74–80.

237. Fidler, 2004, p. 14 (noting that by June 2003, SARS had been "[s]topped dead in its tracks").

238. Institute of Medicine, 2003, p. 8.

239. This account owes much to the work of Robert L. Paarlberg, who has written extensively about the politics of genetically modified food and its impact on developing countries. See Paarlberg, 2000, 2001, and 2003. We are also grateful to Diahanna Post for her insights and helpful comments. See Post and Da Ros, 2003, and Post, 2005. A committee of the U.S. National Academy of Sciences examined these issues in depth: National Research Council, 2000.

240. Commission Regulation (EC) No. 1829/2003 of Sept. 22, 2003, 2003 O.J. (L268) 1; Commission Regulation (EC) No. 1830/2003 of Sept. 22, 2003, 2003 O.J. (L268) 24.

241. Post, 2005, p. 137; see also Statement of Policy: Foods Derived from New Plant Varieties, 57 Fed. Reg. 22984 (May 29, 1992).

242. Commission Regulation (EC) No. 1830/2003 of Sept. 22, 2003, 2003 O.J. (L268) 24.

243. See Guidance for Industry, "Voluntary Labeling Indicating Whether Foods Have or Have Not Been Developed Using Bioengineering" (Draft Guidance distributed for comment purposes only), http://www.cfsan.fda.gov/~dms/biolabgu.html (site accessed May 28, 2006).

244. Carter and Gruere, 2005, p. 9.

245. http://europa.eu.int/comm/food/food/biotechnology/index_en.htm.

246. http://www.cfsan.fda.gov/~dms/biolabgu.html.

247. National Organic Program, 7 C.F.R. pt. 205 (2006).

248. Winickoff et al., 2005, p. 87.

249. Paarlberg, 2000, p. 29.

250. "WTO Rules EU Import Ban Illegal," *International Herald Tribune*, February 7, 2006, http://www.iht.com/articles/2006/02/07/business/gmo.php (site accessed May 6, 2006).

Bibliography

Addison, J. T., & Blackburn, M. L. (1994). The Worker Adjustment and Retraining Notification Act: Effects on Notice Provision. *Industrial and Labor Relations Review*, 47(4), 650–662.

Addison, J. T., & Blackburn, M. L. (1997). A Puzzling Aspect of the Effect of Advance Notice on Unemployment. *Industrial and Labor Relations Review*, 50(2), 268–288.

Adkins, G., Huff, D., & Stageberg, P. (2000). *The Iowa Sex Offender Registry and Recidivism*. Iowa Department of Human Rights, Division of Criminal and Juvenile Justice Planning and Statistical Analysis Center.

Advisory Panel to Assess Domestic Response Capabilities for Terrorism Involving Weapons of Mass Destruction. (2003). *Fifth Annual Report to the President and the Congress: Forging America's New Normalcy*.

Akerloff, G. (1970). The Market for "Lemons": Quality Uncertainty and the Market Mechanism. *Quarterly Journal of Economics*, 84(3), 488–500.

Alman, A. C., Jr. (2001). The Limits of Globalization and the Future of Administrative Law: From Government to Governance. *Indiana Journal of Global Legal Studies*, 8, 379.

Altshuler, A. A. (1997). Bureaucratic Innovation, Democratic Accountability, and Political Incentives. In A. A. Altshuler & R. D. Behn, *Innovation in American Government: Challenges, Opportunities, and Dilemmas*. Washington, D.C.: Brookings Institution.

Anderson, T. L. (2004). Markets and the Environment: Friends or Foes? (Symposium: The Role of Market and Government). *Case Western Reserve Law Review*, 55, 81.

Apgar, W. C., & Calder, A. (2005). The Dual Mortgage Market: The Persistence of Discrimination in Mortgage Lending. In X. de Souza Briggs (Ed.), *The Geography of Opportunity: Race and Housing Choice in Metropolitan America*. Washington, D.C.: Brookings Institution.

Arnett, M. B. (1992). Risky Business: OSHA's Hazard Communication Standard, EPA's Toxics Release Inventory, and Environmental Safety. *Environmental Law Reporter*, 22(7), 10440–10491.

Ashford, N. A., & Caldart, C. C. (1985). The "Right to Know": Toxics Information Transfer in the Workplace. *Annual Review of Public Health*, 6, 383–401.

Association of Community Organizations for Reform Now. (2005). *The High Cost of Credit: Disparities in High-Priced Refinance Loans to Minority Homeowners in 125 American Cities*. Washington, D.C.: Association of Community Organizations for Reform Now.

Avery, R. B., Canner, G. B., & Cook, R. E. (2005). New Information Reported Under HMDA and Its Application in Fair Lending Enforcement. *Federal Reserve Bulletin*, Summer, 344–394.

Ayers, I., & Braithwaite, J. (1992). *Responsive Regulation: Transcending the Deregulation Debate*. New York: Oxford University Press.

Ball, R. (2001). *Infrastructure Requirements for an Economically Efficient System of Public Financial Reporting and Disclosure*. Brookings-Wharton Papers on Financial Services. Washington, D.C.: Brookings Institution.

Baram, M. (1984). The Right to Know and the Duty to Disclose Hazard Information. *American Journal of Public Health*, 74(4), 385–390.

Baram, M. (1996). Generic Strategies for Protecting Worker Health and Safety. *Occupational Medicine: State of the Art Reviews*, 11(1), 69–77.

Bardach, E., & Kagan, R. (1982). *Going by the Book: The Problem of Regulatory Unreasonableness*. Philadelphia: Temple University Press.

Bebchuk, L. A., & Jackson, R. J. (2005). Executive Pensions. *Journal of Corporation Law*, 30, 823–855.

Becker, G. (1968). Crime and Punishment: An Economic Analysis. *Journal of Political Economy*, 76(2), 169–217.

Becker, G. (1983). A Theory of Competition Among Pressure Groups for Political Influence. *Quarterly Journal of Economics*, 98(3), 371–400.

Bennear, L. S. (2005). *Strategic Response to Regulatory Thresholds: Evidence from the Massachusetts Toxics Use Reduction Act*. Working Paper, Nicholas School of the Environment, Duke University.

Benston, G. J. (1973). Required Disclosure and the Stock Market: An Evaluation of the Securities Exchange Act of 1934. *American Economic Review*, 36(3), 132–155.

Benston, G. J., Bromwich, M., Litan, R. E., & Wagenhofer, A. (2003). *Following the Money: The Enron Failure and the State of Corporate Disclosure*. AEI-Brookings Joint Center for Regulatory Studies.

Bluestone, B., & Harrison, B. (1983). *The Deindustrialization of America: Plant Closings, Community Abandonment, and the Dismantling of Private Industry*. New York: Basic Books.

Blustein, P. (2003). *The Chastening: Inside the Crisis That Rocked the Global Financial System and Humbled the IMF*, rev. and updated ed. New York: Public Affairs.

Board of Governors of the Federal Reserve System. (2000). *The Performance and Profitability of CRA-Related Lending*.

Boase, J., Horrigan, J. B., Wellman, B., & Rainie, L. (2006). *The Strength of Internet Ties*. Pew Internet and American Life Project.

Bodie, Z., & Clowes, M. (2003). *Worry-Free Investing: A Safe Approach to Achieving Your Lifetime Financial Goals*. New York: Financial Times/Prentice-Hall.

Bostic, R. W., Mehran, H., Paulson, A., & Saidenberg, M. (2002). *Regulatory Incentives and Consolidation: The Case of Commercial Bank Mergers and the Community Reinvestment Act*. (WP-02-06). Chicago: Federal Reserve Bank of Chicago.

Bostic, R. W., & Surette, B. J. (2001). Have the Doors Opened Wider? Trends in Homeownership Rates by Race and Income. *Journal of Real Estate Finance and Economics*, 23(3), 411–434.

Botosan, C. A. (1997). Disclosure Level and the Cost of Equity Capital. *Accounting Review*, 72(3), 323–349.

Bradshaw, M. T., Bushee, B. J., & Miller, G. S. (2003). *Accounting Choice, Home Bias, and US Investment in Non-US Firms.* Working Paper, Wharton School, University of Pennsylvania.

Brandeis, L. D. (1932). *Other People's Money and How the Bankers Use It*, 2d ed. New York: Frederick A. Stockes Company.

Brown, J. S. (2002). *The Social Life of Information.* Boston: Harvard Business School Press.

Bryant, R. (2003). *Turbulent Waters: Cross-Border Finance and International Governance.* Washington, D.C.: Brookings Institution.

Bui, L. T. (2002). *Public Disclosure of Private Information as a Tool for Regulating the Environment: Firm Level Responses by Petroleum Refineries to the Toxics Release Inventory.* Working Paper, Boston University.

Bui, L. T., & Mayer, C. J. (2003). Regulation and Capitalization of Environmental Amenities: Evidence from the Toxics Release Inventory in Massachusetts. *Review of Economics and Statistics*, 85(3), 693–708.

Bushee, B., & Leuz, C. (2004). Economic Consequences of SEC Disclosure Regulation: Evidence from the OTC Bulletin Board. *Journal of Accounting and Economics*, 39(2), 233–264.

Bushman, R. M., & Smith, A. J. (2001). Financial Accounting Information and Corporate Governance. *Journal of Accounting and Economics*, 32(1–3), 237–333.

Carpenter, G. S., & Nakamoto, K. (1989). Consumer Preference Formation and Pioneering Advantage. *Journal of Marketing and Research*, 26(3), 285–298.

Carter, C. A., & Gruere, G. P. (2005). International Approval and Labeling Regulations of Genetically Modified Food in Major Trading Countries. In R. Just, J. M. Alston, & D. Zilberman (Eds.), *Economics of Regulation of Agricultural Biotechnology.* New York: Springer Publishers.

Case, D. W. (2001). The Law and Economics of Environmental Information as Regulation. *Environmental Law Reporter*, 31(7), 10773–10789.

Chassin, M. R. (2002). Achieving and Sustaining Improved Quality: Lessons from New York State and Cardiac Surgery. *Health Affairs*, 21(4), 40–51.

Chassin, M. R., Hannan, E. L., & DeBuono, B. A. (1996). Benefits and Hazards of Reporting Medical Outcomes Publicly. *New England Journal of Medicine*, 334(6), 394–398.

Coase, R. (1960). The Problem of Social Cost. *Journal of Law and Economics*, 3, 1–44.

Coffee, J. C., Jr. (2002). Racing Towards the Top? The Impact of Cross-Listings and Stock Market Competition on International Corporate Governance. *Columbia Law Review*, 102, 1757.

Coglianese, C., & Nash, J. (2004). *The Massachusetts Toxics Use Reduction Act: Design and Implementation of a Management-Based Environmental Regulation.* Regulatory Policy Program, Center for Business and Government, John F. Kennedy School of Government, Harvard University.

Coglianese, C., Nash, J., & Olmstead, T. (2003). Performance-Based Regulation: Prospects and Limitations in Health, Safety and Environmental Protection. *Administrative Law Review*, 55(4), 705–730.

Cohen, M. A. (2001). Information as a Policy Instrument in Protecting the Environment: What Have We Learned? *Environmental Law Reporter*, 31, 10425–10431.

Commission of the European Communities. (2001). *Proposal for a Regulation of the European Parliament and of the Council on the Application of International Accounting Standards*.

Commission of the European Communities. (2002). *Final Report of the Public Perceptions of Agricultural Biotechnologies in Europe (PABE) Project*.

Committee on Appropriate Test Use. (1999). *High Stakes: Testing for Tracking, Promotion, and Graduation*. Washington, D.C.: National Research Council.

Commons, J. R., & Andrews, J. B. (1916). *Principles of Labor Legislation*, 4th ed. New York: Augustus Kelley.

Congressional Research Service. (2003). *Homeland Security Advisory System: Possible Issues for Congressional Oversight*. Washington, D.C.: Congressional Research Service.

Congressional Research Service. (2005). *Lead in Drinking Water: Washington, D.C., Issues and Broader Regulatory Implications*. By M. Tiemann. RS21831. Washington, D.C.: Congressional Research Service.

Cooper, I., & Kaplanis, E. (1994). Home Bias in Equity Portfolios, Inflation Hedging, and International Capital Market Equilibrium. *Review of Financial Studies*, 7(1), 45–60.

Corrado, A., Mann, T. E., Ortiz, D. R., & Potter, T. (2005). *The New Campaign Finance Sourcebook*. Washington, D.C.: Brookings Institution.

Cutler, D., Huckman, R. S., & Landrum, M. B. (2004). *The Role of Information in Medical Markets: An Analysis of Publicly Reported Outcomes in Cardiac Surgery*. Working Paper 10489, Cambridge, Mass.: National Bureau of Economic Research.

Decker, C., Nielsen, D., & Sindt, R. (2005). Residential Property Values and Community Right-to-Know Laws: Has the Toxics Release Inventory Had an Impact? *Growth and Change*, 36(1), 113–133.

Degeorge, F., Patel, J., & Zeckhauser, R. (1999). Earnings Management to Exceed Thresholds. *Journal of Business*, 72(1), 1–33.

De León, I. (1999). An Alternative Approach to Policies for the Promotion of Competition in Developing Countries. *Southwestern Journal of Law and Trade in the Americas*, 6, 85.

De Marchi, S., & Hamilton, J. T. (2006). Assessing the Accuracy of Self-Reported Data: An Evaluation of the Toxics Release Inventory. *Journal of Risk and Uncertainty*, 32, 57–76.

Derby, B. M., & Levy, A. S. (2001). Do Food Labels Work? In P. N. Bloom & G. T. Gundlach (Eds.), *Handbook of Marketing and Society*. Thousand Oaks, Calif.: Sage Publications.

Di Noia, C. (2001). Competition and Integration Among Stock Exchanges in Europe: Network Effects, Implicit Mergers and Remote Access. *European Financial Management*, 7(1), 39–72.

Dorsett, K. A. (1998). Kansas v. Hendricks: Marking the Beginning of a Dangerous New Era in Civil Commitment. *De Paul Law Review*, 48, 113.

Dranove, D., Kessler, D., McClellan, M., & Satterthwaite, M. (2003). Is More Information Better? The Effects of "Report Cards" on Health Care Providers. *Journal of Political Economy*, 111(3), 555–588.

Ehrenberg, R., & Jakubson, G. (1990). Why Warn? Plant Closing Legislation. *Regulation*, 13(2), 39–46.

Ellerman, D., Joskow, P. L., Schmalensee, R., Montero, J., & Bailey, E. M. (2000). *Markets for Clean Air: The U.S. Acid Rain Program*. New York: Cambridge University Press.

Environmental Protection Agency. (1999). *25 Years of the Safe Drinking Water Act: History and Trends*. EPA 816-R99–007. Washington, D.C.: Environmental Protection Agency.

Environmental Protection Agency. (2000). *Assessment of the Incentives Created by Public Disclosure of Off-site Consequence Analysis Information for Reduction in the Risk of Accidental Releases*. Washington, D.C.: Environmental Protection Agency.

Evans, P. B., & Wurster, T. S. (1997). Strategy and the New Economics of Information. *Harvard Business Review*, 75(5), 71–82.

Evans, P. B., & Wurster, T. S. (2000). *Blown to Bits: How the New Economics of Information Transforms Strategy*. Boston: Harvard Business School Press.

Fagotto, E., & Fung, A. (2003). Improving Workplace Hazard Communication. *Issues in Science and Technology*, Winter, 63–68.

Ferrell, A. (2003). *Mandated Disclosure and Stock Returns: Evidence from the Over-the-Counter Market*. Working Paper, Harvard Law School.

Fidler, D. P. (2004). *SARS, Governance and the Globalization of Disease*. New York: Palgrave Macmillan.

Fielding, J., Aguirre, A., Spear, M. A., & Frias, L. (1999). Making the Grade: Changing the Incentives in Retail Food Establishment Inspection. *American Journal of Preventive Medicine*, 17(3), 243–247.

Fischoff, B. (2002). Heuristics and Biases in Application. In T. Gilovich, D. Griffin, & D. Kahneman (Eds.), *The Psychology of Judgment: Heuristics and Biases*. Cambridge: Cambridge University Press.

Fishbein, A. (1995). A Fair Lending Symposium: Litigating a Mortgage Lending Case (Fair Housing Conference: Home Mortgage Disclosure Act Report). *John Marshall Law Review*, 28, 343.

Fisher, M. L., Raman, A., & McClelland, A. (2000). Rocket Science Retailing Is Almost Here – Are You Ready? *Harvard Business Review*, July–August, 115–124.

Flower, J., & Ebbers, G. (2002). *Global Financial Reporting*. Basingstoke: Palgrave.

Fountain, J. (2001). *Building the Virtual State*. Washington, D.C.: Brookings Institution.

Fox, S., & Fallows, D. (2003). *Internet Health Resources*. Pew Internet and American Life Project.

Frankfurter, F. (1933). The Federal Securities Act: II. *Fortune*, 8(53), 108.

Freeman, R., & Medoff, J. (1983). *What Do Unions Do?* New York: Basic Books.

Fung, A., & O'Rourke, D. (2000). Reinventing Environmental Regulation from the Grassroots Up. *Environmental Management*, 25(2), 115–127.

Fung, A., Graham, M., & Weil, D. (2002). *The Political Economy of Transparency: What Makes Disclosure Policies Sustainable?* Occasional Paper, Institute for Government Innovation, John F. Kennedy School of Government, Harvard University (OPS-02-03).

Fung, A., Weil, D., Graham, M., & Fagotto, E. (2004). *The Political Economy of Transparency: What Makes Disclosure Policies Effective?* Occasional Paper, Ash Institute for Democratic Governance and Innovation, John F. Kennedy School of Government, Harvard University (OP-03-04).

Garretson, J. A., & Burton, S. (2000). Effects of Nutrition Facts Panel Values, Nutrition Claims, and Health Claims on Consumer Attitudes, Perceptions of Disease-Related Risks, and Trust. *Journal of Public Policy & Marketing*, 19(2), 213–227.

Gelos, R. G., & Wei, S. J. (2002). *Transparency and International Investor Behavior*. Working Paper 9260, Cambridge, Mass.: National Bureau of Economic Research.

General Accounting Office. (1992a). *Occupational Safety and Health: Employers' Experience in Complying with the Hazard Communication Standard*. GAO/HRD-92-63BR. Washington, D.C.: General Accounting Office.

General Accounting Office. (1992b). *Drinking Water: Consumers Often Not Well-Informed of Potentially Serious Violations*. GAO/RCED-92-135. Washington, D.C.: General Accounting Office.

General Accounting Office. (1999). *Labor Management Reporting and Disclosure Act: Status of Labor's Efforts to Develop Electronic Reporting and a Publicly Accessible Database*. HEHS-99-63R. Washington, D.C.: General Accounting Office.

General Accounting Office. (2000). *Department of Labor: Administering the Labor-Management Reporting and Disclosure Act*. HEHS-00-116. Washington, D.C.: General Accounting Office.

General Accounting Office. (2001). *Information Management: Progress in Implementing the 1996 Electronic Freedom of Information Act Amendments*. GAO-01-378. Washington, D.C.: General Accounting Office.

General Accounting Office. (2002). *Protecting the Public's Interest*. GAO-02-601T. Washington, D.C.: General Accounting Office.

General Accounting Office. (2003a). *GAO Forum on Governance and Accountability*. GAO-03-419SP. Washington, D.C.: General Accounting Office.

General Accounting Office. (2003b). *The Worker Adjustment and Training Notification Act: Revising the Act and Educational Materials Could Clarify Employer Responsibilities and Employee Rights*. GAO-03-1003. Washington, D.C.: General Accounting Office.

General Accounting Office. (2004). *Homeland Security: Communication Protocols and Risk Communication Principles Can Assist in Refining the Advisory System*. GAO-04-682. Washington, D.C.: General Accounting Office.

Gerhart, P. (1987). *Saving Plants and Jobs: Union-Management Negotiation in the Context of Threatened Plant Closing*. Kalamazoo, Mich.: WE Upjohn Institute for Employment Research.

Gigerenzer, G., & Reinhard, S. (Eds.). (2001). *Bounded Rationality: The Adaptive Toolbox*. Cambridge, Mass.: MIT Press.

Giles, J. (2005). Internet Encyclopedias Go Head to Head. *Nature*, 438(15), 900–901.

Goldwater, B. (1961). The Legislative History and Purposes of the Provisions of LMRDA. In R. Slovenko (Ed.), *Symposium on the Labor-Management Reporting and Disclosure Act of 1959*. Baton Rouge, La.: Claitor's Bookstore Publishers.

Gomes, A., Gorton, G., & Madureira, L. (2004). *SEC Regulation Fair Disclosure, Information, and the Cost of Capital*. Working Paper 10567, Cambridge, Mass.: National Bureau of Economic Research.

Gompers, P. (1995). Optimal Investment, Monitoring, and the Staging of Venture Capital. *Journal of Finance*, 50(5), 1461–1489.

Gorman, S. (2002). Bipartisan Schoolmates. *Education Next*, Summer.

Gormley, W., & Weimer, D. (1999). *Organizational Report Cards*. Cambridge, Mass.: Harvard University Press.

Government Accountability Office. (2004). *Drinking Water: Experts' Views on How Federal Funding Can Best Be Spent to Improve Security*. GAO-04-1098T. Washington, D.C.: Government Accountability Office.

Government Accountability Office. (2005a). *Information Management: Implementation of the Freedom of Information Act*. GAO-05-648T. Washington, D.C.: Government Accountability Office.

Government Accountability Office. (2005b). *Vehicle Safety*. GAO-05-370. Washington, D.C.: Government Accountability Office.

Graham, M. (2001). *Information as Risk Regulation: Lessons from Experience*. Occasional Paper, Institute for Government Innovation, John F. Kennedy School of Government, Harvard University (OPS-10-01).

Graham, M. (2002a). *Democracy by Disclosure: The Rise of Technopopulism*. Washington, D.C.: Governance Institute, Brookings Institution.

Graham, M. (2002b). The Information Wars. *Atlantic Monthly*, 290(2), 36–38.

Graham, M., & Miller, C. (2001). Disclosure of Toxics Releases. *Environment*, 43(8), 8–20.

Graham, M., & Miller, C. (2005). Disclosure of Toxic Releases in the United States. In T. de Bruijn & V. Norberg-Bohm (Eds.), *Industrial Transformation*. Cambridge, Mass., & London: MIT Press.

Grant, D., & Jones, A. P. (2004). Do Manufacturers Pollute Less Under the Regulation-Through-Information Regime? *Sociological Quarterly*, 45(3), 471–486.

Green, J., & Wintfeld, N. (1995). Report Cards on Cardiac Surgeons – Assessing New York State's Approach. *New England Journal of Medicine*, 332(18), 1229–1233.

Greenstone, M., Oyer, P., & Vissing-Jorgensen, A. (2004). *Mandated Disclosure, Stock Returns, and the 1964 Securities Act Amendments*. Working Paper, Stanford University.

Gross, J. A. (1981). *The Making of the National Labor Relations Act*. Albany: State University of New York Press.

Grossman, S. (1989). The Informational Role of Warranties and Private Disclosure About Product Quality. *Journal of Law and Economics*, 24(3), 461–483.

Grossman, S., & Hart, O. (1980). Disclosure Laws and Takeover Bids. *Journal of Finance*, 35(2), 323–334.

Gunningham, N., & Grabosky, P. (1998). *Smart Regulation: Designing Environmental Policy*. Oxford: Oxford University Press.

Hadden, S. G. (1989). *A Citizen's Right to Know*. Boulder, Colo., San Francisco, & London: Westview Press.

Hagel, J. III, & Brown, J. S. (2005). *The Only Sustainable Edge*. Boston: Harvard Business School Press.

Hail, L., & Leuz, C. (2006). International Differences in the Cost of Equity Capital: Do Legal Institutions and Securities Regulation Matter? *Journal of Accounting Research*, 44(3), 485–531.

Hamilton, J. T. (1995). Pollution as News: Media and Stock Market Reactions to the Toxics Release Inventory Data. *Journal of Environmental Economics and Management*, 28(1), 98–113.

Hamilton, J. T. (2005). *Regulation Through Revelation: The Origin, Politics, and Impacts of the Toxics Release Inventory Program*. New York: Cambridge University Press.

Hamilton, J. T., & Viscusi, W. K. (1999). *Calculating Risks?* Cambridge, Mass.: MIT Press.

Hammit, J. K. (1999). *Residential Building Codes, Affordability and Health Protection: A Risk-Tradeoff Approach*. Joint Center for Housing Report. Cambridge, Mass.: Joint Center for Housing Studies, Harvard University.

Hammit, J. K., & Graham, J. (1999). Willingness to Pay for Health Protection: Inadequate Sensitivity to Probability? *Journal of Risk and Uncertainty*, 18(1), 33–62.

Hannan, E. L., Kilburn, H., Jr., Racz, M., Shields, E., & Chassin, M. (1994). Improving the Outcomes of Coronary Artery Bypass Surgery in New York State. *Journal of the American Medical Association*, 271(10), 761–766.

Hannan, E. L., Sarrazin, M. S. V., Doran, D. R., & Rosenthal, G. E. (2003). Provider Profiling and Quality Improvement Efforts in Coronary Artery Bypass Graft Surgery. *Medical Care*, 41(10), 1164–1172.

Hannan, E. L., Stone, C. C., Biddle, T. L., & DeBuono, B. A. (1997). Public Release of Cardiac Surgery Outcomes Data in New York: What Do New York State Cardiologists Think of It? *American Heart Journal*, 134(6), 1120–1128.

Hanushek, E. A., & Raymond, M. E. (2004). *Does School Accountability Lead to Improved Student Performance?* Working Paper 10591, Cambridge, Mass.: National Bureau of Economic Research.

Hayek, F. (1945). The Use of Knowledge in Society. *American Economic Review*, 35(4), 519–530.

Healy, P. M., & Palepu, K. G. (2001). Information Asymmetry, Corporate Disclosure, and the Capital Markets: A Review of the Empirical Disclosure Literature. *Journal of Accounting and Economics*, 31(1–3), 405–440.

Hogarth, R., & Kunreuther, H. (1995). Decision-Making Under Ignorance. *Journal of Risk and Uncertainty*, 10(1), 15–36.

Hunter, R., Kersey, P., & Miller, S. (2001). *The Michigan Union Accountability Act: A Step Toward Accountability and Democracy in Labor Organizations*. Midland, Mich.: Mackinac Center for Public Policy.

Hunter, R. J., Jr., & Mason, P. (1996). Law, Ethics and Public Policy in the Creation of an Environmental Imperative: The Hazard Communication Standard Insuring Workers' Rights. *Thomas Jefferson Law Review*, 18.

IASC Standards Assessment Report. (2000). *Report of the Technical Committee of the International Organization of Securities Commissions*. IASC.

Institute of Medicine. (1990). *Nutrition Labeling: Issues and Directions for the 1990s*. Washington, D.C.: National Academies Press.

Institute of Medicine. (1992). *Emerging Infections: Microbial Threats to Health in the United States*. Washington, D.C.: National Academies Press.

Institute of Medicine. (1999). *To Err Is Human: Building a Safer Health System*. Washington, D.C.: National Academies Press.

Institute of Medicine. (2003). *Learning from SARS: Preparing for the Next Disease Outbreak*. Washington, D.C.: National Academies Press.

International Accounting Standards Committee Foundation. (2003). Annual Report.

Jeske, K. (2001). Equity Home Bias: Can Information Cost Explain the Puzzle? *Federal Reserve Bank of Atlanta Economic Review*, Third Quarter, 31–42.

Jha, A. K., & Epstein, A. M. (2006). The Predictive Accuracy of the New York State Coronary Artery Bypass Surgery Report-Card System. *Health Affairs*, 25(3), 844–855.

Jin, G. Z., & Leslie, P. (2003). The Effect of Information on Product Quality: Evidence from Restaurant Hygiene Grade Cards. *Quarterly Journal of Economics*, 118(2), 409–451.

Jin, G. Z., & Leslie, P. (2005). The Case in Support of Restaurant Hygiene Grade Cards. *Choices: The Magazine of Food, Farm and Resource Issues*, 20(2), 97–102.

Jin, G. Z., & Leslie, P. (2006). *Reputational Incentives for Restaurant Hygiene*. Working Paper, University of Maryland.

Joint Center for Housing Studies, Harvard University. (2002). *The 25th Anniversary of the Community Reinvestment Act: Report for the Ford Foundation*. Cambridge, Mass.: Joint Center for Housing Studies.

Kahneman, D. (2003). A Perspective on Judgment and Choice: Mapping Bounded Rationality. *American Psychologist*, 58(9), 697–720.

Kahneman, D., Slovic, P., & Tversky, A. (Eds). (1982). *Judgment Under Uncertainty: Heuristics and Biases*. New York: Cambridge University Press.

Kahneman, D., & Tversky, A. (1996). On the Reality of Cognitive Illusions. *Psychological Review*, 103(3), 582–591.

Kahneman, D., & Tversky, A. (Eds). (2000). *Choices, Values, and Frames*. New York: Cambridge University Press.

Kane, T., & Staiger, D. O. (2002). The Promise and Pitfalls of Using Imprecise School Accountability Measures. *Journal of Economic Perspectives*, 16(4), 91–114.

Karkkainen, B. C. (2001). Information as Environmental Regulation. *Georgetown Law Journal*, 89, 259–370.

Kearns, D. K., & Harvey, J. (2000). *A Legacy of Learning*. Washington, D.C.: Brookings Institution.

Kennedy, R. F. (1960). *The Enemy Within*. New York: Harper.

Keohane, R. O. (2002). *Power and Governance in a Partially Globalized World*. London & New York: Routledge.

Kern, A. (2002). *Establishing a European Securities Regulator: Is the European Union an Optimal Area for a Single Securities Regulator?* Working Paper No. 7, Carnegie Endowment for Research in Finance.

Khanna, M., Quimio, W. H., & Bojilova, D. (1998). Toxics Release Information: A Policy Tool for Environmental Protection. *Journal of Environmental Economics and Management*, 36(3), 243–299.

Kim, S. Y., Nayga, R. M., & Capps, O., Jr. (2001). Food Label Use, Self-Selectivity, and Diet Quality. *Journal of Consumer Affairs*, 35(2), 346–363.

Kingsbury, B., Krisch, N., & Stewart, R. (2004). *The Emergence of Global Administrative Law*. International Law and Justice Working Paper 2004/1, Global Administrative Law Series, New York University School of Law.

Kleindorfer, P. R., & Orts, E. W. (1998). Informational Regulation of Environmental Risks. *Risk Analysis*, 18(2), 155–170.

Kolp, P. W., Sattler, B., Blayney, M., & Sherwood, T. (1993). Comprehensibility of Material Safety Data Sheets. *American Journal of Industrial Medicine*, 23(1), 135–141.

Kolp, P. W., Williams, P. L., & Burtan, R. C. (1995). Assessment of the Accuracy of Material Safety Data Sheets. *American Industrial Hygiene Association Journal*, 56, 178–183.

Konar, S., & Cohen, M. A. (1997). Information as Regulation: The Effect of Community Right to Know Laws on Toxic Emissions. *Journal of Environmental Economics and Management*, 32(1), 109–124.

Kripke, H. (1985). Accounting: What Does It All Mean? The Commission's Biggest Failure. In S. A. Zeff & T. F. Keller (Eds.), *Financial Accounting Theory*, 3rd ed. New York: McGraw-Hill.

Kristal, A. R., Levy, L., Patterson, R. E., Li, S. S., & White, E. (1998). Trends in Food Label Use Associated with New Nutrition Labeling Regulations. *American Journal of Public Health*, 88(8), 1212–1215.

Kung, F. H. (2002). The Rationalization of Regulatory Internationalization. *Law and Policy in International Business*, 33, 443.

Lang, M. H., & Lundholm, R. J. (1996). Corporate Disclosure Policy and Analyst Behavior. *Accounting Review*, 71(4), 467–492.

Leuz, C. (2000). *IAS Versus US GAAP: A "New Market" Based Comparison*. Finance and Accounting Working Paper Series No. 48, J. W. Goethe University, Frankfurt.

Leuz, C., & Verrecchia, R. E. (2000). The Economic Consequences of Increased Disclosure. *Journal of Accounting Research*, 38, Issue Supplement, 91–124.

Levin-Waldman, O. M. (1998). Plant Closings: Is WARN an Effective Response? *Review of Social Economy*, 56(1), 59–79.

Levine, L. (2004). *The Worker Adjustment and Retraining Notification Act (WARN)*. Congressional Research Service Report for Congress. CRS Report-RL31250. Washington, D.C.: U.S. Government Printing Office.

Levinson, M. (2006). *The Box: How the Shipping Container Made the World Smaller and the World Economy Bigger*. Princeton, N.J.: Princeton University Press.

Linden, L., & Rockoff, J. (2006). *There Goes the Neighborhood? Estimates of the Impact of Crime Risk on Property Values from Megan's Laws*. Working Paper 12253, Cambridge, Mass.: National Bureau of Economic Research.

Logan, W. A. (2003). Sex Offender Registration and Community Notification: Emerging Legal and Research Issues. *Annals of the New York Academy of Sciences*, 989, 337–351.

MacKenzie, W. R., Hoxie, N. J., Proctor, M. E., Gradus, M. S., Blair, K. A., Peterson, D. E., Kazmierczak, J. J., Addiss, D. G., Fox, K. R., Rose, J. B., et al. (1994). A Massive Outbreak in Milwaukee of Cryptosporidium Infection Transmitted Through the Public Water Supply. *New England Journal of Medicine*, 331(15), 161–167.

Madison, J. (1910). In G. Hunt (Ed.), *The Writings of James Madison*, Vol. 3. New York: G. P. Putnam.

Magat, W. A., & Viscusi, W. K. (1992). *Informational Approaches to Regulation*. Cambridge, Mass.: MIT Press.

Magaziner, I., & Reich, R. (1982). *Minding America's Business: The Decline and Rise of the American Economy*. New York: Harcourt, Brace, Jovanovich.

Mantel, S. P., & Kardes, F. R. (1999). The Role of Direction and Comparison, Attribute-Based Processing, and Attitude-Based Processing in Consumer Preference. *Journal of Consumer Research*, 25(4), 335–352.

March, J. G., & Simon, H. A. (1958). *Organizations*. New York: Wiley.

Marshall, M. N., Shekelle, P. G., Leatherman, S., & Brook, R. (2000). The Public Release of Performance Data: What Do We Expect to Gain? A Review of the Evidence. *Journal of the American Medical Association*, 283(14), 1866–1874.

Masters, M. F. (1997). *Unions at the Crossroads: Strategic Membership, Financial, and Political Perspectives*. Westport, Conn.: Quorum Books.

Masters, M. F., Atkin, R. S., & Florkowski, G. W. (1989). An Analysis of Union Labor Reporting Requirements Under Title II of the Landrum-Griffin Act. *Labor Law Journal*, 40(11), 713–722.

Mathios, A. D. (2000). The Impact of Mandatory Disclosure Laws on Product Choices: An Analysis of the Salad Dressing Market. *Journal of Law & Economics*, 43(2), 651–677.

McKenzie, R. (1982). *Plant Closings: Public or Private Choices?* Washington, D.C.: Cato Institute.

McTague, J. (2005). Cloud Hovers over Fed's Record on Transparency. *Barron's*, 85(47), 12.

Mead, P. S., Slutsker, L., Dietz, V., McCaig, L. F., Bresee, J. S., Shapiro, C., Griffin, P. M., & Tauxe, R. V. (1999). Food-Related Illness and Death in the United States. *Emerging Infectious Diseases*, 5(5), 607–625.

Meier, D. (2000). *Will Standards Save Public Education?* Boston: Beacon Press.

Milgrom, P. (1981). Good News and Bad News: Representation Theorems and Applications. *Bell Journal of Economics*, 12(2), 380–391.

Mill, J. S. (1861). *Considerations on Representative Government.* London: Parker, Son & Bourn.

Mitchell, R. B. (1994). *Intentional Oil Pollution at Sea.* Cambridge, Mass.: MIT Press.

Mitchell, R. B. (1998). Sources of Transparency: Information Systems in International Regimes. *International Studies Quarterly*, 42(1), 109–130.

Moorman, C. (1998). Market-Level Effects of Information: Competitive Responses and Consumer Dynamics. *Journal of Marketing Research*, 35(1), 82–98.

Moynihan, D. P. (1998). *Secrecy.* New Haven: Yale University Press.

Mukamel, D. B., & Mushlin, A. I. (1998). Quality of Care Information Makes a Difference. *Medical Care*, 36(7), 943–954.

Mukamel, D. B., & Mushlin, A. I. (2001). The Impact of Quality Report Cards on Choice of Physicians, Hospitals, and HMOs: A Midcourse Evaluation. *Joint Commission Journal on Quality Improvement*, 27(1), 20–27.

Mukamel, D. B., Weimer, D. L., Zwanziger, J., Huang Gorthy, S. F., & Mushlin, A. I. (2004). Quality Report Cards, Selection of Cardiac Surgeons, and Racial Disparities: A Study of the Publication of the New York State Cardiac Surgery Reports. *Inquiry*, 41(4), 435–446.

Mukamel, D. B., Weimer, D. L., Zwanziger, J., & Mushlin, A. I. (2002). Quality of Cardiac Surgeons and Managed Care Contracting Practices. *Health Services Research*, 37(5), 1129–1144.

Munnell, A. H., Tootell, G. M., Browne, L. E., & McEneaney, J. (1996 (originally released 1992)). Mortgage Lending in Boston: Interpreting HMDA Data. *American Economic Review*, 86(1), 25–53.

National Academies. (1996). *Shopping for Safety, by the Transportation Research Board.* Washington, D.C.: National Academies Press.

National Academies. (2002). *Rating System for Rollover Resistance – An Assessment, by the Transportation Research Board.* Washington, D.C.: National Academies Press.

National Community Reinvestment Coalition. (2001). *CRA Commitments.* Washington, D.C.: National Community Reinvestment Coalition.

National Community Reinvestment Coalition. (2005). *Fair Lending Disparities by Race, Income, and Gender in All Metropolitan Areas in America.* Washington, D.C.: National Community Reinvestment Coalition.

National Environmental Education and Training Foundation. (1999). *The National Report Card on Safe Drinking Water.* Washington, D.C.: National Environmental Education and Training Foundation.

National Highway Traffic Safety Administration. (2005). *NHTSA's NCAP Rollover Resistance Rating System*. Paper No. 05-0450. Washington, D.C.: National Highway Traffic Safety Administration.

National Research Council. (2000). *Genetically Modified Pest-Protected Plants: Science and Regulation*. Washington, D.C.: National Academies Press.

National Research Council. (2002). *Making the Nation Safer*. Washington, D.C.: National Academies Press.

Natural Resources Defense Council. (2003). *What's on Tap? Grading Drinking Water in U.S. Cities*. Washington, D.C.: Natural Resources Defense Council.

Nayga, R. M., Jr., Lipinski, D., & Savur, N. (1998). Consumers' Use of Nutritional Labels While Food Shopping and at Home. *Journal of Consumer Affairs*, 32(1), 106–120.

Northwest Regional Educational Laboratory, Planning and Program Development. (2002). *School, District, and State Report Cards: Living Documents for Public Discourse*. Portland, Oreg.: Northwest Regional Educational Laboratory.

Norton, J. J. (2001). International Financial Institutions and the Movement Toward Greater Accountability and Transparency: The Case of Legal Reform Programmes and the Problem of Evaluation. *International Law*, 35, 1443.

Nye, J. S., Zelikow, P. D., & King, D. C. (1997). *Why People Don't Trust Government*. Cambridge, Mass.: Harvard University Press.

Oberholzer-Gee, F., & Mitsunari, M. (2003). *Information Regulation: Do the Victims of Externalities Pay Attention?* Working Paper, Wharton School, University of Pennsylvania.

Occupational Safety and Health Administration. (1991). *The Comprehensibility of Material Safety Data Sheets*. Final Report by the Kearney/Centaur Division of A. T. Kearney, Inc. Washington, D.C.: Occupational Safety and Health Administration.

Occupational Safety and Health Administration. (1997). *Hazard Communication: A Review of the Science Underpinning the Art of Communication for Health and Safety*. Final report for OSHA by Toxa Chemica, International. College Park, Md.: The Environmental Health Education Center, University of Maryland Medical School.

Occupational Safety and Health Administration. (2004). *Hazard Communication in the 21st Century Workplace*. Washington, D.C.: Occupational Safety and Health Administration.

Oleinick, A., Fodor, W., & Susselman, M. (1988). Risk Management for Hazardous Chemicals, Adverse Health Consequences of Their Use and the Limitations of Traditional Control Standards. *Journal of Legal Medicine*, 9(1), 1–103.

Olson, M. (1971). *The Logic of Collective Action: Public Goods and the Theory of Groups*. Cambridge, Mass.: Harvard University Press.

Olsterholm, M. T. (2005). Preparing for the Next Pandemic. *Foreign Affairs*, 84(4), 24–37.

O'Reilly, J. T. (2000). *Federal Information Disclosure*, 3rd ed. St. Paul, Minn.: West Group.

O'Rourke, D., & Macey, G. P. (2003). Community Environmental Policing. *Journal of Policy Analysis and Management*, 22(3), 383–414.

Paarlberg, R. L. (2000). The Global Food Fight: Food for Thought. *Foreign Affairs*, 79(3), 24–38.

Paarlberg, R. L. (2001). *The Politics of Precaution*. Baltimore: Johns Hopkins University Press.

Paarlberg, R. L. (2003). Reinvigorating Genetically Modified Crops. *Issues in Science and Technology*, 19(3), 86–92.

Paarlberg, R. L. (2006). Let Them Eat Precaution: Why GM Crops Are Being Over-Regulated in the Developing World. In J. Entine (Ed.), *Let Them Eat Precaution: How Politics Is Undermining the Genetic Revolution in Agriculture*. Washington, D.C.: AEI Press.

Pacter, P. A. (1985). The FASB After 10 Years. In S. A. Zeff & T. F. Keller (Eds.), *Financial Accounting Theory*, 3rd ed. New York: McGraw-Hill.

Patten, D. M. (2002). Media Exposure, Public Policy Pressure, and Environmental Disclosure: An Examination of TRI Data Availability. *Accounting Forum*, 26(2), 152–171.

Payment, P., Richardson, L., Siemiatycki, J., Dewar, R., Edwardes, M., Franco, E., et al. (1991). A Randomized Trial to Evaluate the Risk of Gastrointestinal Disease Due to Consumption of Drinking Water. *American Journal of Public Health*, 81(6), 703–708.

Payne, J., Bettman, J., & Johnson, E. (1993). *The Adaptive Decision Maker*. New York: Cambridge University Press.

Pedersen, W. F. (2001). Regulation and Information Disclosure. *Harvard Environmental Law Review*, 25, 151–211.

Peterson, E. D., DeLong, E. R., Jollis, J. G., Muhlbaier, L. H., & Mark, D. B. (1998). The Effects of New York's Bypass Surgery Provider Profiling on Access to Care and Patient Outcomes in the Elderly. *Journal of the American College of Cardiology*, 32(4), 993–999.

Petro, S. (1959). *Power Unlimited: The Corruption of Union Leadership*. New York: Ronald Press Company.

Phillips, C., Wallace, B. C., Hamilton, C. B., Pursley, R. T., Petty, G. C., & Bayne, C. K. (1999). The Efficacy of Material Safety Data Sheets and Worker Acceptability. *Journal of Safety Research*, 30(2), 113–122.

Polinsky, M., & Shavell, S. (2000). The Economic Theory of the Public Enforcement of Law. *Journal of Economic Literature*, 8(1), 45–76.

Post, D. (2005). Regulating Biotech Foods: Government Institutions and Public Reactions. In M. P. Egan (Ed.), *Creating a Transatlantic Marketplace: Government Policies and Business Strategies*. Manchester: Manchester University Press.

Post, D., & Da Ros, J. (2003). Science and Public Participation in Regulating Genetically-Engineered Food: French and American Experiences. *Cahiers d'Economie et Sociologie Rurales*, 68–69, 75–101.

Previts, J. G., & Merino, B. (1998). *A History of Accountancy in the United States: The Cultural Significance of Accounting*. Columbus: Ohio State University Press.

Public Agenda. (2000). *Reality Check 2000*. Washington, D.C.: Public Agenda.

Putnam, S., & Wiener, J. B. (1995). Seeking Safe Drinking Water. In J. Graham & J. B. Wiener (Eds.), *Risk vs. Risk: Tradeoffs in Protecting Health and the Environment*. Cambridge, Mass.: Harvard University Press.

Pytka, E. (2005). Publicly Posted Health Inspection Grade Cards. Research Report 2005-R-0403. Hartford, Conn.: Connecticut General Assembly Office of Legislative Research.

Rainie, L., Cornfield, M., & Horrigan, J. (2005). *The Internet and Campaign 2004*. Pew Internet and American Life Project.

Reinicke, W. H. (1998). *Global Public Policy: Governing Without Government?* Washington, D.C.: Brookings Institution.

Robb, R. (1961). LMRDA Section 505: Amendment to LMRDA Section 302 on Crimes of Extortion and Bribery. In R. Slovenko (Ed.), *Symposium on the Labor-Management*

Reporting and Disclosure Act of 1959. Baton Rouge, La.: Claitor's Bookstore Publishers.

Robins, T. G., Hugentobler, M., Kaminski, M., & Klitzman, S. (1990). Implementation of the Federal Hazard Communication Standard: Does Training Work? *Journal of Occupational Medicine*, 32(11), 1133–1140.

Romano, P. S., Rainwater, J. A., & Antonius, D. (1999). Grading the Graders: How Hospitals in California and New York Perceive and Interpret Their Report Cards. *Medical Care*, 37(3), 295–305.

Rottenstreich, Y., & Hsee, C. (2001). Money, Kisses, and Electric Shocks: On the Affective Psychology of Risk. *Psychological Science*, 12(3), 185–188.

Ruder, D. S. (2001). *Worldwide Convergence in Accounting, Auditing, and Independence Standards*. Paper presented at Conference on Securities Regulation in the Global Internet Economy, presented by the SEC Historical Society, November 14–15.

Sage, W. M. (1999). Regulating Through Information: Disclosure Laws and American Healthcare. *Columbia Law Review*, 99, 1701–1743.

Samuelson, W., & Zeckhauser, R. (1988). Status Quo Bias in Decision Making. *Journal of Risk and Uncertainty*, 1(1), 7–59.

Schafer, R., & Ladd, H. F. (1981). *Discrimination in Mortgage Lending*. Cambridge, Mass.: MIT Press.

Scherbina, A. (2005). *Analyst Disagreement, Forecast Bias and Stock Returns*. Working Paper, Harvard Business School.

Schneider, E. C., & Epstein, A. M. (1996). Influence of Cardiac-Surgery Performance Reports on Referral Practices and Access to Care: A Survey of Cardiovascular Specialists. *New England Journal of Medicine*, 335(4), 251–256.

Schneider, E. C., & Epstein, A. M. (1998). Use of Public Performance Reports: A Survey of Patients Undergoing Cardiac Surgery. *Journal of the American Medical Association*, 279(20), 1638–1642.

Schroeder, E. P., & Shapiro, S. A. (1984). Responses to Occupational Disease: The Role of Markets, Regulation, and Information. *Georgetown Law Journal*, 72, 1265–1266.

Schwartz, B. (2004). *The Paradox of Choice: Why More Is Less*. New York: HarperCollins Publishers.

Sebenius, J. K. (1984). *Negotiating the Law of the Sea*. Cambridge, Mass.: Harvard University Press.

Seligman, J. (1995). *The Transformation of Wall Street*. Boston: Northeastern University Press.

Senate Governmental Affairs Committee, Full Minority Staff, Senator Joseph I. Lieberman, Ranking Member. (2003). *State and Local Officials: Still Kept in the Dark About Homeland Security*.

Shapiro, A. (2005). Who Pays the Auditor Calls the Tune? Auditing Regulation and Clients' Incentives. *Seton Hall Law Review*, 35, 1029–1095.

Simmons, B. A. (2001). The International Politics of Harmonization: The Case of Capital Market Regulation. *International Organization*, 55(3), 589–620.

Simon, C. J. (1989). The Effect of the 1933 Securities Act on Investor Information and the Performance of New Issues. *American Economic Review*, 79(3), 295–318.

Simon, H. A. (1997). *Models of Bounded Rationality*. Cambridge, Mass.: MIT Press.

Simon, P. A., Leslie, P., Run, G., Jin, G. Z, Reporter, R., Aguirre, A., & Fielding, J. E. (2005). Impact of Restaurant Hygiene Grade Cards on Foodborne-Disease Hospitalizations in Los Angeles County. *Journal of Environmental Health*, 67(7), 32–36.

Slaughter, A. (2004). *A New World Order*. Princeton, N.J.: Princeton University Press.

Slovenko, R. (Ed.). (1961). *Symposium on the Labor-Management Reporting and Disclosure Act of 1959*. Baton Rouge, La.: Claitor's Bookstore Publishers.

Smith, R., & Emshwiller, J. (2003). *24 Days: How Two Wall Street Journal Reporters Uncovered the Lies That Destroyed Faith in Corporate America*. New York: HarperBusiness (HarperCollins).

Sobel, A. C. (1994). *Domestic Choices, International Markets, Dismantling National Barriers and Liberalizing Securities Markets*. Ann Arbor: University of Michigan Press.

Sparrow, M. (1994). *Imposing Duties: Government's Changing Approach to Compliance*. New York: Praeger.

Sparrow, M. (2000). *The Regulatory Craft: Controlling Risks, Solving Problems, and Managing Compliance*. Washington, D.C.: Brookings Institution.

Stavins, R. (2004). *The Political Economy of Environmental Regulation*. Cheltenham, U.K., & Northampton, Mass.: Edward Elgar.

Stigler, G. J. (1964). Public Regulation of the Securities Markets. *Journal of Business*, 37(2), 117–142.

Stiglitz, J. E. (2000). The Contributions of the Economics of Information to Twentieth Century Economics. *Quarterly Journal of Economics*, 115(4), 1441–1478.

Stiglitz, J. E. (2002). *Globalization and Its Discontents*. New York: W. W. Norton.

Stillman, N. G., & Wheeler, J. R. (1987). The Expansion of Occupational Safety and Health Law. *Notre Dame Law Review*, 62, 969–1009.

Strauss, P. L., et al. (1995). *Gellhorn and Byse's Administrative Law: Cases and Comments*, 9th ed. Westbury, N.Y.: Foundation Press.

Sunstein, C. R. (1993). Informing America: Risk, Disclosure, and the First Amendment. *Florida State University Law Review*, 20, 653.

Sunstein, C. R. (2001). *Republic.com*. Princeton, N.J.: Princeton University Press.

Sunstein, C. R. (2005). *Laws of Fear: Beyond the Precautionary Principle*. Cambridge: Cambridge University Press.

Surowiecki, J. (2005). *The Wisdom of Crowds*. New York: Anchor Books.

Thaler, R. (1991). The Psychology of Choice and the Assumptions of Economics. In R. Thaler, *Quasi-Rational Economics*. New York: Russell Sage Foundation.

Thaler, R., & Sunstein, C. R. (2003). Libertarian Paternalism. *American Economic Review*, 93(2), 175–179.

Tiebout, C. (1956). A Pure Theory of Local Expenditures. *Journal of Political Economy*, 64(5), 416–424.

Tietenberg, T. (1998). Disclosure Strategies for Pollution Control. *Environmental and Resource Economics*, 11(3), 587–602.

Tietenberg, T., & Wheeler, D. (2001). Empowering the Community: Information Strategies for Pollution Control. In H. Folmer, H. L. Gabel, S. Gerking, & A. Rose (Eds.), *Frontiers of Environmental Economics*. Cheltenham, U.K., & Northampton, Mass.: Edward Elgar.

Turner, L. E. (2001). *Disclosure and Accounting in a Global Market: Looking to the Future*. Issues paper presented at Conference on Securities Regulation in the Global Internet Economy by the SEC Historical Society, November 14–15.

U.S. Department of Justice. (2000). *Freedom of Information Act Guide & Privacy Act Overview*. Washington, D.C.: U.S. Department of Justice.

U.S. Department of Labor. (1986). *Economic Adjustment and Worker Dislocation in a Competitive Society: Report of the Secretary of Labor's Task Force on Economic Adjustment and Worker Dislocation*. U.S. Secretary of Labor's Task Force on Economic Adjustment and Worker Dislocation. Washington, D.C.: U.S. Department of Labor.

U.S. Securities and Exchange Commission. (1997). *Report on Promoting Global Preeminence of American Securities Markets*. Washington, D.C.: U.S. Securities and Exchange Commission.

Van Hulle, K. (2004). From Accounting Directives to International Accounting Standards. In C. Leuz, D. Pfaff, & A. Hopwood (Eds.), *The Economics and Politics of Accounting*. Oxford & New York: Oxford University Press.

Variyam, J., & Cawley, J. (2006). *Nutrition Labels and Obesity*. Working Paper 11956, Cambridge, Mass.: National Bureau of Economic Research.

Viscusi, W. K. (1979). *Employment Hazards: An Investigation of Market Performance*. Cambridge, Mass.: Harvard University Press.

Viscusi, W. K. (1991). Age Variations in Risk Perceptions and Smoking Decisions. *Review of Economics and Statistics*, 73(4), 577–588.

Viscusi, W. K., & Magat, W. A. (1987). *Learning About Risk: Consumer and Worker Responses to Hazard Information*. Cambridge, Mass.: Harvard University Press.

Viscusi, W. K., & Moore, M. J. (1990). *Compensation Mechanisms for Job Risks: Wages, Workers' Compensation and Product Liability*. Princeton, N.J.: Princeton University Press.

Von Hippel, E. (2006). *Democratizing Innovation*. Cambridge, Mass.: MIT Press.

Weber, M. (1946). *Essays in Sociology*. Translated and edited by H. H. Garth & C. Wright Mills. New York: Oxford University Press.

Weil, D. (2002). *The Benefits and Costs of Transparency: A Model of Disclosure Based Regulation*. Working Paper, Transparency Policy Project, John F. Kennedy School of Government, Harvard University.

Weil, D. (2005). Individual Rights and Collective Agents: The Role of New Workplace Institutions in the Regulation of Labor Markets. In R. B. Freeman, L. Mishel, & J. Hersch (Eds.), *Emerging Labor Market Institutions for the 21st Century*. Chicago: University of Chicago Press.

Weil, D., Fung, A., Graham, M., & Fagotto, E. (2006). The Effectiveness of Regulatory Disclosure Policies. *Journal of Policy Analysis and Management*, 25(1), 155–181.

Weiler, P. (1983). Promises to Keep: Securing Workers' Rights to Self-Organization Under the NLRA. *Harvard Law Review*, 96(8), 1769–1827.

Weiss, J., & Gruber, J. (1984). Deterring Discrimination with Data. *Policy Sciences*, 17(1), 49–66.

Werner, R. M., Asch, D. A., & Polsky, D. (2005). Racial Profiling: The Unintended Consequences of Coronary Artery Bypass Graft Report Cards. *Circulation*, 111(10), 1257–1263.

Wilson, J. Q. (1980). *The Politics of Regulation*. New York: Basic Books.

Winickoff, D., Jasanoff, S., Busch, L., Grove-White, R., & Wynne, B. (2005). Adjudicating the GM Food Wars: Science, Risk, and Democracy in World Trade Law. *Yale Journal of International Law*, 30(1), 81–123.

Wolf, M. (2004). *Why Globalization Works*. New Haven: Yale University Press.

World Health Organization. (2001). *Global Health Security – Epidemic Alert and Response.* 54th World Health Assembly, A54/9.

World Health Organization. (2002). *Global Crises, Global Solutions: Managing Public Health Emergencies of International Concern Through the Revised International Health Regulations.* Geneva: World Health Organization.

Zeckhauser, R. J., & Marks, D. V. (1996). Signposting: The Selective Revelation of Product Information. In R. J. Zeckhauser, R. L. Keeney, & J. K. Sebenius (Eds.), *Wise Choices: Games, Decisions, and Negotiations.* Boston: Harvard Business School Press.

Zeff, S. A. (2002). "Political" Lobbying on Proposed Standards: A Challenge to the IASB. *Accounting Horizons,* 16(1), 43–54.

Zeff, S. A. (2003). US GAAP Confronts the IASB: Roles of the SEC and the European Commission. *North Carolina Journal of International Law and Commercial Regulation,* 28, 879.

Index